Samuel Milton Jones

The New Right

A plea for fair play through a more just social order

Samuel Milton Jones

The New Right
A plea for fair play through a more just social order

ISBN/EAN: 9783744755191

Printed in Europe, USA, Canada, Australia, Japan

Cover: Foto ©Suzi / pixelio.de

More available books at **www.hansebooks.com**

THE NEW RIGHT

A PLEA FOR FAIR PLAY THROUGH
A MORE JUST SOCIAL ORDER

BY

Hon. SAMUEL M. JONES
MAYOR OF TOLEDO, OHIO

INTRODUCTORY AND A CHAPTER ON CO-OPERATION BY HIS FRIEND

N. O. NELSON, OF St. Louis

Illustrated

NEW YORK
EASTERN BOOK CONCERN
1899

PREFACE.

I HAVE no apology to offer for writing a book. I desire to explain that I have been led to do it, not by reason of a belief that I have a peculiar fitness as a teacher of teachers, but because of the feeling that in some measure I have a message for *the plain people*, of whom I am one. During the last few years I have come to see that there is a divine purpose respecting all humanity, all-inclusive, all-pervading, and that in due time order and harmony are to be wrought out of the present chaotic social conditions that surround us. Though I cannot fully argue it out, still I am deeply impressed with the belief that the people of these United States are to lead the people of the world into a new conception of the purpose of government, the meaning of liberty and justice, and into a larger realization of freedom during the next twenty-five years than the most fanciful imagination has yet pictured. To set forth this belief in order, to give the reason why it is entertained, the processes by which the programme may be wrought out, and to lead those who shall read these pages to pin their faith more firmly to the fundamental, imperishable fact of the Fatherhood of God and the Brotherhood of Man, is the purpose of this volume.

I believe that I can truly say that the best thing in the book is the contribution of my friend and co-worker for Equality, who has kindly contributed the chapter on "Co-operation and Profit-Sharing." If you read that and digest a very small part of it, I shall feel that you have gotten the full cost of the book. For the comfort of the reformers who do not believe in *taking profit*, I have pleasure in saying that every penny of the author's profit from this book will be used to spread the principles of Human Brotherhood and Equality of Opportunity for All of the People. Due acknowledgment of the efficient service rendered by Mr. Herbert N. Casson in editing, and of Mr. W. J. Ghent in revising, this work is here recorded. Without their help the book would hardly have been possible at this time.

TOLEDO, O., *August*, 1899.

ILLUSTRATIONS.

	Page.
Samuel M. Jones,	Frontispiece
Mrs. Helen Beach Jones,	15
The Proctor & Gamble Co., Cincinnati, Ohio,	33
Equity Road, Leicester, England,	34
"The Fort,"	67
Stone Cottage, "Ty Mawr,"	68
Mr. and Mrs. Jones, and their Son Paul, with the Doves at St. Mark's, Venice,	101
The Acme Sucker Rod Factory,	102
A Story of Six Young Men,	135
A View of the Assorting Department of the Government Post-Office, Washington, D. C.,	136
A Social Problem,	169
And This is Free America!!	170
The Man with the Hoe,	203
Edwin Markham,	204
Homes of the Workers Employed by H. C. Frick Coke Company, near Scottdale, Pa.,	237
A Millionaire Residence Section, Fifth Avenue, New York,	238
Illustrative Picture,	271
The "Flow" from an Oil Well Just Torpedoed,	272
A 30,000 Bbl. Oil Tank on Fire, Pennsylvania Oil Regions,	272

Illustrations.

	Page.
Municipal Electric Light Plant, Jacksonville, Fla.,	289
Municipal Light Plant, Logansport, Ind.,	290
Electric Light Tower, Fairfield, Iowa,	307
Municipal Light Plant, Lansing, Mich.,	308
Municipal Market, New York,	309
Municipal Quarry, Hartford, Conn.,	310
N. O. Nelson,	327
Leclaire, Ill.,	328
National Cash Register Co., Dayton, Ohio,	345
Home of the Workers Employed by the National Cash Register Company, Dayton, Ohio,	346
A Group of Prominent Reformers,	427
Mr. Jones Addressing a Vast Audience at Grand Central Palace, New York, upon the Subject of "The New Right,"	428
Jane Addams,	445
A Sunday Afternoon Meeting in Golden Rule Park,	446

CONTENTS.

CHAPTER I.
INTRODUCTORY — BY N. O. NELSON.   Page.

Failure of the let-alone policy — Material advancement — Twentieth century problems — The secret of Mayor Jones' influence — The Toledo Mayor as a business man and politician — His especial mission — A social crusader — His political victories — His honesty of purpose and far-reaching sympathy 17

CHAPTER II.
AUTOBIOGRAPHY.

A toiling childhood — Gaining knowledge under difficulties — Exciting days in the oil regions — Hunting in vain for employment — Samuel Miner — A vanished city — Bread and beans — Marriage — The little cottage on the farm — Death enters it — The methods of the Standard Oil Company — Inventions — An awakening — Nailing up the Golden Rule — Golden Rule Park — Trips to Mexico, California, and Europe — Election as Mayor — Reforms attempted and accomplished — The second campaign — The triumph of principle over party............. 37

CHAPTER III.
THE RIGHT TO WORK.

The next right to be established — The cry of the unemployed — Letters from the unfortunate — The evolution of the tramp — Social injustice causes poverty — The means of employment monopolized — The waste of manhood — Ridpath's "Cry of the Poor" — The industrial battlefield — Effects of idleness upon character — What might be done if all labored 113

CHAPTER IV.
CHARITY OR JUSTICE.

Low motives for charity — Cost of our philanthropic institutions — The workers are always the poorest — The line at Fleischmann's — Gilman's defense of charity answered — The worker's contempt of charity

— Methods of helping the unemployed in Paris, Australia and New Zealand — Increase of homeless citizens — Futility of helping individuals — The unchronicled charities of the poor — The remedy...... 153

CHAPTER V.

THE EIGHT-HOUR DAY.

The eight-hour day in the oil regions — Long hours of London carmen and cabmen — "The Man with the Hoe" — Eight hours the former workday — Physiological basis for the eight-hour day — The increasing burden of machinery, and its effect on art and life — Proved effects of shorter workdays — Still shorter workday ultimately necessary.... 185

CHAPTER VI.

THE ORGANIZATION OF LABOR.

What a trade-union is — The good accomplished by labor organizations — Injustice of the wage system — Growth of parasitism — A word about the boycott — Necessity of political action — The ultimate of trade-unionism 205

CHAPTER VII.

THE COMPETITIVE SYSTEM A FAILURE.

Industrial peace impossible while competition lasts — Modern society organized warfare — Monopolies inevitable — Injustice of the present wage system — The fallacy of the competitive incentive to progress — Uncertainty of business — The gambler and the merchant at the same game — Apologies for competition — Fair competition an impossibility — Inequalities of birth — Degrading influence of poverty — No necessity for either poverty or competition — Our deplorable ignorance 219

CHAPTER VIII.

TRUSTS.

Monopolists like wreckers — Destruction of whole towns — Lawlessness of Standard Oil Co. — How trusts corrupt politics — Industrial feudalism — Trusts cannot be destroyed or regulated — Public ownership the only remedy — New York Tribune on combination — Advantages of industrial organization — Get all the people inside the trusts — The Co-operative Commonwealth 253

CHAPTER IX.

SHOULD A CITY OWN ITSELF?

Evils of private ownership of public franchises — Creates an industrial aristocracy — Society like a human body — Legal aspect of the franchise question — Municipal ownership prevents corruption — Is more economical — Success of municipal ownership in England — Electric light statistics — Public markets, baths, parks, theatres, etc. — Objections answered — Reforms in New Zealand and Glasgow — Civic patriotism — Improvement of citizenship — The children of the slums — The ideals of democracy 279

CHAPTER X.

CO-OPERATION AND PROFIT-SHARING — BY N. O. NELSON.

The co-operative principle — Co-operation in the United States — Co-operation in Great Britain — Low salaries paid — Extent and progress of the societies — Providing homes — Raising their own produce — Advantages of the cash system — Protection against adulteration — Method of procedure — Origin and inception of the movement — Attitude toward education — Attitude regarding the land — The movement makes for public ownership — A matter of experience, adjustment and good faith — The co-operative press — Profit-sharing....... 323

CHAPTER XI.

PROGRESS AND POLITICS.

Significance of Toledo election — Corrupt business the cause of corrupt politics — What a business men's government means — Party machines should be abolished — Neither party has a moral issue — Politicians evade real issues — How to prevent bossism — The duty of breaking up party fetich worship — The mission of America..................... 357

CHAPTER XII.

THE GOLDEN RULE.

Edwin Markham's creed — The tyrannical rule of gold — Is the teaching of Christ practicable in business? — Putting the Golden Rule into practice — The failure of success — The communism of the early Christians — The tangle wherein we are all caught — Social effects of religious revivals — The prayer of self — Why people don't go to church — Force cannot reform people — No excuse for militarism — The victories of love 395

CHAPTER XIII.
THE BROTHERHOOD OF MAN.

How the new inventions make for brotherhood — Labor organizations contribute to brotherhood — All — from highest to lowest — people — The race problem — Equal rights of black, white, brown and yellow — Peace and fellow-love the solution — A plea to the men of the South — True greatness among humble men — The workers not intrinsically more moral than the idlers — Real education needed — Always believed in people — An economic system that denies liberty — The real incentive for work — The ideal of the common good — Our common responsibility — Preaching Christianity and practicing Paganism — More thoughtless than heartless — Service for service the only just recompense — No immediate panacea — The curse of private property — America's task — The movement onward and upward............ 439

THE NEW RIGHT.

SAMUEL M. JONES.

"Give me the pay that I have served for.
Give me to sing the songs of the Great Idea.
Take all the rest."

"O, Trade! O, Trade! would thou wert dead!
The time needs heart — 'tis tired of head:

* * * * * * * *

"Yea, what avail the endless tale
Of gain by cunning and plus by sale?
Look up the land, look down the land,
The poor, the poor, the poor, they stand
Wedged by the pressing of trade's hand
Against an inward-opening door
That pressure tightens evermore:
They sigh a monstrous, foul-air sigh
For the outside leagues of liberty,
Where Art, sweet lark, translates the sky
Into a heavenly melody.
'Each day, all day' (these poor folk say),
'In the same old year-long, drear-long way,
We weave in the mills and heave in the kilns,
We sieve mine-meshes under the hills,
And thieve much gold from the Devil's bank tills,
To relieve, O God, what manner of ills?
The beasts, they hunger, and eat, and die;
And so do we, and the world's a sty';
Hush, fellow swine: why nuzzle and cry?
'Swinehood hath no remedy'
Say many men, and hasten by,
Clamping the nose and blinking the eye.
But who said once, in a lordly tone,
'Man shall not live by bread alone,
But all that cometh from the throne?'
Hath God said so?
But trade saith no:
And the kilns and the curt-tongued mills say, 'Go,
There's plenty that can, if you can't, we know;
Move out if you think you're underpaid.
The poor are prolific; we're not afraid;
Trade is trade!'" — *Sidney Lanier: The Symphony.*

MRS. HELEN BEACH JONES.

CHAPTER I.

INTRODUCTORY.

CHAPTER I.

INTRODUCTORY.

By N. O. Nelson.

WE have had a century of political freedom, and theoretically we have been our own masters. With all its shortcomings, this freedom has led to tremendous personal activity. We have pioneered and settled the frontier, we have ribbed the country with steel rails, we have made ourselves a nation of inventors and manufacturers and even of letters.

The Declaration of Independence and the Constitution took every pains to guard the individual's rights against the aggressions of those in authority. Kings and rulers and even majorities were told to keep hands off. So fearful of power were Jefferson and the fathers, that they hedged it about with the novel political contrivance of three co-ordinate powers, the legislative, the executive and the judicial, neither of which could act without the concurrence of the others. This co-ordinate system and the rigid written Constitution have proved, if not our ruin, a most serious danger. New conditions have developed a rapidly growing population of mixed antecedents, the strictly rural population becoming urban, and agricultural pursuits being overtaken and passed by the industrial occupations. These changes have made the rigid Constitution of 110 years ago an onerous burden. We have been unable to adjust ourselves to the new conditions. The written Constitution gave rise to equally rigid political parties, thrusting absolute power in the hands of party leaders. In no country in the world is party power so absolute as in the United States. It is long since the fiction was seriously urged, that party management was devoted to the good of the people or that platforms were intended to be carried out. The Republican party was brought into existence by the pressure of the slave power, and its spirit and leadership were anti-slavery. Yet, in the winter of 1860–61, a large number of its leaders in Congress voted for an amendment that should fasten slavery perpetually in the States where it then existed, and prohibit the right of petition or consideration in any manner by Congress. We have seen Mr. Cleveland, who was elected on a bimetallic platform, actually block the wheels of government to resist bimetallic legislation.

In this same period of constitutional party rule, we have built up an industrial power, which far more directly concerns the welfare of the people than the political power or the party power. True freedom cannot exist where masses of men are depending upon masters and wages for the means of living. The old-time independent farmer has divided into two classes. Either he is a petty farmer or he employs hired hands. The small shopkeeper has become the great manufacturer. From being neighbors with those who worked with him, he has come to be a great capitalist, living in a mansion in the West End, or perhaps in a distant city, or in Europe. Large bodies of men work in the factories for the most part ten hours a day, at the same monotonous daily task. All responsibility is taken from the wage-worker's mind; he has no interest in his work, because he makes no complete thing and has no interest in the product.

This century of ours is conspicuous for its devotion to science. The work done by Wallace and Darwin broke the shackles of authority from the human mind, never again to be restored. The startling discoveries of evolution following close upon those of steam and electricity, gave an impetus to scientific investigation and to the invention of contrivances for utilizing the natural forces that the scientists had discovered. The economy of labor and the increase of productive power have had the effect of placing unlimited material resources within our grasp. The age of invention has compelled organization. The small shop has become the large factory. The individual capitalist with a few hundred dollars has been replaced by the great corporation with its large capital. The former independent workmen and domestic producers have become the wage-earners of highly specialized trades. Labor unions have become spokesmen for rights which would be imperilled were each workman to stand alone. Thus we have consolidated capital on the one hand and great bodies of organized labor on the other. How much of vitality and character has been lost by the merging of the independent man into the stockholder and the hired workman, cannot well be overestimated. The organization of labor has culminated in the formation of local unions into national unions and then federation of the nationals into the American Federation of Labor. Capital has consolidated, first by the merging of individual capital into joint-stock companies, then consolidating into corporations, and finally consolidating into trusts, which aim to control the greater portion of their line of production. The great retail stores, now usually called department stores, have similarly consolidated the retail trade. Thus along the entire line we have organization and federation, until the individual is lost sight of.

Something more than a century ago, the let-alone policy was the favorite one in manufacturing countries. The manufacturers said to the government, "Hands off, let us alone; let there be free trade in buying and selling labor as well as in buying and selling merchandise." It was soon found that this tended to make the workers abject slaves and the employers heartless masters. The system of laws beginning in England and followed by this country, known as the "Factory Acts," throw such limitations around the workman as at least to preserve reasonable safety of life and health. The right to work has never been considered. The let-alone policy proved a blank failure and has been abandoned by all the commercial nations.

We have gone along all these years trying to palliate and alleviate the inevitable outcome of the capitalistic system. When land and capital are owned by private parties and operated for private profit, it cannot be a matter of wonder that work is spasmodic, that there are conflicts over wages and hours, that factories are dismal in appearance. The country has shown its wonderful growth in the magnificence of its city structures and the splendor of its Pullman trains, and yet the city slums have grown more and more picturesque in their squalor. Had a prophet looked ahead from 1799 and seen a vision of the mechanical and labor-saving improvements of the century, he would have said that we could work half as long hours as formerly and everybody have an abundance. So far from this being the result, there is infinitely more real poverty in proportion to population and wealth now than there was a hundred years ago or fifty years ago. The propertyless man who has steady work at union wages is not poorer but richer than a similar workingman was during the first half of the century, but of the wage-earning class there is a much larger proportion who are out of work, and there is a larger proportion of the propertyless to the well-to-do.

Since the pressure of poverty in this land of abundance has forced itself upon the attention of thinkers and leaders, sociology has become a department of scientific study. The duty that lies before the people of this country is to make the coming century one of scientific study of distribution and of life. It behooves us to introduce co-operation in the place of competition. Already public ownership has taken possession of the people's minds. They stand ready in many of the States to take over the municipal public services. In San Francisco, in Chicago, in Detroit, in Des

Moines, in Denver and in Haverhill as well as in Toledo, the city elections have been carried by sweeping majorities on the issue of municipal ownership. This expression has reference to the public utilities necessarily monopolistic only, but it will be a short step from the natural monopolies to the artificial monopolies. Iowa has erected a binder-twine factory because the trust put up the price of twine. May we not expect Illinois to build a steel mill and Ohio a match factory? We are in the midst of an active propaganda for co-operation in public service.

The writings of Ruskin, and Morris, and Bellamy, and Blatchford have not only taught the people, but have awakened a spiritual fervor in the people's hearts that is taking account of suffering humanity as well as property. General education has been one of the chief elements in the progress of the nineteenth century. In the twentieth we must teach our children not only the rules of literature and the laws of science, but we must teach them the rules of life and the laws of ethics. We must tell them, and our teachers must tell them, that property is a means, not an end; that the making of happy and virtuous lives is to be their life-work, and not at all the accumulation of material things. We must enlarge the co-operation which we have already begun.

In England, voluntary co-operation is taking the private business field. The largest and best factories in the realm belong to the co-operative associations. The membership and the capital and the business done have been for fifty years increasing at approximately ten per cent. annually. For twenty-five years the acquisition of municipal monopolies has been going on. Birmingham and Glasgow and Manchester and Huddersfield have all acquired the street-car, the lighting and the water systems, and some of them large areas of city property, which they have either leased or built upon. London has been under Progressive control for about ten years. It seems probable that by the end of the first quarter of the twentieth century, Great Britain will have taken all the public utilities into public control, and the voluntary co-operative associations will have absorbed all the private business, the nation thus becoming a completely socialized industrial and educational one.

In this country public ownership seems more likely to be the outcome. There is every indication of a rapid expansion in this field. The corrupting influence of the great masses of franchise values, the power of the great consolidations of capital, the resentment of the growing mass of mere wage-earners, all tend to awaken the people and make them ready for a rapid change.

The twentieth century must cultivate peace. War is utterly barbaric, serves no rational purpose, settles no right, and in the Hague Conference we may hope to see the beginning of the end. International arbitration followed by disarmament should take the place of the barbaric armies and navies. From the conflicting interests of the nineteenth century we may hope to find harmony of interests in the twentieth. Reforms do not come at their best from either the top stratum or the bottom stratum of society. The two should be united. It is this virtue that is important in the co-operative movement, that it raises men from common ranks into leadership but retains them as leaders from their own class. The growth in the last part of this century of profit-sharing between private capitalists and their employees has given direction to many employers. A large and growing number of them have been casting about for a better way than the everlasting money-making grind.

The explanation why Mayor Jones is listened to as attentively and welcomed as cordially by many business men as by laboring men, lies in the fact that his out-spoken application of the Golden Rule in his factory meets a response in their innermost feeling. It is not so much the five per cent. in addition to regular wages as it is the distinct message that wages do not settle the account. Still more to the point is the eight-hour day. Sixteen hours or twelve hours or ten hours a day leave neither time nor inclination for much else than work. Work becomes a tread-mill affair, and life loses all of its fragrance. When Mayor Jones wrote his song, "Divide the Day," and put it into practice in his factory and in the oil field alongside of his neighbors with a ten-hour day and a twelve-hour day, he said in effect, "I will do the right whether my neighbors do or not. An employer can do the right whether his competitors do or not. It may reduce his profits, but it need not break him."

Then, instead of building a new factory alongside of the old, he bought the acre of ground and turned it into a park. Here was an investment of private capital in unproductive property, unproductive in money, but highly productive in life. Here the children of the neighborhood may play at any time. Here the people of the neighborhood meet on Sunday afternoons to hear music and lectures. Here they see and meet the man who preferred to make Golden Rule Park alongside Golden Rule factory, rather than an imposing factory building, to glorify the business success of Jones. It has been truly said that a rich man has no neighbors. Undoubtedly Mayor Jones has neighbors in and about Golden Rule Park.

In a lecture program in Chicago one of the subjects was "The Saloon, the Greatest Enemy to the Cause of Christ and Morality." To this a clergyman, who was invited to deliver a lecture, took exception and took as his text, "The Greatest Enemy to Christ and Morality not the Saloon, but Pharisees." Mayor Jones has been criticised for not making a sufficiently severe war upon the saloons, and I think his explanation or apology would be something in the nature of Rev. Tuckerman's defense. He has said that while we have the profit-making factory where the children and the girls work ten hours a day between dingy walls, while the workingman has no place to go for relief from the daily grind of the factory, the saloon answers a real social need and that it at least need not be singled out for attacks. I can well understand why Mayor Jones is a friendly supporter of all the churches, though he is strenuously assailed by some of their pastors. He will not voluntarily leave the church. Believing in and practicing Christ's doctrine, he maintains his right to remain. If he goes, he will have to be driven out. In such case, he would not be the first man to be driven out by the incongruity between the preaching from the pulpit and the practice from the pew, between the Sermon on the Mount and the business of the mart. Many of us who have gone out have the kindest of feelings for the individual members of the church, as many of the preachers and laymen are radical reformers, but the church as an institution by no means fulfills its mission.

That Mayor Jones has come to regard profit-making business as a contradiction of our boasted freedom is only a symptom of the times. Numbers of business men feel the injustice of it, suffer from the hardship of it, and wish they had never gotten into it. Taking business at its best, it violates the Golden Rule, it commonly violates even the commercial code, and taken at its worst it is no better than piracy. Business is war, and war is cruelty. Thousands of business concerns go down every year after a prolonged and disastrous struggle with fate. The families and employees are disorganized, involving all sorts of disappointments and hardships. This business mortality is a matter of cold statistics in the commercial reports. The twentieth century sociologists and statesmen will take account of it in its effect on life. We have said all sorts of great and glowing things about equality. We have asserted it as being the first principle of freedom. We have defined it as being equality before the law. This consisted in being tried by the same rules, guarded by the same police officers and confined in the same jail or penitentiary. May it not be a good deal more than this? Is there any of the substance of equality between the factory girl with her four dollars a week and her home in the slums, and the daughter of the tobacco millionaire with her carriage and servants and mansion in the city and her fifty-thousand-dollar cottage and golf grounds in the mountains? To mean anything, equality must mean equality of conditions, the actual conditions of living.

The right to work is the slogan of the Toledo mayor. It needs to be defined that the worker shall have at least so much as the average product, and that nothing shall be taken out of it for those who do not work. Mazzini put duties before rights. We should make it a duty for every one to work or starve. As mayor, Mr. Jones has had to decide in what spirit he would enforce penalties of the law. During his two-year term, arrests in Toledo have declined about one-third. We need not infer that Mayor Jones has infected the Toledans and made them less disposed to crime and misdemeanor. I think the lessened number is due to the mayor's belief that it is better to send a drunken man to his home than to the jail. It is less expensive to the city and more likely to bring favorable results. That punishment does not prevent crime is well illustrated by the prevalence of crimes which were punished by death less than a century ago in England. There were something over 100 capital offenses, and these offenses were never so prevalent before or since. I once heard Prof. Royce, the Harvard psychologist, say that he had never felt so much like doing a violent thing as when he saw a "Don't" sign up over his grass grounds in Cambridge. Believing really and truly that all the people in Toledo are his brothers, entitled to a brother's kindly interest, Mayor Jones has imbued the police force with the same feeling, the result being much less police force business and less crowding of the jail.

I wonder if I can correctly explain why Mayor Jones has received so hearty a welcome by people of all classes in all sections of the country. When I visited Toledo, I was surprised to find that a business friend of mine, although a strong partisan in politics, was an ardent supporter of the mayor. At a later date I met another leading business acquaintance who also was for Jones, knowing him to be an honest man. I have heard Jones speak alongside such speakers as Mr. Bryan, Miss Addams and Father McGlynn. In each case the Golden Rule speaker seemed the favored. I think it is because he talks straight, simple morality, something that every individual heart feels. He deals not with methods so much as purpose. The church is a method, the party is a method, while brotherhood and actual equality are substantial elements of life.

Then, simplicity is a marked characteristic of the mayor. He talks good, plain English, easily understood by every one. He has escaped the pitfall that Mr. Ruskin tells us he fell into in his youth, that of trying to write a pretty style. The plainness of speech, plainness of manner and plainness of dress are typical of the faith and practice of the man who feels an individual responsibility for all that he says and all that he does.

The author of this book has made a platform of his own. It is not a new platform in all its parts, nor is he the first public man to announce it. But the man and the platform differ from their predecessors in this respect: they harmonize with each other and with their time and place. Were I called upon to write the platform in broad terms, it would read this way:

"Love is the law of life. Co-operation is the social method of love. Competition is war. Parties are warring armies. Punishment is brutal. You can trust the people. The right to work is inalienable. Art is the expression of pleasure in work."

My introduction of the man would be like this:

"He knows what he is talking about. He proposes nothing but what he understands clearly and believes sincerely. He loves all living beings, he loves the beautiful, he lives truth, he hates nothing but wrong."

When the author's ideas are brought to bear on the public questions now before us, he denounces private control of public utilities, long working hours, child labor, riches and poverty, competitive business, war. He believes in municipal ownership, direct employment, an eight-hour day, equality in living, co-operation in business, and international arbitration.

Henry George was an economist possessed of an analytical mind. Land monopoly was illogical, transportation was a public function, free trade was a right. His books are masterpieces of economic reasoning. When Tom Johnson first read "Progress and Poverty," he could hardly believe his senses. He told his lawyer to read the book and point out the flaws. He said there was no flaw, and Johnson became a disciple. But George was also a passionate hater of injustice — with religious fervor he preached the right of all God's children to God's gifts. Mayor Jones is first of all a social crusader. It does not take statistics to prove the viciousness of our system; the evidence obtrudes itself on every hand. Whether the poor are growing poorer is immaterial. If one brother is in want, one sister degraded, one child neglected, that one must be relieved, the cause must be removed. "Does it pay to spend so much money for educating the children of the poor?" said a taxpayer to Horace Mann. "If it were your son, would the price be too high?" answered the educator. I think Ruskin's contempt for political economy was largely because it disclaims any moral purpose and seems to dull men's sympathies.

For the Malthusian doctrine, or the doctrine of Survival, neither George nor Ruskin nor Jones has the slightest forbearance. God's provision is ample for all His children if only men do not play the dog in the manger. Ruskin has been considered reactionary in attacking machinery and factories, for their paralyzing effect on workmen, their desecration of beauty and refinement in art and landscape. Neither Henry George nor Mayor Jones is suspicioned of reactionary tendencies, yet this extract from "Social Problems" would as readily be credited to Jones or Ruskin as to George:

The tendency of all the inventions and improvements so wonderfully augmenting productive power is to concentrate enormous wealth in the hands of a few, to make the condition of the many more hopeless; to force into the position of machines for the production of wealth they are not to enjoy, men whose aspirations are being aroused. Without a single exception that I can think of, the effect of all modern industrial improvements is to production upon a large scale, to the minute division of labor, to the giving to the possession of large capital an overpowering advantage. Even such inventions as the telephone and the typewriter tend to the concentration of wealth, by adding to the ease with which large businesses can be managed, and lessening limitations that after a certain point make further extension more difficult.

The tendency of the machine is in everything not merely to place it out of the power of the workman to become his own employer, but to reduce him to the position of a mere attendant or feeder; to dispense with judgment, skill and brains, save in a few overseers; to reduce all others to the monotonous work of automatons, to which there is no future save the same unvarying round.

Under the old system of handicraft, the workman may have toiled hard and long, but in his work he had companionship, variety, the pleasure that comes of the exercise of creative skill, the sense of seeing things growing under his hand to finished form. He worked in his own home or side by side with his employer. Labor was lightened by emulation, by gossip, by laughter, by discussion. As apprentice, he looked forward to becoming a journeyman; as a journeyman, he looked forward to becoming a master and taking an apprentice of his own. With a few tools and a little raw material he was independent. He dealt directly with those who used the finished articles he produced. If he could not find a market for money he could find a market in exchange. That terrible dread — the dread of having the opportunities of livelihood shut off; of finding himself utterly helpless to provide for his family, never cast its shadow over him.

Consider the blacksmith of the industrial era now everywhere passing — or rather the "black and white smith," for the finished workman worked in steel as well. The smithy stood by roadside or street. Through its open doors were caught glimpses of nature; all that was passing could be seen. Wayfarers stopped to inquire, neighbors to tell or hear the news, children to see the hot iron glow and watch the red sparks fly. Now the smith shod a horse; now he put on a wagon tire; now he forged and tempered a tool; again he welded a broken andiron, or beat out with graceful art a crane for the deep chimney-place, or, when there was nothing else to do, he wrought iron into nails.

Go now into one of those enormous establishments covering acres and acres, in which workmen by the thousand are massed together, and, by the aid of steam and machinery, iron is converted to its uses at a fraction of the cost of the old system. You cannot enter without permission from the office, for over each door you will find the sign "Positively no admittance." If you are permitted to go in, you must not talk to the workmen; but that makes little difference, as amid the din and the clatter, and whirr of belts and wheels, you could not if you would. Here you find men doing over and over the selfsame thing — passing, all day long, bars of iron through great rollers; presenting plates to steel jaws, turning, amid clangor in which you can scarcely "hear yourself think," bits of iron over and back again sixty times a minute, for hour after hour, for day after day, for year after year. In the whole great establishment there will be not a man, save here and there one who got his training under the simpler system now passing away, who can do more than some minute part of what goes to the making of a salable article. The lad learns in a little while how to attend his particular machine. Then his progress stops. He may become gray-headed without learning more. As his children grow, the only way he has of augmenting his income is by setting them to work. As for aspiring to become master of such an establishment, with its millions of capital in machinery and stock, he might as well aspire to be King of England or Pope of Rome. He has no more control over the conditions that give him employment than has the passenger in a railroad car over the motion of the train. Causes which he can neither prevent nor foresee may at any time stop his machine and throw him upon the world, an utterly unskilled laborer, unaccustomed even to swing a pick or handle a spade. When times are good, and his employer is coining money, he can only get an advance by a strike or a threatened strike. At the least symptoms of harder times his wages are scaled down and he can only resist by a strike, which means, for a longer or shorter time, no wages.

I have spoken of but one trade; but the tendency is the same in all others. This is the form that industrial organization is everywhere assuming, even in agriculture. Great corporations are now stocking immense ranges with cattle, and "bonanza farms" are cultivated by gangs of nomads destitute of anything that can be called home. In all occupations the workman is steadily becoming divorced from the tools and opportunities of labor; everywhere the inequalities of fortune are becoming more glaring. And this at a time when thought is being quickened; when the old forces of conservatism are giving way; when the idea of human equality is growing and spreading.

When between those who work and want and those who live in idle luxury there is so great a gulf fixed that in popular imagination they seem to belong to distinct orders of beings; when, in the name of religion, it is persistently instilled into the masses that all things in this world are ordered by Divine Providence, which appoints to each his place; when children are taught from the earliest infancy that it is to use the words of the Episcopal catechism, their duty toward God and man to "honor and obey the civil authority," to "order themselves lowly and reverently toward their betters, and to do their duty in that state of life in which it has pleased God to call them;" when these counsels of humility and contentment and of self-abasement are enforced by the terrible threat of an eternity of torture, while on the other hand the poor are taught to believe that if they patiently bear their lot here God will after death translate them to a heaven where there is no private property and no poverty, the most glaring inequalities in condition may excite neither envy nor indignation.

But the ideas that are stirring in the world to-day are different from these.

Near nineteen hundred years ago, when another civilization was developing monstrous inequalities, when the masses everywhere were being ground into hopeless slavery, there arose in a Jewish village an unlearned carpenter, who, scorning the orthodoxies and ritualisms of the time, preached to laborers and fishermen the gospel of the fatherhood of God, of the equality and brotherhood of men, who taught his disciples to pray for the coming of the kingdom of heaven on earth. The college professors sneered at him, the orthodox preachers denounced him. He was reviled as a dreamer, as a disturber, as a "communist," and, finally, organized society took the alarm, and he was crucified between two thieves. But the word went forth, and, spread by fugitives and slaves, made its way against power and against persecution till it revolutionized the world, and out of the rotting old civilization brought the germ of the new. Then the privileged classes rallied again, carved the effigy of the man of the people in the courts and on the tombs of kings, in his name consecrated inequality, and wrested his gospel to the defense of social injustice. But again the same great ideas of a common fatherhood, of a common brotherhood, of a social state in which none shall be overworked and none shall want, begin to quicken in common thought.

Governor Pingree came down from Detroit to speak for Jones just before his re-election campaign. These two men differ very much in the main points of their political aims and methods, but they are as one in wanting to improve the lot of the common

THE PROCTOR & GAMBLE CO., CINCINNATI, OHIO.
(Partly profit-sharing.)

EQUITY ROAD, LEICESTER, ENGLAND.
(Homes owned by co-operative workingmen.)

people, and in their opposition to arrogant commercialism. Pingree believes in parties, and Jones doesn't, but there is manifestly a strong impulse of humanity in the Michigan Governor. He made no mistake so far as his own prospects are concerned in giving a lift to the Toledo Socialist. Prof. Herron has spoken at different times in Toledo under Mayor Jones' auspices. Herron and Jones are at the opposite extremes in the manner of expressing themselves, but they are in marked harmony in their social views. Jones gives credit to the Iowa professor for having done much to bring him into the new life. In delicate sensibilities and poetic temperament, these men bear a remarkable resemblance.

There was an amusing illustration of journalism at the close of the re-election campaign. The Saturday before the election, one of the local papers devoted an entire page to exposing the public and personal rascality of the candidate. On the day after the election, the same paper accounted for the enormous majority Jones received by his well-known uprightness, kindness and sincerity. It added that it was all right for people of all classes to express themselves in unequivocal tones for Jones, but they need not have "hollered so loud."

The simple way in which Mayor Jones expresses the largest aims in his speeches and his interviews and papers, seems to fascinate all sorts of people. He talks from the heart and through a face that carries unmistakable evidence of sincerity. In breaking with the party machine, he broke it to pieces, and he also settled his own mind against party organization. For a quarter of a century, he says, neither of the great parties has had any moral issue. They are run as a business, for the profit of a few managers and office-holders. They make war and hate between people who have nothing against each other, and who want only the good of all. By party, Mr. Jones means, of course the regular party organizations as we know them. It does not include the bringing of people together for a specific purpose. The fact that they are together in that purpose does not bind them to be together in everything else or anything else.

Golden Rule Park adjoins Golden Rule factory. It is a quarter of a block, with some shade trees, a speaker's stand, and a lot of seats. Here, during the summer, meetings are held, with music and speeches. Distinguished speakers are caught on the wing as they pass between the East and the West, and sometimes they are specially brought out. Mr. Jones is always present as the leading spirit, giving out the songs and making some appropriate remarks.

His sympathies are always with the man who is down. Such a man may always depend on getting a little more help than by the rules of the game he may be entitled to. Applicants for aid are of all sorts, those wanting public appointments, those wanting work, those wanting money, and I saw a letter from a woman who wanted a husband. She described herself in detail and also explained carefully what she wanted. Mr. Jones impresses every one as a man to whom to tell your troubles, and he gives advice or other help as though he likes to do it. His protest is not against individuals, but against the system; against what he calls the rules of the game. Besides being unjust, the game is uninteresting and doesn't pay.

CHAPTER II.

AUTOBIOGRAPHY.

The good Bishop [Butler] lived in an age when a man might write books and yet be permitted to keep his private existence to himself; in the pre-Boswellian epoch, when the germ of the photographer lay in the womb of the distant future, and the interviewer who pervades our age was an unforeseen, indeed unimaginable, birth of time. At present, the most convinced believer in the aphorism, " He that has well kept hidden has lived well," is not always able to act up to it. An importunate person informs him that his portrait is about to be published and will be accompanied by a biography which the importunate person proposes to write. The sufferer knows what that means; either he undertakes to revise the " biography," or he does not. In the former case he makes himself responsible; in the latter, he allows the publication of a mass of more or less fulsome inaccuracies for which he will be held responsible by those who are familiar with the prevalent art of self-advertisement. On the whole it may be better to * * * do the thing himself.—*Huxley: Autobiography.*

CHAPTER II.

AUTOBIOGRAPHY.

I DO not know of what particular consequence it is to the people who read this book just when or where or why I was born, but, quoting from "Copperfield" and following the general custom, I will say that "I was born, as I was told and have reason to believe," on August 3d, 1846, in a small stone house still standing, known as Ty Mawr (big house), about three miles from the peaceful village of Bedd Gelert, Caernarvonshire, North Wales. Three years ago I had the privilege and pleasure of visiting the rude house where I was born, the floor of which was composed of rough flagstones — rougher by far than any I have ever seen used in a common sidewalk — yet worn smooth by the tramp of the feet of the tenantry that have polished them through their service, the main result of which has been that they have earned rent for the landlord and incidentally have eked out an existence for themselves. I am glad that I left the place at such an early age that I cannot recall any of the hard experiences that my parents must have had there.

When I was three years of age they emigrated to America. As I understand the situation, and as the story has been told to me, they were what would now be classed as "assisted" emigrants, who are to-day denied the right to land. My father, hearing the stories of prosperity and happiness that came as the result of toil in the new world, was stirred with the ambition to try to better his hard lot in it, and, to accomplish this object, resorted to the taking up of a collection among his friends in order to pay the fare.

The passage across the Atlantic was made in the steerage of a sailing vessel and the voyage completed in the unusually fast time of thirty days. From New York passage was taken in a canal boat up the Hudson river through the Erie canal to Utica, whence they went by wagon forty-five miles to the northward and settled in the vicinity of Collinsville, Lewis county. In Wales my father had worked in the slate quarries, and so he naturally drifted into the stone quarries and stone mason work in this country; soon afterward he became a renter of tenant farms, with the result that he usually succeeded in getting a tolerable livelihood for himself and family, but that was about all.

I went to the village school as soon as I was old enough, and I recall that it was during these early years of my life the schools were made free in New York State; for when I was about ten years of age, I remember a citizen interrogating me as to why I was not in school. I told him that I had to stay out to work, whereupon he replied that he should think my parents could afford to send me to school now since a recent law had made education free in New York State. This was less than fifty years ago, and I merely call attention to this fact in this place in order to emphasize what I say in the chapter on "The Right to Work," that education has only so recently been made free, it is not one whit a larger undertaking to make free work to-day than it was to make free education fifty years ago.

Long Hours at Uncongenial Work.

From my earliest recollection I had a strong dislike for farm work, and this disliking was called by another name by my family and the neighbors; they called it "laziness," but I now assert that I have not now and never had a lazy hair in my head; it was simply the rebellion of a free soul against the injustice of the kind and quality of labor so sought to be imposed upon me. As I recall my experience in those days, I am led to say that serious injury has been and is being done to thousands of children through attempting to force them into work, into callings and professions for which they have neither inclination nor fitness, and no more important responsibility rests upon parents and teachers than this one of finding out what sort of service their children are best calculated to render to society and then doing their utmost to put them into a position where they can have free play for their natural talents.

> 'Tis education forms the common mind,
> Just as the twig is bent, the tree's inclined,

ran the old couplet, and it is true; but it is also true that a great oak is both more beautiful and useful if allowed to take its natural course and shoot straight upward toward heaven, than if its top were bent to the ground and the living force were expended in growing itself into a distorted shape. Innumerable cases might be cited of men and women who have broken away from every barrier placed around them by parents and teachers, vainly supposed to be "for their good," and, by reason of having done so, have lived to bless the world in song and story, in music and in art, in fact, in almost every field of human endeavor; whereas, if they had followed the course mapped out for them by fond parents, wise(?) tutors and advisers, their lives would have been a failure and the world would have been cheated out of its just due.

At ten years of age I worked by the month for a farmer who used to get me out of bed at four o'clock in the morning. It is true that my work was not of the heaviest kind—that is, I was not required to carry things that I could not lift—but I was dragged out of bed at an unearthly hour when a growing boy should be sleeping, and started off after the cows, and my day's work was not ended until sundown; and for this service I received the munificent salary of three dollars per month. I went to the schools in the winter, more or less, and there got my start for an education that I am still acquiring. I have not yet graduated and never expect to graduate; I am far more of a student to-day than I ever was at any earlier period of my life. I recall that one winter, in order that I might work daytimes, my sister and I took private lessons from a neighbor, who proposed to teach us for a stated sum (very small), provided that we furnished a candle to give light, and I remember that on going to the neighbor's house we would find him and his spouse sitting in darkness, waiting for the candle which was a part of the fee that we paid. As nearly as I can remember, I went to school, all told, about thirty months; during that time I did not get beyond fractions in arithmetic, and I have never studied grammar in or out of school an hour in my life. The education I have acquired has been gained under the severe handicap of a lack of technical training in the fundamental rules.

Invading the Oil Regions.

When I was fourteen years of age I worked in a saw mill twelve hours a day, sawing barrel heading, and one day I brought the little finger of my right hand in contact with the saw. I still bear the marks of the wound as a memento. Shortly after this I secured a boon I had longed for for years; that was a job on the steamer L. R. Lyon, running on the Black river between Lyon's Falls and Carthage. I had a mechanical turn of mind, and was very ambitious and hopeful that some day I might rise to the exalted position (as it seemed to me) of a steamboat engineer. The getting of this job, which was that of "wiper and greaser," seemed like the beginning of the realization of the hopes of future happiness. I spent the greater part of three summers on this boat and got some little knowledge of mechanical engineering that proved useful to me in after life; indeed, it was the advice of a steamboat engineer who had spent the winter of 1864-65 in the oil regions of Pennsylvania that in all probability was instrumental in changing the course of my life; for it was he who said to me one day, " Sammy, you are a fool to spend your time on these steamboats; you should go to the oil regions;

you can get four dollars a day there." A little conversation with him soon led me to determine that his advice was worth considering, and a few days later I landed at Titusville, Pa., the headquarters and gateway, practically, of the oil regions, with fifteen cents in my pocket and without the benefit of the acquaintance of a single individual in the city. Leaving my gripsack at a convenient grocery store near the depot and inquiring where I should find the oil wells, I was directed to the Watson flats, just below the city, on Oil creek; and I well remember how I spent that afternoon literally running, not walking, from oil well to oil well in search of a job as an engineer. In the course of my travels I had to cross and recross Oil creek on a foot bridge, where I was required to pay a toll of five cents for each trip, and, of course, the three trips left me bankrupt. By this time night was coming on, with no sign or promise of a job and my heart as heavy as my pocket was empty.

Those were exciting days in the oil regions, and the town was filled with people. I remember, and shall never forget, the feeling of utter desolation that possessed me as I walked up the crowded street of the bustling town with my grip in hand, not knowing how or where I was to pass the night. Coming in front of the American House, the leading hotel of the place, something like an inspiration seemed to possess me. I walked into the office, and placing my satchel upon the counter, inquired of the clerk if I could get a room for a few days; upon his replying in the affirmative, I courteously asked what rate was charged; he replied, " Two dollars and fifty cents a day," and I wrote my name in the register as an indication that I accepted the terms. The hour must have been somewhat late, for he asked me if I would have supper, and calming my agitation as much as possible at the prospect of a square meal, I replied that I would. I remember it as though it were yesterday. I had beefsteak and onions, and like Oliver Twist, after I had finished the first portion I asked for more, and the girl brought me a second order.

The next morning I was up bright and early, out upon one of the most disheartening of all errands that any child of God ever undertook, looking for a job among strangers—a task, too, that I do not believe God intends that a man shall waste his time on, for I fancy that in the divine order, in the Kingdom of Heaven on Earth, in the condition of social justice that is yet to prevail, there will be such a scientific ordering of the affairs of society that no man will waste time tramping from door to door in the heart-breaking, soul-destroying business of begging for work, looking for something to do. I do not know just how it is going to be fixed, but I know it was all easy in the beginning; when God said to Adam, "in the sweat of thy face shalt thou eat bread," Adam certainly did not have to go out and look for a job. There were the land and the natural opportunities, and I am sure that some way, somehow, God, working through his accredited agents, men — men who love their fellow-men —

> Will yet unfold a plan
> That will make work free to every man.

A Word of Cheer.

Friday, Saturday and Sunday, the first three days in Titusville, were three of the busiest days of my life spent in this fruitless search for work. Every hour that passed by added conspicuously to the discouragement that possessed me. At first I wanted to select my work; I wanted nothing but a job at my profession as an engineer, and I proudly exhibited the recommendation papers that I had, with the feeling that the beholders would be overawed into producing a job at once; but as the hours and the days went by my hopefulness gave way to a growing feeling of despair. I can easily understand how Carlyle could say that a man looking for work, wanting work and unable to find work, is the most pitiable object that ever encumbered the face of God's fair earth.

In this time of hopelessness and despair there occurred an incident, that, as I now recall it, looms up like an oasis in the desert. I remember that although I had been trained to a religious observance of the Sabbath, it did not deter me from pursuing my hunt for work. During the course of the day, seeing a man in an office over which was the sign "Office of the New York Oil Co.," I went in and asked for a job. The man turned a kindly face upon me and said he was sorry that he had nothing for me to do. Evidently discerning from my looks that I was getting somewhat discouraged, he began to ply me with questions, asking where I came from, what I worked at, what my experience had been, etc., and finally asked if I were out of money. I evaded the question and said that I soon should be if I did not get work. This kind-hearted man, Samuel Miner — peace be to his ashes and all honor to his memory! — then said: "Well, my boy, you must not be discouraged; you are in a good country and you will get on. I will do the best thing I can for you; I will give you a letter to a friend of mine in Pithole City, twelve miles away, and I think he may be able to give you work. You know there are many men employed at Pithole, as there is great excitement there this summer, and I would advise you to go right to Pithole."

Perhaps the kind words of this sweet-spirited man have had their influence upon my life, and by reason of what he said to me on that Sunday afternoon, I have been led to feel for the many thousands of hopeless men and boys that I have seen pursuing this despairing trade of looking for work. At any rate, I have made it a point in my life, no matter how busy I have been, to try to find time at least for a kindly word for the man out of a job, and that heart-breaking sign which I have sarcastically called the great American sign of prosperity, "No help wanted," has never defaced and never shall deface the walls of any establishment with which I have to do. I really hope that the day is not far distant when this sign will take its place among the relics of a forgotten past, along with "Keep off the grass," "Beware of the dog," and other unhealthy "dont's" of our callow civilization. I hope that the employers who will do me the honor to read this book will take the thought suggested here to heart. Put yourself in his place and ask how you would feel if, at the end of a weary day of tramping the streets of a city from one shop to another in search of work, the first thing to greet you on a workshop door, as you hurried your weary body along to make one more trial before going to your desolate home, should be the words of this dispiriting signal. It is true you may never be in his place, but remember, my brother, there is no possible scheme by which you can make it a moral certainty that your child or, at best, your grandchild, may not take the place of the man out of work, no matter how well "fixed" you are or how carefully you provide. Remember that the man is your brother.

A Perplexing Financial Problem.

Returning to the hotel, I wrote a letter to my mother. I remember what a weary heart I had, and yet I tried to give the letter a cheerful tone. Among other things I told her that I had not yet found work, but expected to to-morrow. The letter finished, the most perplexing financial problem that I have ever faced confronted me — that was the obtaining of the three cents required to purchase a postage stamp. Still wrestling with this problem, I saw a gentleman who had been busily engaged in writing letters evidently making ready to go to the post-office to mail them, and my wit suggested a way out of the dilemma. Addressing him I said, "Are you going to the post-office, sir?" "Yes," said he. "Will you have the kindness to mail this letter for me along with yours?" "Certainly," said the gentleman, while I fumbled in my pocket for the three cents that were not there, fully expecting that he would do just as he did, which was to say, "Never mind, I will stamp it." Now, I do not believe that a condition of life that would drive an honest boy to trickery of this kind to obtain a three-cent postage stamp is worthy to be called "civilization." Yet we are reared up to the belief that poverty, deserved or undeserved, is a disgrace, deny it as we may; we all feel it when it comes home to us as keenly as I felt it on that desolate Sunday afternoon. I was in no way responsible for the poverty and disgrace that were inflicted upon me, and certainly the deception that I practiced upon the hotelkeeper and upon the man who gave me the postage stamp must have been damaging to my morals at that early period in my life. Why should there not be such a condition of loving sympathy and trust among people who are all brothers of one common family that an honest person might make his wants known and have them supplied as readily in one part of the civilized world as in another? Such a time the world will yet know, and already we can see the signs of the dawning of this better day. Whitman says:

My spirit has passed in compassion round the whole earth,
I have looked for lovers and equals and found them ready for me in all lands.

Work at Last.

On Monday morning, without the ceremony of bidding adieu to my landlord, I started for a twelve-mile tramp to Pithole. In those days all of the oil produced was barrelled and transported overland in wagons, and the road for the entire distance between Titusville and Pithole was lined with teams struggling to get through mud, which in many places was well-nigh impassable. I reached Dawson Centre, a suburb of Pithole, about ten o'clock, and seeing a sign, " Office of the St. Louis & Pithole Petroleum Co., Capt. E. D. Morgan, Supt.," I went in and asked for a job as an engineer. Capt. Morgan was behind the desk, and looking out at me inquired, "Are you an engineer?" I said, " Yes, sir." " What kind?" said he, " a sawmill engineer?" with an evident sneer in his voice. With conscious pride I replied, " No, sir, a steamboat engineer," displaying my papers of recommendation as evidence of my experience. "Well," said he, "you may be just the man we want; we have a lot of inexperienced men running our engines. What wages do you want?" I replied that I should like to have the "going wages," and I have often since thought that, under the circumstances, this was a surprisingly wise answer. As a matter of fact, poverty had reduced me to such a degree of humility that I should certainly have accepted anything in the way of wages that any one might offer rather than pursue my disheartening task of looking for a job; but, somehow, I seemed to reason that if he wanted me at all, this man would pay me the "going wages." My reasoning proved correct, for he replied, "Well, if you suit us at all, we will pay you four dollars a day. Do you think you could pump an oil well?" and my heart stopped beating as I said, "I can run an engine, and I think I can pump an oil well." I was engaged and started to work at noon, my turn continuing from noon till midnight. During the course of the first evening my partner, the young man who ran the engine the other twelve hours of the twenty-four, came around and asked me to take his watch from midnight till morning, saying that if I would do so he would pay me two dollars, informing me, at the same time, that he wanted to " set in a poker game," out of which he could make a good deal more than two dollars. Of course, I accepted the opportunity and sold myself to him from midnight till morning, and Tuesday morning saw quite a changed being. Though I had lost an entire night's sleep, I had earned six dollars, and the feeling of hopeless despair that possessed me Monday morning was replaced by the feeling that I was in a fair way to have the "world by the throat" in a short time.

The company for whom I worked paid weekly, and the next Saturday I was paid twenty-four dollars. On Sunday I hied myself to Titusville, explained the situation to the hotel clerk where I had left my grip, paid my bill and went back to my work. This was a good start, and the difficulty of getting a job to-day as compared with that time cannot be more strikingly illustrated than by my experience. I really believe that an inexperienced man, as I was in the oil business, would be more likely to get struck by lightning on a pleasant day than he would be to get a job to-day such as I found waiting for me on that Monday morning in Pithole. Four dollars a day for pumping one oil well! Why, I know a fairly wealthy man in the oil fields within thirty miles of Toledo, who paid a pumper only thirty-five dollars per month for pumping fourteen wells last summer; when the man remonstrated and asked for a raise, the employer informed him that if he was not satisfied he could quit, as a man could be got who would do the work for thirty dollars. This is the way labor-saving machinery has been a blessing to the working men in the oil regions — a left-handed blessing, indeed, as I show more fully in the chapter on "The Eight-Hour Day."

A Mushroom City.

I think it will be of interest to my readers to know something of the Pithole City of 1865. Those were the boom days in the oil region, and the story of this town reads more like the story of the Lamp of Aladdin or some other Arabian Nights' tale than an actual occurrence within the memory of many men yet living and yet young. The boom was started by the striking of the United States well on the Holmden farm in April of that year. The location was on Pithole creek, about eight miles up from the Allegheny river. There was no railroad nearer than Miller farm, about eight miles, and Titusville, about twelve. To these two points and to the Allegheny river all the oil production of Pithole was hauled in wagons, though the first pipe line, a two-inch line to Miller farm, was laid during the latter part of this year. Within six months of the striking of the United States well on the Holmden farm there was built on this and adjoining farms a city, said to have a resident population of from eight to ten thousand people, with a correspondingly large floating population. A government was organized, streets and water-works were built, "modern improvements" of all sorts were put in, a daily newspaper was published, churches, hotels, theatres, saloons, concert halls, gambling rooms and stores of all sorts flourished, and the business of the post-office for the third quarter of the year, I am told, was the third largest in the State. Stories of the fabulous wealth made from the Pithole oil wells went out over the country, hundreds, even thousands, of stock companies were organized to "bore for oil," and thousands of wells were drilled in that part of Pennsylvania without any regard whatever as to whether or not they were favorably located for getting oil. They were located so as to "skin" the stockholders, the unwary, the confident and the simple, who are ever the prey of the cunning and strong; that was the business of the promoters in 1865 as it is to-day. I shall never forget the busy scene Pithole presented in those summer days; the ceaseless din of hammer and saw and the swish of the carpenter's plane ring as clearly in my ears to-day as they did thirty-four years ago, as I stood on the hillside and looked down on this city of mushroom growth, whose streets were filled with a surging throng of people, every one, almost without exception, eagerly engaged in a scramble to get something for nothing from his fellow-men.

I recall with pleasure that there were some few exceptions, for I remember very well a few devoted souls who went to Pithole for a more noble purpose than money-getting, went there to expend their energies and force, as best they knew how, to make men rather than to make money; chiefly among them I remember Alex. Kinnard, superintendent of the Blanc Farm Oil Company, superintendent of a small Sunday school, and a friend of the "boys," one who gave them wise counsel and advice in health and helpful sympathy and loving care in sickness — a man to whom business was an incident, not the purpose of life. Such a soul was this canny Scot, yet living and yet in the service of the Standard Oil Company in the city of Cleveland.

THE CITY VANISHES.

The decline and fall of Pithole was no less surprising and wonderful than was the story of its rise and growth, for the bubble that rested upon such an insecure foundation was not long in bursting, and as the limits of the richly productive oil pool were discovered and hundreds of dry wells began to be reported, the people realized that they had been buncoed, that they had purchased a "gold brick." Values began to decline. Those who found "suckers" to buy their property quickly unloaded, and those unable to dispose of it in this way began to turn it over to the insurance companies, with the result that nightly the wild cry of "Fire! Fire!" rang out upon the air. By the middle of the summer of 1866 half the buildings of the town had either been burned or torn down and transported to other localities. Within a very few years almost the last vestige of the village had disappeared.

I visited the place about eight years ago, and nothing but farm fields, well fenced and fairly tilled, met my gaze; not a single landmark, except the eternal hills, that I could recognize as Pithole, save one thing, a church upon the hillside that was built largely by money produced by oil, and partly maintained by an endowment left by an oil man. The effect upon me was passingly singular. I could not realize that this was the place where I had seen such wonderful sights, and it was with difficulty that I could convince myself that I should not awake and find the whole thing a dream. And as I thought of the experience that had taken place there, the hopes and fears, the ambitions and aspirations, the scheming, conniving and planning that had been done, the sacrifices and hardships that had been endured in the foolish scramble for wealth, it served to impress upon me more deeply than ever the one truth above all others that I am anxious to impress upon the people who read this book, and that truth is that life does not consist in "things," in property.

A Difficult Winter.

The St. Louis & Pithole Petroleum Company was evidently a "boom" company, for on going to the office as usual for our pay one Saturday afternoon a few weeks later, we found it locked, the superintendent gone and the sheriff's notice on the door. Then followed some more weeks of looking for work, with more or less casual work until winter. On account of the decline of business, of which I have told, there were, of course, thousands of men out of employment. In company with four others I took possession of a shanty and entered into a communistic arrangement to live through the winter, agreeing to share and share alike until spring should open. We made the best of a hard case, but even then about the best fare that our combined efforts could provide was one of bread and beans, which one of the oil region poets has thus characterized in rhyme:

> For breakfast they had bread and beans,
> For dinner, beans and bread;
> And then a lunch of bread and beans
> Before they went to bed.

To provide even this scanty fare we tramped many weary miles in search of an occasional job, and I do not know that we should have gotten through at all, had it not been for a chance for a "raise" that I was fortunate enough to discover. Our cabin was located near a bridge crossing Pithole creek. The planks in the bridge became so badly damaged as to make it impassable. I suggested to one of the boys that we get a stock of planks from an abandoned derrick, repair the bridge, and charge the teamsters who were hauling oil ten cents toll for crossing. Without any

particular regard for the " sacred rights of property," we lifted
the planks, repaired the bridge and put up our toll gate. At
first the teamsters were glad to pay, and, indeed, they continued
to be glad until they began to think we were getting too much of a
good thing; then five of them combined to resist further payment
and made a demand for a free bridge. Like a genuine monopolist
I stood my ground at the pole until I saw that the people (the
teamsters) were against me, when I said to my associate, "Johnnie,
they are too many for us; let us make a break for timber," and we
took to our heels, and I think that has been a " free bridge " ever
since. However, I remember that by our monopolistic venture
we levied tribute upon the hard-working teamsters to the sum of
$27.10 for the use of some other man's lumber and about two
hours' actual work; even then we were not satisfied, and I presume
would have been taking toll to this day had not the teamsters
asserted their rights; but the $27.10 furnished a sufficient
supply of beans and bread to carry us through the winter and
bring us to the time when, as an Irishman who was a member of
the company used to say, " there would be smoke out of every
man's chimney," meaning, of course, that the summer would soon
be here and all chimneys would be alike.

MARRIAGE AND LOSS BY DEATH.

From 1865 to 1870 I had a varied experience, working as driller,
pumper, tool dresser, pipe liner, in fact, doing all kinds of work
in the oil region and for about six months working as a tool
sharpener on a " rock job " in the construction of a new railroad
in northern New York. Returning to Pleasantville, Pa., in the
summer of 1868, I was fortunate enough to strike a steady job,
that boon which the toilers of earth so much crave and which
they are so often denied. In the two years that followed I saved
a few hundred dollars and " started in for myself," moving about
from place to place as new oil fields were discovered — from
Pleasantville to Parker's Landing, and from there to Turkey City,

Clarion county, where I lived for six years and where I secured quite an important part of my literary education in the meetings of the Turkey City Literary Club, of which I was a member and part of the time president. It was while I lived there that I married, October 20, 1875, the wife of my youth, Alma Bernice Curtiss, of Pleasantville, as sweet-spirited and helpful a soul as ever inhabited this world of ours, with whom I lived for ten years. She bore to me three children: Percy, born at Turkey City in February, 1878; Eva Belle, born at Duke Centre, August, 1879; Paul, born at the same place, May, 1884. Our little girl, Midgie we called her, died shortly after she was two years of age, and her mother's death followed in December, 1885.

The separation from these two souls was the greatest trial and severest shock of my life. The little girl, in the first place, had somehow gotten nearer to my heart than any other creature, and the cloud that obscured the sunshine from my sky had scarcely cleared away during the four years that followed her death, when the greater trial came in the death of the wife of my youth. I think now that my suffering was greatly intensified by the confused notions I then held regarding life and its purposes. I now no longer think of them, or of any of the many friends who are gone, as dead, as I then thought of death. Then I believed, or professed to believe, in immortality, but my notions of it were vague and confused. I have since then learned to accept the sayings of Jesus concerning life and death as meaning just what they say. I was greatly helped about that time by reading " After Death in Arabia," " He and She " and other poems of Edwin Arnold's. This passage in " After Death in Arabia " carries a most helpful philosophy:

> Faithful friends! It lies, I know,
> Pale and white and cold as snow,
> And ye say "Abdallah's dead!"
> Weeping at the feet and head,

> I can see your falling tears,
> I can hear your sighs and prayers,
> Yet I smile and whisper this:
> "*I* am not the thing you kiss;
> Cease your tears and let it lie;
> It *was* mine, it is not I."

The thought here suggested did a great deal to rob death of its terrors for me, to help me know that the life that was still is, and to help me to believe, as Henry Ward Beecher once said, that perhaps our departed friends in the other life, with quickened perceptions and enlarged capacity, are working in and through us to accomplish the noble purposes that engaged their attention while visible to us. This thought, suggested by the great preacher, seems to me to be thoroughly in line with the teaching of Jesus and so much more in harmony with the scientific idea of life than the thoughts I once entertained, that I have no feeling now stronger than this one, that I do not want any one to think of me when I am gone as I once thought of those who are dead. I cannot now think of death as anything but birth into a new life, just as orderly and just as natural as birth into this life. I have come to realize and believe that I understand the truth so tersely stated by Job, "though after death worms destroy my body, yet in my flesh shall I see God." And so I ask you, dear friend, to think of me when I am gone, not as dead, but as our own Hoosier poet has said:

JUST AWAY.

> I cannot say and I will not say that he is dead,
> He is just away.
> With a cheery smile and a wave of the hand,
> He has stepped away to the better land,
> And left us wondering how very fair
> It needs must be since he lingers there.

Taking a backward glance over the twenty-four years that have passed since my first marriage, I do not recall any happier years than were the first three which we spent in a small cottage, our first home, on the Shoup farm, about one-half mile outside of Turkey City, where I had a small interest in an oil lease. I pumped an oil well, cultivated a small garden and assisted my wife with the washing, which we used to do jointly at the boiler-house, where I had steam and hot water convenient for the purpose. She repaid me by watching the engine while I was gone to town on necessary errands, and together we dug a part of our living out of the small garden; in addition to this, my wife taught music to two girl friends and presided at the organ in the Sunday school that was held in the hall of the literary club. We lived quite a natural life, comparatively free from the care and burden of "things," and being so, we were at liberty to contribute our share to the common welfare of the community, and we had the best kind of times in so doing. I merely make mention of this because I want to impress the thought upon the minds of young people that the simpler life is, the better it is, and the greater its possibilities in an artistic sense. Jesus made no mistake when he said that "life does not consist in things."

Removal to Lima.

From Duke Centre, in the Bradford oil fields, McKean county, to which we had moved in 1878, and where we lived for six years, I moved, after the death of my wife, to Bradford, and one year later, in 1886, to Lima, O., being induced to do so mainly by my friends, who thought that a change of scene would serve to divert my mind from the great sorrow that had come upon me in the separation referred to. I at once engaged in the oil business in Lima, leasing lands, and drilled what was known as the "first large oil well" in Ohio; it was known as the Tunget well, located about three miles east of Lima, and it started at about 600 barrels per day. The Standard Oil Co. was the only buyer of Lima oil at that time, and was paying forty cents a barrel for it, but on the day after the Tunget well was struck the price declined to thirty-seven and one-half cents and a few days later to thirty-five cents.

When I arrived in Lima, there were but twenty oil wells in the State of Ohio. The marvelous growth of the business in this and the adjoining State of Indiana will be but faintly understood when I say that since that time more than 30,000 oil wells have been drilled in a strip of country running southwest of Toledo about 150 miles, and varying from three to eight miles in width. The amount of labor involved in the development of this enormous industry is altogether past the comprehension of those who are not familiar with it.

A Lesson from a Great Trust.

The development of oil in the Ohio field marked an important epoch in the history of our greatest oil trust, the Standard Oil Company. Prior to 1886, this company had never been a producer of petroleum — merely a buyer, manufacturer and shipper — but soon after the drill had demonstrated that Ohio and Indiana contained vast areas of prolific oil territory, it entered the field as a producer. And right here I want to say that I have been familiar with the development and growth of this company from the beginning, and that while there has always been vigorous and pronounced opposition to it and to its methods, much of this opposition has seemed to me to be a "waste of powder;" for I have always observed that as soon as those who were most pronounced in their antagonism to the Standard Oil Company and its methods were taken into the fold and made to share in the profits of the concern, their complaints suddenly ceased.

Long ago, before I knew anything about the economic situation, indeed many years before I knew that there was an "economic situation" or an economic question, in the days when I thought the only problem worth a man's attention was the attainment of the great American ideal — making money — I seemed to understand that the opposition to the Standard Oil Company, like most of the opposition to trusts and combines, lacked a moral purpose. It arose from the fact that those making it were not sharers in the profit or plunder. No general movement has yet been made in this country proposing to overthrow corporate interests for the benefit of all of the people; there have been those who claimed that as their purpose; but, as I have said, they lacked a moral basis. We are a nation of Mammon worshippers, worshippers of things, "property," success; and in our eagerness to protect the thing that we worship, in our anxiety for the "sacred rights of property," we have lost sight of the sacredness of human rights. The methods of the Standard Oil Company are the methods of "business," and there is no immorality that can be laid at its door that cannot find its counterpart in the methods of business in all parts of the country hundreds of times daily. There is an ethical code for business, it is true, but it is a distressingly low one; its maxim is, "Get all you can, and keep all you get;" and from an intimate knowledge of the methods of the Standard Oil Company, covering twenty-five years, and the methods of business generally, I feel that as a Socialist, as a man who believes in brotherhood, simple justice requires me to say that the ethics of that corporation are simply a reflex of the ethics prevailing in the business world and that guide and control the business men of to-day. The most serious charge that can be laid at its door is that it has succeeded; it has outwitted its competitors who sought to play the same game but had not so thoroughly mastered the art.

Our trouble is not with the bosses, with the aristocrats, with the corporations or the Standard Oil Company, but with a system that denies brotherhood and makes a weaker brother the legitimate prey of every strong man. The Standard Oil Company recognized the fact from the first that competition is a failure, and by resorting to the methods of warfare common to the business world, it has well-nigh eliminated competition, it has set aside its competitors and mastered the situation. Let the people learn a lesson from it and the other trusts, and by orderly means proceed in an intelligent manner to take that which is their own, that which they have paid for, and for all time put an end to competition by owning and operating all of the trusts for the benefit of all of the people. My experience as an oil operator in the Ohio and Indiana fields has been that of hundreds of others. I have simply taken advantage of opportunities offered by an unfair social system and gained what the world calls success — that is, I have accumulated some property. I was one of the original incorporators of the Ohio Oil Company, now the producing department of the Standard Oil Company, and in proof of what I have just said, I will say that in its early history the Ohio Oil Company had the opportunity before it practically to capture the Ohio oil field. It was composed of experienced oil producers, men who knew every detail of that business, but who lacked the ability to go forward and carry the thing through to the success that has been realized by the Standard Oil Company. We did not understand the art of competition, and so we surrendered (sold out) to the Standard.*

---

* The appearance in the columns of some of the newspapers of this reference to the methods of the trusts printed from advance sheets of the book, has brought to me several letters of friendly criticism, suggesting that in my goodness of heart I am disposed to deal too kindly with "our old enemy," the Oil Trust.

Many thoughtful people believe that the Standard Oil Company and kindred organizations are responsible for the introduction into business methods of various phases of crime that were unknown before, and that they, therefore, and not the system, are responsible for the grosser evils from which we suffer. Without in any manner attempting to shield any form of wrong, organized or unorganized, I must say that this reasoning seems to me fallacious. The trusts and the combinations are, as it appears to me, the legitimate outgrowth of the competitive system in industry that our laws have been utterly powerless to prevent. As I have already suggested, it is a matter of common notoriety that the worst charge that has ever been laid at the door of any "criminal

Remarriage and Removal to Toledo.

In 1892 I married my present wife, Helen L. Beach, of Toledo, who has been to me a helpmeet, and to my children everything that their own mother could have been, except that she did not bear them. At that time I moved from Lima, where I had made my home for six years, to this city. During 1892 and 1893 I spent a great deal of my time in the oil fields among the wells and invented some simple but valuable improvements in oil-well appliances, and in 1894 I began the manufacture of these and other oil-well appliances at 600 Segur avenue, where the work is still carried on under the name of the Acme Sucker Rod Company.

---

trust" might be successfully charged against the methods of business hundreds of times daily, if the facts were only known.

The ethical code of business under the competitive system is far below that of such brutal sports as football and prize-fighting, against which there is such an outcry on the part of respectable people. Football, as well as all other athletic games, is subject to rules that have been carefully thought out by men familiar with the art; these rules are designed to give each side an equal opportunity. Prize-fighting is guarded by the most carefully prepared, scientific rules to secure to each combatant a fair chance in the battle; but there are no Marquis of Queensbury or London Prize-Ring rules to protect the contestants in the daily competition (war) of business. In the battles of the prize ring it is sought to match the combatants as nearly equal as possible; their qualifications as to size, age, weight, and experience are all looked into, and if there is any special difference in favor of one over another, this is sought to be equalized by some sort of a handicap. John L. Sullivan, in his palmy days, used to challenge all comers to stand before him for four rounds, and the man who was able to do so was declared the winner of the test. During such battles each side has trained representatives to guard and watch his interests, and there is a referee, skilled in the art of rendering a decision as to who has fairly won.

There is no "weighing in" of the contestants in a business battle; there are no rules classifying the entries; there are neither seconds, umpires, time-keepers nor referee, and the call of "time," in order that the contestants may have a breathing spell and get the benefit of a cooling sponge and a refreshing drink, never interrupts this merciless battle. Into this conflict

My First Awakening.

Prior to this time I knew little about "labor conditions." As a rule, labor in the oil fields had enjoyed fair wages compared to similar work outside, and, having passed most of my life in small towns, I had seen little real suffering among the working people. I think the first real shock to my social conscience came when the swarms of men swooped down upon us begging for

---

skilled and unskilled, the simple and the cunning, crafty and confiding, weak and strong, old and young, are pitched in a hurly-burly scramble for the largest share of the plunder (profit) that is passing from hand to hand in the thing called commerce and industry. In such a battle, it does not require a special skill or training to "pick the winner." If you are in a prize-fight and happen to be down on one knee, the friendly call of "time" gives you an opportunity to put yourself in position more successfully to meet the assault of your antagonist, but in the business battle, the extremity of one is the opportunity of the other, and the brother man who is "down," or partly so, is considered the legitimate prey of his vigorous, healthy, prosperous rival. It is the rule of our competitive life that the time when the business rival is on the downward road — when creditors are pressing him hard, when banks are clamoring that he shall meet his paper, when the sheriff is threatening to close his doors — this is the opportunity for the other rival to strike the finishing blow and make merchandise out of the misery of his fellow-man.

It is true that the instincts of humanity are all violated by this program, for as I have said and repeat, and love to repeat, humanity is loving, gentle and kind; but the exceptions to the picture I have painted only prove the rule, and all experience is conclusive as to the position I have taken, that the "criminal trust" is the legitimate product, the poisoned fruit of the competitive system that denies the fundamental truth of the brotherhood of all men, and asserts the right of one man to convert his fellow-men into instruments of profit for his supposed benefit.

The saving effected by the trust, which, as I say elsewhere, is a social product and belongs to society and not to the trusts, is an economic development and strictly in the line of progress, and the only way we shall avail ourselves of it is by owning the trusts, not by the making of laws against labor-saving associations. We must cease the senseless battle and set up a new order by which, through the operation of love as law, we shall establish the Co-operative Commonwealth, the Kingdom of Heaven on Earth.

work, soon after signs of life began to be manifest around the abandoned factory which we rented for our new enterprise. I never had seen anything like it; their piteous appeals and the very pathos of the looks of many of them stirred the deepest sentiments of compassion within me. I felt keenly the degradation and shame of the situation; without knowing why or how, I began to ask myself why I had a right to be comfortable and happy in a world in which other men, by nature quite as good as I, and willing to work, willing to give their service to society, were denied the right even to the meanest kind of existence.

I began to think about the thing called wages, and as I learned that men were employed at common labor at one dollar a day and even less, the whole hideous wrong of the wage system began to reveal itself to me. I saw at once that it was a purely arbitrary arrangement, in which the man who had nothing but his labor to sell had no choice; he must accept what his employer offers, the alternative being usually starvation for himself and his children. I resolved that the " going wages " rule should not reign supreme in the Acme Sucker Rod Company, but rather, I said, we would try to recognize the rule that every man is entitled to such a share of the product of his toil as will enable him to live decently, in a way that he and his children may be fit to be citizens of a free republic of equals; and since that time, as best I know how, I have tried to be true to this principle.

I soon discovered that I was making the acquaintance of a new kind of man. Always a believer in the equality of the Declaration of Independence, I now for the first time came into contact with workingmen who seemed to have a sense of social inferiority, wholly incapable of any conception of equality, and this feeling I believed it was my duty to destroy. Without any organized plan, and hardly knowing what I was doing, I determined that this grovelling conception must be overcome; so we began to take steps to break down this feeling of class distinction and social inequality. The first year we began to "get together" with little excursions down the bay; we invited our workmen and their families and also some other people, who live in big houses and who do not work with their hands, or anything else for the matter of that; we sought to mix them, to let them understand that we are all people — "just people," you know. As our business increased we took in new men; we made no special effort at selection; there were always plenty of "out of works" (always will be so long as the present competitive system continues), willing and waiting to rent themselves out to us, that is, to allow us to use them to add to our wealth and incidentally to get an existence for themselves. We asked no questions as to their habits, their morals or their religion; we ignored the sacred rules of business, that go so far in some cases as even to submit the men to physical examinations in order to avoid the risk of responsibility incurred through physical weakness. In fact, we were going along in a sort of free and easy way, occasionally giving the boys a word of caution, perhaps printed on a pay envelope, or a little letter expressing good will and fellowship, and a word of friendly advice.

THE GOLDEN RULE POSTED.

It was the distress of mind occasioned by seeing a string of rules a yard long in another factory, at the tail of every one of which was a threat of dismissal, that led me to say to my wife, " I am going to have a rule for our shop; I am going to have the Golden Rule printed on a piece of tin and nail it up as the rule that governs the place." It was not any belief in my own goodness of heart or my ability to reach the lofty ideal of doing to others as I would be done by, but it was the reaction that came from the contemplation of the outrageous injustice that was practiced upon my fellow-men by the iron-clad rules to which they are made abject slaves in order to gain the right to a bare living, that led to the putting up of the Golden Rule on our wall. At that time I did not realize the limitations that are placed upon our better natures by the economic conditions that surround us. I did not know that the competitive system of industry was calculated to bring out everything that is bad and to suppress all that is good in us, as I now know that it is. The putting up of the Golden Rule was the first radical move that was made at the Acme Sucker Rod factory. There were several things about that that may properly be called radical. In the first place, it was acknowledging a basis of equality for all about the premises; next, it was ignoring the time-honored precedent of "doing as other people do;" finally, it was an assumption, at least, that this fundamental rule of conduct, given us by the founder of Christianity, was a livable and practical thing.

As I have said, we ignored the well-established rule of business in inquiring into every man's history before giving him employment; we simply took him in and assumed for the time being that he was a man, and undertook, so far as we knew how, to treat him as a brother. In doing this, of course, we got men who had been victims of all sorts of injustice from their infancy up, and, as a consequence, many of them were far from perfect; but I think it is well for us to remember that the best of us have our faults, and if our opportunities had been the same as those of our brothers and sisters whom we criticise as "worthless and drunken," etc., there is sound reason for believing that our characters would not have been any improvement upon theirs.

We frankly stated that making money was only one of the objects of carrying on the work of the Acme Sucker Rod Company; the other, and by far the more important, being that of "making men." In spite of the hindrance of environment, in spite of the evils of competition that force all who are in it to more or less of a daily denial of the truth of brotherhood — in spite of all this, we believe we have sound reason for saying that the moral reform that has been wrought in the hearts of employers and employed by this departure from the usages of business is of incalculable value to all of us, and we fondly hope that it is destined to be a blessing to generations yet unborn.

GOLDEN RULE PARK OPENED.

Perhaps the most helpful thing of all has been the opening of Golden Rule Park and Playground. This is a lot of ground only 150 feet square, adjoining the factory, at the corner of Segur and Field avenues. Some fine old forest trees made it possible to convert this into a little park for the people and playground for the children, and it has been used and enjoyed to the utmost. The Sunday afternoon meetings for the people have been most delightful experiences. Brotherhood and Golden Rule, and Golden Rule and Brotherhood have been the popular themes we have been preaching from its platform. We have now supplemented the Golden Rule Park with a Golden Rule Hall, which was opened last Thanksgiving day, where we hope to join in the teaching and study of this idea of brotherhood that is yet to save the world that Jesus died to redeem. We wish to have it distinctly understood that we do not lay claim to having done anything for which we either desire or deserve any credit. No man wants or deserves credit for having done what was simply his duty, and we cannot lay claim to having done more; in fact, we do not feel that we have lived up to our convictions. We started out by joining in the universal admission that "something is wrong." The wronged men and women and children have been and are so constantly before us, whether asleep or awake, that we have been impelled by an irresistible power to do what we have done in the hope that we might uncover something that would correct the wrong. In following this impulse, we have uncovered something; we have found the source, the evil, that we believe to be the cause of all the misery, wretchedness, want, poverty and crime that afflict this fair earth to-day. The cause of all this horrid category of evils is found in Social Injustice, springing out of a denial of brotherhood; from this social injustice proceed the causes which produce and perpetuate all the miseries that I have enumerated.

Suffering Due to the Denial of Brotherhood.

It may be said that all of our troubles are due to the denial of brotherhood. Once let us admit brotherhood and we shall spurn the idea of having, while our brothers are in want — but this is a truth that has been stated so often as to be regarded as a platitude. I must be more specific. My purpose in defining "social injustice" is to try to help others who are studying along the same lines, the question of how to bring about reform. In order to do so, let us look at the form of injustice that made the success of the Acme Sucker Rod Company possible, the injustice of a patent. In the ideal society that yet awaits us, in the co-operative commonwealth that is to be realized, in the kingdom of Heaven *that is to be set up here on this earth*, there will be no patents, no railway passes, no reserved seats, no "free list," no franchises, contracts or special privileges of any sort to enable a select few of the people to live off the toil of others. The poet Tennyson saw the new earth that is to be and sung of the time

> When the schemes and all the systems, kingdoms and republics fall,
> Something higher, holier, nobler — all for each and each for all.

In that sort of a civilization no one will want special privileges, for we shall all live as members of a loving family now live, each striving to help, instead of each striving to rob, the others.

The Heresy of "Superior Ability."

What heresy can be more fallacious than the prevailing one that superior ability entitles one to the right to live at the expense

Copyright, 1899, by Eastern Book Concern.

STONE COTTAGE "TY MAWR"
(Where Mayor Jones was born), near Bedd Gelert, North Wales.

of his fellows? After all, what foundation in fact is there for this boasted claim of "superior ability?" Let us look at the myriad hands whose help we must employ in order to convert this "superior ability" into a marketable product. For instance: The Acme sucker rod joint is made from iron, and in order that this "invention" might be a profit to the inventor and be utilized in industry, it was necessary that some one should make the tools, with which I see men mining the ore in the Lake Superior regions; then I see other men loading this ore into carts, while others transfer it to railroad cars, that were made by other hands; I see it transported over a railway, built by still other hands, drawn by a locomotive that involved the inventive genius of a Stephenson and hundreds of others to bring it to its present state of perfection; I see the train manned and the ore hauled to the lakeside, where I see it transferred to ships built by men's hands, guided by others, who have studied the laws of navigation, down the inland seas, and landed at Toledo or Ashtabula; I see the cargo discharged by yet other hands, transferred to the care of other men, transported over still another railroad to Pittsburg, and unloaded at a blast furnace; I see the science of the metallurgist employed to convert this ore into pig iron, when it is again, by the art of the puddler and roller, converted into bars, and transported by other hands to Toledo. In the meantime, I see all along down the ages the development of the art of making malleable iron; I see the men's hands that are employed in that industry, which must be joined with others in order to give this "superior ability" an opportunity to display its genius (?); then I see the men who "manufacture" the Acme sucker rod, and the part they perform in this drama; and then the other hands that drill the oil wells and the hands that transport the rods to the place where they are to be used. I see the hands that built the streets and bridges that we have to use; I see the telegraph and the post-office that we must employ in order to carry on this small industry, and I find that the inventor with his much-vaunted "superior ability" is, after all, only a very dependent creature, much the same as all the rest of us — just a very small cog in the social wheel.

It seems foolish for us to plead for a continuance of our present unholy and unrighteous system of robbing one another. If there were to be improvements in sucker rods, why may we not reasonably expect that there is room for improvement in social relations? I know that the conservative mind of the world has always been against improvement of any sort, but conservatism has had to give way before the ceaseless march of progress, and in no department of human activity is there the imperative call for improvement to-day that there is in that of our economic and social relations. As a matter of fact, some of the most thoughtful men and women on earth believe that there must be radical improvement, or that the race is destined to go out in darkness. Such a profound philosopher as Huxley said just a few years ago, "If I did not believe that there was destined to be a great improvement in the moral and social condition of the race, I should regard the advent of a friendly comet that would sweep the whole thing away, as a consummation much to be desired."

Conditions that Compel Crime.

Why should we consider the work of creation with respect to our economic and social conditions a finished job, and why should some of our best people regard any reference to the conditions of social unrighteousness, that are so flagrantly before us all the time, as the next thing to treason? The disciples of the *laissez-faire*, or let-be, school have brought us face to face with social conditions that are little less than calamitous. Pauperism and crime are frightfully on the increase. Men and women voluntarily commit themselves to prison in order that they may be warmed and fed. Our latest poet of the people, Mrs. Charlotte Perkins Stetson, has stated the case very pertinently:

> With charity we would prevent this poverty and woe,
> But find the more we've fondly spent, the more the poor ao grow.
> We've tried by punishment full sore to mend the case they're in;
> The more we punish them the more they sin and sin and sin!
> We make the punishment more kind, we give them wise reform,
> And they, with a contented mind, flock to our prisons warm.

A few winters ago an able-bodied, self-respecting man about fifty years of age searched for work on the streets of Toledo until he was well-nigh famished with hunger. Feeling unable to endure the pangs longer, he applied to the infirmary for relief. He was told that relief was not given to able-bodied men. "You are able to work," said the officer, "and we have no right to relieve you." He replied that he was unable to find work. He was met with the answer that that was no part of the business of the department for the relief of the poor. With a heavy heart he turned again into the chilly streets and made a few more applications for work, with the same result that had met him for days — failure. He next went to the police judge and requested to be given a sentence to the workhouse; that official denied his request, saying, "You have done no crime, and I cannot sentence you to prison." He walked hopelessly away from the station, but the experience had quickened his perceptions, and by the time he had reached the corner of St. Clair and Jefferson streets, he had reasoned out a way of relief; he had learned that society will aid a criminal to a living. but will not lift its hand to help the same person while he is an honest man. In a moment his mind was made up; he decided to become a criminal, and suiting the action to the word, he took up a brick and hurled it through a hundred-dollar plate-glass window in a vacant store room, formerly occupied by the Holcomb National Bank. A watchful guardian of the law saw the act, and hastily crossing the street, marched the culprit to the police station in triumph, entering against him the charge of malicious destruction of property. He was housed and fed at public expense at the police station, the first housing and feeding he had been able to obtain for days. Next morning he was placed on trial and received his longed-for sentence of ninety days in the workhouse.

Now, dear reader, in all candor, is this a rational state of affairs? Is it the best we can do with the thing called government? Of what avail is our boasted liberty to men caught in the stress of circumstances that drove this man, a brother, to crime? Am I an Anarchist, a disturber of the peace, a dangerous man, because I venture to suggest that it would be wiser, cheaper, more humane and Christian to provide a plan to take care of such men, or to aid them in taking care of themselves before they become criminals, rather than to continue to destroy men and women in this cruel and heartless fashion? If it is wiser, more humane, more Christian, and above all, in this money-worshipping age, if it is cheaper, ought we not to give heed and do something to change a social order so clearly wrong? I maintain that it is the plain duty of the legislature of the State of Ohio at its next session to deal vigorously with the question of the unemployed and to extend the functions of the Labor Bureau to such a limit that employment will be provided for those unable to provide for themselves in time, at least, to save them from the necessity of starving, stealing, or committing a worse crime. If we are so busy as individuals in the scramble for gain—"business," "trade" — that we have no time to consider and provide for the welfare of our fellows, then it is clearly the business of society — all of us, the state — to see to it that her citizens are not forced into pauperism or crime.

The matter of detail must be wrought out by the legislators; it is clearly within the province of that body; it is easily within their reach and their manifest duty to face this question of questions boldly, and at once place outside the domain of problems the matter of whether or not a man willing to work can obtain a decent livelihood. The state should provide a place where any man driven to that extremity could go and find public work, the result of which would, at least, keep soul and body together.

In other words, the state should provide productive labor for the unemployed, either at building roads or in some class of service that would add to the wealth of the community. It is an opportunity for an expression of the highest form of patriotism. The time is ripe, the call is loud upon the legislators of Ohio to lead in this great work of reform, and the people are patiently awaiting their action. I believe that the legislators will respond to the call, and that Ohio will be among the first states of the Union to take this forward step toward a higher and nobler conception of patriotism.

Journeys to Mexico and California.

Ever since my boyhood days I had longed for an opportunity to travel and see and study something of the world about me, for I have always been a student, as I always expect to be. In the spring of 1895, this opportunity came, and with my wife and part of my family, I made a trip first to the Republic of Mexico and later to the Pacific coast. The visit to Mexico was an "eye-opener" in a truly educational way. I had heard and read something of "pagan Mexico;" I believe that to some small extent I had contributed to the support of missionaries in that country, and I was surprised to find that I had gained quite a false impression of social conditions as they really exist in that progressive republic.

Mexico has been called the Egypt of America; there is much that is old about its civilization, and many of the mechanical improvements that are so conspicuous a feature in our life have not yet made their way there. Notwithstanding the fact, however, that in some parts of Mexico they still plow with a stick, use great wheels that are sawed from the end of a log for their carts, transport their freight on the backs of burros, drink pulque and live in adobe huts — notwithstanding all this, I say, there are many features of their social life in which they lead the people of the United States. In a small city of 35,000 inhabitants, Aguas Calientes, I visited their beautiful free public baths, one for men and another for women, and I remember counting twenty-six men in the swimming pool at one time. In Toledo we have 135,000 inhabitants, and we provide no place for swimming; if one of our citizens invades the sacred waters of the Maumee for that purpose, he is promptly arrested. The same little city furnishes music in the plaza twice a week for the people.

Free music in the public plaza is one of the *common* things in Mexico; of course, being free and in a public place, it is enjoyed by rich and poor alike. Their public markets, museums, libraries, schools and other features of municipal Socialism, indicate that the social conscience of these people is awakening and keeping pace with the march of progress in other parts of the world. In the Guadalajara penitentiary, which we visited, we were told that prisoners having families were paid a certain small wage, which went toward the support of the family during the confinement of the prisoner; and Mr. Joseph Byers, secretary of the Ohio State Board of Charities, who visited Mexico in the winter of 1898-99, told me that the new penitentiary which was opened in the city of Mexico about that time is more nearly ideal than anything we have in the United States. With the opening of that prison, the republic has, I believe, also abolished capital punishment.

My first trip to California, in 1895, enlarged my conceptions of the vastness and grandeur of our country very greatly, and more vividly than anything else I remember having seen there is impressed upon my mind the incomparable beauty of the Yosemite Valley. I feel that I should be untrue to my better self if I did not speak in the strongest terms of the scenery of this valley. Nothing that I have seen in any part of the world that I have visited since has made anything like the lasting impression upon my mind that it did; indeed, it is the one spot the memory of which awakens

> A nameless longing and vague unrest,

and a desire to hie myself thither at the first opportunity. To the traveller who journeys to California, I say, by all means go to the Yosemite, even if you have to walk. Perhaps some day, under government ownership of the railways, the cost of a journey across the continent will have been so reduced that the beauties of the Yosemite may be brought, if not within the reach of all, at least within the reach of multitudes of our people from whose longing eyes they are as effectually shut out as if they were located in the moon.

Journey to Europe.

The trips to Mexico and California seemed to sharpen my appetite and quicken my desire to see more of this beautiful world of ours and to know more of the conditions of life that surround its inhabitants, and so during the summer of 1896, in company with my family, I visited the land of my birth, making a tour through England, Scotland, and Ireland as well; afterward making a somewhat extensive journey into Europe, visiting France, Switzerland, Italy, Austria-Hungary, Germany and Roumania. The visit to the capital of Roumania, Bucharest, was specifically to investigate the oil fields of that country, and the same object took me to Galicia, a northern province of Austria.

It was during this trip that the photographs were made which form a part of the illustrations of this book. To those who are familiar with the method of oil production in this country, these illustrations will prove an interesting object lesson showing the backward method of producing oil still in vogue in far-away

Roumania. Cheap labor, cheap human life and low standards of living account for the difference. The lower standards of living have not yet been accepted by the artisan class of American workingmen, and may God grant that we may get our eyes opened to the iniquity of a social system that is forcing low standards of living upon us, before we shall have sunk to the degraded social state of the countries I have referred to.

I tried to make the most of the opportunity that was before me during this time of travel to study the social life of the people wherever we went. Having some knowledge of German, I was able to do this much better than had I been confined to one language. Nearly everywhere we went, I found German-speaking people, and the facility with which the people of those foreign countries acquire different languages is so nicely illustrated by an incident that occurred one day when we were on the way from Bucharest to Budapesth, that I feel it is worthy to be made a matter of record. A family entered the compartment that we occupied, one of the members of which was a bright little girl, who chatted pleasantly with two other little girls who were her travelling companions. As she was speaking German to the little girls and I had heard her speaking the Roumanian language to her mother, I addressed her, saying, "You speak German also." With an air of the utmost nonchalance she said, "Ich habe vier sprache" (I have four languages). "So," I said, "what are your four languages?" "Roumanian, French, German and Italian." Expressing surprise, I said, "How old are you?" and you can well understand that my surprise was well founded when the reply came, "Ich bin acht yahre alt" (I am eight years old), and the mother assured me that she spoke the four languages fluently.

The Lower Standards of Living Abroad.

The study of the life of the people in the various countries through which we passed convinced me that while there is much that we of America may learn from the people of Europe in the way of municipal and state Socialism — lessons that have come to them because they are so much older — yet on the whole, distressing as are the conditions of the poor in our own country, they are infinitely worse in all the other countries that I have visited. True, it is no easier to starve in one place than another, but I have seen people reduced to the verge of starvation from want of work in our own country, and six months or a year later I have seen them earning, perhaps, three or four dollars per day. I do not wish to convey the idea that this is a common instance, but it is not uncommon in the business with which I have been most closely connected, that of oil producing. That the standards of living among the American workingmen are infinitely higher than of those of any foreign country, I think all are ready to admit. I mention this fact because it is one from which we may take courage. It is one that bids us hope that the time is not far distant when the standard of living now possible to an American workingman who is fortunate enough to have a steady job will be within the reach of all who are willing to work; for we shall have come to understand our social relations so thoroughly that we shall amend the system under which we are living to such an extent that a reasonably human life will be easily obtainable by all who are willing to render an equivalent in service for it.

The Remedy in Political Action.

The state, or political division, is the only agency through which all of the people may be served; it is the only agency, indeed, through which the people can adequately express their love and care for one another. The people have dimly understood this principle ever since governments were established among men; but the prevalence of the competitive idea has, to a great extent, thwarted their efforts to put it into practice, and never, so long as the competitive idea is the rule and guide of our daily life, have we any right to hope for the survival and supremacy of any but the cunning, the strong, and the unscrupulous, and the consequent enslavement of the confiding, the simple, the gentle, and the loving. The state is the only organization that reaches All of the People, of which All of the People are a component part. Every subsidiary agency, no matter how lofty its purposes, is necessarily limited in its scope. Charity organizations, churches, lodges, guilds, fraternal societies, and political parties — all come within this classification. No matter, then, what may be the professions of the platforms or sects, or what declarations of principles may be set forth by any select few, their real purpose must be antagonistic to the purposes and conceptions of the state.

With the competitive idea uppermost it has been urged that self-preservation is the first law in nature. (I admit this is true with respect to wild beasts.) Of course, it will follow in the minds of those who recognize this first law, so-called, that the second law must be to preserve the thing nearest to yourself, which is usually your political party, or, perhaps, your lodge, or some other division of society. This reasoning has brought me face to face with the fact that there is grave danger that a person may unwittingly be guilty of disloyalty to the state through a mistaken conception of duty to minor organizations, such as I have mentioned. Indeed, there is reason for believing that the commonest form of disloyalty to the state is found in the mistakenly excessive loyalty to one's own family. This is not a new idea; it has been sarcastically immortalized in the well-known jingle alleged to have been the prayer of one of this sort of disloyal people:

> Lord, bless me and my wife,
> My son John and his wife;
> Us four and no more. Amen.

The man who can feel or utter that sort of a prayer is guilty of treason to the state (All of the People).

My Entrance into Public Life.

The revelations of truth that came pouring in upon me as a consequence of my experience with the swarms of hungry men looking for work about the Acme Sucker Rod factory brought me more and more every day to a realization of the truth that I have talked so much about, the truth of brotherhood and the equal right of every man to a place upon the earth, as well as an equal right to live an entire human life. It was the result of these revelations and reflections and my seeking some way of escape from the guilt of the dreadful system in which we are all caught, that led me, in the conduct of the work of our own business, to take such steps looking toward a mitigation of these evils, as I have already outlined. The social gatherings, wherein we made an attempt to break down the absurd notion of social distinctions between employer and employed; the shortening of the term of labor to a fifty-hour week; the practicing of a little profit-sharing at Christmas time,* and during the last year the giving a week's vacation with full pay, are measures we have

---

* [A copy of the Christmas dividend letter to the workingmen of the Acme Sucker Rod Company.]

Toledo, Dec. 25, 1898.

Mr. John Smith:

Dear Brother.— Following our custom for the past few years, we inclose herein our check in your favor for the sum of ...., that being 5 per cent. on the amount that has been paid you in wages by this company during the past year. This is not intended as a charitable gift; it is an expression of good-will, a recognition of faithful service, and an admission that the present wage system is not scientific; therefore, not a just system; further, it is doing the best we know at the present moment in the way of making a beginning that will finally lead us to a condition of life (brotherhood), where the question of what a person shall receive as a reward for his labor will no longer be a mere matter of chance, depending upon the necessity

employed in the hope of moralizing the system of industry in our plant. I now see that all these measures, while they are steps in the right direction, are insufficient. Fundamentally and scientifically, as well as according to all Christian conception, it is plain that every man is entitled to *all* the fruit of his toil. It follows, therefore, that neither I nor any other man has a right to take profit from his fellows, nor shall we want to in a just social order.

It was the application of these principles at the Acme Sucker Rod factory that brought my name with some degree of prominence before the Toledo public. In the spring of 1897 the Republican convention, to which I had been chosen a delegate, assembled in the city for the purpose of nominating a city ticket. There were three candidates for the office of mayor. After four ballots there was no choice, and two of the candidates looked about for a man upon whom they could combine their forces to defeat the third, who was likely to be the winner in the next ballot. In this emergency my name was placed before the convention, and I was nominated on the fifth ballot. I had been a resident of the city a little more than four years, had never been in a convention before, was not a member of a single club or

---

of the one and the greed of the other, as is the case at present, but where justice will prevail and where every man will be secure in the enjoyment of all of the fruit of the labor of his hands. If in the future there shall appear a better way to contribute to this end, we hope to be as ready to adopt it as we were to adopt this little division of profit.

Accompanying this dividend, we hand you a little booklet, our fifth annual Christmas greeting, wherein you will find our views upon the subject of social relations somewhat fully discussed, and we commend the same to your thoughtful consideration.

We wish you all always a merry Christmas and a useful, that is, happy New Year.

Very faithfully yours,
S. M. JONES,
For the Acme Sucker Rod Company.

fraternal society, and as my time had been largely spent outside the city, in the oil fields, I had, of course, but a limited acquaintance. The politicians and the wise men who fancied that they knew how it was all going to turn out were simply astounded; they could not by any possibility account for such a strange performance, that an entire stranger, who had never done anything for the party, a comparatively unknown man, should walk in and capture a plum so longed for and so highly prized; should jump, as it were, right over the heads of faithful party workers who had toiled long and patiently during many weary years to serve the party. It passed their understanding.

And yet it was all due to a little effort put forth to deal justly with our fellow-men, and the workingmen, the toilers who produce all and have so little, were quick to realize, keen to appreciate and anxious to place the seal of their approval upon even this small effort in behalf of the right.

Being unacquainted with the city, I decided at once that the wise course for me to pursue was not to attempt the organization of a political machine, but to start out at once to tell some of the truths that had been crowding in upon me, speak my mind, make a plea for a better social order, for fair play, for a Golden-Rule deal all around. In line with this policy I entered upon the work of the campaign, and, though unused to public speaking, made many speeches in various parts of the city, in parks, factories and little halls over saloons where I could assemble men together. On one occasion I addressed a Democratic club, advocating non-partisan municipal politics. (I have gone only a step further now that I am advocating absolute non-partisan politics under all circumstances, the absolute destruction of partisan politics as the necessary first step to the realization of free government.) Though vigorously opposed by the forces of individualism, and particularly by the saloon-keepers, who feared, on account of the fact that I was known to be a member of a church, that a drastic policy would follow my election, I was elected by a majority of 534.

A Desire and Attempt to Serve All the People.

Installed into office, my first thought and constant care from that day to this has been to serve the people. I made no effort from the very first day to serve the Republican party. I did not try to administer the office in the interest of any party, sect, clique, or clan; but strove, as best I knew how, to take the high ground that I was elected to be the servant of All of the People, and the boss of none. I had gone into the office absolutely a free man, without a promise, direct or implied, of any sort to any person on earth, and I had unusual opportunities for inaugurating a more lofty program than commonly prevails among those who are elected to public office. I claim no credit for the course I pursued. I was exceptionally favored in the way I have recited. It was easy for me to do right; it would have been hard for me to do wrong. Under existing conditions to-day there are few of us who are free men and women in any capacity. We are either in economic bondage or in servitude to some party, sect, corporation or individual, or else we are in the worse position of a boss or ruler of our fellow-men. I want, therefore, to be plain when I say that I deserve no credit. I had an opportunity for freedom of action that seldom comes to a man in public office, and I sought to be worthy of the trust reposed in me.

Believing that the great need of our municipalities, the great need, indeed, of our social and national life to-day, is ideals; seeing that we are a nation of Mammon worshippers, with Gold as our god, and that we have been long enslaved by it, I sought to lift the public mind in some measure into the domain of art and idealism. I believe that it is the artistic idea of life that helps us to see the possibility of a social order in which all life, *every* life, may be made beautiful; and having this conception, I sought to lift the minds of the people toward it, to encourage them to look forward to the better day, the realization of which is sure to dawn upon us. I advocated some few measures looking toward social justice in the management of the affairs and work of the city; I strongly advocated the shorter workday, and at least two important departments are now operating under it, the police department and the water-works department. I advocated, and the police commissioners adopted, the merit system, instead of the spoils system that had for years kept the police department a wrangling, fighting, jarring collection of men hating one another instead of loving one another. Many things that I did and the measures I advocated were called "radical," but, on the whole, the administration was well received by the people of the city, and that portion of the country outside that knew anything about it.

Second Annual Message.

Toward the close of my term I submitted to the common council my second annual message, embodying recommendations of such remedial measures as seemed to me not only desirable but practicable. The program, to some who will glance at its scope and detail, may seem a large one; but I believe that there is no measure named in it which is not urgently needed; none which will not contribute greatly to the welfare of every citizen of Toledo, and none which is not possible of immediate accomplishment if only the people will resolve to give over their prevalent notions of individual strife and selfish gain and consider their real welfare in the light of the collective welfare of all.

The following is the substance of the recommendations made:

The establishment of a city plant for the manufacture of fuel gas.
The control and operation by the city of the electric-lighting plant.
The establishment of civil service in all departments of the municipality.
The enactment by the legislature of laws that will give the city such a measure of home rule as will enable it to "bring out the best that is in its own people."

No grant or extension of franchises to private enterprise without the approval of the people.

The abandonment of the contract system on all public work, such as paving, sewers, etc.

The compilation and publication of the city directory by the municipality itself.

The establishment of kindergartens as part of the public school system.

A larger appropriation for street improvement.

The sprinkling of the streets by the city itself.

The passage of the ordinance for the appointment of building inspector.

A larger appropriation for public parks.

An appropriation for music in the parks.

The establishment of playgrounds for the children.

The establishment of free public baths.

Improved facilities for those who market in Toledo.

The erection of a city building.

The uniting of all the people to the end that the Ohio Centennial may be made a grand success.

The revision of the city license laws.

The repeal of the ordinance licensing employment agencies in Toledo.

The veto power to be abolished and the referendum to the people substituted in its place.

It is a pleasure to record (and I hope I am not trespassing on the patience of the reader in doing so) that this message was received with considerable interest in many parts of the world. Among the letters regarding it which I received were one from our well-beloved novelist and humanitarian, Mr. William Dean Howells, and another from Count Leo Tolstoy, to the latter of whom I had sent a copy of the message, accompanied by a letter expressing my appreciation of his work. I take the liberty of publishing these two greetings. The quaint diction of Count Tolstoy's will be noticeable:

FROM WILLIAM DEAN HOWELLS.

40 W. 59TH ST., NEW YORK CITY, Dec. 18, 1898.

MY DEAR SIR.—I know of no public paper in these times of greater value than your annual message, of which some unknown friend sent me a copy. It is full of good sense springing from the humanity which is the source of all good sense. With yourself and Governor Pingree in official life we cannot quite lose courage, even when the republic is trying to turn itself into an empire.

If there were any form in which one might congratulate the city of Toledo upon its mayor, I should like to offer it my felicitations, and wish it long years of you.

Very sincerely,
W. D. HOWELLS.

FROM COUNT LEO TOLSTOY.

YASNAIA POLIANA, 24 January, 1899.

DEAR FRIEND.— I beg you to pardon me for not answering your letter, which gave me great pleasure, for such a long time. Please to receive my warmest thanks for it and for the pamphlets. It is a great joy for me to know that such ideas as those that are expressed in your address are approved by a great majority. I am not so hopeful as you are on the results of the Czar's note, and have explained my reason for it that I will have the pleasure to send to you when it will be translated.

Thanking you for your sympathy to my activity, and hoping that a part of what you say about it would be true, I am, dear friend,

Yours truly,
LEO TOLSTOY.

DETERMINE TO MAKE A SECOND RACE.

As the time approached the closing of my first term, I began to be convinced that our greatest hope for relief from social evils lies in political action, and I determined to be a candidate for re-election. Three months before the election I so stated to the chairman of the Republican committee, adding that my reason for being a candidate was found in the fact that I thought there were a lot of people in Toledo who believed in the principles that I tried to stand for, and I thought they should have a right to vote for them. I said that, inasmuch as I had been the candidate of the Republican party when I was elected to office, it seemed, as a matter of courtesy, that I should again be their standard-bearer. I said that if we were granted the open primary, provided for by law in Ohio, where the people may vote directly, without a delegate system, for the candidate to be nominated, and I should be defeated by the Republican voters, I, while laying no special claim to Republicanism, would stay out of the race. But I added that if I were defeated or turned down by a delegate convention, I would be an independent candidate, because I knew how the best man on earth may be beaten in a delegate convention, and to abide by any such decision would be an injustice to the people in not allowing them to express their will on the question.

Believing that the history of this Republican convention and the Independent campaign that followed, which resulted in my election, is of sufficient importance to be made the subject of permanent record, I now present a succinct account of the circumstances, beginning with my proclamation of candidacy and ending with the election.

Announcement of Candidacy.

On the 18th of February I addressed the people of the city through the columns of the newspapers in the following letter:

TOLEDO, O., Feb. 18, 1899.

To the People of Toledo:

I am a candidate for renomination and re-election to the office of mayor.

I know there is a large number of people in the city of Toledo whose sympathies on the general subject of government and the need for a more just social order are with me, and I believe these ought to have an opportunity to express their convictions through the ballot. I ask the nomination at the hands of the Republicans, because I am entitled to it according to the usages of the party in this city, where a second nomination has always been conceded to those whose administration has been satisfactory to the people. The nomination that led to my election came to me unsolicited, and I claim that I have not unworthily represented either the party or the city.

I am a Lincoln Republican. I believe in the people as he believed in them, and trust them as he trusted them. I have been the mayor for all of the people, high and low, rich and poor, black and white, employed and unemployed. My experience in the office has served to strengthen every conviction to which I have ever given expression regarding the brotherhood of all men. I believe that we are in the beginning of a time when, through the administration of love as law, we are to realize in a larger degree the kind of liberty that Lincoln believed in and died for.

I believe that the wealth created by the people should be used for the people's benefit. The streets are the common property of all of the people. Every wire, every pole, every conduit, every rail — everything permanently in or on the streets should be for the common benefit of all the people, not for the private benefit of a few.

The contract for lighting the streets of Toledo expires with this year. The city should at once take steps to own and operate its own lighting plant. We are now paying $90 each for about 800 arc lights; the city can furnish them for $60, thus saving about $25,000 a year.

I believe in the shorter workday as the most practical step now possible looking to the solution of the problem of problems — the problem of the unemployed. The eight-hour day should at once be adopted and rigidly adhered to on all public work. It is wiser, more humane and cheaper to provide a plan to let men work and add to our wealth than to keep them in idleness either as tramps, beggars or dependents on our overworked charities.

Believing that a large majority of Republicans would indorse these principles, I said to the chairman of the committee having the matter in charge that, if the primaries were called under the straight Baber law, I would abide by the result. This law provides that the primaries shall be publicly conducted by the board of elections exactly the same as any regular election is carried on, and the system has been adopted by every metropolitan city in the state outside of Toledo. The committees, however, have taken the matter entirely out of the hands of the board of elections, and the primary election will be in charge of a committee of five persons; delegates will be chosen to the convention, which is called for the 4th of March, and these delegates will select candidates for the offices to be filled.

It is reported that I have said I would not be a candidate for the Republican nomination. This is not true; I never said anything that could be construed to be an intimation of the kind. I am a candidate, and ask that all who believe in the principles that I have here outlined and who trust the justice of the Golden Rule and the Declaration of Independence, assist me with their support for the nomination.

Very sincerely yours,
S. M. JONES.

THE COMMITTEE OF FIVE.

The Republican central committee had appointed a supervising committee of five to conduct the primaries for the ensuing nomination. To this committee was delegated "full power and authority," and it was ordered to "exercise general supervision over the primary election, arrange and order all the details, decide all questions and determine all matters relative thereto." As if this were not explicit enough, the committee's commission further read: "The supervising committee of five shall canvass the returns of the primary election and shall certify the list of delegates so chosen at the primary election to the temporary chairman of the convention." The majority of the members of this committee was understood to be opposed to my nomination.

My friends were alarmed at the menace involved in the giving of such powers to a committee. It suggested a deliberate plan of manipulating the election of delegates. Open charges to this effect were made. The chairman of the committee of five now offered me the privilege of stationing watchers at the primary polls. To this offer I replied as follows:

TOLEDO, O., March 1, 1899.

Hon. J. H. DOYLE, *Chairman, Committee of Five, Toledo, O.:*

MY DEAR SIR.— I am pleased to acknowledge the receipt of your note of yesterday and thank you for the courtesy that inspired it. It seems to me that to be consistent, I must decline the privilege you offer. I have not questioned the integrity of the committee of five; my objection from the beginning has been to a dishonest system of conducting the primary elections,— a system that takes the primaries out of the hands of the regularly constituted election officers, and substitutes in their stead a privately chosen committee of officers. A system that distrusts the ability of the people to such an extent is neither republican nor democratic, but essentially autocratic; it is the quintessence of ring rule, which is only one remove from king rule. This is my objection to the present system; it denies to the people the free exercise of the sovereignty vested in them by the Constitution and Declaration of Independence, and seeks to lodge the power in the hands of a few — the cunning and the strong — and opens the way to and makes possible, if not extremely probable, the practice of all sorts of villainy and corruption. The mere counting of the ballots is only an incident. This part of the work may be honestly done and yet the will of the people be entirely subverted, as you well understand, and as every one at all familiar with modern business methods applied to politics very well knows. Entertaining this view of the case, it does not seem to me proper to enter into any system of espionage proposing to watch one door only while dozens of others are wide open.

Assuring you of my confidence in the integrity of your purposes, I am,

Very sincerely yours,

S. M. JONES.

THE CONVENTION.

The opposition to my nomination had centred almost wholly upon Charles E. Russell, a young real-estate dealer, although J. D. R. Lamson, a prominent merchant, carried some support. The result of the primaries seemed to throw in doubt the results of the forthcoming convention, for a number of delegates were looked upon with suspicion, and it was thought they would vote for the side upon which they conceived their interests to lie. Moreover, reports came to me from every section of the city of the grossest manipulation of the polling booths and of the actual returns.

The Republican convention, which assembled on March 4th, at Memorial Hall, was a monster gathering. Long before the doors were opened, great crowds of men stood waiting, and the sentiment for my renomination was pronounced and persistent. From the first there were loud cries of " Jones! " " Jones! " whenever opportunity offered, and, as the meeting progressed, this sentiment became more and more pronounced. The committee of five had issued orders that no one, except holders of tickets, was to be admitted to the convention floor. This was a new rule in Toledo, and, like many other laws and rules made by self-constituted authorities for the government of the people, it withstood the pressure of public opinion but a short time, for the surging mass took matters into their own hands, removed the doorkeepers, pushed the doors open and filled the body of the hall; but nothing that could be called disorderly, beyond the incident of breaking in the doors, occurred at any time in the proceedings.

On the first ballot for permanent organization, the vote stood, Harry E. King, 126, and T. P. Brown, 125. Mr. Brown, who was the temporary chairman, and represented the forces opposed to my nomination, promptly decided that there was "no choice," in effect saying that 126 was not more than 125. In justice, it should be said that Mr. Brown quoted a rule of the committee of five, which read, "Necessary to a choice, 127." This, however, referred to the number of delegates necessary to a choice in the selection of candidates, and obviously had nothing whatever to do with the organization. During the hubbub that followed this decision, "business methods," well known to manipulators of conventions, were brought into play, and on the next ballot Mr. Brown had a clear majority.

It was freely charged that the votes necessary to accomplish this change were purchased outright. It is impossible to say whether the money was actually paid on the floor of the convention or not; I believe that it was, and the great majority of disinterested spectators believe as I do. Such a procedure is so common to conventions in both political parties that it is a subject hardly worthy of remark.

Nominations were now in order for candidates for mayor. When my name was presented, cries from the opposition arose, asking if I would "stand by the ticket." I replied, "My service in the past is the only promise for the future."

Isn't it a rather striking commentary upon the conceptions we have of political loyalty that the Republican convention two years before placed my name in nomination absolutely unsolicited, absolutely without question, and that now a convention majority stood in the face of an unchallenged record in the administration of the mayor's office for two years, asking if I would "support the ticket?"

On the first ballot the vote stood: Jones, 124 9-11; Russell, 125 2-11; Lamson, 3. Agents of the opposite side and representatives of the leading corporations were actively engaged working with the delegates, and the second ballot stood: Jones, 124 9-11; Russell, 126 2-11; Lamson, 2. On the third ballot a choice was made of Mr. Russell, by a vote of 130 to 123 for myself.

I announced from the platform of the convention that I would appeal from the decision of the committee of five to the decision of the Committee of the Whole People.

Independent Announcement Made.

On the same evening I wrote the following address to the people of Toledo, which contains substantially the platform upon which I made the campaign:

Toledo, O., March 4, 1899.

To all the People of Toledo:

The Republican convention of this city has to-day repudiated the administration of the mayor's office for the last two years.

The principles that have guided me, and upon which I shall go before the people as an Independent candidate, are:

Equal opportunities for all and special privileges to none.

Public ownership of all public utilities: the wealth created by the people should be for the people's benefit rather than for the private profit of the few.

No grant of new or extension of existing franchises.

The abolition of the private contract system of doing city work — a source of corruption equally as great as that occasioned by the granting of franchises — and the substitution therefor of the day-labor plan, with

A minimum wage of $1.50 per day of eight hours for common labor; organized labor to be employed on all public work.

The Republican convention has made history. The cause of reform is becoming more respectable every day. Thousands of people whose attention had not been called to the infamy of the present system will now join in the work of reform, no matter what their party affiliations. In the convention to-day I made the battle of my life to enlist the support of the Republican party for these principles, but the cunning of manipulators won the day, and, I believe, stifled the will of a majority of Republicans.

As no criticism has been entered against the administration of the mayor's office, it follows that my defeat for renomination in the convention to-day is a repudiation of these principles. The methods employed to accomplish my defeat were so notoriously corrupt as to excite the indignation of all classes of the entire community, irrespective of party. The unqualified promise of support from these is a comforting assurance that government by the people has not yet perished from the earth.

The experience of to-day convinces me that a good measure to put an end to business corruption in our politics would be to amend the bribery laws, punishing only the bribe-giver, letting the poor victim of this despoiler of our liberties escape.

The city of Toledo should at once take measures to own and operate its own lighting plant; the present contract for lighting our streets expiring with this year, and competition being impossible, we are at the mercy of the present contractors.

The movement to defeat me found its chief inspiration in my well-known opposition to the extension of the franchises of the street-railway company and those sought for by the Water street railway, as the plans of men of " eminent respectability " will be seriously interfered with if these schemes are blocked.

Asking for the support of all who believe that the people and not the machine should rule, I announce myself as an Independent candidate for the office of mayor, promising in the event of an election to be in the future, as in the past, the mayor of all the people.

S. M. JONES.

REASONS FOR THE STEP.

A few days later I sent to the chairman of the committee responsible for the manipulation of the convention the following letter:

TOLEDO, O., March 7, 1899.

Mr. WALTER BROWN, *Chairman, Republican Executive Committee, Toledo, O.:*

DEAR SIR.— On or about February 15th, I called on you at your office and stated that I would again be a candidate for the Republican nomination for the office of mayor; that I had no desire to be the candidate unless a clear majority of the party desired that I should; and I asked that the primaries be called under the straight Baber law, that gives the voters the right to vote directly for the candidate of their choice. I also asked you to say to the committee of which you are chairman that if a primary was held and I was not the choice of a majority of the Republicans, I would loyally abide by their decision; but I added: "I will not submit to a turn-down at the hands of political manipulators of a delegate convention, for I know how it can be done, and I cannot fight with or by their methods; if I am defeated that way I will be an independent candidate." You carefully repeated my words, and said: "You are saying this to me, as chairman of the committee, and wish to have me so report to the committee, do you?" I replied in the affirmative, and you said you would so report at your next meeting. A member of the committee declares that you made no report of the kind to the committee at all. At any rate, my request for "fair play" was ignored. The call was issued for a privately conducted primary; and a private committee of five, four of whom were known to be as reliably solid against me as they are against the people, was chosen to conduct the primaries, instead of the regularly constituted bi-partisan board of election officers.

Six months ago I received notice that orders had gone out from the head machinist that I was to be turned down at the Republican convention for my published expression of sympathy for Governor Bushnell last winter, when he was the subject of the most shameful and unwarranted attack ever made on a high-minded public official since the days of political martyrs. Evidently the selection of a private committee of five was the first move in a scheme, conceived in iniquity, born in sin, and carried out in injustice at the primaries and the convention last Saturday to accomplish my defeat. The discovery of the presiding officer, when the first ballot was taken for permanent chairman, of a kind of arithmetic in which 126 is not a majority in a vote of 251 would seem to indicate that even an elementary knowledge of figures is dangerous in the hands of some men.

The high-handed outrage of that convention has shocked the moral sensibilities of all decent people without regard to party, as thousands of our citizens who were present testify by their indignant denunciation, their brotherly words of sympathy and offers of help. The American people believe in fair play, and they are ready to use the machinery of government to extend it to the humblest citizen. The attempt of the committee of five and the convention that grew out of it, to subvert the will of the people and to set up in its place the will of a few manipulators, will prove one of the greatest blessings that has come to Toledo in many years, and its influence will never end, for it will go on and on until not only the dreams but the visions of prophets and seers will be realized, and it will hasten the day when business will be friendship and government will be love,

> " When man to man the world o'er,
> Will brothers be for a' that."

There will be a wonderful clearing of the atmosphere as a result of this convention. It will be easier to locate " dangerous men " and to determine who are the real Anarchists. The anarchy that stands in the way of, and is a constant menace to, free government is the anarchy of those corporations who send their agents into convention halls, courts and legislatures to bribe, corrupt and intimidate the representatives of the people. These Anarchists who would destroy free government and bind the people for all time in unbreakable chains as mere instruments of profit to be used for their selfish purposes, either for a consideration or a price — these are the forces that are at the bottom of the movement that accomplished my defeat at Saturday's convention.

I point with pride to the fact that during the two years that I have been in office as a Republican mayor, there has been no trifling away of the people's property to further enrich this by far the most dangerous class of all lawbreakers, no grant of new or extension of existing franchises having been recorded during the last two years. I congratulate the people that, in the effort that culminated in the convention last Saturday, the extreme viciousness of a system that puts a constant premium upon dishonesty was revealed so clearly that the unjust purposes that inspired it are doomed to certain and ignominious defeat at the hands of a wronged people, when they register their will at the polls on election day.

To those Republicans who ask why I would not pledge myself to support the ticket, I reply that my record was a sufficient guarantee to the people of Toledo for my conduct in the future. I went into the mayor's office absolutely without promise of any kind to any man, and death on the platform at Memorial Hall last Saturday would have been infinitely preferable to wearing the collar that would bind me to loyalty to the organized selfishness that is conspiring to put the city of Toledo in bondage to insatiable greed. The attempt to exact a promise from me as to my future conduct in the face of an unchallenged record in an office where I had honored the party who called me there, was so farcical as to be morally grotesque, and merited the contempt with which I treated it.

The foregoing will enable you to understand why I appeal from the committee of five to the Committee of the Whole People. If loyalty to the principles herein set forth is sufficient to debar me from further affiliation with a party that I have always voted with, I shall accept the result cheerfully, confident that I shall find a resting place with that larger party, of which we are all a part, and whom I have tried faithfully and loyally to serve as a Republican mayor during the last two years — the party known as All of the People. To them I now submit my case.

Very sincerely yours,
S. M. JONES.

THE CAMPAIGN OPENS.

Petitions favoring my candidacy were distributed the day following the convention, and in a few days several thousand signatures were obtained. The Democrats had nominated Capt. Patrick H. Dowling, and a three-cornered contest was assured. The campaign began in earnest. A headquarters was established in the Valentine Building, under the efficient charge of Lem. P. Harris, former city clerk, and a candidate for the nomination of mayor two years before. Hundreds of citizens called to assure me of their support, and many volunteered services or money, among the latter being hundreds who could ill afford a contribution from their meagre earnings. Among the first volunteers were two bands — the Libbey and the Marine.

ATTITUDE ON PUBLIC LIGHTING.

My position on the question of municipal public lighting, to which I had given considerable attention, had been repeatedly attacked by a local paper. I had proposed a plan, drawn from that successfully begun and now about to be successfully accomplished, by the citizens of Springfield, Ill., for the erection and maintenance of an electric-lighting plant. The following letter on this subject will be found self-explanatory:

TOLEDO, O., March 10, 1899.

Editor Toledo Blade:

DEAR SIR.— In Tuesday's "Blade" you have editorially addressed the following questions to me:

"FACT vs. THEORY."

"Will Mayor Jones come down to facts and state his plan for what he calls 'public utilities' under the ownership of the city?

"Does he expect to confiscate those already existing? If so, what method does he propose? Does he expect to buy them, or to construct new plants?

"In either case, where is the money to come from to buy or build?

"Is there any way to get it except by the issue of more bonds, with a consequent increase of the annual interest burden?

"Is the experience of the city with the 'public utilities' it already owns, such as to render it a good business proposition to go in deeper?"

The only public utility that I am recommending to be placed at the present time under municipal ownership is a public lighting plant, and this is the situation with regard to it: The contract for lighting the streets of Toledo expires with the close of this year. The law governing electric lighting in Toledo provides that no person can submit a bid for lighting our streets until the question whether they may bid or not shall first be submitted to a vote of the people at an election, and to carry it must have a majority of all votes cast at that election. A majority of all votes cast on the electric-lighting question is not sufficient; it must be a majority of all votes. The indifference of many voters is a guarantee that they will neglect to vote on the question of electric lighting. Such a question is usually printed on a separate ballot, and the result has been that this city in the past has been shut out from any possibility of getting even a pretense of competition in this important branch of public service. There is but one way of escape for the people of Toledo from the monopoly now enjoyed by the electric-lighting company, and that is through municipal ownership. This situation is fully explained in my message to the council on October 3d last.

Some months ago, acting under the direction of the common council, Mr. Thomas Cook, superintendent of water-works department, made a report on the subject of a municipal lighting plant, in which it is set forth that such a plant can be located at the water-works, where we already have the land and a building in which to install it without a dollar of expense. Mr. Cook also furnished an estimate of cost, which he says is only approximate but near enough to meet the requirement of the report, which was simply to show to the council the entire feasibility and economy of a municipal plant located at the water-works, owned and operated in connection with the water-works by the city, to provide the city streets with light at actual cost instead of continuing a system of lighting by contract by a private corporation whose only purpose in furnishing us with light is to make private profit, and of course the more profit the better. This is no criticism of the lighting company, but an attempt to reveal the wrong of private contract for private profit against public ownership for the benefit of all the people. The council ordered Mr. Cook's report printed, and that was the end of it.

Some months ago, Mr. Braunschweiger introduced the following resolution:

"Resolved, By the common council of Toledo, that, whereas the contract for lighting the city expires in 1900, and municipal ownership of lighting plants is not an experiment but a pronounced success, Be it resolved by the common council that the best interests of the public demand that the city of Toledo shall own and control its own plant, together with the necessary poles, wires, conduits and other appurtenances for the proper lighting of its streets and alleys. And the mayor and city solicitor are hereby appointed a committee to report a plan to the common council for raising the necessary funds to properly equip, maintain and operate an electric-lighting plant, in accordance with the estimates submitted by Superintendent Cook of the waterworks department.

"Adopted December 27, 1898.

"Attest: Lem. P. Harris, City Clerk."

On January 9, 1899, a report was returned, from which I quote:

"We beg leave to report that the resolution is so comprehensive in its scope that we are unable to report a definite plan at present, owing to a lack of time, but will do so as soon as our time will admit of a careful study of details. As this question is one of interest to all of the people of the city of Toledo, we recommend that it be submitted to a popular vote at the coming election, and in pursuance of such recommendation, submit the following resolution.

"(Signed.)   S. M. JONES, Mayor.
"WM. A. MILLS, City Solicitor.

"Resolved, By the common council of the city of Toledo, Ohio, That the mayor be and hereby is authorized and requested to issue a proclamation submitting the question of the construction by the city of a municipal lighting plant to the voters of said city at the next regular spring election, and the city clerk of said city is hereby authorized and directed to certify a copy of this resolution to the board of elections of said city."

The resolution passed the council and came up at the next regular session of the board of aldermen, when it was "laid on the table."

On February 27th, I introduced the following resolution in the board of aldermen, asking that it be placed on its passage as the time before the spring election was getting short.

"Resolved by the common council of the city of Toledo, Ohio, That the mayor of said city be and is hereby authorized and directed to issue and cause to be published in two newspapers of general circulation in said city a proclamation calling upon the electors of said city to vote at the next regular spring election, to-wit, April 3, 1899, upon the question of said city constructing, erecting and operating its own municipal electric-lighting plant, providing the same can be done without the issue of bonds.

"Resolved, That the city clerk of said city be and is hereby authorized and directed to certify a copy of this resolution to the board of elections of said city."

Objection being raised to its passage, I stated to the members that the resolution explained itself; it merely asked that the people be permitted to say whether they believed the city ought to own a municipal plant, provided it could be had without a bond issue to cover the cost of building the plant. There was a full, fair and free discussion of the question by the members, and finally, in response to a question from one asking " how a plant could be had without a bond issue," I replied that " I will provide a construction company, who will install an electric-lighting plant, complete, ready to start, turn it over to the city without asking the down-payment of a dollar. Let the city run the plant and continue to pay monthly for lighting $90 per arc light, the price we are now paying, and the construction company will take their pay out of the saving effected under the price we are now paying until the debt is discharged. I further stated that I would, and I now repeat I will, become personally responsible for the proposition to provide a reliable construction company who will enter into such a contract.

Notwithstanding this manifestly just and fair proposition, the resolution was defeated; by a vote of eight to seven the aldermen decided that the people ought not to be permitted to vote on this question, and, let me add, it was not due to the "corrupt politics" that we hear so much about, as the vote against the measure was equally divided, four Republicans and four Democrats. If corrupt corporations will keep their agents away from our convention halls, council chambers and courts, we shall soon cease to hear this talk of corrupt politics, for the real trouble will be located in a corrupt system of private ownership of public properties that opens the way to all sorts of corruption and puts a premium on dishonesty in public officials in order to keep the people in perpetual bondage to those corporations who seek to use them as mere instruments to make profit out of, as mere grist for the inhuman mill of greed.

Superintendent Cook's report states that the arc lights of 2,000 candle power can be furnished under municipal ownership at $60. Competent electricians assure, and the experience of other cities convinces me, that it can be done for less. We now have over 800 arc lights in the city and ought to have 1,000. With 1,000 lights, a saving of $30 per light would mean a saving to the city of $30,000, and this saving would clear the debt from our plant in from six to ten years, and give us our own public lighting plant, owned and operated by the city for the benefit of all of the people instead of a privately owned one for the private profit of the few. The issue is clear. Shall we pay the lighting company $30,000 per year more than we can do the work for ourselves; shall we add $30,000 a year to the burden of the taxpayers, to still further enrich the lighting company? That is the only question now before the people of Toledo on the subject of municipal ownership. I believe they will answer it in a way that indicates the ability of the American people to govern and serve themselves unaided by the paternal care of corporations or their paid attorneys. The world is full of honest men. Give us a system that will let them live according to their best instincts.

Very sincerely yours,
S. M. JONES.

Answer to the Ministers.

My conduct of the office of mayor had not given unalloyed satisfaction to the ministers. A committee from their organization now determined to " sound " the various candidates on their attitude in respect to the saloons, the gambling-houses and the houses of ill-fame. The Republican candidate, when approached, promptly declared his intention of rigorously closing these places, and the Democratic candidate returned an answer considered to be evasive. My own answer is contained in the following letter:

TOLEDO, O., March 16, 1899.

Rev. G. A. BURGESS, *Chairman:*

MY DEAR BROTHER.— Replying to your committee of ten clergymen who called on me yesterday, asking that I sign a written pledge to enforce the laws with respect to the saloons, the gambling and bawdy-houses, etc., I desire to repeat what I said in the conversation:

It seems to me, in view of the fact that I have been your mayor for two years and my record is before you, it would be puerile to outline by promise what it will be in the future. Men are judged by what they do rather than by what they say. In the coming election the ballots will indicate what the people of Toledo think of the administration of the mayor's office, as we have had it during the last two years. In my case the service I have already rendered is what I must abide by; that is the only promise the people will fairly accept. If the administration has been a mistake or a failure, the people will so decide and put one of the other candidates in my place, and I must accept the verdict, and I will still trust the people. I have been guided by the same principles that actuated me in the conduct of our private business, believing that it was because of what I had done differently from the usual methods of business in private life that the people called me into their public service. I have sought as best I know how to apply the Christ philosophy to the conduct of the affairs of the city.

The records of the police court in this city reveal the fact that there have been many attempts in the past to enforce various phases of the saloon laws with the practically uniform result of a failure to make a case and the saddling of the costs on the city. This simply proves a well-known truth that, no matter what law is on the books, the only law that can be enforced is the law that the public sentiment of the community will uphold. On this point I shall be explicit. I have enforced and shall continue to enforce all the laws according to the standard of existing public sentiment.

I shall always hold myself open to any new revelation of truth that may be presented and always be ready to give careful attention to any appeal or plan that has for its purpose the betterment of the conditions of the people of our city.

I have done my best so to lead and direct in the administration of the affairs of the office as to secure the blessings of good government to all of the people, and I believe that the result has been attained to a greater extent than we had a right to expect two years ago. About one year ago the saloon question was up for discussion, and the city council, by a vote of forty-three to two in both bodies, repealed all the ordinances having any bearing on the Sunday question; following their action came the spring election, when we had two police commissioners to elect. It was currently reported that the Republican candidates favored a more drastic enforcement of the laws against saloons, and the Democratic candidates were advertised as "wide-open" men. The entire Republican ticket was elected by varying majorities of from 2,000 down, except the two candidates for the office of police commissioner; these were defeated by more than 600, and the so-called "wide-open" men elected. Simple justice to these men requires me to say that they have rendered excellent service to the city, and that I have seen nothing in them inconsistent with the character of fair-minded gentlemen. I voted for the Republican candidates, with both of whom I was personally acquainted.

Up to the beginning of the present administration the police department had been used as a clearing-house for the payment of political debts, and had frequently been the scene of the most shameless and unblushing outrage against the commonest instincts of humanity in the wholesale discharge of faithful officers, who were "fired" simply to carry out the

MR. AND MRS. JONES, AND THEIR SON PAUL, WITH THE DOVES OF ST. MARK'S, VENICE.

terms of a business arrangement between itical managers. The logical result of this sort of thing was a demoralized department, where envyings, jealousies, bickerings, back-biting and a desire to "get even" were the marked and important characteristics, service for the city being evidently a secondary consideration. From the start I pleaded for a peace policy and, after a time, succeeded in getting the merit system of civil service adopted, the Republican commissioners voting against it. We next introduced the eight, instead of the twelve-hour day, without increasing the expense or reducing the pay of the men, and not long after the men were given canes instead of clubs, with the result that there has been a marked improvement in the character of the entire department. I have sought to impress upon the patrolmen that they are the public servants and not public bosses; I have told them individually and collectively, and especially impressed upon the new men, that the duty of a patrolman is to do all in his power to make it easy for the people to do right and hard for them to do wrong, and I have added, "an officer can often render better service by saving the city the necessity of arresting one of her citizens by helping a prospective offender to do right instead of waiting for him to be overtaken in a fault, in order that he may be dragged a culprit to prison. The result may be seen in the number of cases in the police court; there has been a decline of more than 1,000 cases, about 25 per cent., for 1898, as compared with 1896, and 500 less arrests are recorded than for the corresponding period ten years ago, when the city had one-half its present population. I know that those who believe that the path of peace is by the way of Jorgensen rifles, Gatling guns and torpedo boats will say that this decline in arrests only proves that the law has not been enforced and that we have a "lawless town." Of course, it is idle for me to reply to this charge, for the people who make it will not accept my statements; but my appeal for refutation of this slander is to the patriotic people who love our city, who visit other cities, and who take a broad view of life and try to comprehend the condition of all of the people; and upon these I confidently rely to support my affirmation that our city is composed of as orderly, well-governed, liberty-loving and loyal people as any city of similar size on this continent. I firmly believe that we have a police department that is second to none in the country, and I make this statement after having personally investigated many of the chief cities from the Atlantic to the Pacific coast since I have been mayor of Toledo. For confirmation of what I say in regard to the efficiency of this department, I refer especially to Mr. Robinson Locke, proprietor, and Mr. Locke Curtis, city editor of the "Blade," both of whom have told me within two months that there had been a vast improvement in the department and that the so-called morals of the town were infinitely better than ever before. Reference to the editorial columns of the "Blade" will confirm all that I have here said.

Regarding the charges that are bandied about and believed by many good people, I will say that there is no open gambling in Toledo; by open gambling I mean places running "wide open," such as Hanner's, on St. Clair street, and the one over the Wabash saloon, on Summit street, which were running at the time of my election, and had been for years previous. The gamblers are not running the town, but there are respectable thieves who are trying very hard to get a chance to run it. I am not, nor have I ever been, in collusion with, nor have I, directly or indirectly, authorized any one for me, to enter into any sort of collusion with any man, or set of men, to make any deal providing for any evasion of or "letting up" on any law. I do not know five saloon-keepers in the city. I have never had any kind of a conference with saloon-keepers since my election, nor have I authorized any one to do any of these things for me. I have never made anything like an attempt at organization to forward my election, nor spent nor authorized the spending of a dollar for such a purpose prior to the late Republican Convention.

This is the truth with respect to the questions that your committee propounded. The saloon is not an issue in this campaign. It is sought to make it an issue by those who are moving heaven and earth and resorting to every sort of infamy to accomplish my defeat and clear the road for a wholesale era of franchise-grabbing unparalleled in the history of the city. It is a false issue, raised to divert the public mind from the main question. "In vain doth the fowler spread the net in the sight of any bird."

The net is too plain, but the prize they are playing for is nothing less than one of the most gigantic schemes of franchise-grabbing ever concocted — that contemplates not only a new electric-lighting franchise, but the Water street railway, an extension of the existing street-railway franchises, and involves not only turning over the city to those profit-gatherers, but would make the great centennial itself and the people of the great State of Ohio mere grist for the profit-gatherers' mill. The saloon issue has been raised to help forward this cause, and any force that seeks to defeat the Independent ticket in this campaign may rely on these agencies for sympathy and cash.

The bare idea that the Traction company with their Sunday beer at the Casino are enlisted on the side of "law and order" ought to afford a clue to the real animus of the movement to defeat me, and I think it will. I do not believe that the Christian people of Toledo are going to be caught with any such bait.

I went into the mayor's office absolutely without promise or pledge of any kind to any person or set of persons. I have faithfully tried to be, in the best sense of the word, a mayor for all of the people. If I am elected on the 3d of April, it will be on exactly the same conditions. I cannot be bound by any promise more definite than that I will use every power of head and heart to be in the future, as I have been in the past, the mayor for all of the people.

Very faithfully yours,
S. M. JONES.

LABOR A PRACTICAL UNIT.

The labor unions were prompt in rallying to my support. Some of them indorsed my candidacy openly, and others, prohibited by their constitutions or by-laws from the formal favoring of candidates for political office, indorsed the declaration of *principles* upon which I based my candidacy. Among these was the Central Labor Union, composed of delegates from the several unions, and their action was practically unanimous. To this body I replied as follows:

TOLEDO, O., March 17, 1899.

Central Labor Union, Toledo, O.:

GENTLEMEN.— I am in receipt of your communication announcing the adoption of the resolution by the Central Labor Union, indorsing me as an Independent candidate for the office of mayor. I take pleasure in saying that so far as there is anything personal in this campaign, I feel a deep sense of obligation to the organized labor in Toledo. The spontaneous and outspoken manner in which the principles I stand for have been indorsed by the various locals has impressed me deeply, and now that the Central has, by this resolution, confirmed the acts of the local bodies, making organized labor practically solid for the Independent movement, we are fully justified in saying that organized labor in Toledo stands in the forefront of the great movement now fairly started in this country to bring about the equality that the founders of the government intended, when, in the Declaration of Independence, they said that " all men are created equal and entitled to certain inalienable rights, among which are life, liberty and the pursuit of happiness."

I believe that organized labor has done more than any other agency during the last twenty-five years to bring men to a better understanding of the purposes of government, the meaning of justice and liberty and what we have a right to expect as the fruit thereof. I believe that we have the right to expect and that in the near future we are going to realize a condition in this country that every man willing to work may find work and the means to live in a manner becoming a self-respecting citizen of a great republic.

Thirty years ago John Ruskin wrote: "The wealth of a nation may be estimated by the number of happy people that are employed in making useful things." I believe it is the manifest destiny of the United States of America to show to the world a practical demonstration of a nation rich because of this kind of wealth — wealthy because all of her people are employed in doing useful things. This is the only way in which we can be a really great people; great in our knowledge of how to serve one another — this is government — and great in our love for one another. Then we shall have justice. To this work I am fully committed. I believe it to be the hope of the nation and the world. It shall have the strength of my remaining years.

Awaiting your commands, if in any way I can serve you, I am,

Very sincerely yours,

S. M. JONES.

Invasion of Sam P. Jones.

One of the spectacular features of the campaign that attracted wide attention was the series of meetings held for two weeks and a half in the Armory by the revivalist, Sam P. Jones. Mr. Jones took very pronounced ground against my candidacy, he having been led to believe that I was in league with the devil, and that it was owing to my inefficiency and lack of " backbone " that there was a demand in the city of Toledo for saloons, gamblers and houses of prostitution. I do not believe that the extirpating method to which Mr. Jones pins his faith is either the Christian or the scientific method. I believe that the only way in which evil will be overcome is the strictly Christian way, which is to overcome it with good. I believe the only way in which the saloon evil will finally disappear will be through the growth of the loving spirit in mankind, which will provide an opportunity for people to live decently human lives, provide equality of opportunity for all; and then no one will want to live a degraded life, either in the slums of the rich or in the slums of the poor.

Mr. Jones' violent attacks upon my policy greatly alarmed some of my friends. One timid little white-ribbon woman, who believed in me and my interpretation of the gospel of love, came to the office one day, relating that she had had an interview with Brother Sam P., pleading that he would cease his attacks upon me, telling him that he did not understand me, etc. Grasping me by the arm, she said: " Now, Mr. Mayor, he is just awful; he told me that if you did not promise the ministers this afternoon that you would enforce the law against the saloons, he would cut wide open on you, and you would be the worst-licked man that ever ran for office in Ohio." As best I could, I calmed the dear sister's agitation, assuring her that we could safely leave the matter in the hands of the people, that they would decide. " But," she asked, " you will put them off with some kind of a promise, won't you? "

I was told by one of the ministers who said that he handled every card at the Sam P. Jones meetings, that less than two hundred men, women and children, all told, signed the cards even professing to believe in the gospel of a man who, after reference to the Golden Rule mayor, said, " I believe in the Golden Rule, too, *to a certain extent,* but then I want to take up the hickory club and shotgun." This does not sound to me like the gospel of love of the lowly Nazarene, who said, " Love your enemies," " Do good to them that hate you," " Pray for them that despitefully use you," and finally, " A new commandment I give you, that ye love one another even as I have loved you." It is a hopeful sign, promising much for the future of our beloved country, and filled with promise for the waiting peoples, that but two hundred persons signed cards indorsing the gospel which Mr. Jones preached with such venom and vigor for two weeks and a half to thousands of Toledo citizens. Love redeemed, and will yet save the world.

Mr. Jones, getting his cue from unofficial sources, announced again and again in Toledo, and far and wide in other places, that there were 840 saloons in this city. This led me to make an investigation of this question, which revealed the following facts, which were published in the Toledo "Commercial" of March 29.

TOLEDO, O., March 29, 1899.

To the Editor of the Commercial:

I desire to bring to your attention, since yours is one of the journals that has been so persistent in declaring the existence of 840 saloons in Toledo, that an investigation of the books of the county auditor, instituted by me to-day, utterly refutes this statement.

There are to-day in force in this city 608 licenses for the sale of liquor or beer. Beginning with the 1st of March, each year, there is always an increase in the number of these licenses. The increase continues until June 1st, when it falls off moderately, the number decreasing during the autumn and winter, and increasing again as spring opens. The number in force to-day is about the same as on March 29, 1898. There are no means now available of giving the exact figures for that time.

But the official figures for the time approximating the beginning and the end of my term in office — and the only figures available for comparison, on account of the time of footing up totals in the auditor's office, are as follows:

December 20, 1896, 589.
December 20, 1898, 581.

This number includes every place of business — wholesale or retail, restaurant, drug store, grocery or side bar — wherein any class of liquor or beer is sold.

Since you and others have repeatedly declared or implied that the alleged increase in the number of saloons was due to a certain policy imputed to me, it is but just to point out that the figures show a decline of eight, instead of an increase of 240.

The ingenious gentleman who figured up the total of 840 has apparently included the 219 discontinuances of licenses made since May, 1898, and these not being sufficient, has evidently made another addition, subtracting it from his imagination.

Sincerely yours,
S. M. JONES.

CAMPAIGN OF EDUCATION.

The campaign was truly a campaign of education. Clubs and committees were organized in every ward, and meetings were nightly held. I usually addressed two, and often three and four meetings, in one evening in the different wards. The size of the meeting was almost invariably measured by the size of the room or hall, and the enthusiasm of the men of toil, the workers, knew no bounds. I shall never forget the intense feeling that was manifested in these meetings, the earnestness with which the auditors would listen to my description of a government that is yet to be realized, a government that I have so often spoken of as the time when the Golden Rule shall be the supreme law of the land, and when business will be friendship and government will be love.

The three notable meetings of the campaign were the one on Saturday evening, March 18th, in Memorial Hall, the one on the Thursday evening before election in the Armory, and that in Memorial Hall again on the following Saturday.

The first Memorial Hall meeting was the first general meeting of the campaign. The hall was filled, and the enthusiasm was rampant, giving us the satisfaction of seeing that the tide had set in our direction. Rev. John H. Grant, a colored minister, and one of the two ministers who publicly supported me, presided, making a strong plea for the success of the Independent movement. I followed in a forty-minutes' address. Then came the great speech of the evening, by Mr. Clarence Brown, one of the ablest of Toledo's lawyers, a masterly orator and a believer in the principles of human liberty, who contributed freely of his service for this glorious work.

The night of the Armory meeting there was to have been an industrial parade. During the afternoon a snowstorm set in, and as the evening drew on the storm increased until, at seven o'clock, the hour set for the assembling of the parade, the streets were one blinding sheet of falling snow. The general sentiment expressed among the people was that there would be no parade, but, of course, it was decided to go on with the meeting, though we felt sure there would be but few people there. Contrary to all expectations, the labor unions and independent bodies began to assemble in the streets, the bands playing, the horns tooting, and the people gathering, when they took their places in line and the procession moved. The sight as they filed along the street was one never to be forgotten. The falling snow, with many of the paraders carrying umbrellas loaded down with two or three inches of it, the red fire, the ascending rockets, the blare of trumpets, the playing of the bands, the hurrahing of the enthusiastic people determined to love one another, and to manifest their love for one another under any circumstances, made an impression upon the mind of the beholder and hearer never to be forgotten. Conspicuous among all the paraders were the girls of the Laundry Workers' Union, who, nothing daunted, pinned up their skirts and joined their brothers in the march, singing the "Industrial Freedom."

The Armory reached, they filed in by twos, fours and tens, until the great building was filled to overflowing, while many hundreds turned away unable to gain admission. The addresses at the Armory kept up the enthusiasm that had inspired the paraders in the street, and the meeting broke up at a late hour, every one feeling that it was good to have been there.

The second Memorial Hall meeting was surprisingly well attended considering that the great Armory meeting but two nights before had called out so large a part of the population. Brief speeches were made by nearly all of those who had taken part in the campaign, and it was seen that the enthusiasm was yet at flood tide.

Predictions and Results.

The last issues of the capitalistic, corporation, and political machine papers on Saturday evening and Sunday predicted the election of the respective candidates that the papers represented, assuring their readers that the Jones cause was hopeless, that the people had stood loyally by the old parties, etc., to the end of the painful chapter. Our own forces were confident of success, though few anticipated the real degree of it. The election passed off quietly. The result is believed to be a matter worthy of record in these pages, and the figures are hereunto appended:

Total vote	24,187
Jones, Independent	16,773
Russell, Republican	4,266
Dowling, Democrat	3,148

The Independent ticket received 70 per cent. of the total vote, carrying every precinct but one in the city.

What the Result Means.

The day after the election I gave the following statement to the public press as my view of the situation, and the time that has since elapsed has tended to confirm the convictions then expressed on the subject:

> The overwhelming victory that has resulted in the election of the Independent candidate for mayor in this city by a majority of more than 9,000 votes over the two party candidates in a total vote of 24,000 is a great triumph for the common people and indicates the beginning of a movement for equality of opportunity that is destined to sweep this country. It cannot be accounted for on the narrow hypothesis of the "personal popularity of the candidate," as the partisan press of this city is seeking to show. It is the triumph of principle over party. It is the dawn of the day that is to see the emancipation of the people from the long night of bondage to party superstition, class hatred and slavery to the corporations.
>
> I want it to be distinctly understood that this campaign has been fought out on the broad basis of equality as set forth in the Declaration of Independence, the still broader proposition of the brotherhood of all men, and the declaration that every man willing to work has a right to live and the right to such a share of the fruit of his labors as will let him live a decently human life.

The declaration of principles upon which the independent campaign was conducted and to the support of which the people rallied so magnificently involved:

Public ownership of all public utilities;

No grant of new or extension of existing franchises;

The abolition of the contract system of doing the work of city improvement;

The substitution of the day-labor plan, with a minimum wage of $1.50 for an eight-hour day, and

The employment of organized labor on all public work.

The victory indicates that the people believe in these things, that they have tired of ring rule in the interest of corporations, that the crack of the whip that places party above principle no longer has any terror for men born free, and that the people are eager that their legislators and leaders shall incorporate these principles into law and give them an opportunity to express their love for one another through the thing we call government. To lead in this work is the manifest destiny of these United States, and the municipalities must be in the forefront of progress.

All the disreputable tactics of guerrilla warfare were resorted to by the partisan press of the city in their frantic and vain effort to divert the minds of the people from the real issue. The fair name of our beautiful city was besmirched with every vile calumny and slander that could be laid against it, but the people kept their minds on the issue of whether we should have the Golden Rule of all the people, or the rule of cash by a few of the people — and the verdict has been rendered once for all by the heroic Toledans in favor of the Golden Rule of all the people.

On one side of this question stood organized labor in a solid phalanx and with organized labor practically all of the working people and the intelligent masses who believe in fair play and do not ask anything more for themselves than they are willing to grant to others. Over against them stood both political machines, the partisan press of the city, and the franchise-hungry corporations. The victory proves that the people will yet have their own.

Long live the people.

CHAPTER III.

THE RIGHT TO WORK.

"Behold us here, so many thousands, millions, and increasing at the rate of fifty every hour. We are right willing and able to work; and on the Planet Earth is plenty of work and wages for a million times as many. We ask, if you mean to lead us toward work; to try to lead us — by ways new, never yet heard of till this new, unheard-of-time? Or if you declare that you cannot lead us? And expect that we are to remain quietly unled, and in a composed manner perish of starvation? What is it you expect of us?" This question, I say, has been put in the hearing of all Britain; and will be again put, and ever again, till some answer be given it.

Unhappy Workers, unhappy Idlers, unhappy men and women of this actual England! We are yet very far from an answer, and there will be no existence for us without finding one. A fair day's-wages for a fair day's-work; it is as just a demand as governed men ever made of governing. It is the everlasting right of man.— *Carlyle: Past and Present.*

CHAPTER III.

THE RIGHT TO WORK.

THERE is talk of a new kind of right. It is in the air. We hear it on every hand. It is the *right to work*.

It is not a *newly conceived* right. It has been postulated before, it has been preached before, it has been maintained before, by thousands of the world's great teachers and prophets.

But it is *new* in the sense that it is coming to be accepted by all humane men as a necessary right; indeed, fundamental and precedent to those rights declared in the Declaration of Independence — for only by the concession of the right to work can a man live, enjoy liberty and pursue happiness; and it is *new* in the sense that it is to be the next right incorporated into the law of our Republic.

Until this right is as well established in this country as the right to vote, and work is as free as education in the public schools, our boasted liberty is, and will remain, largely a myth.

Appeals for Work.

The present social system has failed, as every thoughtful man who comes in contact with real life is ready to admit. *The public offices in our cities to-day are living charnel-houses.* The cry of the poor and disinherited never ceases in their corridors. Work! Work! Work! is the plaintive cry. Denied it in one office, they turn to another, to meet the same denial. This experience is repeated until hope has fled from the man's bosom, and there is no man left; and he goes out to become a criminal, or perhaps to seek escape in a suicide's grave.

The other day I received a pathetic letter from a wife and mother in our city; it is yet unanswered, simply because I do not know what to say; it is a counterpart of hundreds that come to the mayor's office and of hundreds of thousands that go to the office of every public official and employer throughout our land; it is the appeal of a wife and mother coming to the help of a husband and father, who has become disheartened in the hopeless search for work. She says:

> My husband has looked in every shop and every store and every new building in the city, and he *can't get as much as a pleasant look.* They act as if you had asked for their pocket-book when you ask only for work, etc.

Actually the warfare is so fierce in the competitive scramble for "trade" that the modern business man cannot afford the time for either a pleasant look or a pleasant word unless there is money (business) in it.

Here is another letter:

> DEAR SIR.— Please excuse me for troubling you, but it's a case of *don't know what to do.* I am a widow, with three children — two boys, one sixteen and the other seventeen, and a little girl of twelve. We could get along nicely if my boys could get work, but they have looked and looked all summer long and found nothing. We have advertised in the papers, and they have answered every advertisement we have seen, but all to no use. My boys are good boys, and I want them to stay good boys. I don't want them to become corner "bums," but unless they get work soon, I am afraid they will drift into evil ways, as so many have done. I work for —— ——, but, of course, don't get much these hard times, etc.

Here is a mother, pleading that her boys may have what is clearly the *right* of every man,— the right to work, pleading that her boys may not be driven through enforced idleness into lives of crime. Put yourself in her place; she is your sister; think of the pathos of the situation, and then see if you can satisfy your conscience by saying "it has always been so," while you complacently draw your robes of luxury about you.

Every day's mail brings letters to the mayor's office, begging for employment or pleading for immediate help. It is a revelation of misery. Men and women, altogether human, and well-educated, as can be readily seen from the composition of their letters, are suffering unspeakable agonies of mind and even the actual physical pangs of starvation, for the lack of a few pitiful dollars.

Husbands plead for work that their wives may not go hungry; mothers implore assistance for their children, that they may be kept from shivering in the winter's cold; sons declare themselves willing to do any kind of labor to save their white-haired parents from the poorhouse.

It is a constant wail of anguish, and it would take so little to transform it into a song of thanksgiving. Any one would think that work was the elixir of life. Men plead for it as though it were the greatest boon in the world. Work! Work! Work! What can be more pathetic? Willing to dig ditches, to delve in treacherous coal-mines, to sweep refuse off the streets, to run any risk, to endure any hardship, to submit to any conditions, however inhuman, so that a few precious dollars may be earned to shake in the face of poverty!

Here are three sample letters, selected at random from among hundreds, showing the way in which our people are being driven over the precipice.

A heart-broken woman from Grand Rapids, Mich., says:

> As a drowning man catches at a straw, I catch the thought that by appealing to you something may be done. My husband is an old locomotive engineer. He is well and favorably known among railroad men. Seven years ago his health broke down, and he became a physical and mental wreck, partially paralyzed and half blind. He will never again be able to earn a dollar.
>
> I was obliged, some years ago, to give a chattel mortgage upon our furniture, and until now I have been able to pay the interest. I raised $250 at 8 per

cent. But I can no longer pay any more, and we owe $50 for the rent. Besieged upon all sides for money, I don't know which way to turn. Every one I know wants money, but I cannot hope to get any unless some friend of humanity will lend it to me until I can pay him back. Only the bitterness of necessity causes me to write this to a stranger. I am in desperate circumstances or I would not dare to appeal to you. I will repay you every cent. With an anxious heart I shall await your reply.

Here is another, from an Ohio town:

I take the liberty of asking you if you could give me employment *at anything*, as I have a family depending on me for support. I have done nothing all winter, and I am at the end of my means,— no money left. If you can get me work, for God's sake do, and I will remember you as long as I live. I was in the oil-refining business, but was crowded out by the Standard Oil Company. I must either work or starve. I will be faithful to you if you will please be kind enough to give me a chance. I should have sent you stamps for reply, but have spent the last money I had in the world to send this letter

And this is one from our own city of Toledo, dated November 21st:

I suppose you hear a great many hard-times stories, but I feel as though I must tell you mine. My husband had just one day's work last week, and we have not had fire enough to keep warm. We have been living on dry bread and not enough of that. We have a family of eight, and five of them are without shoes. The truant officer compels us to send them to school, and we cannot send them barefoot and hungry and cold. I asked for help and was refused. If you come to our house you will see that I am telling you the truth. Part of my children sleep on the floor because there is no bedstead for them. If we had an old one we would be thankful. We pay our rent and that is something. I am sick abed, and I can't bear to see the children so cold and unhappy. We must have shoes and food until my husband gets regular work. If you can help us quietly, please do. If not, we can suffer the same as we have been doing.

Such are the stories that come from thousands of families. To blame the unfortunate creatures themselves, to pharisaically point to their lack of thrift, their large families, and so forth, is to treat a large subject in a trifling way. Poverty is too widespread a disease to account for it by cataloguing a few individual frailties. These touching appeals come from the victims of an unrighteous social system.

The continued appeals for work from so many men, their repeated offers to "work for anything," their piteous pleading for their needy and distressed wives and little ones, the abject and servile deference that many of them manifested in the presence of those who had the power, as they believed, to give or withhold the precious boon for which they sought, was to me, when I marked them first, a new and very distressing revelation of the life of the people about us. Morning, noon, and night the same story was repeated,— nay, is still being repeated — and always by a new crop of men. My business friends who had long lived in the city and had, in a manner, become used to the "hard-luck stories," as they called them, tried to comfort me by saying that "it has always been so," or that "they are looking for work and praying that they shall not find it," or that "they are a drunken and worthless set and no good anyhow;" but these answers did not and do not satisfy the awakened social conscience. Most of my business friends enjoy the comfortable seclusion of an inner office, and as business men cannot afford to listen to appeals for work, that unpleasant duty is turned over to a servant or to the still cheaper and more comfortable sign-board on the outer wall labelled with the legend that has proved a heart-breaker to many a man who has walked weary miles only to feel hope die within his breast as his eyes fell on this indictment of modern industrialism, this cold-blooded denial of *Brotherhood*,—"NO HELP WANTED." I knew that the explanations offered by my friends did not furnish a true reason for the existence of such an army of unemployed men. It is not true that "it has always been so;" and if it were true, my reply would be that it has therefore been wrong, and that it is our duty to change it.

We Know Not How the Other Half Lives.

It was the actual contact with ragged, starving men, your brothers and mine, willing and anxious to do any kind of work, that opened my eyes to the iniquity of our social arrangements. As some poet has said:

> Evil is wrought by want of thought,
> As well as want of heart.

Too many of us confine our lives to a small, select circle of friends. The real lives of the people in the city where we live are as unknown to us as the manners and customs of the Patagonians. All the folk outside our own little clique are regarded as necessary automatons, not as human beings with the same joys, sorrows, virtues and frailties as ourselves.

> We live for ourselves and think for ourselves,
> For ourselves and none beside,
> Just as if Jesus had never lived,
> As if he had never died.

If we only knew the tragedies that take place probably in our own ward or street, if we only knew the bitter heart-ache of the poorly dressed woman who touches elbows with us on the sidewalk, we should endeavor to live larger and less self-centred lives. Our duties are not fulfilled when we love our families and remain true to our friends. "Thy brother is he who hath need of thee."

We are members of the human race, and "humanity is more than any man." The very complexity of our civilization brings with it a thousand social duties, the ignoring of which will bring bankruptcy and disaster to us as a nation and as individuals.

Vast Development Which Has Meant Only Want to the Workers.

During the last fifty years America has seen a wonderful materialistic development. A nation of inventors, we have led the world in making marvelous machines which have been and are the wonder of the age, each displacing the labor of many men. In the old time, a man with skill at his trade, made in his shop the whole of a thing, whether it was a wagon, an axe, or a pair of shoes. Now a worker in any of our large factories makes and has skill to make only the twentieth part of a thing. He himself becomes a machine, going through the movements many times a day, day after day, week after week, and month after month, with no stimulus of brain to inspire him to aim at an artistic and finished creation, but merely to turn out as' many pieces of a thing as a piece-price wage, or an exacting foreman, demands.

We have developed great wealth in this nearly completed nineteenth century (will it not seem strange in one more year to write 1900?) but it is the wealth of individuals — millionaires and multi-millionaires, who hold in their hands a dangerous power, in this money-worshipping age, which can, if it wills, corrupt courts and legislatures, and can and does frequently menace and crush out private interests which stand in the way of desired ends.

Ruskin says: "The wealth of a nation, first, and its peace and well-being besides, depend on the number of persons it can employ in making good and useful things."

Does this apply to us as a nation? Yet, who shall say when a man has reached the limit of right in the amount of his possessions? Who can set the mark for a definite stopping-place in the scramble for wealth?

Thoughtful men and women who are close students of social conditions tell us that in the evolution of society in this country the great middle class, which has constituted the stability of our nation (a nation which in its founding was created by this same so-called "middle class"), is gradually lessening in numbers and prosperity, and will eventually cease to be, unless we change our social system. Wealth is more and more being massed in the hands of the few, and the armies of the poor and of absolute pauperism daily grow in numbers. More than 300,000 people exist in one square mile of the city of New York. In Chicago, men run over one another to get a chance to cut ice at a dollar a day, and board themselves: hard and cold work, and those who want the job are thinly clad and poorly fed.

Men tell us that times are better; that there has been a fine trade, and we hope it is true, and are glad; yet the army of the unemployed is still here. To-day there are steam shovelers on the docks that load and unload each as much coal and ore as formerly took fifty men to handle.

The Modern Tramp.

In this way we have developed the modern American tramp. There must have been tramps in bonnie Scotland one hundred years ago, or Robert Burns would not have written the "Jolly Beggars;" but the modern tramp is a different creature. He has been and is still the subject of many a jest and cartoon in our papers, humorous and otherwise, and Weary Waggles has become a well-worn and familiar friend. The tramp to-day may occasionally be the idle and worthless fellow we have come to think him, but in the main, very largely indeed, he is the man who, thrown out of employment through conditions wholly beyond his control, after a vain attempt to find work in his own town or city, is driven through his own desperate need or that of a wife and little children who suffer with him, to start out to find a "job" in some other locality, and at once he becomes a tramp. Without means, he is arrested by railroad detectives if found trying to steal a ride, or in the cities as a vagrant, and told to move on, or worse still, thrown into the workhouse. What think you of his state of mind if he has left behind wife and little ones whom he loved? He may be among the incapables — naturally they would be the first to be thrown out by the development of machinery, and saving of hand labor,— but they must live. He is usually ragged and forlorn — how could he be otherwise?

The objection, " he does not want to work," is simply a polite bit of evasion with which we try to soothe our troubled consciences. It is belied in a thousand ways by our daily experience. The army of unemployed furnish the recruits for every new enterprise that is started. No man would be afraid to start a mill, factory, or blast furnace because a thousand men were needed and he feared they could not be found; the supply of labor is always "long;" whatever other market may be "cornered," this one never has been and never will be while the competitive system of industry remains.

The late Myron W. Reed, of Denver, Col., whose bright book, "Temple Talks," has furnished much inspiration for reformers, said:

> The tramp is often dirty, uncombed, and generally unpleasant. The slouch and shuffle and unmanly front are not necessarily there because of a lack of brains or heart. The lack of a shirt will account for it. George Washington, in continental coat and powdered hair, fronts the world with a Virginia look. But let him hit the road, sleep in hay stacks, eat cold victuals, and the father of his country will not be recognized by his child.

The American tramp is far from being an ideal man, but as a rule he is not only willing, but anxious to work. In our own Humane Society lodging, out of more than 3,000 men fed and housed from one to three days during last winter, less than a dozen refused to perform the stipulated amount of work upon the streets, which was done often under humiliating conditions.

with jeers and gibes of lookers-on at the "hobos." Yet they comprised many intelligent but unfortunate men, from every walk of life.

How Tramps Are Made.

In an agricultural machine factory 600 men can to-day do the work that twenty-five years ago required more than 2,000. Men are being displaced in all lines of manufacture. Toledo is a bicycle town, and competition has become so sharp here and elsewhere that the prices of wheels have fallen more than half; yet there is not enough work to keep men busy all the year, and the factories close down a part of the summer.

The immense wheat farms of Minnesota, the Dakotas, and California raise tramps as well as wheat. In harvest, the proprietor requires hundreds of men; when harvest is over he requires perhaps ten. The extra force tramp. Their fires can be seen all the way from San Francisco to Minneapolis.

Social conditions at present make it a hundred times easier for a man to do wrong than right. I was at the workhouse recently, and while there saw one-third of the men confined in the prison working at the brick machines for the revolting and blood-curdling crime of jumping on freight trains. A man comes into the city looking for work. He cannot find it. He is hungry. If he is caught begging, we arrest him and send him to the workhouse; if he steals, he is imprisoned and branded as a criminal. So he does the next best thing,— he tries to get out of town. Then he is arrested for jumping on a freight train, and caged like a wild animal. We catch him coming and going. We punish him if he will, and we punish him if he won't. We refuse him the right of being a respectable and industrious citizen, and then send him down for vagrancy. We turn the hose on him, and then arrest him for being wet. What kind of a system do you call that? Is that the way to make a good citizen? Every tramp is a good citizen spoiled.

Men do not become social outcasts for pleasure, nor because of any innate and unconquerable depravity. An irresistible social pressure is forcing our people by thousands over the precipice. I believe it is natural for both men and trees to grow straight, and not crooked. Release men from the burden of this iniquitous profit-system, and tramps will be as rare as lepers. Restore comfort, hope, and ambition to the laboring classes, and trampology will become a lost art.

A young boy, or young man perhaps, starts out in search of employment. He goes from place to place from day to day, week to week, month to month, and year to year. At first he is respectable, well clad, ambitious perhaps; he is unable to secure any employment, or at best to secure but casual work. He goes out with bright hopes of getting a good job by which he can lay up a little something. He does not know that for every one chance in favor of his becoming rich, there are literally thousands against the possibility that he will be able even to make a comfortable livelihood for himself, and thousands more against the possibility of his ever being able to have a home in which to bring up a family. It does not take long for his clothing to become shabby; his last shirt disappears, literally worn off his back, and he pins his coat under his chin to cover his nakedness. He does just about as you and I should do if we had been forced to go through his experience. He does not become so lost to reason but that he can tell that riding beats walking, so, driven from one city, he starts for another; he takes the head end of the "blind baggage" or freight car in preference to walking; of course, there are laws against this; he is a law-breaker; but what would you do in his place? Would you be a law-abiding citizen? Could you maintain your self-respect while denied the right to a place to stand on the earth, as thousands of American citizens are to-day? I think not; I do not think you would try; you would see that every man's hand was against you, and naturally your hand would be against every man.

An Instance of a Homeless One.

A New York gentleman relates the following typical incident, showing the condition of thousands of our people:

I was hurrying along William street, headed toward the bridge, when a man addressed me with, " Say, Mister, wouldn't you help a poor fellow out?" I passed along unheeding. Again he spoke: " Say, Mister, I haven't slept in a bed in two nights!" As I continued to turn a deaf ear to his entreaties, he continued: " You won't listen to me; you won't even look at me!" A sob in his throat brought a note of anguish into his voice which made me stop, both to listen and to look at him. He was not a pleasant sight. The ragged clothes, battered hat, weather-beaten, unshaven face, the sunken eyes, with a half-starved look in them, that made one suddenly silent with a realizing sense of the awfulness of such a condition of life, all made me forget that the man was talking to me while I was studying him.

" My father was born in this country before me," I heard him saying. " My crime is that I am an uneducated man. Nobody wants to listen to me; nobody wants to look at me; nobody wants to help me; what shall I do?

" Well," I said, " you say you have not slept in a bed in two nights; why not?" " Well, I haven't," said he; " and I'm hungry, too. If you, sir, will help me, I will not spend the money for drink. The trouble with you, like all the rest, is that you class all as unworthy; you do not take time to investigate — if you care!"

By this time the man's despair lent eloquence to his argument. He continued: " Here in this big city I have tried for days and days to find work; nobody wants me; if I go a second time to the police station, where I have once been for help, they will send me to the Island, and I don't want to go there. Sir, work is what I want! In the great churches they are taking up collections to feed the heathen and educate them, giving ministers gold watches and chains, and letting thousands starve at their very doors!"

Unconsciously enough, he had struck home with me. The Sunday morning before I had heeded the appeal from the pulpit and put a dollar in the church collection for "foreign missions," and here was a man telling me my duty as a citizen of this great city, to him as a man and brother, an unfortunate one, a dirty, disreputable-looking one, yes, but a man who probably spoke truly and with a fervor born of great necessity. By this time I had given him what he named as a sum sufficient for supper and a bed — to my regret, it was only a quarter — and I listened further.

"Now," said he, "I worked on the snow gang. With no money in my pocket, and the delay, I had to have my order cashed, and the man who did it took a good part for giving me the money. I come from Colorado," he went on, "used to work in the mines there. What did they do? Brought over gangs of Italian laborers who would work cheaper, and I had to get out. I have no recommendation; nobody will hire me without; what am I to do? Starve, or go and jump off the dock into the river?"

I told him that I did not employ any men myself; that the treatment he received in his distress and need was not directed against him as a man, but as one of a class — one of the thousands who day and night haunt the streets until their appeals are unheeded, hardly heard, because of the great number of them. As I spoke, the meaningless platitudes sounded so empty. But I did not know of a place to send him, nor, in my acquaintance, a man who would give him a chance.

No Place for Them on the Earth.

A few of us have corralled the opportunities for work so that we have become like gods upon the earth, holding the lives of our less fortunate fellow-men in our grasp. The dreadful hardships of enforced idleness and inevitable poverty are being endured by thousands who are as worthy and industrious as any of us.

For days and weeks and months they have tried every avenue of escape, doing everything within their power, until finally the awful truth dawned upon them that there was no place for them on the earth,— no pen, or hammer, or shovel, or plow, or other tool that they could use to get the necessities of life for themselves and their loved ones. Then they become desperate and commit some crime, even a prison seeming to them as a place of refuge; or, if their nature rebels against a criminal life, they pass into the future life by the *short-cut of suicide*.

Every day, upon the streets of our cities, you will see throngs of discouraged men. They have lost hope. The ambitions of their youth are only cinders in the ashes of a burnt-out past. Civilization to them seems organized hate. They are on the wrong side of every door, and every man's hand is against them.

They used to hope for a better time coming, but now they simply exist hour by hour and look forward to nothing. To them, America is another word for disappointment. They feel like the prisoner in the terrible cell, used in the Middle Ages, the walls of which gradually approached nearer and nearer, until the helpless victim was crushed to death between them. I can look out of the window of the mayor's office and see the unemployed men standing on the streets with their hands in their pockets, an idle, hopeless, listless look in their eyes; and many of them have no home but the public highway. They come to the office; they besiege me with their pathetic words and their hopeless, hungry looks. They ask for work. They try to add emphasis to their request by telling me of a sick wife and small children.

I repeat the stale old platitude that I am sorry for them, and tell them that work is a luxury beyond my power to give. Every day there is a new crop of people in the office. Where they come from and where they go I cannot tell. Many of them struggle through the winter, half frozen, borrowing a little warmth from the saloons and existing on free lunches and hand-outs.

And all these are *people*, not cattle nor machines. They are sons, husbands, brothers, fathers. Loving mothers nourished them through infancy and cared for them through childhood. They are nineteenth century human beings, having all the feelings and faculties of men.

How Can the Waste of Manhood Be Justified?

How can we justify this waste of manhood? If a single copper penny were dropped on the sidewalk, it would be picked up in a moment; but men, *men* with bright minds and strong, skilled hands, are allowed to stand and rot in idleness upon the streets of our unchristian cities. Men reared in our American civilization and educated in our public schools are to-day without any alternative than to steal or starve. I meet them every day.

They are good men — just as good as most of the pious men of the churches, but they are unfortunate. They are not to blame. When business is a lottery, some people must get the blanks. They failed, not because they were immoral or unskilled or lazy; but because an inhuman system of industry picked them up and threw them on the dump-heap.

It is not necessarily our best men who rise to the top, nor our worst men who sink to the depths. No business man can be sure that he or his children will not before ten years be enlisted in the ragged army of vagrants. The bright-faced young lads now preparing for life in the high schools may find themselves thrust to one side as if it were a crime to be alive. The great Juggernaut car of business has no mercy, and none can be sure of escaping from its crimsoned wheels.

Idle men throng the market places and congregate on the street corners, and yet on every hand there is work in abundance that needs to be done. Many of the city streets are in dire need of improvements, some of them being almost impassable, but there has been such a terrific howl about taxes, mainly on the part of rich men, that there seems to be a dread to propose the work of improvement that is needed. The rather anomalous spectacle confronts us, that, while our streets are full of idle men, our banks are full of idle money. Never in the history of the country, perhaps, have the bank balances been so large as at the present time. Thus far we seem to be unable to unite these two idle forces to do the work that is so much needed, both by the city at large, and by the workers themselves.

Begging for Leave to Work.

Begging for leave to toil is not a new profession, but it is one wholly at variance with any just conception of democracy or brotherhood, and inconsistent with our claim to being a republic of equals; and nothing can be more certain than that if we are ever to realize that condition of equality that the founders of our government forecast in the preamble of the Declaration of Independence, it must be through a realization of perfect democracy in government,— what Lincoln called, "A government of the people, by the people, and for the people," for all of the people, not alone for a few of us.

A man begging for leave to toil, which is in other words leave to live, cannot be a good citizen; it is impossible for him to have any proper feeling of love of country; patriotism in the best sense cannot live in the heart of such a man, for how can he love a country that does not afford him and his little ones a right to live, in return for the service he stands ready to offer? Such a country is unworthy to be loved, because it is unloving.

We are beginning to see that so adroitly have the captains of industry managed for themselves, to-day the toilers who produce all the wealth are not only deprived of any fair share in it, but many are denied even a place to stand upon the earth. All over this broad land of unparalleled richness, men — industrious, honest, earnest men, willing workers — are compelled to tramp in enforced idleness and vainly beg, not for a share in the wealth their hands have produced, but for the poor privilege to work that they may still further add to the wealth of others that they may not enjoy, and incidentally that they and their little ones may eat bread and not die. One hundred and twenty-five years ago Robert Burns wrote:

> See yonder poor, o'erlabored wight,
> So abject, mean and vile,
> Who begs a brother of the earth
> To grant him leave to toil,
> And see his lordly brother worm
> His poor petition spurn,
> Unmindful though a weeping wife
> And helpless offspring mourn.

Ridpath's "Cry of the Poor."

When I think of the misery which exists among the many, and the hardened apathy of the few, I am reminded of John Clark Ridpath's "Cry of the Poor":

Oh, ye money lords of the United States! Oh, ye men of unbounded wealth and license, ye men who reap where ye have not sown and gather where ye have not strewn, ye men who have arrogated to yourselves the right of establishing a despotism over American society, ye men who have banded together to destroy the great Republic and to rebuild on its ruins the abandoned, owl-haunted fabric of the past, ye men who are the foes of human liberty, who do not believe in the democracy of man, who trample down truth and crush the aspirations and hopes of 70,000,000 people under your gilded Juggernaut, ye men whom nothing will satisfy but to gather up the total earnings of your countrymen and consume them in the attempted gratification of your insatiable greed and luxury, ye men whom preachers preach to and teachers teach and lawyers plead for and orators flatter and journalists glorify, ye men who have purchased the organized powers of society and who use them as the dumb pawns of the gambler's board, who think you can buy the world and convert it one-half into a slave market and the other half into a park, ye men who own all the railways and all the bonds and all the sugar and all the petroleum and most of the cotton — heaven save us! — of the United States, ye men whose intolerable pride overtops that of the feudal lords and whose unmitigated selfishness devours the lives of others as the Roman gluttons devoured humming birds and snails, ye men who fear neither the proclamation of truth nor the appeal of innocence in torment, ye millionaires and multi-millionaires and billionaires about to be, whose spoliation of the human race goes on unchecked and whose arrogance already grins defiance out of the ironbound windows of your arsenals, stop — stop now!

The time has come for you to pause and listen! The low murmur which you hear in the distance, so sad and far, is the cry of the poor. They who cry are your fellow-beings. They are as good as you are. They have as much right to the blessedness of life as you have. They have brothers and sisters and children, as you have a few. They have hearts, as some of you have. They are patient and true, as you are not. They are not arrogant and envious; they are humble and sincere. If there be a God they are His loved ones, and now, by the goodness of heaven, you shall hear their cry. We serve upon you a modest and generous notice to hear that cry. You shall do it. The nation will make you do it. You are not the lords of the world; you are not the proprietors of nature. You are simply men as are the rest of your brothers. Your brothers will do you no harm, but you shall hear their cry. You shall not be liars and say that there are no poor; you shall not be casuists and say that it was always so and always will be, for civilization will either abolish poverty or be abolished by it. You shall not be hypocrites and say that God will take care of those whom you have robbed of their labor and their hope, as though He were your confe 'erate. Hear ye, hear ye, the cry of the poor and answer that cry with justice and compassion! Otherwise the future will come down on you like night, and your children's children, visited with a fate worse than that which you now inflict on the children of the poor, will damn you for your sin and folly.

Beginning to Be Ashamed of Profitable Idleness.

Thousands of us are beginning to understand that the right to work is an inherent right, like the right to breathe. All over this broad land people are feeling a sense of ignominy and shame that the workers who produce all the wealth, who make all the useful and beautiful things, should have so little of the product of their toil. Many of us are beginning to be ashamed of living in idleness on profits gathered from the toil of little children, overworked women, and underpaid men.

Great numbers of thoughtful people feel like hanging their heads and hiding their faces as they contemplate the hopeless despair of the army of unemployed that throngs our public highways and our city streets, repeating its piteous plea for employment.

The thing we stand in need of just now is not more territory, not expansion nor imperialism, but a system of government which shall so order and regulate industry that every man shall be free to work, and be protected from the profit-monger in the product of his toil. It would pay us a thousand times better to provide work for our own people than to *purchase insurrections from Spain*, and squander the public money on Gatling guns and battleships. The real battle, which our people are being allowed to fight unaided, is against poverty and bankruptcy. Our self-respecting workers are not asking for charity, like the Italian lazzaroni, but only for the chance to sweat and toil at some productive occupation.

No honest, self-respecting man can be content to live at the expense of other people's toil. I do not believe there is any way in which a man can show his love of country except as he manifests it to his fellow-men. Both our religion and our patriotism are measured by our attitude towards one another, and not by a professed veneration for the flag or the Creator. Such conceptions of patriotism as I got in my boyhood days are a delusion, pure and simple, and instead of aiding me to a helpful and proper understanding of citizenship, they proved almost insurmountable barriers. The impression is given to our children that, as the thing called government is perfected, there is therefore no responsibility upon them beyond the pure perfunctory work of voting on election day, of proclaiming in season and out of season that we have the best government on earth, and constantly keeping before the minds of our fellow-men the assertion that we "can lick everybody." If we have the best government, which I do not question, it does not necessarily follow that even that may not be still improved. If we can "lick everybody," even that is not of necessity the highest ideal toward which a nation may strive. It is even possible that we may demonstrate our greatness in a far more substantial mannner by manifesting our ability so to organize and associate ourselves together in the thing called government as to show the world that we can love everybody, and that we love them so thoroughly and so scientifically that we have a government that is ready to listen to the cry of the weakest child as to the clamor of the most powerful organization on earth; and a government in which and under which every man, great or small, may have equal and exact justice; and when that condition shall have been attained, the cry of the pauper and mendicant and the pitiable appeals of the workless throng will forever cease in our land.

Idleness Destroying Men.

The most glaring and immoral fact in our present civilization is the army of the unemployed — an army created largely by the development of machinery and the perfecting of all the means of production and transportation, multiplying the capacity of labor many fold without any adequate reduction in the hours of labor, or any attempt at economic adjustment by raising the pay of the workers. This condition of affairs cannot continue many years longer without serious injury to the government itself. It has been for years doing irreparable damage to our wage-workers. Lack of employment, with all its accompanying worry and discouragement, simply destroys men. It takes all the manhood out of them, and leaves them mere wrecks on the highway of life.

Why should we bestow so much sympathy and honor and glory upon the victims of militarism, and entirely ignore the victims of industry, who are ten thousand times more numerous? In almost every American city and town there is a monument to the soldier boys who never came back. It is an appropriate token of appreciation, and reveals one form of patriotism which is very necessary for the upbuilding and welding together of any country. But where is there a single monument to workingmen who have been killed while doing their work? Why are there no statues to the soldiers of the plow and hammer? Why do we not recognize that service is service, whether rendered with a pick and shovel or with a Springfield rifle and Gatling gun? Let us prove that it is the *man* we honor, and not merely the uniform he wears. Many a young volunteer has recently discovered that the public did not appreciate his worth as highly when he wore a workman's smock and overalls as when he wore his military

A VIEW IN THE ASSORTING DEPARTMENT OF THE GOVERNMENT POST OFFICE, WASHINGTON, D. C.

(The largest business institution in the world, conducted by the National Government.)

clothes. He has found that the country he went to defend will not now even guarantee him a job.

England spent twenty-five million dollars in rescuing one of her citizens from the interior of Africa, while the same money would have saved the lives of thousands of citizens at home, in London, Manchester, and the other great English cities. Are we not in danger of making a similar blunder?

Why Cannot We Provide a Plan of Universal Work?

We have been skilful enough to provide a plan whereby all of the people, without distinction of color, wealth, or education, shall have their letters carried and delivered in an orderly and scientific way, and our present great task is to provide a plan whereby every man shall have a chance to work without any more uncertainty than now attends the delivery of a letter.

Every man has a right to the public streets, parks, and highways. The poorest laborer in any city has the right to receive the aid of the fire department, without being obliged to pay a cent for the expense.

We have already fought for and obtained the right to vote, to exercise freedom of speech, to worship as we please, and to receive a free public-school education. The next right, which is really more important than any of the others, is the right to labor and to receive the full, fair value of what we produce.

Every right necessary for the continuance of life has been, through the growth of democracy, granted to every man, except the right to steady employment, but the denial of the latter makes all the others of little value. Men cannot eat votes, or pay their rent by free speech, or buy clothing by prayer. The freedom of starvation is the bitterest kind of slavery.

The social evolution of the last hundred years has no meaning unless it goes further and bestows upon every citizen the right to at least self-support. A nation of free citizens, nine-tenths of whom have no legal claim to a livelihood, could not possibly exist without a series of revolutions that would terminate finally in a military despotism that would crush out every instinct of freedom.

THE RIGHT TO WORK AS AFFECTED BY THE CONTRACT SYSTEM.

The right to work is not to be considered as established merely when all men are employed. We must consider *how* they are employed, and for *whose benefit*. The right is not fully granted when willing workers are transferred from idleness to a condition of service wherein they toil long hours and for trifling rewards, the profits of their exertions going to others. The right to work carries with it the right to decent work, to useful work, to work to which the toiling one is adapted, and the right to the full recompense thereof.

I believe one of the best methods for restoring the wage-worker to his rightful place is by the abolition of the contract system. This prevents him from being sweated by middlemen, and cuts out direct profit on labor.

The evils of the contract system are the evils of special privilege. Any system that is adopted by society, either as custom or law, that grants to one man or set of men, a privilege that is by force of circumstances denied to other men, is a denial of the equality guaranteed to the people of this government in the Declaration of Independence, and is, moreover, a violation of divine justice.

This iniquitous system is one to which many of the cities of our country are chained by law. In my own city we are bound by a state law to let all work amounting to more than $500 to that ideal robber, the lowest bidder, and similar laws and customs prevail with regard to nearly all of the public work, municipal, state and national. This law would seem to have been framed especially for the benefit of those who are capable of influencing, purchasing and bribing boards, departments or legislatures. The popular idea, of course, is that it has been framed in order to give the community the most work for the least money, but in practice it works in exactly the opposite direction; for, as I have already intimated, it is the contractor's business, not to see how cheaply he can do the work and do it well, but first, to see how much he can get for doing it, and next, how very little he can pay the laborer and how poorly he can do the work in order to increase his profits. The result of this unscientific system is damaging and destructive in innumerable ways; the most direct damage of all proceeding from it is the wholesale robbery of labor. Instead of affording the free competition that its advocates claim for it, it has been shown by practical experience that the inevitable result of the system is monopoly through a combination of business interests into rings, combines and trusts.

Where in a single instance the monopoly fails, as sometimes occurs, the result then is the wholesale robbery of the laborer. In one city of Ohio last year the contractors failed to "get together" in bidding for the work of a large sewer. The warfare between them was bitter, and the contract was finally let at a figure so low as to threaten the ruin of the man who secured it; but, acting under the impulse of the greed that has been developed by the competitive system, the man shifted the consequence of his wrong-doing upon the poor laborers. Instead of employing them by the day at a living wage, he put them in competition with one another for the privilege of digging the sewer by the linear foot, with the result, as I was told by the Civil Engineer of that city, that the poor laborers who dug the sewer received less than fifty cents a day for their pay. And this is freedom! This is under the best government on earth! This is liberty, is it? Liberty for what? Liberty to what? Liberty to exist on a crust and live the life of a dog.

It seems to me that the city that sells to the lowest bidder the privilege of plucking its people, is placing itself on a par with the robber barons of old, who sold the privileges of highway robbery in the narrow passes and mountain crags of their possessions; and the poor laborer to-day under the contract system is a more helpless victim in these United States than were the travelers of old, who were made the legalized objects of plunder by the robber barons. But this system does not exist because men hate one another; it exists because we have not yet learned the source of our distress. Our social system ministers to selfishness and greed, and in every conceivable way we have sought to divert attention from the real question, first by this false issue and then by that.

At every recurring campaign a new cry of "stop thief!" has been raised to divert attention from the real thief; at one time it is the tariff question, at another the money question, at another the question of our foreign policy, and while we still point our fingers at these vanishing myths and cry loudly "stop thief!" we are all the time filling our pockets with unrighteous gains at the expense of the toilers and producers.

State Elimination of the Contractor.

In New Zealand the government carries on public works on the co-operative principle, directly employing those who are able and willing to work upon them. It is found that this system is cheapest; that contractor's profits are saved to the state, and the men paid the ruling standard of wages in the open market. One thing the co-operative labor system has certainly done. It has relieved the congested state of the labor market in all the large centers of population, and cleared the streets of thousands of men who were formerly driven to a state of enforced idleness in consequence of the limited channels of private employment, in winter time more especially.

There are a few cities, notably Boston, Baltimore, Worcester, Mass., Fall River, Mass., Brockton, Mass., Evansville, Ind., and

Manchester, N. H., which report that the contract system is very seldom used, and that practically all the work of the city is done by direct labor.

In Birmingham the health committee, which is responsible for sanitation, has not only entirely eliminated the contractor from the cleaning and repairing of the streets and removal of refuse, but from the laying down of granite paving and flagging. once a most profitable item of his business. The gas committee is not content with employing hundreds of men to make gas, but also keeps its own staff of carpenters, bricklayers, blacksmiths, tinmen, painters, fitters, etc., to execute its numerous works. The improvement committee has its own carpenters, fitters, bricklayers, paperhangers, plasterers and zinc-workers, while the water committee, besides a regular staff of mechanics of all kinds, is now actually engaged in constructing several huge dams and reservoirs near Rhayader, two tunnels and various water towers and syphons, together with workmen's dwellings to accommodate a thousand people, stables, stores, workshops, a public hall and recreation room, a school, two hospitals and a public-house — all without the intervention of a contractor. Liverpool has had a similar experience. Almost all the city engineer's work is done by men directly employed by the city government. After a cruel experience in doing the work of sewer construction by contract, it now does the work by direct employment.

During the Crimean War, the clothes furnished by the contractors to the English army were of the poorest quality. They hung in rags upon the soldiers; and public sentiment was so thoroughly aroused against the contract system that a clothing factory was built at Pimlico, which has ever since supplied both the sailors and soldiers of the British Empire.

The progressive Municipal Council of Paris has for several years allowed a trade union, or any responsible association of workingmen, to make bids for public work, thus shutting out the contractor and encouraging co-operative effort.

A System that Cannot Endure.

"Unemployment exists," says Alfred Russel Wallace, "because of the fact that production is carried on not at all for the sake of supplying the wants of the people, but for the sake of making money for the capitalist." This is the vital weakness in the contract system of doing the work of public improvement. I have no quarrel with the capitalist. I have no quarrel with the contractor. Under our existing business system, it is the business of the capitalist and contractor to get the best end of the bargain, and to my mind all inflammatory and denunciatory appeals directed against "the capitalist," "the contractor," "the money power," are idle and of no avail. Our warfare should be upon an unholy system, a system, too, that is as unscientific as it is unholy, a system that hopes to perpetuate itself through ministering to greed, a system that is a daily warfare, that is calculated to make men hate one another — men who are the children of one Father, whose natural instincts are to love one another and who will yet demonstrate that in spite of all the devils in our special privilege laws or in hell itself, they *will* love one another. The contractor, the franchise-grabber, the briber, who invade our halls of legislation and courts of justice, the political plunderer, the business plunderer and all of the "monsters of greed" to whom we charge our distress to-day, are the legitimate products of this vicious system that makes our pretended democracy a travesty, and exhibits our life and practice as a denial of democracy and brotherhood.

A Plea for the Well-to-Do.

Hitherto I have argued chiefly for the disinherited, the millions who have to confess themselves beaten in the game of life, and who, for that reason, are living the most miserable of all miserable lives — a life of enforced idleness. I now want to enter the plea for another class, the well-to-do, the wealthy, who are leading lives of idleness that, while not calculated to excite our pity as does the life of a man unable to find employment, who has a wife and little ones dependent upon him, are yet just as pitiable, equally deserving of sympathy from all who have any just conception of life and its purposes.

In every city there are hundreds — thousands — of young men and women who are practically rotting on their feet, living upon incomes derived from the fruit of other people's toil, having no more part or lot in the common life about them than the marble statuary that adorns their homes, or the painted faces that hang on their walls; and these have come to have my sympathy to an equal extent with those at the other end of the social line. These rich men's sons and daughters have a right to work, to have a share in the creative work going on around them. How can they, any more than the others, love a country that they have had no part in making, but which has been built up by the toil of other hands? If they reflect at all, they must reflect not only that they have not contributed to the creative work about them, but that they have been, indeed, a burden upon the body politic, drones in the social hive, rendering no service whatever in return for that which is given to them; and so I now want to include in my plea every one of God's creatures, whether rich or poor.

The right to work is a natural right in which we all have a right to share, and ought to share. Work is a necessity in the creation of a human being, and the more useful the work that contributes to the building up of the physical man, the more human the man will be; and many of our rich men have learned through bitter experience that the very money that has enabled them to raise their sons and daughters in idleness has been a curse rather than a blessing to them. William Morris says that " it is right and necessary that all should have work to do, work that should not be over-wearisome nor over-anxious, and which of itself should be worth the doing," and I agree with Morris that, "turn this claim over as I may, look at it as I will, I cannot find that it is an exorbitant or extravagant claim; on the contrary, it is a most just claim."

The necessity for work in order to produce a normal, healthy human being is generally recognized, and we have all sorts of schemes for providing artificial work for the well-to-do to whom useful work is not available. We know we can make mere bone, muscle, and sinew by providing artificial work, such as is found in every well-equipped gymnasium, but I do not believe that sort of work has the moral worth or brings with it the satisfaction that comes from the feeling that we have contributed to the making of the material world about us, to the beautiful and useful, to the sum total of the comfort of our fellow-men. And so these reflections have led me to the point where I can say that my sympathies are equally divided between the two classes of unfortunates at either end of the social line — the unfortunate poor and the unfortunate rich. Indeed, many of the latter are living lives of enforced idleness, and, in addition, they are living wholly artificial lives, entirely out of sympathy with the common life about them, growing up in ignorance of the needs of the world about them, growing up without the knowledge that they have need of work, thanking their stars that they have been born above the working classes, and yet growing up with the belief that they can in some way share in the common stock of patriotism, that they can share the same patriotic impulses and love of country that are felt by people who have made sacrifices to build up the country and to raise up its institutions. But any thoughtful person knows that this is impossible, that in no just sense can we appreciate the blessings that surround us, whether they be spoken of in more general terms as the blessings of liberty or the more ordinary blessings of home and home comforts, except as we have contributed to them through real service.

We have to learn that "service brings its own reward." Illustrating the pressure that there is for place under existing conditions and the unfair competition that the poor have to meet, I relate an instance: A well-to-do gentleman called upon me with the request that I give his son employment "in almost any capacity." "I want him to think that he is earning something. Pay him $40 a month, and I will send you my check for that amount monthly," said he. This man knew the value of work and was willing to pay for it. "An idle brain is the devil's workshop" is an old saw and a true one; it is equally true whether the idler be poor or rich. God never made a place for drones in human society. God never provided a plan whereby a human being could be happy and be idle. Any social system that enforces or permits idleness and non-productive life on any of its citizens is as unscientific in theory as it is vicious and wrong in practice. I hail with delight the signs that I see of the dawning of the day of industrial freedom, when every man shall be as free to exercise the right to work as he is to-day to exercise the right to vote or the right to worship.

Set the Idle to Work on Road Building.

If we are the great people that we are said to be, we shall demonstrate our greatness by getting together the idle millions of the millionaire on the one hand, and the idle men on the other, and putting both to work. Work is man's normal condition, as natural for a healthy man as play for a healthy child; but work under reasonable conditions, mind you; I am not talking of the work of a serf or a slave, but of the work of a man; not ten, twelve, or fourteen hours' work, for eight hours for the present is enough for the proper development of any man. Moreover, work is a thing that is as much needed by one man as it is by another. If you know a man who will not work, remember he is what we have made him by our vicious social system. Our rich men have never had a better opportunity to demonstrate their patriotism, their love of country, than they have in these days. I do not see why patriotism does not call for the millionaire to give up the service of himself for a while and to invest his money in road building, just as much as it calls for him to set himself up for a target to be shot at in front of Santiago. I cannot see why a man who would give his life, or a part of it, to the service of making such roads as would enable the people to go to and fro freely through the country, ought not to be loved by his fellow-men just as sincerely as the other man who gives his life to the rusting idleness of the camp. And I believe that the country will love and honor, and build monuments too, to that man or those men who give up the selfish scramble for money for which they have no use and which they know can only be obtained at the expense of those who have none to use, and instead, will turn their attention and their talents to the service of their fellow-men in providing by their skill and business ability such socializing agencies as good roads.

I know that the millions of our tramps who are to-day denied the right to work will love them; I know that millions more who recognize the tramp as a brother man, however low he may be descended in the human scale, will love them; I know that this thought is in strict line with the correct idea of democracy, which is that the individual shall sink himself for the benefit of his fellowmen; I know that we must lay hold upon this truth if we are to realize a perfect democracy in this country. We must understand that millionaires on the one hand and tramps on the other will not exist in any perfect order of society.

Association is the word that is to save this nation and the world, and good roads contribute to, and help forward, the work of association. Macaulay says that "every improvement of the means of locomotion benefits mankind morally, and intellectually, as well as materially, and not only facilitates the interchange of the various productions of nature and art but tends to remove national and provincial antipathies, and to bind together all the branches of the great human family." This is our great need to-day, to be bound together. Good roads, through facilitating the means of getting together, making country districts equally accessible at all seasons of the year, will aid in the work of building up a nobler and purer patriotism. Men will love a government, local, state, or national, that provides them with such things as contribute to their comfort, that does something for them. In every section of the country where they have good roads, particularly in many of the counties of Indiana, noted for their fine graveled pikes, I find all of the people pointing with pride to these properties of the people. In Ireland I found a poor peasant who seemed to take pride in showing me the 90,000-acre farm of Lord Kenmare, but the things that a people with any true conception of liberty take pride in are the publicly owned properties. Our public highways ought to be first. The adoption of a plan by the general government for aiding in the work of road building would be beneficial to the people in every respect. It would furnish employment for idle men and idle money, and the labor so employed would benefit every class without injuring any.

A NEW CONSCIENCE NEEDED.

After all, I find that the consideration of the question of good roads lands me at the same place as the consideration of any phase of the subject of the improvement of social conditions; namely, this: we can only improve our roads by improving our morals. We shall only have better roads as we have a better understanding of social relations and the obligations of patriotism; only as the social conscience is awakened in our people and we come to a knowledge of right relations and break away from the slavery of ancient tradition and live as brothers, love one another in time of peace as well as when we are at war with a foreign nation, shall we come to have better roads, better government, better social conditions, or anything better. To get better roads or better anything else, we must turn our thoughts from the debasing idea of making money at the expense of our fellows to the nobler idea of making men of them.

Let me illustrate with a quotation from the remarkable address of Mr. Henry D. Lloyd on "The New Conscience," which will give us a picture of what we could do were the idle labor of the world employed:

> If the idle labor of the world could be employed, if the idle soldiers of the world could be set to work, and if all the other idlers could be turned from their idleness, we could do anything in the world that we wanted to do. The first year, we could take the women and children out of the shops and factories, and send them home, to stay home. The second year, we could buy up all the monopolies and begin to administer them for the benefit of the people. The third year, we could rebuild the slums in all the cities of the world. The fourth year, we could give every child the beginning of an education, which could go on to college and university. The fifth year, by applying labor adequately to cleanliness and isolation, and proper nursing, we could abolish all the contagious diseases. The sixth year, we could pay all the national debts of the world. And the seventh year! the seventh year, we could do what we are told the Creator of the Universe did after His six days' labor of creation. We could rest, and look upon our work and behold that it was good.

Labor Ordained by God.

The labor question is as old as time. We first hear of it at the very dawn of creation when God said to Adam, "In the sweat of thy face shalt thou eat bread." This declaration of the Almighty defined the most important and indefeasible of all the rights that man is heir to, the first great right, the right to work, the right to help carry on the great but never-ending work of creation. When God spoke to Adam there were no "jobs" available, except such as were found in the natural resources. There were the earth, the air, the sunlight, and the rain; there was no boss "to hire him;" there was no shrewd "business man" on hand to organize industry and " make work " for Adam on the one hand, and to make profit out of him on the other. Clearly, if he was willing to work, he might work. Moreover, it naturally followed that he might have the whole product of the toil of his hands.

It seems to me that this lesson in the history of primitive man is a very valuable one for us to consider to-day. It is certain that we cannot go on indefinitely with the present social system. It is admitted by all thoughtful people that a social system, based on competition, has failed to provide a plan whereby all who are willing to work may work and may live, and the consequence is that in our country to-day there is an ever-increasing army bearing the " curse of the wandering foot."

THE RIGHT TO WORK IS THE RIGHT TO WORSHIP.

" The secret place of the Most High is in the depth of human need." I am excited to more reverence when I stand in the workshop or factory, watching the work of men's hands, than when I stand in the nave of the grandest cathedral. The right to work! the right to work! — this is the right that must be established and for which we need a new Emancipation Proclamation. The millions of toilers, who are now tramping our streets, highways, and alleys have a right to share in the creative work that is going on about them. They have a right to have a hand in building a country that they are asked and expected and want to love. Men are brothers. That they should live in a state of competition is a denial of brotherhood; that this system of social warfare must be succeeded by co-operation — a system in which men can be brothers — is as certain as that to-morrow's sun will rise. We may hasten its coming by proclaiming, by spreading, the gospel of brotherhood. We cannot retard it, however reactionary may be our purposes.

These are the reflections of a plain man of the world who comes in contact with the people, who knows the people, BELIEVES IN THE PEOPLE, and will never cease to raise his voice in their behalf. The right to vote, over which we have expended much spread-eagle eloquence, is as small dust in the balance when compared with the right to work. Why shall I vote if I am denied the right to work? There is no reason, unless there shall be a market for votes when the market for labor has ceased. "But they do not want to work," is the apologetic plea often flung back at me, usually by those who are living in comfort on the fruit of other people's toil. I know it is a thoughtless remark. I know that the people who make it are, in the main, good people, and they would like to see some easy way out of our present difficulty. Let me say, however, that my experience put the lie to this statement that "they do not want work." I have been permitted to see thousands of them tried, and not 1 per cent. are unwilling to work under half-way decent conditions. I protest against a continuance of this suicidal policy that this competitive system is waging against the young men of America to-day.

Let me not be misunderstood. In the juster order of society that is coming, the right to work will not involve slavish drudgery for eight or ten hours a day, but the right to participate in creating the world about us and the right to such a conception of art as that of which William Morris gave us a definition when he said that "art is the expression of man's joy in labor." That is the kind of work that all have a right to share in; that is the kind of liberty that we are yet to know through the larger recognition of social obligation that is coming to us, and coming with whirlwind speed in these closing years of the nineteenth century.

NOTE.— The six young men, whose picture appears on page 135, furnish a striking example of the inefficiency, waste and criminality of the present social order with regard to the question of employment for our people. They came into my office one morning last winter, and from their appearance I judged them to be a committee of some labor union, perhaps. They were all fairly well-dressed, bright and intelligent-looking. The facts, however, were these: They had each made application at a local employment agency for work. Their applications had been filed for from two to eleven weeks, and they had been putting in time every day searching for work. It had been their regular custom to call at this employment agency every morning. In this way, these six young men, who were all strangers to one another, became acquainted. Every morning they found the sign of "Help Wanted" outside the employment agency, but the "manager" always reported that the class of service on demand was something that "none of them could do." They, therefore, were led to believe that the agency was merely a "graft" for working money out of those least able to bear that sort of a tax. The business of the agency is perfectly legal, and, of course, I could offer them no relief. They kindly consented to co-operate with me to the extent of going over to the photograph gallery to have their pictures taken. I might add that along with it I took their history. Every one is American born, every one is a voter. Two of them had been school teachers and all were willing to contribute useful service to society, but society had no place for them. Suppose one of them were your son, your boy, how would you like it?

CHAPTER IV.

CHARITY OR JUSTICE.

People are perpetually squabbling about what will be best to do, or easiest to do, or advisablest to do, or profitablest to do; but they never, so far as I hear them talk, even ask what it is *just* to do. And it is the law of Heaven that you shall not be able to judge what is wise or easy unless you are first resolved to judge what is just, and to do it. That is the one thing constantly reiterated by our Master — the order of all others that is given oftenest — "Do justice and judgment." That's your Bible order; that's the service of God. * * * The one Divine work — the one ordered sacrifice — is to do justice; and it is the last we are ever inclined to do. Anything rather than that! As much charity as you choose, but no justice. * * * Christian Justice has been strangely mute, and seemingly blind; and, if not blind, decrepit, this many a day; she keeps her accounts still, however — quite steadily — doing them at nights, carefully, with her bandage off, and through acutest spectacles (the only modern scientific invention she cares about). You must put your ear down ever so close to her lips to hear her speak; and then you will start at what she first whispers, for it will certainly be: "Why shouldn't that little crossing sweeper have a feather on its head as well as your own child?" Then you may ask Justice, in an amazed manner, how she can possibly be so foolish as to think children could sweep crossings with feathers on their heads? Then you stoop again, and Justice says — still in her dull, stupid way — "Then why don't you, every other Sunday, leave your child to sweep the crossing, and take the little sweeper to church in hat and feathers?" Mercy on us (you think) what will she say next? And you answer, of course, that "You don't, because everybody ought to remain content in the position in which Providence has placed them." Ah, my friends, that's the gist of the whole question. *Did* Providence put them in that position, or did *you?* You knock a man into a ditch, and then you tell him to remain content in the position in which Providence has placed him. That's modern Christianity. You say, "We did not knock him into the ditch." How do you know what you have done or are doing? That's just what we have all got to know, and what we shall never know, until the question with us every morning is, not how to do the gainful thing, but how to do the just thing; nor until we are at least so far on the way to being Christian, as to have understood that maxim of the poor, half-way Mahometan, "One hour in the execution of *justice* is worth seventy years of prayer."— *Ruskin: Crown of Wild Olives.*

CHAPTER IV.

CHARITY OR JUSTICE.

WE read and have many times been told that "the Lord loveth a cheerful giver," "it is more blessed to give than to receive," and "he that giveth to the poor lendeth to the Lord;" and this pious phraseology has generally been construed to mean, and has often been urged upon the benevolent as a guarantee, that whoever responded liberally to appeals for aid was sure of a good bargain with the Lord.

In this materialistic age of highly wrought competitive energy, when the policy of "each man for himself," "save your own soul," etc., is the mainspring and inspiration of most of our lives, it is not to be wondered that liberal contributions are made in the name of charity. When the ordinary avenues of business turn out so many failures, the speculative instinct is apt to respond to the invitation to invest in any enterprise that has the appearance of a "sure thing." This desire to play a "sure-thing game" must in large part account for the enormous investments in the name of charity that are annually made by the rich and prosperous classes of our people. I believe that a very large percentage of the twenty-two millions said to have been expended in the State of New York during the last year was given (?) as an investment pure and simple because of the belief that it would pay. The constant iteration in one form or another of the army of solicitors, who are burdened with the work of carrying on charity organizations, that "the Lord will bless you," and the flood of "ghost stories" that have gone the rounds of the country telling how God had blessed this, that and the other "liberal men," leads to a superstitious belief that God will especially interest himself in prospering the givers to charity. I have known of a case where this belief was so deep-seated in a gambler that he religiously practiced giving to the unfortunate and distressed a portion of his winnings in the hope of courting the favor of the fickle goddess, called "Good Luck."

Far be it from me to attempt to belittle any generous impulse. For we have altogether too little of it, and my object is to awaken real benevolence, a benevolence that will be satisfied with nothing less than justice to every one of God's creatures. When we shall have reached a conception of that kind and learned to express it through government, the thing that is now called charity will be known only as a relic of a distressing stage of civilization that the race has happily passed by.

Rev. George C. Lorimer, of the Tremont Temple Baptist Church, Boston, said recently in a baccalaureate sermon before the senior class of Brown University:

> The stress on organized charity is an example of the sophistries which the scholar needs to expose. I am in favor of real charity, but that charity is misnamed which compels a man to turn his soul inside out to charity officials before he can get a crust of bread; that charity is misnamed which forces a woman to give her history before she can get a garment to clothe her naked child.
>
> What society wants to-day is not charity, but justice — justice between man and man. Do you say we must clothe the naked? I tell you, give men justice, and there will be practically nobody to clothe. Do you say we must feed the hungry? Make justice to reign, and men will not be hungry.

COMPETITIVE SYSTEM THE CAUSE.

The competitive system is the cause that constantly horrifies us and shocks our finer sensibilities with its outrages upon the weak and incapable brothers of society. Annually and periodically we are horrified with appeals for the "starving miners of Ohio," men willing to work, driven into enforced idleness as a direct result of the competition growing out of human greed. They and their wives and children made paupers, driven into vice, immorality and crime of every sort, are a perpetual protest against the continuance of a system that has failed. The state is derelict in its duty if it fails to take cognizance of these conditions. I see no possible solution for the troubles perpetually harassing us by the wrongs and injustice done to the coal miners, except that the government own all of the mines and operate them for the benefit of all the people. Every man willing to work has a right to live on the fruit of the toil of his hands, and no government has a right to deny him this right. It is a sacred heritage given to him when God said to Adam, "In the sweat of thy face shalt thou eat bread." Able-bodied men ever walk the streets, alleys and highways of our country pleading for work, yet there is no lack of useful and beautiful work that ought to be done.

In all of our cities too many men, and women, too, are up against a stone wall; they have reached a point where they can go no farther. Their labor, which is the only thing they have to sell, is a drug on the market which none will buy. They must buy the necessaries of life from a monopolized market. As they cannot sell their labor, and their chattels are in the possession of the pawnbroker and the mortgage shark, they are face to face with the fact that their liberty is a mockery, is not even the liberty to beg, for that is a crime.

My observations in America and in foreign countries have convinced me that no matter where you go, *the same class of people are down*. No matter whether they have good money or bad, whether it is gold or silver, hard or soft, the wage-earners and producers are down, while the traders, the bankers and the speculators are up. In all countries the bees who make the honey are smoked out of the hives. Labor and wealth have been divorced; what justice has joined, our unwise laws have put asunder.

Labor-saving machinery has wrought great havoc among the laboring classes everywhere. As John Stuart Mill has said, it is doubtful if all the machinery of the world has lightened the labor of the workers by a single hour. Machinery has done more for profits than it has for wages. It has added intensity to the day's work. Instead of giving leisure to the operator, it has in many cases made him work faster, and at lower wages. Machinery has been a great benefit to those who *buy*, but a great injury so far to those who make.

As Henry George has shown, progress and poverty have gone hand in hand, by some inexcusable blunder in our system of distribution. The brighter the light which civilization has shed upon the avenues, the darker is the shadow which falls upon the alleys. The palace-towers and glittering steeples are built higher and higher toward the clouds, while the dingy cellars where the ragged outcasts gather are dug deeper and are becoming more crowded every year.

Charity and Drunkenness.

Charity agents and temperance reformers have much to say concerning the direful tendency to poverty caused by the drinking habit. Doubtless many men know of some person or persons who have been made poor through excessive drinking. But for one instance of an individual made a pauper through drink, there are instances of whole classes made drunkards by poverty.

The frightful conditions prevailing in the slums of the great cities — the insecurity, hopelessness, hunger and want of the dwellers therein — draw them with irresistible force to indulgence in liquor as a sole relief for their woes. So true is this that recognition of it is now made by the best authorities. The tables compiled by Prof. A. G. Warner, in his "American Charities," show that intemperance is the cause of poverty in but from one-fifteenth to one-fifth of all the cases noted. Other statistics show that but 16 per cent. of the 156,000 paupers in New York city became such through the liquor habit. The great temperance apostle, Miss Frances E. Willard, came to see before her death, and made repeated announcement of her belief, that poverty was the cause of drunkenness rather than drunkenness the cause of poverty.

For many years I contributed my influence and means to the " destruction of the accursed traffic," battling along the conventional lines. Fight! fight! fight! was the war cry continually raised, and believed I was doing God's service. I do not seem to learn any lesson by the failure of the fighting tools; one form of the fight had no sooner failed than I was ready to take up some other form, with the same old tools. But I have come to see more clearly the forces that make for drunkenness; I have come to regard it as an effect rather than a cause, and I have reached a stage from which my previous attitude and methods appear to me wrong and futile.

I agree with all Christian people as to the evils of the liquor traffic. It is an unmitigated curse; but it will continue to exist so long as the people want it. The saloon is here because the people want it here. If the people want it away they can soon put it away, not only on Sunday, but on every other day.

When justice is done to the disinherited of earth, when well-paid, useful and agreeable work is provided for every child of God, the crowds that now turn to the saloon for solace will find, through the larger outlook of life, other desires than that of drink and other gathering places than that of the saloon.

If all the rich church members would do their utmost to give these the unemployed work they would accomplish more for temperance than they do by attacking saloons. There are many ways in which this could be done. Persons with bank accounts could paint their houses a little oftener than usual and make improvements in their stores and dwellings; they could clean up and beautify their grounds and feel all the better for the expenditure which would afford paying employment for people who are now walking by the churches idle, starving and ragged. As a city, we could build and adorn streets, boulevards and parks and so set in circulation the idle money now hoarded in our banks, and serving no useful purpose for humanity. The door which idleness and poverty open to the saloon would then be largely closed, and the door from the saloon to the jail and poorhouse would seldom turn on its hinges.

CHARITY ONLY PALLIATES.

Students of social phenomena understand that the thing we call charity in no sense tends to eradicate the evils of poverty. Many, indeed, see, on the contrary, that the most carefully conducted charitable organizations tend only to delay the day of our deliverance from the injustice of the present economic system, and they are coming to see, as Mrs. Stetson says, that —

> The love that fed poverty, making it thrive,
>   Is learning a lovelier way;
> We have seen that the poor need be with us no more,
>   And that sin can be driven away.

Our unparalleled power of organization, that has exhausted itself very largely in building up the individual during the last half of this century and has amazed the civilized world by its triumphs, is one of the sources that we must look to for relief from the social distress of the present hour. To get this relief, the great power of organization of our captains of industry must be moralized, and the patriotic impulse, the love of country, which is the love of our fellow-men, must be relied upon to use this power in a more rational way in socializing the energy of our cities, our state and our nation, so that our phenomenal ability may be made a blessing to all of the people, may build up the city, state and nation through the development of a better and nobler type of manhood, instead of letting it go on in the present hopeless plan of mere money getting, which, as a matter of fact, from any scientific standpoint, is not a blessing to even those who are temporarily successful.

It is an indication full of promise for the future that so many in this, the next to the last year of the nineteenth century, are coming to see that the success that depends for its continuance upon the failure of others is not in any true sense success at all. We are getting ashamed of our extremes of wealth and poverty. We have boasted of our ability in the art of production. We should be ashamed of our ignorance in the art of distribution. Millions have been made in a few weeks in the New York Stock Exchange on stocks that derive their value from the toil of underpaid men, overworked women and in some cases from the labor of little children who are robbed of their childhood. We are becoming so patriotic, we are learning to love one another so well, that we are getting ashamed of this kind of profit and are coming to see that it is the "price of blood."

There is no permanent peace by pursuing a system of profit getting that depends upon the destruction of human life for its continuance. In no collective capacity have we any plan that considers the good of all of the people with respect to the most important, the most fundamental thing in our common life. This is the right to earn one's daily bread. Neither as a nation, state or municipality have we yet given serious consideration to this important question. We have the post-office, that provides a plan whereby we may send and receive our letters safely and promptly. It is carried on without profit for the good of the people, and rich and poor are served alike by this beneficent agency. We have the public schools in the various states, which provide free education for our children.

In many places even we teach them to work, how to be useful members of society, and when they are thus equipped turn them out into the fierce competitive warfare of the present day to struggle for themselves, to enter into a contest against trained men of experience for the possession of property, where strong and weak, simple and cunning, wise and unwise, are pitted together in the "grab-all," "catch-as-catch-can," "every one-for-himself," "devil-take-the-hindmost" scramble for things (property). In such a contest it does not require a prophet or seer to "pick a winner."

Of course, the little ones, the weak, the helpless, will be numbered among the unfortunates, and I fancied as I looked at the 200 hopeless men waiting for their dole of bread at Fleischmann's bakery in the chilling rain of a January midnight, that I could see Christ, the Carpenter of Nazareth, with sympathetic mien, pointing to this sad, sad sight and saying in tones of profoundest pathos to me, to every man and woman to-day living in reasonable comfort in this land of liberty, "Inasmuch as ye did it not unto the least of these (hungry men), ye did it not unto me."

The Unsocial and Un-American Spirit.

Yet there are some writers who claim to be cultured and well-informed who assure us that there is no remedy for poverty save the spasmodic charity of the rich; and a few even go farther and maintain that charity is a superior and elevating method of removing social evils.

Mr. N. P. Gilman, author of "Socialism and the American Spirit," vehemently opposes Socialism on the grounds that self-help and independence will come to an end if monopolies are owned and operated by the nation. In the midst of his eulogies of self-help, however, we find him preaching the enervating gospel of charity as a cure for social evils. He says:

> Let the men of wealth look about, each man in his town or city, to find what he can do in the way of endowing schools of various kinds; building libraries and stocking them with books; assisting promising young men and women through college; establishing hospitals; supporting homes for the

destitute; laying out parks and play-grounds; or in a hundred other charities and philanthropies which will be sure to do more good than harm.

Let them establish trade-schools, like Messrs. Pratt, Drexel and Armour. Let them endow music, like Mr. Higginson, of Boston; or theology, like the Scottish Lord Gifford. Let them open new avenues of wise philanthropy by endowing newspapers that shall be clean, able and independent of party, or periodicals of too high a grade for a small subscription list to support.

Let them aid research in natural and in social science. Let them help in the publication of books needed only by the few, and in the support of men of mind engaged in investigations likely to be of use to many, but only hindered by the lack of means.

The rich man should seek the close alliance of the man of science and the man of sagacious humanity, who can do him no greater service than to show him where to employ his surplus fortune for the public good. Every man who follows the laudable custom of giving while he is able to direct his gift aright, and see its good results, is a practical apostle of peace and good-will among men.

If this is the most optimistic gospel we can preach, then democracy is a failure and the Declaration of Independence was a mistake. Mr. Gilman would push America back to where Europe was in the seventeenth century, when literature, art, music and poetry were dependent upon the whims of dull-witted kings and dukes. The learning and genius of that period are tainted with servility and cringing homage to the possessors of wealth and power.

THE ECONOMIC INDEPENDENCE OF GENIUS.

Already our colleges, our magazines, our pulpits, and our artists depend too much upon the owners of wealth. I believe in *the economic independence of genius*. Every millionaire who is at all philanthropic has constantly around him a circle of whining, clamoring, flattering professors, ministers, artists, authors, etc., holding out their hats for a checque — the eminently respectable beggars of society.

If " promising young men and women " are to be helped financially, the money should come from the city or state, and not from an individual money-maker, who, in return for the money advanced, will expect to dictate the opinions of those whom he assists.

The public recognition of genius is never regarded as charity; it honors the recipient instead of degrading him. The watchful care of a kindly government over the interests of all the people does not interfere with any of the sturdy virtues that spring from self-help and self-reliance. But the paternalism of a few patronizing millionaires, who reward the cunning sycophant and pass over the independent thinker who dares to speak the truth with regard to the origin of these great fortunes, is a form of philanthropy which ought not to be encouraged. Nothing is endangering freedom of thought and speech in our universities so much as the fatal philanthropy of millionaires. Professors who dare to investigate honestly the causes of poverty and the nature and methods of private monopolies, are discharged if they venture to declare their convictions. Ask any artist who paints for love of his work and not for money, what effect the patronage of the wealthy has upon art, and he will tell you that it is destructive of good work. It leads artists to paint pictures merely to sell — to please men who have no natural appreciation of the beautiful, and who frequently order their paintings by the square yard and their books by the hundred. Pressed hard by poverty, artists are driven to betray their ideal to the Pilates and Herods of wealth for a few pieces of silver.

As long as money and its owners rule the world, true art will be compelled to hide in garrets for years before the nation discovers and rewards it. Commercialism leads to the building up of "art factories," where oil paintings are made to order "while you wait."

Ask any conscientious or clear-sighted magazine writer or author what effect the patronage of the wealthy has upon literature, and he will reply that it creates an unofficial censorship which prohibits the impartial discussion of the real economic issues of the day. There are certain things which wealthy advertisers will allow to be said, and certain other things, equally true, which they will not permit to be mentioned.

Mr. Gilman's eulogy of charity might do much good in a country like Russia, where governmental restrictions make self-help impossible, and where a fraternal democracy scarcely exists even in imagination; but in the land of Jefferson and Lincoln such sentiments are an impertinence.

Millionaires and Paupers Abnormal Creatures.

Our chief task is not to coax and wheedle a few thousands from the rich to help the poor, but to consider the means by which the rich have become rich, and the poor have become poor. Millionaires and paupers are both abnormal creatures, and the republic will never prosper until both are made as scarce as buffaloes in Rhode Island. The question we are asking concerning the enormous fortunes which a few trust-makers have piled up in twenty or thirty years, is not, "What will they do with it?" but, "How did they get it?" We question the righteousness of their claims. It is not enough that they have acquired possession, and escaped the jail. We shall not stop the pursuit because they now and then throw out a few dollars from their millions. We are not after their money; we are after justice.

Mrs. Stetson aptly describes the real nature of a great deal of our charity in the following poem:

> Came two young children to their mother's shelf
>   (One was quite little, and the other big),
> And each in freedom calmly helped himself,
>   (One was a pig).
>
> The food was free and plenty for them both,
>   But one was rather dull and very small;
> So the big smarter brother, nothing loath,
>   He took it all.

> At which the little fellow raised a yell
>   Which tired the other's more aesthetic ears;
> He gave him here a crust, and there a shell,
>   To stop his tears.
>
> He gave with pride, in manner calm and bland,
>   Finding the other's hunger a delight;
> He gave with piety — his full left hand
>   Hid from his right.
>
> He gave and gave — O blessed Charity;
>   How sweet and beautiful a thing it is!
> How fine to see that big boy giving free
>   What is not his!

The Workers' Attitude Toward Charity.

Prof. John Graham Brooks says:

> I have spoken during the past year to many labor organizations, and everywhere this angry note against charity methods and against anything like charity for the unemployed makes itself felt. The reasons for this hostility are at bottom the stigma which has come to be associated with charity; the idea that charity, being voluntary, the recipients are supposed to be grateful for such helps, but even more the fact that the very respectable and well-conditioned people in the community administer the charities. Here is the arch offense. The traditional charity carries with it, as a fatality, a sense of distributing favors. It is a gift from success to failure, from superiority to apparent inferiority; from one who pities to one who is an object of pity.

The working classes have quite a clear knowledge of the fact that without labor there would be no wealth, and that every loaf of bread was created by the strength and skill of farmers, millers and bakers, and not by the fiat of a financier. It is the remembrance of this that causes sullenness to take the place of gratitude when any favors are received from the wealthy.

They know that something must be wrong when the industrious are obliged to depend upon the bounty of idlers; and they bitterly resent being placed in the position of beggars and dependents. Why should well-to-do spendthrifts give them patronizing lectures on thrift and economy? Why should young ladies who have never earned by hard work a dollar in their lives, intrude into their shabby homes, and preach to them of industry and perseverance?

Many a charity visitor has felt how natural and well-founded is the resentment of the poor against charity. To quote from an able article on "The Subtle Problems of Charity," by Miss Jane Addams, of Hull House, Chicago:

> The charity visitor is, let us assume, a young college woman, well-bred and open-minded. When she visits the family assigned to her, she is embarrassed to find herself obliged to lay all the stress of her teaching and advice upon the industrial virtues, and to treat the members of the family almost exclusively as factors in the industrial system. She insists that they must work and be self-supporting; that the most dangerous of all situations is idleness; that seeking one's own pleasure, while ignoring claims and responsibilities, is the most ignoble of actions. The members of her assigned family may have charms and virtues — they may possibly be kind and affectionate, considerate of one another and generous to their friends; but it is her business to stick to the industrial side.
>
> As she daily holds up these standards, it often occurs to the mind of the sensitive visitor, whose conscience has been made tender by much talk of brotherhood and equality which she has heard talked at college, that she has no right to say these things; that she herself has never been self-supporting; that, whatever her virtues may be, they are not the industrial virtues; that her untrained hands are no more fitted to cope with actual conditions than are those of her broken-down family.

I want to knock the props clear out from under every person who is harboring the delusion that our charity institutions are evidences of civilization. They may be evidences that we are tending toward civilization; the very need of them is evidence that we are not civilized. The way to help the poor is to abandon a social system that is making the poor. The way to get rid of criminals is to make opportunities for men to obtain an honest livelihood. This we must do through associating ourselves together in the thing called government, or we must lapse into savagery. But we are not going into savagery.

Progress is in Moving Forward.

When the children of Israel were on their march from slavery in Egypt and found themselves on the borders of the Red Sea face to face with impassable mountains on the right and left and Pharaoh's pursuing army in the rear, the command of God came to Moses, saying: "Speak unto the children of Israel that they go forward," and they had but to obey that command and the impassable waters of the Red Sea parted before them, giving them a pathway to cross over into the land of promise dry-shod. Out of the rumble, and roar, and clash, and clang of our great cities, out of the incessant whirr of the railroads and machinery of our busy industries, grinding the lives of men, women and children into capital for private owners, the voice of God is speaking to the thoughtful people of America to-day, saying: "Speak to the children of this republic that they go forward." We look out upon the difficulties upon the right and the left, in the rear and in front, but we have only to obey the voice of God, and the sea of economic injustice made red and hideous by the annual sacrifice of thousands of lives for the sake of profit, will clear away, and we shall find ourselves upon the broad plains of the fair Canaan of promise, the land flowing with the milk and honey of love, in the eternal sunshine of the equality of brotherhood. This is the manifest destiny, the heroic and spiritual future that waits the development of the conceptions of government for which the peoples have long and patiently waited, and to realize which is to be the proud distinction of these United States.

The Delusion of Necessary Poverty.

We have been nursing a delusion. We believed poverty a necessity of civilization, when the very fact of its existence is a crime against democracy. We have believed crime a necessary corollary of virtue, but we are coming to see that poverty and crime are

A SOCIAL PROBLEM.

Grace Church. Fleischmann's Bakery. Department Store.
(In line for free bread at Fleischmann's Bakery — A daily scene on Broadway, New York.)

Copyright, 1899, by Eastern Book Concern.

AND THIS IS FREE AMERICA!:

(Citizens of Columbus, Ohio, waiting at the gates of the State Prison for the refuse food that is left from the tables of the convicts.)

absolutely indispensable concomitants of the present social order, that our charities do absolutely no good so far as removing the hideous blotch of poverty from our civilization is concerned; that at best they are only palliative; that if we are to continue a system of industry and trade that makes millionaires and billionaires on the one hand, we must have paupers and tramps on the other. I want to spare you the necessity of quoting the words of Jesus, "The poor ye have always with you," as an apology for the hideous wrongs of the present system by placing a reasonable interpretation upon this scripture. Jesus could have had no other purpose than to reproach the civilization of his day by this charge, as I reproach the civilization of the present hour that is content with palliating an evil that would quickly vanish upon the adoption of a system of government that would make social justice possible.

To compel or permit an able-bodied man or woman, rich or poor, to eat the bread of idleness is not charity, is not love; it is a crime, and a crime with a capital C. Work is the normal condition of every healthy man and woman as play is normal to a healthy child, and if we, the captains of industry, have so corralled opportunities for work that we deny this right to the poor on the one hand, and to our own sons and daughters who grow up around us actually rotting in the idleness of useless lives on the other, we are not good citizens. We have no right to call ourselves patriots, for by our very system we are pursuing a course that can finally result in nothing short of a condition of anarchy and the overthrow of all semblance of government.

Centuries ago men wandered about Europe with weapons in their hands, demanding food, money and property, and sustaining their demand by force. But to-day the wanderers of our cities trudge from place to place with empty hands, pleading to be allowed to increase the wealth of the world, offering to do the hardest work for any one who will permit them, and asking only for a fraction of their product in return.

And if the condition of the unemployed man be one of misery and despair, what shall be said of the unemployed *woman?* What shall we say of the hundreds of young girls against whom the gates of opportunity have been shut?

As John Burns sternly says:

> Even more pathetic than the unemployed male worker and industrial nomad is the workless woman or girl in search of work in a city of great distances. Trudging from shop to factory with thin boots and slimmer clothes, with little food, without the support that trade-unionism gives to men, lacking the stimulant of association, isolated by her sex, with no organization, often the victim of bogus registry offices, friendless and alone, she searches for work that slowly comes. Before her the workhouse or the street, she bravely suffers in silence, and has no alternative to starvation but the eating of the crumb of charity or the loaf of lust.

Provide Work, and Charity Will Not Be Needed.

I am an exponent of the right to work. I contend that this right to work is an inherent right like the right to breathe, like the right to be. The highest right of every man is the right to do right, and there is no kind of question in my mind but that when a man is compelled to eat the bread of idleness, because social conditions over which he has no control deny him the right of access to work, he is as much a victim of injustice as though he were sand-bagged on his way home and robbed by the highwayman or assassin of the fruit of his daily toil. It is this social injustice that breeds and perpetuates vice, poverty and crime, this trio of hideous monstrosities, this three-headed Cerberus that guards the gate of our social hell, denying us any possibility of escape until we have emancipated ourselves from a superstition that will recognize anything as civilization short of a condition of society in which all shall have equality of opportunity. It is that equality for which prophets have pleaded, for which poets have sung, for which Christ lived and died, for which He asked you and me to live and die when He said: "A new commandment I give you, that ye love one another even as I have loved you;" that equality which the founders of this government saw when they wrote that "all men are created equal;" that equality without which we can never hope to realize a democracy of sovereign equals; that equality that we must realize in this republic, if it is to endure and a government of the people for the people is to be firmly established upon the earth.

A curious old pamphlet published in 1646, entitled "How to Reform Beggars, Thieves and Highway Robbers," shows that the lack of work was the cause of vagabondage, two hundred and fifty years ago just as it is to-day. The pamphlet says:

> It is very lamentable that poor rogues and beggars should be whipped or branded, or otherwise punished, because they are begging or idle, when no place is provided for them to set to work. I have heard the rogues and beggars curse the magistrates into their faces, for providing such a law to whip and brand them, and not provide houses of labor for them. For, surely, many would go voluntarily to such houses to work if they were provided for them. Beggary and thievery did never more abound in this realm, and the cause of this misery is idleness, and the only means to cure the same must be by labor.

The "new right" to work is in fact a very old one — old as the human race; but it is not recognized by the governments of civilization. In spite of all our cleverness, and education, and inventive ability, and Christian creeds, we have not yet found a plan whereby every industrious man may be self-supporting.

Efforts to Provide Work Instead of Charity.

The city of Paris realizes in a measure its obligations to the unemployed. It does not guarantee work, except to a few at its municipal farm colony, which was started in 1891, and has proved very successful. But it has provided, since 1886, free lodging-houses for men and women in search of work. There are two for men, accommodating about 300 each; and one for women. Men are allowed to remain for three nights, and women for an indefinite period of time. Food, baths, and even clothing are provided for all, and all possible assistance is lent in the quest for employment.

This, at least, is an attempt to move in the direction of justice, but it does not go far enough so long as it stops short of employment for every citizen. Clothing, shelter, meals and work are provided for criminals, paupers and lunatics; why not provide at least the latter for honest, able-bodied, sane citizens? This is a question which civilization must answer, if it would outlive the twentieth century.

The colony of Victoria, Australia, possesses a labor colony of 800 acres, with the object of supplying temporary work at subsistence wages to the able-bodied unemployed. A newspaper gives the following particulars of the colony:

> If a man is really "down at heel" in Victoria, and desires work under the authorities, he is sent to the farm and employed in hewing trees, burning stumps, or any other form of agricultural labor of which he is capable. He is paid a "deterrent" wage, ranging from fifty cents to $1 a week; and he is given good food, with fairly comfortable sleeping accommodation. He may not, strictly speaking, stay on the colony more than six months at a time, although exceptions to the rule are occasionally made. When he leaves, he is given the wage-money to his credit, and he can depart at any time if he desires to seek work elsewhere. To secure discipline, it is provided that instant dismissal shall follow insubordination. The men work only eight hours per day, with intervals for smoking and meals. During their stay, every effort is made by the government to secure them employment outside the settlement.

New Zealand has five or more of these state farms for the unemployed, and leads the world in its recognition of the right to work. It has also one of the most beneficent land systems of any civilized country.

Impressed with the necessity of providing land for the people, the government of that colony has entered upon the policy of purchasing large estates from private owners and cutting them up into convenient areas for purposes of close settlement. Several large estates have been acquired in this way, some by amicable arrangement with their owners as to price, and others compulsorily, through the medium of Supreme Court intervention, where the government and the owners of the fee simple are at loggerheads as to the price to be paid for these large estates. For example, if the government of New York State wanted a particular property in order to settle people more closely upon it, it would offer a price to its owner, and if that price was not accepted the question would be decided by the Supreme Court, after taking evidence on the price offered and the valuation placed upon the land and improvements by the individual owner. That represents exactly what happens in New Zealand. The government of that colony has power, under its land laws, to insist upon the cutting up of large estates, and once it acquires these large areas, it cuts them up and lets the subdivided areas to tenants of the Crown, upon what are termed leases in perpetuity, or, in other words, for a term of 999 years. The state becomes the landlord, and the tenants pay annual rentals of 5 per cent. upon the capital value. Suppose a farm is taken up under the lease in the perpetuity system, and the capital value of that farm is assessed at $1,000, the tenant will have to pay a rental of $50 a year.

The system applies equally to agricultural and pastoral lands, the latter being let at proportionately smaller rentals; and to provide for future requirements what are termed small grazing runs are let for twenty-one years, so that they can be used for closer occupation as time goes on. The new system of tenure has created an immense demand for land, and the enormous estates opened up in this way are showing splendid results. Where properties consisting of 100,000 acres, for instance, were occupied by sheep and a few shepherds and station hands only, prosperous homesteads have been established upon them, and thousands of people who were formerly at their wits' end to know how to provide for their families have been made happy and comfortable. Settling upon land has become quite the fashion, and members of every trade are taking to it under the splendid inducements which the lease-in-perpetuity system offers to struggling men. For what is virtually a freehold a man has now to pay an exceedingly small rent, and in addition to this he can borrow money from the government at 4 per cent. to carry out improvements upon his holding. This great reform of the land system was initated by Mr. John McKenzie, the present Minister of Lands in that colony, and the new scheme is working admirably.

What Could Be Done with the Land in America.

This system of small holdings of land is vastly superior to our system, whereby one man owns two million acres while others do not own an inch. It is a sure way of developing an industrious, happy and patriotic population, rescuing them from slumdom and pauperism and crime. We, in America, in spite of our great expanse of territory, refuse our unemployed citizens land until they are dead; and then we grudgingly give them six feet of earth. We grant to the dead what we deny to the living, while New Zealand seeks to prolong the lives of its people by granting every one a chance to produce the necessities of life.

A much better and more scientific way than dividing the land up into small holdings would be to allow ten, twenty or more families to manage a large form co-operatively. It has been abundantly proved, by the owners of the large bonanza farms in the Western States, that a large farm is as much superior to a small one in economy of production as a large factory is superior to a small hand-labor workshop.

The most improved farm machinery is too expensive for a farmer who derives his living from two hundred acres; but some plan of co-operation might be arranged whereby every man might own his own farm, and join in with a score of others in the purchase and use of farming implements.

But whatever be the plan adopted, it is certain that steps should be taken at once to free the land from the grasp of speculators and absentee landlords. It is said that the English nobility own over twenty-five million acres of our western land,— more than the whole of Ireland; and thousands of American citizens pay rent for American soil to English dukes and barons. There should be no alien ownership of land in this republic. If some conscientious and ambitious duke wishes to rise in the world and become a self-supporting American farmer, by all means give him a chance, and do not bar him out because of his unfortunate parentage. But when the titled do-nothings of foreign countries purchase large tracts of our land with money which they obtained from pauperized wage-workers, and endeavor to establish the feudal system under the Stars and Stripes, they should be stopped as promptly as if they had invaded our shores with foreign troops.

As long as one of our own citizens is in need of land, we have none to spare for outsiders, no matter what price they may offer. What would you think of a father who, to make $2 a week, would turn two of his little children into the streets to sleep, and rent their room and bed to a chance stranger? This is the treatment which America accords to thousands of her children, and when occasionally she throws them a nickel, she calls it Christian charity, and expects them to be heartily grateful for the generous act.

America is ceasing to be a nation of *homes*. In our larger cities only 22 per cent. of the families own the houses they live in. Out of every hundred of our citizens, seventy-eight do not own an inch of their native land, or a single board or brick in the house they call their home. In New York city only 6 1/3 per cent. of the families own their homes, and two-thirds of the families have practically no property at all. And let it be remembered that these homeless, landless people are not idlers and parasites, but the industrious workers who have built up all that is material in our civilization. To give them anything short of their just share would be robbery. The 78 per cent. of our people who do the most arduous and disagreeable work pay rent for the houses they have built and the farms they have hewn out of the forest. How can charity pay the claim which they are presenting to society? How can we have the impudence to offer them a soup-kitchen when they ask us for their homes?

A Typical Case of Charity Methods.

Two years of active service in the mayor's office in a city of something like 150,000 people have brought me face to face with many cases of poverty, for it is pretty generally known that in our cities the last resort of the poor and distressed is to the mayor and police. Let me cite a typical case. On the very first day that I took possession of the mayor's office, a man and woman applied for relief. They were married, and the woman was the spokesman. They were what might be called a likely looking pair, about thirty years of age, healthy, rosy complexioned, and having every appearance of being well raised. Briefly, their story was this: they had been in the country two years; came from Wales; he was a roller in a tin-plate mill in New Castle, Pa.; after about a year hard times came on; the mill being unable to make money out of his labor (the only purpose, by the way, for which any mill is carried on), shut down; naturally enough, they did their best to live in New Castle in hopes that the mill would start up, until their money was about exhausted; they then sold what few articles of furniture they had succeeded in buying, packed their remaining goods in a trunk and went to Cleveland, where they spent a week in searching for work; some charitable person in Cleveland very kindly advised them to go to Toledo, I suppose, for the want of knowing something better; after a week in Toledo at a small hotel, their money was entirely gone and their trunk was held for security for the pay of their board; in that condition they came to the mayor's office. One of our infirmary directors happened to be in the office at the time, and I said: "Can you do anything for a case of this kind?" As there did not seem to be the slightest chance to blame them with being the cause of their poverty, he replied: "Oh, yes, we can get them transportation to the next county, and so on until they get back to New Castle."

The poor woman, upon whose face were plainly written signs of the deepest anxiety and concern, listened intently to these utterances until she heard the words, "get back to New Castle," when her countenance fell and a look of hopeless despair crossed her face, as the tears burst from her eyes, and she said, "What do we want to get back to New Castle for? There is no work there."

Inadequacy of Charity.

The question of this poor woman unveils at once the slipshod, make-shift character of our whole miserable social system, conceived in the iniquity of a denial of brotherhood relations with our fellow-men, founded upon the injustice of using our fellow-men for purposes of profit, and then bolstering it up by the petty frauds that we carry on in the name of charity; but we are coming to see that expediency is not a substitute for justice, and that right is the only antidote for wrong. Thoughtful people all over this country are beginning to inquire if, indeed, our charities do any good, or are a positive injury. In the last report of President J. M. Brown, of the Humane Society in my own city, he deliberately charges two religious organizations with doing incalculable harm to the cause of social justice through their mistaken attempts at relieving the distress of the poor.

We are coming to see the utter futility of helping an individual here and there. As well might we try to prevent the Mississippi river from reaching the Gulf of Mexico by bailing it out with a dipper. As fast as one man is picked up, ten more are thrown down. We cannot expect to prevent the miseries of poverty while the great industrial machine is allowed to turn out new victims every hour. Poverty in America was once a rare and startling thing, but to-day it is the chronic condition of thousands of our people. Nothing but national action can remove it, because national action has been the cause of it. The government has permitted and even encouraged the building up of private fortunes at the expense of the working people, and now it must permit and encourage the building up of the working people at the expense, if it must be, of these private fortunes. Individual effort is utterly unable to cope with the problems which confront us.

The greater part of our charity is, after all, only a sort of apology for the unrighteous conditions that we are content to live in,— an apology for our failure to be Christian. The most pathetic words that Christ ever uttered, except perhaps his last expiring cry on the cross, were those words which seem continually to ring in my ears as I contemplate the decadent Christianity of to-day — "Why call ye me Lord, Lord, and *do* not the things which I say?"

Those who defend the immoral methods of our business system think they can square accounts by attending various highly respectable "means of grace," by saying nice things about God, and by throwing an occasional bone of charity to Lazarus who sits hungry at the gate.

Charity is twice curst,— it curses him that gives and him that takes. It breeds a self-righteous condescension on the one hand, and a cringing, servile spirit on the other. The maimed and the sick and the aged can demand assistance as a right, not as a favor; and the young and able-bodied should be supplied with work.

Our charitable institutions are like the pumps in a leaky ship. The pumps may be very effective, but would it not be a thousand times better to stop the leaks? In a well-ordered society the necessity for charity would in a short time entirely disappear.

The Real Charity of the Poor.

Let me digress a moment to say that it is a common mistake to imagine that the wealthy are the most charitable class, because their gifts are paraded in annual reports and in public meetings before the eyes of the world. The charities of the poor are small, but they are innumerable. In proportion to their means, they give away incomparably more than the well-to-do classes; and what is infinitely more, they give one another the charity of personal service. Miss Addams relates an instance of this in the "Atlantic Monthly." She says:

<blockquote>
A woman, whose husband was sent up to the city prison for the maximum term just three months before the birth of her child, having gradually sold her supply of household furniture, found herself penniless. She sought refuge with a friend whom she supposed to be living in three rooms in another part of the town. When she arrived, however, she discovered that her friend's husband had been out of work so long that they had been reduced to living in one room. The friend at once took her in, and the friend's husband was obliged to sleep on a bench in the park every night for a week, which he did uncomplainingly, if not cheerfully. Fortunately it was summer, "and it only rained one night." The writer could not discover from the young mother that she had any special claim upon the "friend" beyond the fact that they had formerly worked together in the same factory. The husband she had never seen until the night of her arrival, when he at once went forth in search of a midwife who would consent to come upon his promise of future payment.
</blockquote>

The Remedy: A Democracy of Sovereigns.

I have made a hasty diagnosis of the disease. The words of Jesus, "The poor ye have always with you," are bound to be especially applicable to social conditions as long as the present competitive order of society shall continue, and there is but one remedy — one and only one — that is a democracy, a government of sovereign equals. The possibilities are within our reach: a government of equals, a government of brothers. "Ah," but you say, "that is so far away — a hundred years, a thousand years." I care nothing for that. It is the ideal for which the people wait and for which I am working, and we who have spiritual desire know that "a thousand years in Thy sight are but as yesterday when it has passed and as a watch in the night." But I do not believe it is far away. "The kingdom of heaven is at hand." "Now is the accepted time." Let us arise and possess it.

In 1859 so hopeful an optimist as Ralph Waldo Emerson said of the institution of human slavery: "The man is not yet born who will see human slavery abolished in the United States," and yet four years later the Emancipation Proclamation of the immortal Lincoln was an established historical fact. So some of us raise our puny hands in alarm at the ideals that I have attempted to depict, and we say "Utopian!" "Absurd!" etc.

Socialism Now a Respectable Word.

Thomas Carlyle tells of a poor woman in Glasgow nearly famished for want of nourishment, who went from one charity to another in search of relief; finally, faint and exhausted with hunger, crept into an alley, sickened with typhus fever, inoculated the alley with it, and seventeen deaths were the result of it. And, says Carlyle, "you denied her relationship, but she inoculated your alley with her typhus, and seventeen of your dead prove her sisterhood." Let us acknowledge this only just and patriotic conception of relationship. Call it Socialism, if you will. I have lived to see Socialism a respectable word and a Socialist a respectable person. Let us deal with these evils that outrage and shock and horrify our waking hours as we would deal with them in our own family. Let us stop dealing with effects and give our attention to causes. Already this work is well under way. A hundred years ago we had no asylums for the poor afflicted insane, worn and distressed until reason had become dethroned in the struggle for existence — we had no way to deal with the poor brother and sister but to take them to the madhouse and practically chain them to a post; but to-day, under the inspiration and impulse of the divine spirit of love latent in every heart, we have provided for these wronged people such institutions and such surroundings as will be most likely to restore the dethroned reason; or, if that is beyond the ken of our weak and undeveloped human intellect, at least provided comfortable and humane surroundings in which the unfortunates may pass the remaining years in peace and comfort.

When the Poor Were Sold at Auction.

Lately I visited the Allen County Children's Home at Lima. Dr. S. A. Baxter, of that city, who accompanied me on the visit, told me that when he was a young man he had many times seen indigent men and women and children auctioned off on the courthouse steps in Lima to the bidder who would care for them at the lowest figure. And in pleasing contrast to the custom of selling poor children to be cared for for profit by the lowest bidder, we saw eighty beautiful, well-fed, and well-cared-for, happy children, the wards of Allen county. But there is yet room for further improvement. At sixteen years of age these children must leave the home and go out into the uncertainty of the fierce competition for a living, only to meet with discouragement through their inability to obtain work, that again lands them upon the care of the state either as paupers or criminals.

The auction block was an incident of the civilization of forty years ago, and in some counties of Ohio this custom has been carried on at a much later date. We regard that as little better than barbarism, and to-day the state, through the county homes and the various institutions, is reaching its loving arms out to care and provide for the helpless and wronged among its citizens. We have only to extend the idea that we have already begun to work out in order to extend equality of opportunity to the weakest child born in all this great republic.

ABSOLUTE EQUALITY THE ONLY SAFETY.

I have a baby, only two years old. I want, for his sake, the rules of the "game of life" to be amended. For, as it is being played to-day, I do not know but he will become a tramp or a pauper or a criminal. There is no way in which I can insure his future. I want more than that. I want such a system of government in this country that not only my baby, but the poorest baby in the country, shall have an equal opportunity to the largest possible life. Absolute equality is the only safety of this republic; unless we can secure that, the republic is doomed.

The social conscience of the cities of our country, the states and the nation at large is awakening. The day of special privileges to build up private fortunes by robbing the people is past. Through enlarging the functions of government to minister to the people in such social necessities as railroads, telegraphs, telephones, water, heating and lighting plants, etc., the people are now beginning to take possession of valuable heritages that have been surrendered to those who had no other purpose than to despoil them.

Inasmuch as private interest and private greed have failed to find a plan that will let all who are willing to work have the right to live, the time seems ripe for collective effort to solve the problem; inasmuch as labor produces all wealth, let us have more wealth. Let us set the example of a state made wealthy in character as well as in property; in short, let us apply ourselves to the task of inaugurating and perfecting a just social system, conceived and carried out upon scientific lines, and poverty, crime, vice and consequent human misery will be things of the past, and the prayer of our Lord will have been realized, the kingdom of heaven will be set up here and His will be done on earth as in heaven.

CHAPTER V.

THE EIGHT-HOUR DAY.

You labor for ten or twelve hours of the day; how can you find *time* to educate yourselves? The greater number of you scarcely earn enough to maintain yourselves and your families: how can you find *means* to educate yourselves? The frequent interruption and uncertain duration of your work causes you to alternate excessive labor with periods of idleness: how are you to acquire habits of order, regularity and assiduity? * * * It is, therefore, needful that your material condition should be improved in order that you may morally progress. It is necessary that you should labor less, so that you may consecrate some hours every day to your soul's improvement.— *Mazzini: On the Duties of Man.*

CHAPTER V.

THE EIGHT-HOUR DAY.

ONE of the most sensible first steps which can be taken, either by individual employers or by legislative bodies, for the purpose of giving work to the unemployed, is the reduction of the hours of labor. In a civilization full of contrasts, not one is more startling or inexcusable than the contrast between the overworked, pleading for leisure, and the unemployed, pleading for work. I believe in the right to rest as well as the right to work.

Two years ago I determined never to drill another well on the twelve-hour plan, or allow one man to work twelve hours while other men were unable to get one hour's work. During these two years we have drilled about fifty wells, and the workingmen who did the work have received in the neighborhood of $2,000 more under the eight-hour plan than they would have received working twelve hours. They all express themselves as highly pleased with it. It makes better men of them physically, morally and intellectually.

The fact that some drillers refuse to adopt the eight-hour plan is not to be wondered at. They are like the negro slaves who clung to their chains and refused to be set free by Lincoln's proclamation.

For the practical information of those who are interested in this subject I may say, if I may be allowed to refer to our own experiment, that we have made the following scale of wages for the eight-hour system:

Drillers, $3 per day, or thirty-seven and one-half cents per hour; tool-dressers, $2.40 per day, or thirty cents per hour. This makes the expense to the employer $16.20 for the services of six men, against $14 for the services of four men.

It costs a little more money, but the effect of it is to give two more men a job on each well; to grant to two little families the right to live decently, and to elevate the lives of six men at every well by transforming drudgery into a reasonable task.

Most of the drillers put in *fourteen* hours, counting the time that is involved in getting to and from their work, and, while they are being worn out and ruined in health by their endless labor, thousands of other men are on the streets, unable to find any work at all, even for one hour a day.

There are cases in almost every oil field where one man is employed to run one or more wells *twenty-four* hours a day, seven days a week, three hundred and sixty-five days a year. True, in such cases he has no severe manual labor to perform, but he is deprived of his liberty, like Prometheus chained to the rock, never knowing a minute that he can call his own. Technically, such a man is a free American citizen; but in fact, he is as much a slave as any negro ever was in the Southern cotton-fields.

The eight-hour plan may not be immediately profitable to employers, but it is *right* and *just*, and yields large dividends in satisfaction and peace of mind. If it were universally adopted, it would do more than any other one thing to furnish employment for the workless thousands who wander with heavy hearts from factory to factory, gradually losing the hope and ambition that makes life worth the living.

The Eight-Hour Day in the Oil Regions.

Nearly three years ago I prepared a little pamphlet on the subject, "The Eight-Hour Day in the Oil Regions," reciting the hardships of the workers and pleading for a shorter workday. I distributed some 20,000 of them through the oil regions and in the city of Toledo during the spring campaign of 1897. The following is the text of the pamphlet:

My first purpose in writing this little booklet was to reach the people of the oil regions (our own are always properly the first objects to claim our attention), but as I thought the subject out it seemed to cover a little outside ground that is within reach, and so the oil region comes in at the close.

There is no industry where a reform in hours of labor is more in demand than in the business of drilling wells and producing oil. Three years ago, by actual count, 600 men were employed in pumping wells at the rate of one man to each one and one-quarter wells; to-day 600 men are pumping wells at the rate of one man to *four and one-third wells.* In other words, 600 men are, by the use of labor-saving machinery, doing an amount of work that would have required more than 1,800 men under conditions existing three years ago. The fact that the wells are smaller and would not pay for operating under the old system has nothing to do with the situation before us. The question is this, what is the man who is displaced by the machine and who is unable to find work, going to do to keep from starving? I reply, divide the day with him, give him a part of the work.

Notwithstanding the enormous strides of improvement that have been made in the last thirty years in drilling and operating oil wells, there has not been one particle of improvement in the condition of the oil-well worker. Wages are the same, or lower, and the hours of work remain unchanged. The gain from improved appliances has all gone to the well owners; and the same thing is true in nearly every industry, all of the benefit arising from the introduction of machinery going to the owners of the machine. *As a rule,* not one particle of the benefit arising from the introduction of labor-saving machinery goes to the worker who operates the machine, and there is no justification for this condition whatever in the domain of *right* and *wrong;* there can be no justification excepting the usual appeal to the traditions of the past, " We are doing as well by our men as others." But in the name of justice and reason, I ask, if there is improvement in the methods of production so that capacity is multiplied many fold, why should there not be improvement in the methods of distributing the earnings of the machine? Now, please stop and look that question squarely in the face and answer it. Think it out. Don't say, " Oh! that's rot." Play fair. Let us reduce the proposition to a *simple*. There are ten men living on an island, all working contentedly and getting a good living from the fruit of their toil. One of the ten invents a machine that does all of the work of the other nine. The owner of the machine hires one of the nine to operate it, takes all the earnings for himself and leaves the other eight to hustle for themselves. There is no other work on the island. They are unable to get away to any other land, and there is but one way of escape from starvation left them: they still have left the divine right of begging from the man who owns the machine, and the brother man who operates it, but that is all. How long do you suppose these eight men will willingly look on and see others living comfortably — nay, luxuriously, while they are denied the right to live at all? I think this is a fair picture of society as I see it to-day. The illustration might be greatly amplified, but I think the point is clear. Both the man who owns the machine and the man who operates it are at fault, and the result will be that the eight men who are in enforced idleness will become totally worthless members of the little society because they are supported in idleness, or if they are denied support they will destroy the only two men who stand between them and the right to work for a living. This is not a plea for sentiment or charity; it is a plea for a scientific solution of one of the gravest questions affecting our national life to-day: "What to do for the unemployed?" I reply — give the man a chance to live — give him a little work.

The solution of the difficulty with the little society of ten on the island is very plain. The man who invented the machine, it will be conceded by all the rest, is entitled to a reward for his genius, but he knows his fellow-men must live, and so instead of hiring one to work all day, he hires all to work a part of the day; they then have an equal chance during their leisure hours for mental improvement, recreation, devising means for bettering conditions around them and so on to the end of the chapter.

The question of wages did not come up at all with this little society on the island. Neither will it cut any figure at all when we are *all* ready for the eight-hour day.

The men on the island were all working contentedly before the machine came into their life, and if the only effect of its coming was to shorten their hours of toil it would serve to increase their contentment. Don't say this is visionary or ideal; it is nothing but plain *horse-sense*. One man or one firm cannot inaugurate the eight-hour day and make it work *justly*, but if all in any given trade or calling will join, it is no longer a problem, and it is no more a question of wages than it was a question of wages with the ten men *on the island*. It is the easiest possible solution of the great question of "*What to do for the unemployed?*" Here is the answer:

Divide the day! Divide the day! Divide the day! *Give them a part of the work.*

Right here let me introduce an extract from my first report as president of the Western Oil Men's Association, presented at their first annual meeting last January:

"Before concluding this report I wish to call your attention to one department of our industry where this association may be useful if it will. I refer to the department of labor. The situation in that field is briefly this: Much has been done in the way of improving methods of drilling wells and handling oil and of operating generally. Let me illustrate by comparison. I am not yet an old man, but I worked at drilling wells when we considered that 100 feet of hole in a week was good work. I received for that work $4 per day. To-day the driller who cannot under favorable circumstances 'string the derrick,' which means make 140 feet within twelve hours, is not in an extreme sense a skilled man. Thirty years ago the labor of the driller on that amount of hole would cost $50. To-day the driller gets a minimum of $4 and perhaps a maximum of $10. I worked on a farm in 1868 where we had twenty-one oil wells. There were forty-two pumpers to operate them. Even three years ago I know of a property of sixty wells that furnished labor for sixteen men to pump and handle them under the boiler and steam box system. To-day a property similar to that is being operated by six men, the pumping power, the surface rod, the pumping-jack and the gas engine all reducing and displacing labor. This is just and proper. In labor-saving machinery is found some of the greatest triumphs of the age, but I am firmly convinced that we, as a people, have failed to appreciate the responsibility that comes to us in the introduction of labor-saving machinery. That the worker who is displaced by the machine, by the pumping power or the gas engine or any improvement, has a right to live as long as he is willing to work, there can be no question, and the responsibility of devising ways and means whereby he may live when he is displaced by the machine that makes the owner more money does not rest altogether with the worker. I am my brother's keeper.

"In the oil fields to-day, notwithstanding all the improved methods, we still cling to the antiquated, barbarous custom of working twelve hours on drilling wells. It seems to me that it would be a step in the right direction, a step that will put a seal of great usefulness upon this association, if we can simply endorse a resolution favoring a more humane and equitable division of the hours of labor and divide the day by three instead of by two, advocating working eight hours instead of twelve, and thus do something to provide for a worthy brother man who is only asking for a living and a right to work for it. I believe the workers throughout the length and breadth of the oil region will kindly take their share of the responsibility and burden of a move of this kind, and I believe that its endorsement by this association will demonstrate beyond question that it has been more largely useful than any and all of its predecessors and will at the same time make its future bright and glorious with promise."

It is gratifying to add that a resolution favoring the adoption of the eight-hour day was unanimously passed, and it is probable that the Western Oil Men's Association is the first organization of employers on record that has taken the initiative in this great work that is yet to play such an important part in the social salvation of our beloved nation.

The melancholy fact must be recorded that, notwithstanding this resolution, the lapse of nearly three years has shown not the slightest change for the better in the condition of the oil workers. The employers simply soothed their consciences by the passage of a declaration favoring a shorter workday, and then left the fulfillment of what they declared to be just, to the processes of nature or a timely miracle.

Long Hours of London Carmen and Cabmen.

An anonymous English writer says in his book, "The Social Horizon:"

None of our men get more than thirteen hours," proudly observed a London tramway official to me when, a year or two back, I was discussing with him some of the points in dispute between the company and its servants, and had incidentally referred to a working-day of fifteen or sixteen hours, that some of the men were reported to be regularly undergoing.

"None of our men get more than thirteen hours!" Just think of it. A man starts on his first journey at 7 in the morning, and he finishes his last journey at 8 o'clock at night — summer and winter, wet and cold, all the year round — stopping and starting a tram car, putting on or taking off the brake, dealing out tickets or pocketing pence. I think of the dreary monotony of such a life.

I found, however, that only by managerial ingenuity could it be made out that thirteen hours was the maximum working day. That was only the time that the man was actually on the car. Ten minutes, or twenty minutes between the journeys was not reckoned in his day. All the little odds and ends of time required for getting his supply of tickets, handing in cash, making reports of accidents, waiting about the office for this, that and the other, none of these things were taken into account, but only just the bare reckoning of the time-table, and of course no account was taken of the time a man required for getting to his work and getting home again. So even where this proud boast could be made, the man who turned out of his home at a quarter of seven in the morning could not expect to get back again till between nine and ten at night, and that week after week, month after month, year after year.

As to the cabmen of London, they are of course less regular. For the most part they have a certain sum of money to make up for their cabs, and after that what they take in is their own. With good luck a man may get moderate hours, but competition is such that they are often compelled to be prowling about, as I have had them express it to me, "pretty nigh all the hours that God A'mighty makes."

Sixteen hours, taking trains and omnibuses and cabs all around, is not so very far out as the working day, and we may adopt this figure for the sake of argument. Suppose that we had reduced the working-day of these 40,000 men from sixteen hours to twelve — long enough in all conscience — is it not a mere matter of arithmetic that at one stroke we should have found employment for 10,000 idle men, probably representing not less than four or five times that number of people, all of them suffering more or less in body and soul from poverty? Take the 40,000 men employed on the vehicles of London, or in connection with them, reduce their hours of work and increase their numbers to 50,000, put them into comfortable uniforms, and set up another government factory for a thousand of the unemployed, or the over-employed and villainously underpaid seamstresses of London; make the uniforms for those 50,000 men, and you will immediately send a new current of life tingling through every vein of the community.

The Man with the Hoe.

When I look out in the early morning or in the hours of evening at the bucket brigades that I see in my own city and the other cities of my land, upon the toilers who produce all the wealth, and reflect upon the meager share that they are permitted to enjoy, my heart is heavy with anguish as I think of the wrongs of such a system; when I look upon the army of cripples, legless, handless, eyeless, sitting about our streets, begging for a dole to eke out their miserable existence, I see in them the products of modern industry, and my mind instinctively turns, as I look upon these shapeless creatures, these distorted human beings, these brethren of mine, to that great poem by Edwin Markham, "The Man with the Hoe." Those of you who have had the privilege of seeing Millet's picture will understand what was the inspiration of this poem. There stands the man in the bare field, bareheaded, wearing coarse wooden shoes, both hands clasping the handle of an old-fashioned hoe, and Markham says of him:

"God created man in his own image; in the image of God created he him."

[By courtesy of DOUBLEDAY & McCLURE.]

> Bowed by the weight of centuries, he leans
> Upon his hoe and gazes on the ground,
> The emptiness of ages in his face
> And on his back the burden of the world.
> Who made him dead to rapture and despair,
> A thing that grieves not and that never hopes,
> Stolid and stunned, a brother to the ox?
> Who loosened and let down this brutal jaw?
> Whose was the hand that slanted back this brow?
> Whose breath blew out the light within this brain?
>
> Is this the Thing the Lord God made and gave
> To have dominion over sea and land;
> To trace the stars and search the heavens for power,
> To feel the passion of Eternity?
> Is this the Dream He dreamed who shaped the suns
> And pillared the blue firmament with light?
> Down all the stretch of Hell to its last gulf
> There is no shape more terrible than this —
> More tongued with censure of the world's blind greed —
> More filled with signs and portents for the soul —
> More fraught with menace to the universe.
>
> What gulfs between him and the seraphim!
> Slave of the wheel of labor, what to him
> Are Plato and the swing of Pleiades?
> What the long reaches of the peaks of song,
> The rift of dawn, the reddening of the rose?
> Through this dread shape the suffering ages look;
> Time's tragedy is in that aching stoop;
> Through this dread shape humanity, betrayed,

Plundered, profaned, and disinherited,
Cries protest to the Judges of the World,
A protest that is also prophecy.

O masters, lords, and rulers in all lands,
Is this the handiwork you give to God,
This monstrous thing distorted and soul-quenched?
How will you ever straighten up this shape;
Touch it again with immortality;
Give back the upward looking and the light;
Rebuild in it the music and the dream;
Make right the immemorial infamies,
Perfidious wrongs, immedicable woes?

O masters, lords, and rulers in all lands,
How will the Future reckon with this Man?
How answer his brute question in that hour
When whirlwinds of rebellion shake the world?
How will it be with kingdoms and with kings —
With those who shaped him to the thing he is —
When this dumb Terror shall reply to God,
After the silence of the centuries?

EIGHT HOURS THE FORMER WORKDAY.

The artisan and laborer of the fourteenth and fifteenth centuries worked only eight hours per day as a rule and were paid for overtime. Professor Thorold Rogers says:

The winter's wages are about 25 per cent. less than those of other seasons, but the winter seems to have been limited to the months of December and January. This fact, which I have frequently noticed, is proof that the hours of labor were not long. They seem to have been not more than eight hours per day, and at a later period in the history of labor the eight hours' day seems to be indicated by the fact that extra hours are paid for at such a rate as corresponds to the ordinary pay per hour for eight hours, being a little in excess. Hence the artisan, if he were minded to do so, would have time during summer for some agricultural employment; it would seem that this occupation for spare time was not unusual, for I have found employers of artisans occasionally purchasing agricultural produce from the mason and carpenter, or from their wives. Extra hours are often paid for when the work is pressing and time was an object. Extra hours, sometimes as many as forty-eight in a week, are frequently paid for by the King's agents (Henry VIII) when hurried work was needed. Even when the Act of Elizabeth and the regulations of the Quarter Sessions prescribed a day of twelve hours all the year round, two and a half hours were allowed for rest, and the day was brought down, on an average, to nine and a half hours.

The quality of the work in the old times is unquestionable. It stands to this day a proof of how excellent ancient masonry was. I am persuaded that such perfect masonry would have been incompatible with a long hours' day. The artisan who is demanding at this time an eight hours' day in the building trades is simply striving to recover what his ancestors worked by five or six centuries ago. It is only to be hoped that he will emulate the integrity and the thoroughness of the work of his ancestors. The working-day of the English artisan in the early part of this century was increased to eleven and fourteen hours. Where the new mill and factory machinery was in use, the hours were far longer. In 1817 the workers in the stocking factories of Leicester were employed fourteen and fifteen hours. Worse still was the condition of the children "apprentices," who toiled from sixteen to eighteen hours daily.

Physiological Basis for the Eight-Hour Day.

That there is a sound physiological basis for the demand for a shorter workday is shown on the high authority of the "British Medical Journal," which in a recent article says:

Few will question that grinding toil from morning till night is most undesirable, and that a reasonable time for recreation and change of scene is necessary for all workers, not least for those whose employment calls into play none of the higher and intellectual sides of the mind, and for those whose work, like that of miners, is of an uninviting and laborious nature.

It is impossible, however, to argue such questions from the more lofty standpoint of theory. Labor problems cannot always be put to the touch of experiment; but in this particular case the experiment has been tried, and its success will do more to convince objectors than any amount of theoretical quibbling. Certain engineering firms in the north of England having determined to give the eight hours' day a trial, took the precaution to agree with the men to reduce their wages by such an amount as would cover half the anticipated loss, the masters bearing the other half. After a few months it was found that there was no loss whatever; the output was as large as before.

Such a result, and it is by no means unique, is not only intensely interesting to the parties immediately concerned, but also opens up a field of physiological research which is almost untouched. It is not often that politics and physiology come into such close relationship. It amounts to this, that when the men worked for nine or ten hours, one or two hours were to all practical intents and purposes wasted.

We do not mean deliberately wasted, but that the natural processes of fatigue operated in such a manner as to lead to a wasteful expenditure of energy. In a shorter day the workmen work with a will, to put it popularly; that is to say, the hours are not sufficiently long to admit of the onset of a time when the voluntary control over the muscles is necessarily lost to a great extent.

The question of fatigue is very nearly related to that of the muscular sense, and few physiological questions have been more keenly discussed. Muscular fatigue is not a purely local muscular condition; the nervous centres are also at fault. Mosso of Turin has gone so far as to suppose that some toxic substance is produced during muscular activity which, passing into the blood and reaching the brain, impairs its activity and the will power associated therewith. He has also, by means of an instrument which he has devised and named the ergograph, shown graphically that the fall in the amount of voluntary contractions is not necessarily a steady one, but may exhibit rises in the course of the downfall. * * *

An eight-hour country need never be afraid of competing with a fourteen-hour country, because the grade of work performed in the latter is certain to be inferior. A shorter day always means a better product. Whenever you buy an overcoat made by an overworked tailor, and it rips up the back in a few weeks, you discover that *jaded men cannot do good work.*

Every week we hear of some accident or explosion caused by the bad work of some tired-out machinist. Many a runaway is caused by the careless stitches of a fagged harnessmaker, who is required to sit and sew for ten long hours a day.

If a man labors from eight in the morning until twelve, and from one to five, he has exhausted his energies for that day. Whatever he does more than this, he must do with strength borrowed from the future. If he crowds five days' work into four, he simply takes a day from his life. No man should be expected constantly to expend his energies without being allowed a chance to recuperate. If it were not for the rest which Sunday brings to the worn-out wage-earners, they would soon be complete nervous wrecks.

The Increasing Burden of Machinery, and Its Effect on Art and Life.

Machinery has added speed, and intensity, and discomfort to production, so that many a factory worker's life is almost equivalent to imprisonment at hard labor. Consider what a machinist's work is like during the hot summer months. In spite of the intense heat, the murky, impure air, the deafening roar of machinery, the grime and sweat and dust, when every second seems a minute and every minute seems an hour, he is expected, for ten long, weary hours every day, to be as accurate as a jeweler and as energetic as a blacksmith. Surely it is not right and Christian for employers, who are finding it difficult to keep cool at the seaside or in the mountains, to require their employees to toil ten and twelve hours a day in the dusty furnace of a city street.

A mechanic's work is not physical only. It is brain-work quite as much as the labor of many a professional man. If post-office clerks, and teachers, and lawyers, and doctors, and preachers, and business men must have vacations, and a chance every day to recuperate, why should not the same privilege be extended to the working people? Their bodies and brains need rest and recreation as much as any.

Machinery is almost driving some branches of art out of existence. It is leading us to lay stress on quantity, not quality. No nation could ever manufacture so many poor articles in so short a time as we can. The combination of machinery and long hours has worked against all that is artistic and original. As John A. Hobson says, in "The Evolution of Modern Capitalism," "It must never be forgotten that art is the true antithesis of machinery. The essence of art is the application of individual spontaneous human effort. Each art product is the repository of individual thought, feeling, effort; each machine-product is not."

The "art" in machine-work has been exhausted in the single supreme effort of planning the machine; the more perfect the machine the smaller the proportion of individual art or skill is embodied in the machine product. The spirit of machinery, its vast, rapid power of multiplying quantities of material goods of the same pattern, has so overawed the industrial world that the craze for quantitative consumption has seized possession of many whose taste and education might have enabled them to offer resistance. Thus, not only our bread and our boots are made by machinery, but many of the very things we misname "art-products."

The same thoughtful writer, in calling attention to the effect of this craze for quantity upon our intellectual life, says:

> By making of our intellectual life a mere accumulation of knowledge, piling fact upon fact, reading book upon book, adding science to science, striving to cover as much intellectual ground as possible, we become mere worshippers of quantity. It is not unnatural that our commercial life should breed such an intellectual consumption, and that the English and American nations in particular, who have, beyond others, developed machine production and the quantitative genius for commerce, should exhibit the same taste in their pursuit after knowledge. Pace, size, number, cost, are ever on their lips. To visit every European capital in a fortnight, see acres of pictures, cathedrals, ruined castles, collect out of books or travel the largest mass of unassorted and undigested information, is the object of such portion of the commercial life as can be spared from the more serious occupations of life, piling up bale after bale of cotton goods, and eating dinner after dinner of the same inharmoniously ordered victuals.

> Our schools and colleges are engaged in turning out, year by year, immense quantities of common intellectual goods. Our magazines, books and lectures are chiefly machine products adjusted to the average reader or hearer, and are reckoned successful if they can drive a large number of individuals to profess the same feelings and opinions and adopt the same party or creed, with a view of enabling them to consume a larger number of copies of the same intellectual commodities which can be turned out by intellectual machinery, instead of undergoing the effort of thinking and feeling for themselves.

So it will be seen that a shorter workday is not only a requirement of the physical nature, but of the intellectual as well. As long as machinery is owned by individuals, and used to increase the volume of production and the amount of profits, we shall have neither the best workers nor the best work. The wonderful, almost self-operating machines ought to give leisure to the many instead of profits to the few; and the most sensible way of giving the whole people the benefits of machinery is by means of public ownership and a steady reduction of the hours of labor in proportion to the progress of invention.

Proved Effects of Shorter Workdays.

Every objection that was made against the ten-hour day has been since found to be a product of prejudice or imagination. It was claimed that men would spend their extra hours of leisure in the saloons, and that the streets would be rendered unsafe by the great increase in the number of drunken men. The very reverse of this has been the fact, in every country where the working day has been made shorter. There is as much drunkenness caused by overwork as there is by idleness.

Liquor is a stimulant, and after a worker has toiled and sweated for ten long hours, it is natural that he should crave the artificial strength that liquor gives. The drunkenness which wrecks so many homes, and breaks the hearts of so many wives and mothers, can never be cured by temperance pledges or prevented by any system of license or prohibition so long as the industrial causes of drunkenness are allowed to continue. The saloon is like a sore that is caused by impure blood, and requires more than local treatment.

As John Rae says of the eight-hour system in Australia, in his book, "Eight Hours for Work:"

> The "go" and energy the workingman is said to put into his work since the reduction of hours is itself good evidence that he does not spend his time in vicious dissipation. If a shorter day in the workshop meant only a longer

day in the tavern he could not possibly show such signs of invigoration, and his day's work and his day's wages would soon have hopelessly declined.

The general opinion in Victoria is that the habits of workingmen have improved and not deteriorated through the short hours. By leaving work early in the afternoon, they are enabled to live out in the suburbs in neat cottages with little gardens behind them, which are almost invariably owned by their occupiers, and they spend much of their leisure tending their little gardens or in some outdoor sport with their families.

The two first effects of the reduction of hours were the multiplication of mechanics' institutes, night schools and popular lectures on the one hand, and the multiplication of garden allotments on the other. Work people had neither time nor energy for such pursuits before — the only resource of the languid is the tavern. But with a longer evening at their disposal, it became worth while devising other and better means of enjoying it.

An English manufacturer writes concerning the reduction of hours:

Soon after our firm adopted the eight-hour system, one of the men came to me and said that, as they had more time in the evenings to themselves, he thought that many would like to buy books to read. A proposal for a book club, to be maintained by weekly contributions from voluntary members, was submitted to the works committee and heartily approved. At the close of the first year over 600 volumes were distributed, and it is anticipated that quite 1,000 volumes will be bought next Christmas. The great bulk of these books, it is certain, would not have been purchased but for this reduction of hours. Here is an interesting suggestion of how, in dealing with one industrial question, the alleviation of another may be assisted. These thousand volumes represent so much work for the papermaker, the printer and the binder, and thus shorter hours have tended to benefit the unemployed.

An English member of Parliament, writing in 1893, says:

An argument which is freely advanced against the interference of the state with the relations of capital and labor, is that it tends to undermine the independence and self-reliance of the class which it seeks to protect, and teaches them to look to the state rather than to their own exertions to remedy evils requiring redress. My answer to this is that the factory operatives of Lancashire and Yorkshire have made greater advances in self-reliance and independence during the past fifty years than any other class of English operatives. Building and benefit societies, co-operative associations, both for distribution and production, have taken their rise and flourish amongst them on a scale of magnitude unknown in any other part of the United Kingdom.

In New Zealand the eight-hour day is already established by law, and the experiment has thus far proved so successful that an agitation has been begun for a still further reduction of hours. It has been found that with an increase of leisure there has come a decrease of crime and pauperism. The liberated workers have now an opportunity to read books and become acquainted with their own children, which was denied to them before.

STILL SHORTER WORKDAY ULTIMATELY NECESSARY.

People ask me what I would do if we had the eight-hour day universally adopted and then there was not work enough to go around? I reply: Divide the day again, and then, if there should still be unemployed men, divide the day again. This is a perfectly logical, rational and reasonable programme. The simple rules of arithmetic will demonstrate that it must be a success.

We must have a chance to think, as well as a chance to labor; else our cities will be mere hives of bees or nests of ants.

Selfishness, and greed, and love of money, grown rampant, have well-nigh consumed us, but the people, the great people, the patient, loving, waiting people, are thinking as they never thought before, and the reign of the people is about to begin. The ideal of the republic, which we find in the well-ordered family, must be realized, and that soon, if the nation is to be saved and the republic is to be permanent. I believe we are coming to this realization at a tremendous pace. The machinery which does the work of the world in one-quarter of the time or less that was formerly required to do it has made it both unnecessary and impossible to provide ten or twelve hours' work for all of the people. The people will not willingly starve or commit suicide. They have a right to live, because they are willing to work; and they have a right to rest, and to enjoyment, and to the use of every good thing their hands and brains have created.

CHAPTER VI.

THE ORGANIZATION OF LABOR.

I confess to having at one time viewed them [labor organizations] suspiciously; but a long study of the history of labor convinced me that they are not only the best friends of the workman, but the best agency for the employer and the public; and that to the extension of these associations political economists and statesmen must look for the solution of some among the most pressing and difficult problems of our times.—*J. E. Thorold Rogers.*

CHAPTER VI.

THE ORGANIZATION OF LABOR.

A TRADE-UNION, as defined by Sidney Webb, is " a continuous association of wage-earners for the purpose of maintaining or improving the conditions of their employment." It is a fraternal, defensive organization, which seeks to make the best possible terms with employers, and to educate and provide for its members. It is not, as a few seem to think, a league of strikers whose endeavor is to drive business out of the country.

Labor organizations date back, in tradition, if not history, to at least 700 years before Christ, when Numa Pompilius allowed the Roman workers to organize. C. Osborne Ward says: "The era covered by the ancient trade-unions is that celebrated as the 'Golden Age.' It was the era of social and intellectual prosperity." In summing up the history and influence of labor unions, Mr. Ward says: "The greater the organization of the working classes for mutual protection and resistance, the higher is the standard of enlightenment in the countries they inhabit."

In our own country, labor organizations are comparatively young, as the necessity for them did not exist until about sixty or seventy years ago; but I believe they have played a great part in the up-building of this nation.

THE GOOD ACCOMPLISHED BY LABOR ORGANIZATIONS.

They have done much to free little children from the sweatshops and factories, to relieve underpaid men and women, to shorten the hours of labor, and to ennoble the working classes with the feeling of solidarity and brotherhood. By means of lectures and labor papers and free discussions, they have educated the workers in matters of industry and good citizenship. They have almost invariably thrown their weight on the side of arbitration, and resorted to strikes only when conciliatory measures failed. The reading-rooms which they have provided for their members have kept thousands of men from lounging on the streets and in saloons.

Without the aid of unions, the working people never could have accomplished the reforms in the factory system, or maintained a high rate of wages as well as they have done in spite of the pressure of the unemployed.

It has been owing to the independent character of organized labor that we have secured the little that we have in the way of helpful legislation for the wronged peoples. I wish I might say that it had been through the help of the churches, but this is not true. "The sinners are with us; it is the saints that are against us," bitterly cried Lord Shaftsbury when he was engaged in the struggle to protect the children of England through factory legislation in Parliament, and so it may be said to-day in this country that progressive legislation to protect children from the factories and sweatshops and to protect life and even property, has been secured by the solidarity of labor organizations.

A few years ago the motormen in the street-car service were standing exposed to the rigors of the wintry winds of our streets on the front end of street cars. The profit-gatherers, the owners and managers, insisted that "no practicable vestibule could be devised or made," that "a man could not safely run an electric car while looking through glass," and as a result of their neglect to provide vestibules, no one knows how may children were orphaned and wives made widows by the lives that were sacrificed through pneumonia and other lung disorders caused by those wintry days. But the labor unions appeared on the scene, the legislators passed a law requiring the men to be protected by a vestibule, and, although for a time it was sought to evade this law by a flimsy subterfuge, the reform was finally accomplished.

The Typographical Union No. 6, of New York city, is this year making its second experiment in cultivating land for the benefit of its unemployed members. It leased 166 acres of land near Bound Brook, N. J., last April, and put fifty of its unemployed members in charge of it. Up to the present time the experiment has proved highly successful. Potatoes, corn, beans, cabbages and tomatoes are being raised, and what is far better, fifty men are taken off the streets and placed where they can earn a living. In this way the contractor and profit-maker are eliminated, and the "men with the hoe" receive directly what they produce. I believe that this kind of activity can be widely extended, with the result of a considerable alleviation of distress. Then, too, organizations of carpenters, bricklayers and plasterers might profitably join in employing their out-of-work members in erecting their own meeting-halls. The Lasters' Union of Lynn, Mass., built and owns to-day the finest labor hall in New England.

Those who would understand the objects and spirit of labor organizations should take notice of the nature of the mottoes which the unions have adopted. The motto which was adopted by the Knights of Labor was: "An injury to one is the concern of all." The favorite motto of all socialistic bodies of workingmen is the famous saying of Karl Marx: "Workingmen of the world, unite." It is an appeal for international brotherhood — a plea for the reign of peace instead of prejudice. The motto of the seamen's union is, "The Brotherhood of the Sea." In every case they urge toward comradeship and helpfulness. The teaching of the trade-union is the only ethical training that thousands of workers receive. Their union becomes their church, and by acts of practical fellowship their moral nature is made stronger.

Injustice of the Wage System.

Trade-unionists speak frequently of " a fair day's wage." This, of course, is a legitimate demand, but it does not cover the ground. A day's wage will never be "fair" so long as an employer subtracts profit from it. Wages should be raised up to a level with earnings.

The wage system is a method of extortion whereby the articles produced by the workers are taken away for a small fraction of their value.

There is no more justification for the payment of dividends when men in the industry get but a dollar a day for ten hours' work, than there is for the highwayman who takes money from the pocket of the victim whom he has sandbagged into insensibility.

There is no good reason why any business should be on the sweat-shop level. When poor sewing-machine women make pants for nineteen cents a dozen they are as much robbed by society as if their houses were burglarized by the police.

A man cannot be an American citizen, and live as a citizen should in this rich country, on a dollar a day. An employer has no right to compel his workers to live like dogs.

Many a wealthy man spends more than a dollar a day on cigars, or theater tickets, or flowers, or wine; and yet we expect a laborer to pay rent and grocery bills and doctor's bills, and clothe and care for a wife and family on the same daily pittance. If the children of these laborers grow up to be ignorant and vicious and criminal, society is to blame. The next generation will not find it easy to deal with the young Goths and Huns and Vandals who are now growing up in the slum alleys.

While wages continue to be paid, and until the establishment of the Co-operative Commonwealth overthrows the entire wages system, the maintenance of a high rate of payment for labor should be one of the first considerations of a government which pretends to represent the people. Low wages mean a low standard of living — a low grade of citizens — an inferior type of civilization.

Twenty cents an hour is a low enough wage for almost any man's labor. Poorly paid work is always poorly performed. No man can do his best work for wages that mean a bare existence. He feels like a horse in a tread-mill, toiling day after day without any hope of promotion or prospect of wealth; and what makes his situation still worse, the threat of discharge continually haunts him. The money he receives on Saturday night is all spent before Thursday or Friday, and a single week's loss of work plunges him into debt and confronts him with actual starvation.

Growth of Parasitism.

A stigma has become attached to honest toil and sweat. Workers have become a separate class, living in a separate part of the city. Their employer is almost as far removed from them as if he lived in the moon. The old ambition of becoming a partner in the firm, which boys used to cherish, seems to-day almost as unreal as a fairy-tale, so separate have the lives of employer and worker become. The former becomes an absolute parasite, living without toil of any kind off the labor of the workers.

To quote from Jean Massart, a Belgian author:

In the factory system the evolution towards parasitism goes its way in open daylight, and under a variety of forms. In proportion as the extension of the market calls for an increase in the scale of production, the more marked becomes the separation of the wage-earners, who are engaged in the actual work of production, from the capitalist master, who retains to himself the task of direction alone. Then comes the moment when those captains of industry delegate their functions to lieutenants, reducing their personal interference in the business to a minimum. One step further and we have the parasitic condition fully achieved; on the one side *work and no prosperity*, on the other side *prosperity and no work*. Then the workers do not even know who the capitalists are, by whom they are exploited, and the exploiters have perhaps never even seen the industrial black-hole or factory of which they are the shareholders.

A Word About the Boycott.

We hear a great deal from the confessedly respectable element of society regarding the wickedness of the strike and the boycott, when they are employed by labor organizations in defense of their principles. The social boycott of those who earn their living by those who live off the earnings of others is a sacred right, a mark of "refinement," a "necessary distinction for the preservation of society," and so on. The blacklisting boycott by railroad dukes and pork-packing marquises and soap-making barons, of toilers who have committed no crime but that of upholding the principles of their unions — a boycott that compels hungry men to tramp wearily from town to town, and state to state, for re-employment — this, of course, is a justifiable protection of the interests of "business." But a boycott levied against the profit-makers who deny men the right to live decently human lives — this is a wicked and pestilent thing which must be suppressed by Krag-Jorgensens, or the jail.

So long as we are separated into warring classes and are inspired by the competitive incentive for individual gain, we shall continue to have just such diverse standards of right and wrong as those I have indicated. A strike is war; a boycott is war. I do not believe that either by class conflict or individual conflict are we to reach the better state to which we all aspire. That goal is to be reached through the growing sense of our common kinship and by our association in collective effort.

Bad as is war, there are distinctions of better and worse to be made regarding it. The same is true of the boycott. A boycott made and carried on in defense of liberty, of humanity, of right conditions of living, has much that may be said in its favor. I wish to quote here from a recent address made by me in Cleveland before the striking railway employees:

> When the Apostle Paul visited the Corinthian Church, he found the people in a great uproar over the question of the eating of meat. This great philosopher quickly proposed a solution of the question in these memorable words:

"If the eating of meat cause my brother to offend, I will eat no more meat while the world stands." Is it not barely possible that there is a conception of patriotism in Cleveland, in Ohio, in these United States, to-day that is saying: "If the running of street cars makes necessary the dehumanizing of my fellow-men, makes necessary the degradation of American citizens to the level of the serfs and below, then I will not ride on the street cars while these conditions remain, while men who operate street cars are forced to be something less than men, less than human."

I have a right to say that I will not ride on cars where my fellow-men are thus outraged — nay, more, I have a right to ask my brother men that they withhold their patronage and place the seal of their condemnation upon organized wrong of this kind against American citizenship. And is it not probable that we are on the eve of the new time when this new patriotism is to take such deep root in all the people that this principle will be extended not only to the street railway service but to every department of industry where human labor is employed; when, realizing our social responsibility, realizing that we are our brother's keeper, we shall make it our business to see that every American works under conditions that grant him the privilege and right to live a decently human life; and that we will refuse to participate in the enjoyment of the fruits of toil in order to furnish ill-gotten gains for private profit-getters?

I believe this is the meaning and the lesson of the boycott. Whether the men win or lose in the end, we shall have learned a valuable lesson by their costly sacrifice, and it is a comfort, at least, to know that if these unfortunate men lose their jobs, no job is lost in the aggregate. The present vicious system of industry is always certain to supply a surplus of the proletariat class who have nothing but their hands and their labor to sell. Thank God, the signs of the better day are plentiful and abundant.

NECESSITY OF POLITICAL ACTION.

In my addresses in the campaign in Toledo I always sought to leave men looking forward to something better than the present hard conditions of life. I know how hopeless is the struggle, how little rainbow and sunshine there is in the life of a man who starts off with his dinner bucket in hand and a crick in his back at 5 o'clock in the morning, and I felt the desire to lead that man to look forward to something better and to get him to contribute of his mite to the bringing about that better time.

The ideal towards which the race is struggling, the ideal which poets, prophets and philosophers have seen is the realization of human brotherhood in human affairs. There is but one way in which we may hope for this realization. *The State is the only instrument through which the people may express their love for one another.* In the work of developing this larger idea of liberty, this nobler conception of government, in this reaching out for justice, organized labor has performed an important part, but there is still greater work to be done. The fields are truly white for the harvest and the laborers are few. It is as true to-day as when Robert Burns wrote that

> Man's inhumanity to man
> Makes countless thousands mourn,

but we are to see the day when man's love for man, through the institution called government, will bring joy and gladness to millions of hearts.

If the workingmen and masses are in economic slavery, in chains to-day, it is because they so will it; it is because preceding economic slavery there has been party slavery, and in each succeeding election the workingmen of the country have been the dupes of the schemers who sought to serve only their own ends. I believe this is the beginning of the end of government that has been bought and sold and run for revenue; that the days of pretended partisan hatred are past; that workingmen can no longer be rallied with the mere hue and cry of "be a Democrat" or "be a Republican."

Let the platform that commands the votes of the workingmen and reform forces be definite and positive, for those things that we know are essential to liberty, such as equal opportunities for all, the abolition of the contract system, the substitution of the eight-hour day and the recognition of organized labor in all skilled departments; and let us repudiate any platform that does not include every one of these principles. Expediency is not a substitute for justice, and right is the only antidote for wrong. Let us be strong and patient in this great work of emancipation. Let us nail to our banners, "Principle before party," the slogan to which the hosts of Toledo rallied in the recent election. Take my word for it, the people are eagerly waiting for an opportunity to respond.

THE ULTIMATE OF TRADE-UNIONISM.

The labor question is larger than the trade-union programme. It means more than the raising of wages and shortening of hours. It means more than profit-sharing. Direct legislation and single tax and free silver do not touch the heart of it. It means the establishment of *national copartnership*.

The disgusting and distracting conflicts known as labor troubles will disappear from civilization before the clear daylight of the sun of public ownership. Who ever heard of a strike among the post-office employees? And yet periodically we are disturbed with strikes among the street-railway employees, the lighting companies, the railroad companies, indeed among all manner of employees who are serving an individual. But where the people minister to themselves, as through public ownership, the people know how the people should be treated; consequently we have decent conditions under which men may labor, we have living wages, and we have such a division of the hours of toil that labor becomes a joy instead of a mere drudgery.

Organized labor has done more in the last twenty-five years to teach the people of these United States the purpose of government, the meaning of justice, liberty and brotherhood than any other organization that I know of, but even organized labor is only a necessity of this system of warfare that we are living in. Competition has become so cruel and heartless that it has become a necessity that labor should organize as for war, and yet, in this particular, labor is ahead of many of our institutions professing to be wholly educational. *Rarely has a labor organization passed a resolution favoring war;* always for peace and generally for public ownership; on the other hand, we have ministers professing to preach the gospel of the lowly Nazarene, preaching against public ownership and telling us that war is a necessity. For my part, I refuse to believe such a libel on the race. I see no more reason for war between nations than between individuals, and I hail with delight the growing sentiment in favor of the reign of the Prince of Peace, and look to the time when the Golden Rule shall be the supreme law of the land. Men do not want to hate one another. Their normal condition is to love each other, and in spite of all the devils in our competitive warfare, in spite of all the devils in hell, this is the glorious future that awaits us in these United States. We have only to be true; we have only to be firm; we have only to be faithful; we have only to believe in men and carry out in our lives the precepts of the lowly Carpenter.

As long as there is an industrious, useful man poor, or a useless idler rich, the labor question is not settled. As long as men are obliged to make poor goods, for sale and not for use, the labor question needs attention. Working people should not be a special class in society. Every one of us should serve our fellows with muscle, or brain, or both. I cannot sum up what I wish to say in words of my own so well as in the following verses by Mrs. Stetson. She says:

> Shall you complain, who feed the world?
>   Who clothe the world?
>   Who house the world?
> Shall you complain who are the world,
>   Of what the world may do?
>   As from this hour
>   You use your power,
>   The world must follow you!

The world's life hangs on your right hand!
    Your strong right hand!
    Your skilled right hand!
You hold the whole world in your hand,
  See to it what you do!
    Or dark or light,
    Or wrong or right,
  The world is made by you!

Then rise as you never rose before!
    Nor hoped before!
    Nor dared before!
And show as was never shown before,
  The power that lies in you!
    Stand all as one!
    See justice done!
  Believe and dare and do!

CHAPTER VII.

THE COMPETITIVE SYSTEM A FAILURE.

To this cheapening of production * * * everything [during the competitive era] was sacrificed — the happiness of the workman at his work, nay, his most elementary comfort and bare health. His food, his clothes, his dwelling, his leisure, his amusement, his education, his life, in short, did not weigh a grain of sand in the balance against this dire necessity of "cheap production" of things, a great part of which were not worth producing at all. * * * Their "labor-saving" machines were made to save labor (or, to speak more plainly, the lives of men) on one piece of work in order that it might be expended — I will say wasted — on another, probably useless, piece of work.— *William Morris: News from Nowhere.*

If you want to know precisely what sort of fruit *unrestricted competition* will bring forth, study the history of English labor during the first quarter of this century. That was a time when "the economic forces" held undisputed sway. There were no laws to restrict freedom of contract; there were no trade-unions, or, if any timidly ventured into being, they were ruthlessly stamped out by the law; there was not much moral sentiment to restrain tyranny and extortion; supply and demand were the only regulative forces. That ought to have been a blessed season of peace and plenty for all. Was it so? For the capitalists it was; not for the laborers. Hear Mr. Thorold Rogers: "Children and women were worked for long hours in the mill, and the Arkwrights and Peels and a multitude more built up colossal fortunes on the misery of labor. * * * High profits were extracted from the labor of little children, and the race was stunted and starved, while mill-owners, land-owners and stock-jobbers collected their millions from the toil of those whose wages they regulated and whose strength they exhausted." * * * These * * * are but part of a leaf out of volumes of horrors. It was to this that unrestricted competition brought the English laborer; and no economic force appeared for his deliverance, nor was there any sign of salvation coming to him from that quarter.— *Washington Gladden: Tools and the Man.*

CHAPTER VII.

THE COMPETITIVE SYSTEM A FAILURE.

THE real impracticable visionaries of to-day are those who imagine that "free competition" can bring prosperity and contentment to the wage-earning masses. Under the present business system, the prosperity of the few necessitates the poverty of the many. It is a capitalistic sophistry to say that "the interests of labor and capital are identical." They ought to be identical, and would be under proper conditions; but every strike and lock-out proves that the present relation between labor and capital is not one of peace and harmony.

Individualism has failed properly to distribute the immense wealth which has been created in the last forty years. It has failed to furnish work for millions of our people. It has failed to reduce the hours of labor for those who were employed. It has allowed loafing schemers to become richer than the princes of India, while industrious and intelligent citizens have become pauperized and outlawed. It has put tiny children in the factory while their fathers sought in vain for work. It has fostered crime, and driven thousands to suicide. It has brought out all the baser passions of human nature, and repressed the nobler, kindlier virtues. The evidences of its failure and collapse are to be seen on every side.

For instance, look at the failure of individualism to manage the coal-mining industry of this country; look at Hazleton, Pa., where two years ago thirty unarmed men were shot down while peacefully walking along the highway. Look at Virden, Ill., where thirteen men sacrificed their lives in an attempt to get work and a living wage only a short time ago. Look at our own great State of Ohio. Listen to the pathetic wail of the wives and children of 600 miners at Jobs, Ohio, who had but twenty-two days' work in five months! Can these people be patriotic? Can they sing with any just conception, " My Country, 'Tis of Thee, Sweet Land of Liberty? "

The People Beginning to See the Light.

I think we have reached a period in the history of the world when people are beginning to understand that the cause of our misery, our woe and want, our poverty and crime lies in social injustice. And I am sure that if we have once properly located the cause, we shall not be long in discovering the remedy. We have heretofore been dealing too much with effects. We have talked about the struggle between capital and labor, forgetting that all capital is but labor, that all created wealth is the fruit of the toil of men's hands, that all of the immeasurable value that we call improvement, all the created wealth of great cities, of magnificent buildings, of railroads and ships, canals and highways — all of these are the product of men's hands. Naked man and natural opportunity have produced them all. We are coming to understand that neither the earth nor the great cities of the earth have been created for the benefit of a few men or for a special class. We are coming to understand that all alike are entitled to so much of natural opportunity as they have need of. There is no dispute on the question of air and sunshine, although something of an embargo is placed on the latter by the tall buildings in our cities; so far, we have free access to certain kinds of air — though it is not always of the best; — but man has been fenced off through private ownership from free access to the earth, the land; and as we study the low estate to which many of our fellow-men have fallen under the influence of the thing we call civilization, we do not have to look very deep before we can find that the cause of a man's wretchedness is generally the denial of an opportunity to exercise the God-given right of working in order to develop and bring out the best possibilities of his manhood. I believe that a government to be worthy the name ought to *guarantee equality of opportunity for every child born in it.*

We have been given to fulsome boasting that we have the best government on the face of the earth. Granted. It does not follow that it may not be made better. A government in which jails, penitentiaries, almshouses and workhouses are filled to overflowing certainly has not realized final conditions in the art of civilizing its inhabitants. We are coming to understand that so much of the thing that we call civilization as we really have, has come in spite of modern industry rather than by reason of it. We have come to understand that a civilized man is a man who cares for the welfare of his fellow-man; an educated man is a man who knows that it cannot be well with him unless it is well for all of his fellows. The old Knights of Labor motto that "An injury to one is the concern of all," is an important fundamental, necessary in the conception of every man who claims to be a good citizen.

The Tramp and the Trust Prove the Failure of Competition.

Modern society is organized warfare, and there is no hope of escape from these conditions through more warfare. Competition has failed; the competitive system is doomed. It seems like a waste of words to repeat a truth that is so apparent to-day. It is proved by our great armies of tramps, paupers, mendicants and criminals who have been squeezed out of the race simply because of their inability to hold their own, and have fallen into the class known as dependents. Charge them all up to competition, which is a denial of brotherhood, and you will have found the cause of all of our distress to-day. Now, shall we find the remedy in more competition? Not at all. The only remedy for the evil arising from competition is the antidote that we find in association, and the people, the great masses, seem to be the last to comprehend this fact. The business man, already discerning the signs of the coming storm that is to sweep the competitive system from the earth, is breaking for cover, and hence we see the great organization of trusts that are springing up daily and almost hourly.

As I say further on, in the chapter on "Trusts," we shall not overcome the evil of the trusts by legislating against them, and compelling a dozen companies to do business where one might do the business. There would be no more virtue in a programme of that kind than there would be in the sympathy of a man who should employ his brother man to carry a pile of bricks first to one side of a lot and pile them up nicely and then back to the other side to repeat the operation. It is said that Stephen Girard actually once did this sort of thing, believing that he was philanthropic in doing so. Useless labor is clearly a curse and not a blessing, and instead of trying to destroy the trust and department store, we must organize our society through the thing called government in such a way as to distribute all blessings, distribute the profit, if you please, of the saving of labor where it belongs, among all of the people. The profits of these organizations are only made possible by the fact that society is here, that the city is here, and no man or organization of men has a right to use the city, state, or nation, or even an individual, simply as an instrument out of which he may squeeze profit. We are realizing the inevitable result of competition, which is always monopoly. In any game or test of strength or skill, first there are many, then there are a few, then there is one; and so we have the prospect before us, if we continue our present course, of one gigantic trust and a nation of wage slaves and paupers.

Let me quote from an article, "The Spread of Socialism," by Washington Gladden in the "Outlook" for May 13th, 1899. Dr. Gladden is known as one of the most conservative, most careful, conscientious and just men to-day in the Christian ministry:

Such a gigantic attempt to bind burdens upon the whole community of consumers must provoke a violent reaction. These billions of watered stock are simply a legalized demand upon the people for contributions of their substance to those who have given them nothing in exchange. The feudal lords of the olden time made no more unjust demand. It will not be endured. And there is terrible danger that these injustices will be swept away by a whirlwind of popular wrath. Prof. Albion W. Small, the head professor of sociology in the University of Chicago, cannot be suspected of reckless enmity toward capitalists, but he has just been testifying that the tendencies of which we have been speaking are ominous. "In this age of so-called democracy," he says, "we are getting to be the thralls of the most relentless system of economic oligarchy that history has thus far recorded. That capital from which most of us, directly or indirectly, get our bread and butter, is becoming the most undemocratic, atheistic and inhuman of all the heathen divinities." Professor Small goes on: "I am not thrusting the dust of my library in your faces; but if you heed the symptoms from bank and office, factory and railroad headquarters, and daily press, you have discovered that the very men who have made these combinations are beginning to be frightened at their shadows. These very business men, who claim a monopoly of practical "horse-sense," have involved themselves and all of us in a grim tragedy. They are asking in a quiet way how it is all going to end. Whether they realize it or not, our vision of freedom is passing into the eclipse of universal corporate compulsion in the interest of capital. The march of human progress is getting reduced to making time in the lock-step of capital's chain-gang. It would make infinitely more for human weal if every dollar of wealth was cleaned off the earth, if we could have instead of it industry and homes, and justice and love and faith, than to be led much further into the devil's dance of capitalization.

Public Ownership the Remedy.

Further on Dr. Gladden says:

Vested rights will be respected, I have no doubt; but vested wrongs may be called to account. It is probable that some new legal maxims will be framed and enforced, and that our jurisprudence will be enlarged and invigorated by a new application of ethical principles. Whether corporations in any sense private will long be permitted to manage public utilities may be doubted; but if they do, they will certainly be required to govern their conduct by a strict regard for the public welfare. " Universal corporate compulsion in the interest of capital" is the goal toward which, in the estimate of Professor Small, our economic world is moving. Of course, we shall not tarry at that goal; probably we shall never reach it. The swifter and stronger the movement toward it, the more prompt and resolute will be the revolt. When the purpose becomes evident, these vast aggregations of capital will be seized, their holdings will be appropriated, and the properties will pass under the control of the people. Industrial feudalism, when it is finished, will be speedily transformed into industrial democracy. Thus it is that the present tendencies in the business world are carrying us toward Socialism at a plunging pace.

The solution of our problem of what to do with the trust and the monopoly lies solely by the way of public ownership. The properties of the people that have been frittered away through legislation nearly always inspired by, and clearly in the interest of, private business, must be again brought into their own possession. Long before the time for the expiration of the fifty-year street railroad franchises, the people will have awakened to a new conception of morality, to a new understanding of business, to a new idea concerning stealing, and they will say, "Well! we thought that was *business* in the old times, but we find now it was simply stealing," and by perfectly orderly methods they will retake the possessions that are rightfully theirs and out of which they have been robbed.

Where Public Ownership Is Tried.

The advantages of citizenship to the average person in the Antipodes, where the principle of public ownership is in the ascendant, is comprehensively summarized by a writer, who, in assuming, for example, that he is a New Zealander, says:

> In that case, I live in a country which is governed in the interests of the people, and not in the interests of monopolists, as England is largely governed in the interests of the ground landlord; I live under an equitable system of

taxation, the burden of which, as far as possible, is in proportion to the pecuniary capacity of the taxpayer. If I am anxious to settle upon the land, I can rent or buy it on favorable terms from the government. Owing to the existence of a vast number of freehold properties, I can be certain that no revolutionary measures will have any chance of acceptance, because so large a portion of the population has a direct interest in the soil, and is likely to be conservative in the best sense of the word. As an owner of land or as a leaseholder — assuming that I have carried out improvements upon my property — I can borrow of the government money at a low rate of interest. If I am an urban worker, I have the benefit of stringent laws which protect me from abuses, whether I work in a factory or a shop. Whether I am an employer or a workman, I feel confident that there are not likely to be any violent disturbances in trade, because I am in a country in which, owing to the compulsory arbitration law, there has been no strike or lockout for a period of four years, and all industrial disputes have been amicably settled. If I want to insure my life, I go to the government, and I know that they can give me the best security. When I make my will, I have no friend whom I can trust, no friend whom I wish to trouble, I can put my property with entire confidence in the hands of the public trustee. Finally, if I am living as an upright citizen of my country, though a poor man, I need have no fear of a miserable old age, because, when I have reached sixty-five, the government will give me a pension of seven shillings a week; and in the meantime I shall save as much as possible, in order that my own modest means, as a supplement to the allowance which I shall receive, may enable me to obtain something beyond the mere necessaries of life.

SERVICE FOR SERVICE INSTEAD OF THE MODERN FACTORY SYSTEM.

Five years ago I dealt with my associates as "employees," but I now know that there is a higher relation between men than master and servant. I have come to see that it is due to a mere accident of an unjust system that I am permitted to have a choice in the matter. An accident of another kind might have made one of the employees the master and me the servant. It might have placed him in the office and me in the factory.

Under the existing social order it is impossible to see how any proper conception of justice can be realized in the factory system. The average factory is a place where wealth is made, and men are unmade. Men are treated as impersonal "hands," not as brothers and fellow-beings. In many cases the employees are numbered like convicts, and locked into the rooms where they work. Overseers watch them with lynx-eyes, and a slight mistake often means an instant discharge. The division of labor makes each worker's daily task as monotonous as the swinging of a pendulum.

The factory system, in its present form, must go. It is too great a strain on our nerves, our health, and our morals. Our better natures cry out against it as an unnatural method of obtaining a livelihood. Whatever is contrary to the spirit of brotherhood must not be regarded as final.

What we call wages is a subterfuge so transparent, when viewed from any just standpoint, that it can only be properly characterized as morally grotesque. The absurdity of the idea that I can organize industry, employ my fellow-man in a capacity that by his labor he makes $25 a day for me and I fancy that I am dealing with him in a Christian manner or carrying out the Golden Rule because I give him $3 a day, is too apparent to be worthy of discussion. Not only is service for service the only Christian basis for social relation between men, but it is absolutely the only scientific basis, and dealing on any other basis is an immorality pure and simple, is a wrong, and no amount of patching or compromise will ever make it right.

> When we shall for service render
> Service of an equal worth,
> Then will all mankind be brothers,
> Heaven will then have come to earth.

Service for service is the divine law, and we plead for public ownership of common utilities because it leaves out the idea of profit. Our people need no padrones to take care of their wages and manage their affairs. They are quite intelligent and moral enough to conduct their own business activities without the dangerous assistance of any capitalist.

During the flurry in the stock exchange in New York in the winter of 1898-99, one man was known to make (?) a million dollars in a day, though we all know that he did not make a thing even of the value of a tooth-pick; while another man, made of the same kind of clay, spent the day in the vain search for an opportunity to work to earn bread for himself and those dependent upon him, and found himself reduced to such extremity that at midnight he stood in a waiting line of hungry men to receive a loaf as a gift of charity at Fleischman's bakery. Such frightful extremes of wealth and poverty indicate more eloquently than words the truth of the popular admission we hear on every hand, even from superficial thinkers, that "something is wrong," that we have not realized the ideals of the founders of this government who declared that "all men are created equal and entitled to * * * life, liberty, and the pursuit of happiness."

The Fallacy of the Competitive Incentive to Progress.

As King C. Gillette says, in his remarkable book, "The Human Drift:"

> There is no greater fallacy in the minds of men than that competition is the life of trade or an incentive to progress. It is just the reverse. It is the most damnable system ever devised by man or devil. It is the cause of every injustice in our social atmosphere, and is the only cause of all ignorance, poverty, crime and sickness. By its maintenance as a system, the world of progress loses the greater part of its brain power; and the whole system is a waste of material and labor beyond calculation. It is responsible for all fraud, deception and adulteration which enters into every article of consumption. It is a system of chaos which no man can reduce to order. It is a complicated machine which has a thousand unnecessary parts to every one that is necessary, and every unnecessary part is a loss of power and labor. No one understands its working, and it grinds out poverty to some, wealth to others and crimes indiscriminately to all.
>
> If I believed in a devil, I should be convinced that competition for wealth was his most ingenious invention for filling hell; but not believing in that much-abused individual, I must conclude that competition for material wealth is maintained simply through ignorance. Competition for wealth or individual power has been the basis of all civilized governments, and, by resulting

oppression, the cause of their final disintegration or destruction; and no government can stand until material equality is secured to the individual, and intelligence and progressive thought are made the only basis of competition.

With competition for wealth, selfishness is born; for material wealth is not divisible without loss. But knowledge is divisible to infinity, and it suffers no loss; and the giver is made richer thereby, for it returns to him increased a thousand-fold.

Private wealth can only be accumulated at the expense of human misery and suffering. The attainment of knowledge deprives no one of his individual rights or happiness, but benefits the individual and humanity. Under a system of control by the people of the production and distribution of the necessities of life, the whole brain power of the people, instead of being concerned in this insane struggle for wealth, would be turned as by magic into the channel of scientific progress. It is impossible for the imagination to conceive what a power for good this change would mean.

The whole world is an arena, and human beings are combatants in constant struggle for existence. The gain of one is the loss of another. Success means luxury and ease; failure, poverty and despair. The weak are trampled under foot by the strong, and their cry for help is unheeded by those who tread them down. It is every man for himself against the world. Crime flourishes like weeds in a tropical bog, and finds its home with both rich and poor. Wealth is the material God of man. With it he can satiate the selfish passions of his nature, which grow in strength with its attainment; for selfishness is the natural sequence of material possession, the result of competition.

Do you still maintain that competition is the life of trade? If you do, you cannot deny its only possible, logical conclusion — the final control of production and distribution by one individual, one company, or by the people, the last being final, naturally; for no one will suppose that the people, as a whole, would submit to the dictation of one man or one company, unless such company were controlled by the people and for the people.

Instead of being based on human nature, competition is contrary to all the better part of our nature which has been developed in the last hundred years. It is human nature that cries out against it.

Precarious Nature of all Business.

Business to-day is a haphazard thing. Success comes generally either by unprincipled craftiness or by pure luck. We are going along in a planless, reckless fashion.

Thousands of business institutions are like water-logged rowboats, with the gunwale only a couple of inches above the water. Most of the income is swallowed up by expenses,—advertisements, clerk hire, rent and so forth.

There never was a time when so much merchandise had to be handled to make a dollar. The large stores and factories set the pace, and the smaller ones have to tear along like bicyclists in a six days' race.

At any moment the death of a millionaire financier, or the failure of a large business institution, may throw investors into a panic. There may be at any time a " Black Friday " around the corner. The average business man feels like a worker in a fulminate factory,— he never knows when an explosion may take place. No one can foretell what the great money-kings will do next; and their pathway is marked with the broken wrecks of their competitors. How is it possible to establish " confidence " in the midst of such conditions? A feeling of alarm and panic is in the air. Anxiety is chiseling grooves in the faces of business men and laborers alike. If poverty were less terrible, uncertainty would bring less fear; but every man realizes the horrors of being moneyless in a nation whose deity is Gold.

Profit, not morals, is the purpose of business. The saloon is run for the same purpose that railroads, stores and factories are,— to make profit. Some of us assume to separate ourselves from our fellows, and say, " I am holier than thou," but are we? If we analyze the source of our wealth, none of us will have to go very far to find that we are all mixed up in an interminable and almost hopeless tangle with the present unjust social system.

Our merchants who sell jewelry, silks and satins to the woman of the street ask no questions as to the source of her income, but quietly pocket the money. Our prohibitionist grocers accept orders from saloon-keepers without the slightest compunction; and no church makes inquiries as to how the money was earned which it receives upon the collection-plate.

All this simply shows us that all life is one, and that the only way we can save one is to save all. We cannot divide our lives up into sections, and label one part religion and one part business and one part home life. The endeavor to do this has led us into a thousand hypocrisies and pretences, and caused us to lead insincere Jekyll-and-Hyde lives, devoid of true peace and satisfaction.

THE GAMBLER AND THE MERCHANT AT THE SAME GAME.

No class of people should be regarded with more pity, not to say contempt, than the gamblers; yet how can we draw a clear line between the gambling that is illegal and the common processes of ordinary respectable " business? "

What is many a stock company but a large nickel-in-the-slot machine? What is many a real-estate office but a place where bunco-steering has become a respectable profession? How much superior is many a legal battle in the courts to a game of poker or baccarat? What essential difference is there between the morality of the stock exchange and the morality of a gambling dive?

Is not the greater part of business a species of " gold brick " game? Is not every one endeavoring to get as much as he can for as little as possible? Are we not all striving to obtain something,— merchandise, money, or labor, without rendering an equivalent? What is profit but getting something for nothing?

The manufacture of useful, genuine articles, and the exchange of these for other useful, genuine articles, would be real business. We do not call a skilled sculptor a business man, so remote is our idea of business from what it should be. A " business man " is not supposed to be a producer, but a trader, a schemer, a clever exploiter of other men's labor, an appropriator of the product of other men's hands, a speculator, or in short — a gambler.

Can you imagine, for a moment, Jesus as a modern successful business man? Can you imagine Him foreclosing mortgages, or hiring men for $1.50 a day when their labor was worth $4 to Him?

Is there not a "great gulf fixed" between His teachings and the daily transactions of commerce?

Almost every evil that curses society to-day can be traced directly to the fact that we are living under an economic system which is unfair, dishonest and oppressive. All of our business, reduced to its last analysis, is simply a warfare upon one another. It is the striving of the cunning and the strong so to arrange and order their lives that they may live in idleness and luxury by the toil of others.

But the iniquity of the system does not stop here. While the many are doomed to work long, wearisome hours, to occupy what are called servile and mean positions, utterly destructive of any conception of brotherhood, on the other hand others are condemned to lives of enforced idleness, absolutely denied the God-given right to work.

It is not corrupt politicians that have brought disaster, so much as corrupt business men. The trouble is, that the methods of business have got into our politics, and have adulterated our whole national life. Business, by appealing to the lowest and most sordid passions, has made us worshippers of the golden god of success, with the result that we have a country in which a few are enormously wealthy, more are in what might be called circumstances of reasonable comfort, the masses are on the verge of poverty, and millions are in absolute and hopeless pauperism.

According to Spahr's tables of the distribution of wealth in the United States, about one-half of the families in our country own practically nothing, seven-eighths of the families own a little over one-seventh of the wealth, and 1 per cent. own 59 per cent. of the wealth.

In a country that is rich beyond the dreams of avarice we are confronted by this appalling condition. Our wealth has passed into the hands of a small clique of financiers, not because they have been more useful or intelligent or industrious or thrifty, but because they have obtained special favors from government, or were allowed to form combinations for plunder.

We have built up a social system in which we have assumed that it was possible for all to succeed, when the success of a few can come only from the failure of the many. Such a suicidal policy can only lead to "confusion worse confounded." Business is a chance game, in which the skilled players use loaded dice. The rules of the game favor the strong. They are more unfair and merciless than those of the prize-ring. A pugilist will give a man ten seconds to get up, but in business there is not a moment's respite for the fallen. All our natural American instincts of fair play rebel against the methods of trade.

Apologies for Competition.

A few very able and helpful writers have made the serious mistake of supposing that without competition human liberty would be curtailed. They cannot conceive of government without coercion and corruption. To their minds Socialism means a gigantic, stupid and tyrannical bureaucracy, under which business would be obstructed by knots of red tape, and individual enterprise would be impossible.

One of the cleverest writers who opposed state co-operation was Henry George,— the sturdy opponent of land monopoly, and one of the noblest spirits the social reform movement has known. In his last book he declares modern socialistic reforms to be a result of German thought, and contrary to the American spirit. To apply the principle of public ownership to private industries, he thinks, would be to develop a type of civilization similar to the communism of the ancient Peruvians.

Mr. George underestimates the growth of the democratic spirit. He does not see that such a paternalistic nationalism as that of Peru in the time of the Incas would be impossible in these days, and especially in this republic. In Peru the Inca, or king, owned practically all the property in the country, and provided work and wages for every one of his subjects. There was no starvation, but there was no liberty. Every man had enough for himself and his family, but he had no voice in the affairs of the state. The right to work was acknowledged, but not the right to vote.

Of course such a civilization would not satisfy American citizens, and there is not the slightest danger that public ownership would lead us to such conditions. Political reforms will keep pace with industrial reforms. The public ownership of industries will not lead to governmental despotism, but to a more complete and all-embracing democracy than the world has ever yet known. The word "paternalism" has no place in an American dictionary. It is appropriate in the monarchies of Europe, but the proper expression in a republic is "fraternalism."

Our so-called "representative" government, which has for years failed to represent the great, useful, honest body of the people, will be replaced by a system of direct legislation. All laws will spring from the people, and be referred to them for their approval.

Government ownership will undermine the power of the political bosses. The professional politican, like the professional courtier, will pass into ancient history. Our citizens will begin to take a keen interest in public affairs as soon as government begins to exercise its proper functions, and the senseless partisanship in politics which blocks progress to-day will gradually disappear. We shall commence to vote for measures, not for party triumphs.

It is private monopoly which threatens to establish an objectionable paternalism, and destroy the liberties of all save a few employers. Public ownership is the only escape from this danger.

It is co-operation, not competition, which is the mother of freedom. All strife, whether military or industrial, leads in the end to victory on the one side and defeat on the other, while co-operation benefits all without injury to any.

Already the greater part of our business is organized into great national trusts, and public ownership simply means that the benefits of this organization shall, like the sunshine, be extended to all. Government in the future will mean the management of things, rather than the coercion of individuals. It will become simply the means by which we do our work together.

Free Land Not Enough.

In a just order of society, private ownership of land would be as impossible as private ownership of air. The land was given as a free gift from the Creator, just as water, air and sunshine, and no man has any right to barter or sell it. There would be just as much justice in plotting Lake Erie, and charging the steamers a toll for running across each lot.

We should respect the wishes of the dead, but we should also consider the welfare of the unborn. If we cover the earth with trespass signs and barb-wire fences, what will the next generation do?

The English nobility own probably more land in America than all the wage-workers put together. How can we expect people to be loyal to their "native land," when they do not own a square foot of its surface? We have become a nation of renters and floaters. No civilization can rest upon a stable and enduring foundation where the majority of the citizens have become detached from the soil. A rented flat can never take the place of a home; and not even a public park can atone for the loss of a little grass plot and garden of your own.

Henry George is unanswerably right in demanding that the "unearned increment,"— the value which population gives to the land,— be turned into the public treasury instead of into the private purse of a landlord. That which is created by society

HOMES OF THE WORKERS EMPLOYED BY H. C. FRICK COKE COMPANY, NEAR SCOTTDALE, PA.

should belong to society; but land is not the only property which is in its very nature social and not individual.

Were not the millions of Rockefeller, the Standard Oil magnate, as much created by nature and society as the millions of Astor, the New York landlord? Is not machinery a social product,— the result of centuries of experiment and invention? In short, is not our whole civilization essentially a social product? Back of every inventor stands a thousand others who made his invention possible. Back of every enterprising capitalist stands the entire nation, without which not one of his schemes could succeed. The day of Robinson Crusoes and Daniel Boones has gone by. No man can point to his pile of gold and say: "Alone I earned it." What is called Socialism is not a visionary plan for remodelling society; it is a present fact, which is not yet recognized in the distribution of wealth.

Another Order Wanted.

The time has arrived to establish peace and good-will in business. We have tried to build up a nation on competitive lines, and we have failed. We have built up a few private fortunes at the expense of the nation.

If a nation exists for the enrichment of a few, then competition has been an unparalleled success, for since the world began no fortunes were ever piled up so fast and so high as were the fortunes of our millionaires. But if the happiness and prosperity of the average citizen is to be considered, then a new industrial system must be evolved.

"Every man for himself" is a motto which originated in the dead centuries of war and hate. It is as barbarous as the thumbscrew and the rack. It might appropriately be written in the museums above the war-clubs and spears and stone-axes of prehistoric times; but it has no place in a civilized community.

Our civilization has become so complex and highly organized that it will not stand the uncertainties and rude shocks that are inseparable from a competitive system. "Each for all and all for each" is the motto of the present and the future.

No reform, not even the single tax, will banish poverty and monopoly as long as we have a system that makes every man's life a scramble for dollars. Until we have an orderly and brotherly way of making and distributing our goods, the shrewd and unprincipled will continue to make wage-slaves of their simpler fellow-men, and parasitism will flourish.

There is no fear that America will lapse into a condition of Peruvian feudalism, or, like the Chinese nation, lose the instinct of progress. We have nothing to fear from democracy. "The voice of the people is the voice of God." We have had enough of strife and "smartness," and in a few years more, at the present rate of enlightenment, our people will be prepared for new business arrangements, which will guarantee every man the right to work and the right to be a partner in the industry of the nation.

No well-regulated, loving family would give one of its members a special franchise to make profit from the labor of the other members; neither would any member of the family desire any such franchise, but he would find his delight and pleasure in rendering such service as he could for the benefit of all, realizing by his experience that service brings its own reward.

The family ideal may seem visionary to those who have the dust of the streets in their eyes. Generations may come and go and be forgotten before it is a reality. You and I may never even see the morning star of that brighter day. Yet as surely as the world rolls, it is coming, and, as *I* believe, coming soon. If we can be but the foundation stones of the new structure, sunk in the mire and unremembered, we shall not have lived in vain. Others before us have labored, and we have entered into their labors.

Fair Competition an Impossibility.

An absolutely free and fair competition is an impossibility. Men and women are unequally endowed from birth. One is born with a strong and sturdy constitution, while another is as frail as a lily. One is by nature pushing and self-assertive, and another is modest and timid. One is born a genius, and another is born a dunce.

These are common, every-day facts, and ought to be recognized in political economy. Even allowing that wealth should be the reward of merit, we should distinguish between merit and the accident of birth.

The differences which nature creates are sufficient, without being emphasized by human law and custom. Instead of saying that the cleverest should be the richest, I should rather say that it is the clever who can best do without riches. If nature has already made them rich in intelligence they can afford to be poor in material things.

Government should be the science of compensation. It should endeavor to even up social inequalities instead of creating artificial differences.

To say that the swiftest and strongest and shrewdest should be rewarded by ownership and authority is to place men on the same plane with tigers and wolves. The rule which should regulate human society is this,— " He that would be great among you, let him be the *servant* of all." Life as it was in the forest was a struggle for existence; but life as it should be in our American cities is a co-operation, an education, an opportunity to learn, and help, and love.

Besides the inequalities which are hereditary and unavoidable, there are many others created by environment and partial legislation. One baby is born in a mansion, heir of the family millions. The cradle in which it is rocked costs as much as would pay a workingman's rent for a year. The cushions and covers were bought for a sum that would be sufficient to clothe an entire family for six months. Servants wait upon the child, and when it grows older, professors and private tutors are at its service.

The tiny infant is foreordained, by human law, to untold wealth and irresponsible authority over the lives of thousands of men and women. All this power and privilege come to it not because of merit or thrift or moral worth or business ability, but because of birth alone.

On the same day in which the baby mentioned above is born, another one also sees the light of day for the first time, but under different circumstances. Its father is an unemployed laborer and its mother is a scrub-woman. It is cradled in an old soap box, which has a scrap of carpet in the bottom to make it soft.

The curses of its father and the harsh and bitter retorts of its mother first instruct it in the art of language. It is often left alone for hours, to stare at the dirty walls, and cry itself to sleep with the pangs of hunger. It knows no kindness, no kisses, no love. It has come where it is unwelcome,— where it is regarded as a nuisance and an expense.

As soon as it is strong enough, it is cuffed and beaten. It lives in an atmosphere of terror, and soon learns to oppose force with cunning, and tyranny with falsehood. When it is able to walk it escapes from the dingy room to the street, and there, in the cobblestone kindergarten, it learns the A B C of crime and vice.

What about "free competition" between these two babies? Who will dare to say that their chances are alike in the business world? One is predestined, by human decree, not divine, to be a millionaire, to whom every door is open; and the other is predestined to be a criminal, to whom every door, save that of the jail, is shut.

Take a man with the brain of a Webster or a Shakespeare, put him on the streets of New York without a cent in his pocket, compel him to tramp from factory to factory in search of employment, meeting contemptuous refusals at every office, stand him in the line of hungry outcasts that wait every night at Fleischmann's bakery for a half loaf of bread, allow him to live by charity and free lunches in saloons for six months, and to be shoved here and there by policemen, and both genius and manhood would perish.

Degradation of Enforced Poverty.

We tie a balloon to one man, and a saw-log to another, and then declare that they have an equal chance to rise in the world. It sounds well in poetry to advise the poverty-stricken laborer to

> Break his birth's invidious bar,
> And grasp the skirts of happy chance,
> And breast the blows of circumstance,
> And grapple with his evil star.

But it may be generally noticed that those who give this advice are not doing any "breaking," or "breasting," or "grasping," or "grappling." They know little or nothing about the mind-killing influences of the factory and tenement. They do not understand that the poverty of to-day breaks a man's spirit and stupefies his intellect. It is quite a different thing from the "plain living and high thinking" which is so highly commended by poets and philosophers.

The poverty of our grandfathers was an entirely different thing from the poverty of the city slums. The poverty of the farmer's cabin in the pioneer settlement developed the sturdier and worthier and more self-reliant qualities of manhood and womanhood. There were in those industrious little communities an ambition, an intelligence, and a conscience which are not at least very conspicuous in the slum districts of New York and Chicago.

There was no stigma attached to poverty in the earlier days of this republic, and thus lack of wealth was no bar to advancement. It was possible to go "from log-cabin to White House,"—from splitting rails to the highest honor which the nation could confer. There was "room at the top" in those days, but by some inexcusable legislative blunder we have knocked down the ladders by which it was formerly possible to climb. There never was a time in the history of America when there were so few people and so much money at the top, and when there were so many people and so little money at the bottom.

The poverty of the modern slums is degrading. It does not cultivate the self-reliant virtues, but rather develops the spirit of mendicancy and dishonesty. It destroys self-respect. It makes refinement all but impossible. It transforms hope into a bitter and sullen resignation. It is squalid, unhealthy, and morally poisonous.

There is not the slightest similarity between the poverty of Diogenes, Socrates, Buddha, and Thoreau, and the poverty of a workingman who is out of a job. The whole structure of our civilization is built without any regard for the feelings or the rights or the life of the moneyless man. Life to the poor is an obstacle-race from the start; and an American laborer might almost as well hope to become the heir of a European monarch as to be one of the czars of finance in New York.

Competition the Death of Trade — and of Brotherhood.

No, what we need is not the restoration of " free competition." The rotten old hulk is too unsafe to be repainted and sent to sea with another generation on board. We have given it a fair trial, and it has dashed us on the rocks. We have proved, not once or twice but always, that competition is the death of trade, and what is infinitely worse — the death of brotherhood.

Men are unequally endowed from birth with brains, energy, and wealth. Competition means simply the *massacre of the weak and timid* by the strong and impudent. It inevitably leads to the capture of all property by an unscrupulous few, who combine against the interests of the nation.

Competition leads to monopoly as surely as the river seeks the sea. All systems of warfare and force end in the centralization of power in a few hands. Militarism produces an Alexander, a Caesar, a Napoleon; and industrial competition produces the trust-emperors of New York. You cannot have a lottery in which every one receives a prize; you cannot have a race in which every one wins; you cannot have a fight in which no one is ever defeated.

That is why competition is condemned by the new spirit of democracy. As Whitman says: " I will have nothing that all cannot have their counterpart of on equal terms." So long as this capitalistic system of rent, profit, and interest lasts, industrial democracy is impossible.

It is held out as a prize to all of us that if we accumulate enough money, we can quit doing any useful work and live by the toil of other men and women. What we call an " independence " means nothing else than that we have become dependent upon others for our support.

This system compels us to be either hirelings or parasites. It injures both those who lose and those who win. It obliges us to pile up profits either for ourselves or for other men. We must either wrong or be wronged.

Even if competition were perfectly fair, and all were equally well-armed for the contest, it would be none the less immoral and unworthy of a civilized nation. It would be none the less war and enmity and fratricide. A fair fight is better than an unfair one, but *why should we fight at all?*

> Look at the roses saluting each other;
> Look at the cattle at peace on the plain;
> Man, and man only, makes war on his brother,
> And laughs in his heart at his trouble and pain.

When man had to fight nature with his bare hands; when, as in the days of the cave-dwellers, food and clothing were more difficult to obtain, then competition might have had an excuse for its existence; but it is in these days unnecessary, wasteful, criminal, and absurd. Our bonanza farms, our immense factories, our railroads, our mastery over steam and electricity, our unequaled machinery, and all our scientific discoveries, have made it at last possible for every one of us to have enough. All necessity for scrambling and jostling and grabbing has gone, yet we continue to struggle as if a seven years' drought were upon us.

After thousands of years of slow evolution and discovery, we have reached the banquet-hall of a new civilization. The feast is spread before us, and there are plates enough and to spare; but we have not yet been able to overcome the old instinct of strife, and we are upsetting the tables and trampling on the food in our mad haste to get our share. The old instincts of the forest survive in us still; but they are becoming less and less powerful, and we are gradually learning to trust the higher motives which we have hitherto confined to the narrow sphere of the home. We are learning the wisdom of extending the spirit of family life to the state and nation.

The defeated and disinherited millions are coming to understand the source of their misery. They are realizing that government has been acting as a father to the rich, and as a policeman to the poor. They have discovered that the granting of special favors must inevitably make paupers of many of us. They are no longer feeling personally responsible for their misfortunes, as they formerly did. The blame is being gradually centered where it rightly belongs.

System Can Be Mended Only as Morals Are Mended.

We shall mend our business system only as we mend our morals, and we shall never get it right until we have established collective ownership of every public utility, whether municipal, state, or national. This alone will eliminate profit-making, and require every man to render personal service to his fellows, in return for what he obtains from the public store. Private, competing capital must be replaced by public, co-operative capital; this is the ultimate and only satisfactory remedy for our social evils.

During the days of chattel slavery there were many kind-hearted and worthy men who were slave-owners. They sought by various schemes of checks and balances to eliminate the evil from slavery; some of them who were especially kind made provision for the sickness and old age of their slaves; and others, by coercive legislation, compelled cruel masters to be more lenient; but all this did not relieve us from the curse of slavery.

The trouble was with the institution itself, and not until the foul blot was wiped from our statute books and Constitution by the Emancipation Proclamation and the Thirteenth Amendment did we begin to get rid of the evils of an infamy some of the effects of which still pollute our civilization.

We must deal with the question of monopoly just as we dealt with the slavery question. We can gain nothing by delay and hesitation. We have tried in vain to regulate. We have demanded the non-extension of trusts, and we have been laughed at by the giant monopolies. In this matter our courts seem to be impotent. They can deal with trade-unions, and enforce injunctions against strikers, and send the unfortunate tramp or drunkard to jail, but the monopolist is too big for them. They have no nets to catch whales, so they spend their time catching and punishing the small fish.

There is no solution save public ownership. Retain the admirable organization of the trusts, but administer them for the benefit of all the people. Grant no more profit-making franchises to individuals, *but give every man a franchise which will entitle him to steady and remunerative employment.*

No man can walk straight on a crooked street, and no individual can preserve himself untainted from blame in a civilization that is unjust and oppressive. Individual purity in an unclean world is a monkish dream. It is better to lift your whole city up an inch than to pull yourself up to the skies. Our conception of social reform must be more comprehensive than the old endeavor to rescue an individual here and there.

To-day we are demanding nothing less than the salvation of all the people,— nothing less than the remodeling of our whole industrial structure. In the heaven on earth which we seek to build, no one will be left outside.

We look upon society as a living organism, not as a heap of stones; therefore we seek to act upon society as a whole, by means of legislation and education, striking at the root of social evils, and not merely cutting off a few withered leaves. We are not battling against the church, against institutions, or individuals; but against a social system that has gone to seed, and outrages every conception of justice. To fight individuals would be as futile and childish as was the ignorant rage of the savage, who shot his arrow at the lightning. All individual leaders and rulers are only the representatives of ideas and principles. Overthrow one leader and another will take his place, so long as the idea which created him remains in the minds of the people.

Thought and sympathy are the parents of reform. We cannot do better until we *are* better. The main thing at present is to point out the evils which inevitably result from the competitive system, and explain the possibility and necessity of a higher system in which one man shall not grab the food from another's mouth. Truth and love, like murder, will out, and when our people realize the suicidal effects of competition, it will not take them long to act. There is no doubt about it, the monopolists and special-privilege people must let go. The rising tide in favor of liberty for *all* the people is gaining strength every day and is bound to sweep this country from ocean to ocean within the next ten years.

Almost every man to-day knows something is out of gear in

our industrial machinery. He can see that things are not running smoothly, but he is so busily engaged in scrambling for a living that he has not had time to study out the causes of the trouble.

Before long, some financial panic or industrial tie-up will force the question upon every citizen; and when our people once clearly see into a thing, they are not long in taking action. In these days of the cable and telegraph and daily paper, social changes can take place with startling rapidity.

America has taken two great steps already for humanity's sake,— first, when she wrote the Declaration of Independence, and second, when she proclaimed emancipation to the four millions of colored people. I believe the time is at hand when America will take a *third step,* longer than either of the others, and establish the Co-operative Commonwealth, in which the business of the nation will be organized and managed not to make profit for a few employers, but to serve and benefit all the people.

We cannot come nearer to a just system of production and distribution than by adopting the creed of St. Simon — " From each according to his ability; to each according to his needs."

Social Ignorance Must Be Dispelled.

The distress and suffering of the workers, or what is known as the masses of people, is not necessarily due to the venality of the classes; it is not because of aristocrats or plutocrats or bosses that we are in a social and industrial misery: it is because of our own ignorance. I am not an advocate of any system by which a lightning transformation is to be effected. I am simply an advocate of the people, one who believes in all of the people, and one who sees no possible hope for better conditions for all of the people except and alone through a process of education upon the important foundation principle of right social relation. I believe in the brotherhood of man — all men. The correct family relation is the one social ideal through which we can attain peace. Believing all men to be my brothers, under existing conditions I have no reason to complain of being "short" on poor relations; wherever I go I find lots of them, and there is no prospect that the supply will ever be diminished while the present social system shall continue. "The poor ye have always with you" is and will always remain a safe proposition as long as is kept in motion our social machinery that denies equality of opportunity and annually makes thousands of worthy and willing workers unwilling poor or paupers.

I want to be careful not to make a statement that is not entirely borne out and supported by the facts, and with this preface, I deliberately charge failure against the present social order known as competition. Until we shall speak of competition by its shorter name of WAR, we shall not be able properly to appreciate this statement. Competition has so thoroughly and fully failed as a business system to-day that it is not practiced to any extent except by small traders, and the great army of producers known as the working people; and to this one fact is due that while the classes have abandoned the competitive war as a mode of gain and livelihood, the masses of workers still adhering to this antiquated system of slowly destroying each other, are made the tools of the cunning, the unscrupulous, and the strong in the political world in order that they may be used to perpetuate a system that for centuries has bound them in chains.

Let me repeat: our denial of brotherhood, with its consequent social injustice, is due to the great crime of ignorance; and as there is one great cause, so there is one great remedy; the never-failing antidote for ignorance is education. By education I do not mean at all that thing that is popularly referred to as such; I use the word in a broader sense, and by it I mean a knowledge of the proper relation with your fellow-men, and when the working people understand their true relation to society — that is, to all people — they will no longer be made the dupes and tools of the cunning, the unscrupulous, and the idle, who now live from the fruit of their toil.

Trust the People.

The demand for public ownership is not a grumble from the idle and shiftless; it is not a growl from the vicious; it is a desire for a more just and kindly system of industry, and it comes from the great body of the people. I believe Lowell was right when he said: "I have no fear of what is called for by the general instinct of mankind."

If we cannot trust the people, what agency is there that we can rely upon? Does the "divine right of kings" still inhere in a few of us, and are we to impart virtue to the people by coercion?

As Lincoln said in his first inaugural,— "Why should there not be a patient confidence in the ultimate wisdom of the people? Is there any better or any equal hope in the world?"

This great movement towards equality is taking hold upon the hearts of the people, and at last the toilers, who produce all and who have so little of the product of their hands, are awakening to the fact that they themselves must throw off their chains by united action; that they must no longer be used as mere pawns to play into the hands of those who would enslave them; that the cause of their slavery is, as I have said, their own ignorance, and the one way of escape lies in united action in a step forward and upward to a higher plane and a more intelligent appreciation of the purposes of life.

The Failure Admitted.

The failure of the competitive system to provide a way whereby all who are willing to work may live, is now admitted by all thoughtful persons, and patriotic men and women everywhere are eagerly looking for an improved social order, that instead of destroying the many in order to build up the few, will provide a plan whereby all who are willing to work may live in a manner becoming self-respecting citizens in a republic of equals; that thus the dream of the founders of our government may be realized and we may hasten the day when we may become what we are surely destined to be — a republic of free and truly happy people.

CHAPTER VIII.

TRUSTS.

Socialists regard these colossal corporations and the wealthy bosses that direct them as the greatest pioneers of their cause. By concentrating the economic functions of the country into large masses, they are simply helping forward the socialistic movement. Their mission is to displace the smaller capitalists, but they will thereby eventually undermine capitalism altogether. In proportion as the centralization of industry is pushed forward, the easier it will be for the democratic people to displace its capitalistic chiefs, and assume the control of it for the general good. They are only hastening the time when a vast educated and organized democracy, subsisting on precarious wage-labor, will find itself face to face with a limited number of mammoth capitalists. Such a crisis can have but one result. The swifter, the more complete the success of the most powerful bosses, the quicker will be their overthrow by a democratic society. Such is the belief of Socialists.—*Kirkup: Inquiry into Socialism.*

CHAPTER VIII.

TRUSTS.

THE scholarly pastor of Plymouth Church, Rev. Dr. Newell Dwight Hillis, in a recent sermon, strongly denounced the brutal and destructive methods by which trusts have been created. He said:

When some Samson of industry uses his superior wisdom to gather into his hands all the lines of some branch of trade while others starve, he is like a wrecker who lures some good ship upon the rocks that he may clothe himself with garments unwrapped from the bodies of brave men slain by deceit.

In every manufacturing state in the Union, deserted factories or mills can be seen. The grass grows in front of the doors, and boards are nailed over the windows. Useful machinery, which cost the labor and thought of hundreds of men, lies rusting inside. And what is worst of all, scores of little cottages, built out of the savings of industrious mechanics, stand empty around each factory, while their owners are tramping the streets of some great city, hunting for the work they were robbed of by the trusts.

The displacement of workmen through these organizations has been enormous. Where will those men find re-employment? It is stated by drummers that recent combinations have thrown into idleness 35,000 of their number. What will these men do? Few of them have a trade, and such as have, would, on seeking to re-enter it, find it overcrowded.

The trusts are thus forcing into public concern the question of the right of their victims to work, and they are likewise riveting attention upon the methods by which they achieve their marvellous "success."

Some of them have captured more of other people's property in a year than all the burglars in America. The cleverest lawyers are in their pay, and it is charged that even judges act as the quiet partners of these lawless brigands of industry. There is scarcely a crime against property rights which has not been committed by them.

Read Henry D. Lloyd's unanswerable book, "Wealth Against Commonwealth," and you will see that the Standard Oil Trust was built up by a daring series of crimes, which, if the law had been impartially administered, would have landed its promoters in the penitentiary. Their methods of competing have amounted in some cases to downright confiscation; and scattered throughout this country are men who were once prosperous, and who are now discouraged bankrupts through the legalized burglary of the remorseless Oil Trust.

Mr. Lecky, writing of the methods by which the enormous fortunes of American financiers have been gathered together, says:

> Nowhere else have there been such scandalous examples of colossal, ostentatious fortunes built up by reckless gambling, by the acquisition of gigantic monopolies, by a deadly and unscrupulous competition bringing ruin into countless homes, by a systematic subordination of public to private interests, by enormous political and municipal corruption.

By means of the outrage known as watered stock, the most unreasonable profits have been taken from the people. Instead of a moderate return for invested capital, these corporations have demanded and obtained a higher percentage than any Shylock ever dared to ask.

Says Prof. Herron:

> Watered stock is a *method of high treason*, by which corporations forcibly tax the nation for private profit, and by which they annually extort millions

from American toilers and producers. It is as essentially a system of violence, spoil and robbery as would be the overrunning of the nation by Tartar hordes, laying hands on whatever they chose to take for their own. Although a large part of American industry is organized by this system of watered stock, and we consent to it tamely and ignorantly, it is yet the worst historic form of indirect usurpation and tyranny; and it renders our national wealth in large part purely fictitious.

The New Incursion of Barbarians.

Henry D. Lloyd says:

If our civilization is destroyed, as Macaulay predicted, it will not be by his barbarians from below. Our barbarians come from above. Our great money-makers have sprung in one generation into seats of power kings do not know. The forces and the wealth are new, and have been the opportunity of new men. Without restraints of culture, experience, the pride, or even the inherited caution of class or rank, these men, intoxicated, think they are the wave instead of the float, and that they have created the business which has created them. To them science is but a never-ending repertoire of investments, stored up by nature for the syndicates; government but a fountain of franchises, the nations but customers in squads, and a million the unit of a new arithmetic of wealth written for them. They claim a power without control, exercised through forms which make it secret, anonymous, and perpetual. The possibilities of its gratification have been widening before them without interruption since they began, and even at a thousand millions, they will feel no satiety and will see no place to stop. They are gluttons of luxury and power, rough, unsocialized, believing that mankind must be kept terrorized. Powers of pity die out of them, because they work through agents and die in their agents, because what they do is not for themselves.

Of gods, friends, learnings, of the uncomprehended civilization which they overrun, they ask but one question: "How much?" "What is a good time to sell?" "What is a good time to buy?" The church and the capitol, incarnating the sacrifices and triumphs of a procession of martyrs and patriots since the dawn of freedom, are good enough for a money-changer's shop for them, and a market and shambles. Their heathen eyes see in the law and its consecrated officers nothing but an intelligence-office and hired men to help them burglarize the treasures accumulated for thousands of years at the altars of liberty and justice, that they may burn their marbles for the lime of commerce.

Said Mayor Swift, of Chicago, in an address given on December 28, 1896, to the wealthy commercial club of his city:

Talk about anarchy! Talk about breathing the spirit of commercialism! Who does it more than the representative citizens of Chicago? * * * Who bribes the common council? It is not the men in the common walks of life. It is you representative citizens, you capitalists, you business men. When have they come to the front, either individually or collectively, and inveighed against this manner of obtaining franchises? When did they come to the front individually and ask of the common council to demand adequate remuneration for the city? Never to my knowledge.

The Menace of Irresponsible Wealth.

In the growing power and rule of irresponsible wealth lies the great danger, possibly the only danger, seriously threatening our Republic to-day.

Patriotism must be something more than fire-crackers, tin horns and loud-mouthed declarations that "we can lick everybody." *No man is truly patriotic unless he is doing his utmost to make the conditions of life not only tolerable and enduring, but pleasant for those around him.* Every thoughtful man in this city, and in the country at large, knows that to-day we have thousands upon thousands of good loyal citizens, who are denied the right to work for a living, and are forced into all sorts and conditions of poverty and degradation by this fact; while, on the other hand, we have a spectacle of the great throngs, who, because they were either born with a gold spoon in their mouths, or superior cunning and strength, are in peaceful possession of idle millions, which they contemplate with selfish indifference, while their brothers starve. In view of the fact that the starving brothers are in the main voters, and consequently part of the body politic, I cannot but believe that this condition of arrogant indifference on the part of irresponsible wealth is to-day the dangerous element in our national life. Wealth certainly carries with it the responsibility of good citizenship — certainly no man is a good citizen who devotes his days to piling up wealth, in order that he may say, "This is mine," while he is indifferent to the suffering, starvation and degradation of brother-men all around him.

No Right to So Large a Share of the Social Product.

To quote from Washington Gladden's book, "Tools and the Man:"

> I maintain that no man can accumulate property, in a social order like that in which we live, without incurring a heavy debt to society,— a debt that is by no means discharged when he has paid his taxes. Our fortunes as well as our characters, are due in no small part to our environment. Those who have amassed property in this generation have done so by the use of a vast system of social and industrial machinery, which has been furnished to them without money and without price. They are the heirs of all the past ages of discovery, of invention, of study, of experiment, of organizing intelligence.
>
> Society has brought all these enormous gains down through the generations and laid them at their feet. All these methods of communication, swift and cheap, by which time is multiplied and space is annihilated, all this wonderful utilization of natural force in machinery; all this mechanism of exchange so intricate, and yet so beautiful in its action; all these systems of industrial organization,— what is all this but the costly and magnificent provision made by society for the use of the individual? It is only because this provision has been made that large gains are possible to honest men. In no past time could property be accumulated by honest industry and enterprise as rapidly as it can be to-day. There were rich Romans, but their gains were gotten by rapine or extortion. There are rich Americans, too, whose wealth is mainly plunder; but there are many others who by fairly legitimate means have acquired large possessions. This they never could have done had they not been the beneficiaries of a social and industrial order in which everything was made ready for their hands.

As King C. Gillette says in "The Human Drift:"

> The equal right of individuals to the products of nature and the benefits derived from progress, is based upon the fact that the ever-present progressive condition of mankind is founded upon the efforts of all past generations and not upon present individual effort. Man only builds upon the foundation of accumulated intelligence, and has no moral right to claim special privileges for himself from the benefits arising from this foundation of thought, which

is an inheritance to humanity at large, and should descend with equal justice to every individual.

The individual cannot separate himself from the race, past, present and to come. He is not only " part of all he has met," but part of all that exists, ever did exist or ever will exist. Society as we have it to-day is the result of all the effort and all the accumulated intelligence of the past.

The Useless Contribution of the Capitalist.

When challenged as to the legitimacy of their holdings of such an enormous share of the nation's wealth, our capitalists — or at least such of them as concede the right of the public conscience to inquire into their methods and as to their holdings — allege that they themselves are the producers of everything; that it is *their* intelligence in organizing and directing labor; *their* acumen in determining the public wants; *their* initiative, and *their* generalship which keep the wheels of commerce turning and the wants of the public satisfied.

But in the evolution of the competitive system, the capitalist plays a less and less part in the direct control of industry. The skilled, practical man with money invested in a productive enterprise is a smaller factor than ever before. The capitalist has become a mere financier — a mere investor of money. His ignorance of the details of a business in which he is invited to invest his money is no bar to the investment. He knows that skilled superintendence is in the market for purchase just as corn and potatoes are; and it is upon the skilled foreman and superintendent that he depends for the return to himself of the profit which he demands as the price of his investment. His sole function has become that of using the withheld wages of other men in previous enterprises for the opportunity of withholding further wages from new men in a new enterprise. He plays no useful part whatever. He is as unnecessary as the fifth wheel of a wagon. As a class, he must become extinct. It is a scientific fact that the less effort a plant or an animal needs to put forth in order to secure its food supply, the greater and swifter will be its degeneracy. Nature says to her creatures: "Work or die!" Mere ownership is not work — not social service. It is as absurd to support a man in idleness, because he has great possessions, as it would be to pay a man a pension because he has a large mouth.

And, therefore, we need not become unduly alarmed when capitalists, in answer to the threat to call them to account for the disproportionate share they take of the nation's product, threaten to remove their capital to South America or China. We know that when it goes, it will leave the country and all its real wealth behind it. When James I, in one of his numerous disputes with the officials of the city of London, threatened to remove his court to Oxford, the Lord Mayor cleverly replied: "Provided only your Majesty leave us the Thames."

To quote from "Problems of Modern Industry," by Sidney and Beatrice Webb —

Either we must submit forever to hand over at least one-third of our annual product to those who do us the favor to own our country, without the obligation of rendering any service to the community, and to see this tribute augment with every advance in our industry and numbers, or else we must take steps, as considerately as may be possible, to put an end to this state of things. Nor does equity yield any such conclusive objection to the latter course. Even if the infant children of our proprietors have come into the world booted and spurred, it can scarcely be contended that whole generations of their descendants yet unborn have a vested interest to ride on the backs of whole generations of unborn workers.

A Believer in Trusts.

It may be a surprise to you to hear me say that I believe in trusts, but I do. In the fierce warfare of our competitive system, that was never intended for anything but wild animals, I see nothing to save us from final destruction but some form of trust. The only trouble with the trust, as at present conducted, is the fact that it is not large enough to take us all in on a basis that will let everybody live. But I see in it an indication of the growing social movement toward collectivism. I believe in brotherhood; so do the makers of the trust. They believe in brotherhood for the fellows that are in the trust; I believe in the brotherhood of all men. The trust is the Great American Brotherhood (limited). We shall yet learn to utilize the trust by amending the title, leaving off the last word. Of course, there is no moral purpose in the minds of the men who organize these trusts, but the final result of their work will be to build up an orderly and scientific system of business, which society, for self-preservation, will be obliged to appropriate.

The trust is preparing the way, showing society the great benefits that may be derived through association in industry, both in production and distribution. Any combination of capital or any organization of men which has for its object the saving of useless labor is a blessing. For example, when a dozen companies producing the same article join their forces, it becomes possible to send one man out to sell the product of the organization where twelve men were required before the companies were consolidated. An invention that lightens the burden of the world's toilers and makes it possible for one man to do the work of twelve is called a " labor-saving machine." Does it matter whether the machine is made of wood and iron or composed of organizations and associations of men? If the result is the same it is a labor-saving machine. In this sense the trust is a labor-saving machine. The fact that the owners of the trust capture all the profit produced by the labor-saving machine does not affect the truth of this statement. That is the peculiar tendency of the modern " captain of industry."

Destruction Impossible and Regulation Futile.

In the beginning of this chapter I touched upon the distress and misery caused by these industrial monsters.

As great as the sum of this distress has been or may yet be, there is no remedy immediately available — there is no cure this side of collective ownership. Destruction of the trust is not to be thought of. The trust is an economical development, strictly in the line of progress toward the elimination of competition. We cannot afford to take a backward step toward the individualistic method of production. We cannot do it if we want to. World forces of tremendous impetus would oppose us. The talk of smashing the trust is idle. The department store is a trust. Smash it and you have the single-line dealer. Why not go farther and smash him and give us peddlers? You cannot separate these great aggregations into their original parts. Like the primitive cells that now are the constituent members of a complex body, these parts have become welded into a social organism and cannot be rendered back into their original form.

Thirty-five years ago I saw a mob of teamsters trying to destroy the first pipe line ever built for the transportation of oil. They feared that the pipe line was an "attack upon their craft." The movement for the destruction of the trust rests identically on the same moral and intellectual basis as the rage of a mob against a pipe line or elevators or labor-saving machinery generally, and I predict that it will have the same result in the end.

If destruction is impossible, what is to be said of regulation? Plainly that the trusts cannot be regulated — that in turn they invariably regulate the regulator — and further, that even if we could control them by certain limitations to their activities, we should be merely patching up temporarily a broken and dying system, certain to collapse in the near future, and therefore that all our efforts would be wasted. To declare for regulation is to declare that we must provide further plans to allow the individual to proceed peaceably in the business of private profit-getting. In a thousand ways we have proved by the costly sacrifice of treasure and countless human lives the impotency of law to control organizations of men gotten together for purposes of gain, unmindful of the fact that it is the purpose of business to outwit law, and of the more important fact that even much of what is called legitimate business is in constant violation of heaven's law, of the divine law of Right. For example: we hear much about "legitimate profit." All good people will agree that a man has a right to "legitimate profit," which means the legal profit, and that is nowhere defined, so far as I know, except in the business of money lending, and in that field it is constantly violated in the most flagrant manner by almost every sort of money-lender; but in the ordinary domain of business — commerce, industry, trade — a "legitimate profit" means all the profit one can get, and the inadequacy of laws, rules, regulations, contract stipulations, agreements, checks, balances, to control business men whose appetite has once been properly whetted for profit is so proverbial as to be a matter of the commonest notoriety.

I have said that the trust cannot be regulated, and few things in this world seem to me so plainly evident. In many states laws have been made to suppress them, but they go merrily on; no effort has been spared to enforce these laws, but the trusts are still multiplying. The interstate commerce laws are against pools of railroad earnings, and such trust-like methods. The members of the Interstate Commerce Commission, a group of high-minded men, have for a dozen years been doing their utmost to regulate the transportation business of the country and make the railroads obedient to the laws of the land. Yet the tenth annual report of that commission practically confesses the laws a failure, alleging that wherever a case was found against the railroads, the courts invariably found a way of escape for the offenders.

This is not because the men composing the trusts of our country are lawless or law-defying any more than the rest of us, or because all the judges are venal; it is because of the unscientific quality of a system predicated upon the idea of individual success that seeks first to encourage the individual to build himself up at whatever cost and then undertakes to enact laws to prevent the accomplishment of the very thing that we are all saying that every man has a right to do. In other words, we are all exhorted to strive for success, and so long as the measure of success is only mediocre, the law does not attempt to interfere or inquire particularly into the methods; but as soon as one of us has made a real good success, that is, as soon as we have succeeded in capturing the streets of a city, a railroad across the continent or a system of them, or of corralling the supply of oil, coal or beef, thus putting a city, state, nation, or the world under tribute to one man, then the rest of us seek to make laws to prevent that kind of success.

A striking contribution to the proof that regulation doesn't regulate is found in a recent speech of Martin A. Knapp, the present chairman of the Interstate Commerce Commission. In the "Chicago Times-Herald," August 8, 1899, he is reported as having spoken as follows:

> I undertake to say that if the worst enemy of the railroads whom you can name were elected President of the United States, and if he should pack the Interstate Commerce Commission with the worst Populists of the land, those men would never dare to do the reckless and indecent things which the managers of railroads themselves have done. Can you name any five men so ignorant, so prejudiced, so inimical to the common interests of the country that they would upset the commerce of the country and demoralize rates and business in the way the railroad men have done by putting in the rates that now prevail to the seaboard by way of Galveston from the Missouri River? Would they let the Missouri River rate be as low as the Chicago rate? Would they allow flour to be carried from Minneapolis to the Atlantic cheaper than from Chicago? In such things the railroads are making a fearful misuse of their power.

In the face of this striking indictment (for I fancy that Mr. Knapp's idea of a Populist is the equivalent of the common idea of an Anarchist), I am sorry to say that Mr. Knapp's hope of relief seems to be in more law. We absolutely ignore the fact that in making laws to provide for a few men to use all of the rest of the men of a city, state, or nation, as mere instruments out of which the few shall make profit, we are violating the fundamental law of equal rights provided for in the conception of our government, provided for and demanded in the constitution of ever man — the right of equal opportunity with every other man; that in arranging for the private ownership of great public utilities and seeking to protect private owners in the exercise of special privileges, we are planting a poison at the very foundation of the social and economic structure which, if not removed, will destroy the institution itself. This evil cannot be corrected by more law or by any process, except such processes as are calculated quickly to bring to the people the right to own themselves, the right to the use of every public utility without the paying of private profit to any man or set of men. Hence I do not believe that even temporary relief can be secured for the people by any plan that proposes to evade the inevitable.

No Hope in Palliatives.

I really wish that I could see some hope in palliatives, but I cannot. We have been dealing in social economics with an arithmetic that was wrong at the base, an arithmetic in which sometimes two and two would make four and other times would produce other results. We now know that with such an arithmetic there is no hope of correcting mathematical calculations at all, and this seems to me to be our situation to-day with reference to the question of providing for the people who are thrown out by the organization of trusts and the failure of the competitive system.

The one difference in the present situation as against that of previous years is found in the fact that a different set of people are now added to the army of the unemployed. They are the people who have been occupying positions of responsibility, more or less, as managers, superintendents, salesmen, commercial travelers, etc. In the past these men have been mainly among our contented citizenship; they have been drawing good salaries, while their employers have been making large profits; they have spoken flippantly of the "agitators" as Anarchists, Populists, Socialists, etc. "Hobo," "tramp," and "bum" have been the butt of much ridicule and often the subject of cajolery at their hands, while the army of the unemployed has excited no feeling within them but one of contempt. "Any man can get work who will hustle for it," is a common saying that I have heard from these thoughtless brethren, when I have attempted to plead the cause of "the man out of work."

This reinforcement to the army of the unemployed will prove a valuable factor in solving our social problems. These men have been trained in the art of business; many of them are in possession of valuable secrets of "private business," and so long as they drew good salaries, could ride in parlor cars, eat good dinners and smoke fine cigars, and if the "house" settled the bill they were content. But the situation is changed; now that they are unwilling members of the army of the unemployed, they know more than they did; they have been brought with a dull thud to a realizing sense of the idea of brotherhood; as a consequence, they are already in large numbers getting into the "head push" of the agitation, reinforcing the ranks of those who are protesting against things as they are in the interest of things as they ought to be; they are a valuable ally to the forces of reform; their experience, education and knowledge will now be turned to good account; will, indeed, be delivered to their fellow-men in the form of true patriotism; they will come to understand that there is no peace for a part unless there be some peace for all, and realizing that "no man liveth to himself," will contribute to the salvation of their fellow-men, and by saving their fellows, will save themselves.

I wish I could see some shorter way by which relief could be brought to the wronged peoples, but as "there is no royal road to learning," so it may be truly said there is no cross-lots way to a just social order; there is no way, indeed, except through spreading the idea of love as law until the oppressed peoples shall find a way for their own deliverance through the realization of the sacred relation of brotherhood, through the conscious understanding that every man's welfare is dependent upon the well-being of every other man. I see no escape from the strain and agony and distress that surround us in our present everyday life; but just the joy of knowing that there is a way of escape, that the present conditions are not permanent; just the joy of believing that in these states is to be wrought out the divine scheme of deliverance for the wronged and oppressed, not only of our own land, but of the entire race, and of knowing that it is to be brought about by the realization of the conception of patriotism that will recognize love as the proper basis of the state — just this joy is a sufficient recompense for a life-time of sacrifice and struggle in the service of such a cause. To this joy and to this reward, to the work of spreading this new conception of government, I invite the patriots and the lovers of liberty, not only in America, but in all lands.

What to Do.

What, then, shall we do with the trust, with the continually increasing army of unemployed thrown out by these organizations? I reply, we must organize government (society) in the interest of all, for the good of all, so that we may utilize the economic benefits of the trust.

The problem which now confronts us is not to prevent the formation of trusts, but to bring about an equitable distribution of the savings effected by those organizations — savings which we may term the increment of associated organization.

Under the present system, this increment goes, in the form of increased profits, to the individuals who form the trust. Now, this is obviously wrong, for any advantage which accrues from a more perfect utilization of the forces of nature or from a more economical application of human labor, should belong, not to any individual or number of individuals, but to society as a whole. The profit that accrues to the organizations known as trusts, by reason of the economic production that arises from associating ten or more companies together, does not belong, in any ethical sense, to those who compose the trust. The profit is only made possible because the people are here, the cities are here, and the means of transportation and communication are here and available. Neither the cities nor the earth have been created for the benefit of the trusts. It is clear that the earth and the "natural opportunities" that have resulted in building cities, highways, railways and commerce, were created for the benefit of all alike. This profit that arises is a social product and a social saving, belonging, of right, to the whole mass of the people. To destroy the trust is to destroy an improved method of organization and sacrifice the social benefits made possible by it; to "regulate" the trust, if at all possible, is to clog its machinery, limit its savings and increase the amount of useless, conflicting labor in the world.

There is only one way in which the difficulty may be solved, and that is for society, that is, the municipalities, the states, and the nation — to absorb and own the trusts. We must leave off the word "limited" from the Great American Brotherhood that I have referred to, and own and operate the trust for the benefit of the people, as we now own and operate the post-office trust.

The movement toward municipal ownership, toward public ownership, toward co-operation of every sort, indicates the channel through which the people are to come into possession of their own. When they are thoroughly enlightened, they will simply retake in a perfectly orderly way the properties that have passed out of their hands and become private possessions, usually through the practice of deception and fraud.

The Post-Office Trust.

We point with exultant pride to the splendid work that is wrought by that socialistic enterprise of our government — the post-office. What higher tribute to the integrity of the army of helpers in this work could there be than is found in the cold figures of the post-office reports?

Millions of letters, packages and parcels, containing in the aggregate priceless treasure, are transmitted from one end of the continent to the other, from the great cities to the country cross-roads and obscure hamlets, with hardly the loss of a penny.

What devotion to high and noble purposes, what faithfulness and worth of moral character are portrayed in these facts! And what impudence and dishonesty are displayed by the charge, so often repeated, that the business of the government cannot be managed as honestly as the business of an individual or corporation!

Let the reports of the post-office department give the lie once and for all to such base and groundless accusations. The post-office is the best organized, most efficient, reliable and satisfactory business institution in the country. It treats rich and poor alike. The Standard Oil Company may get rebates from the railroads, but it gets no special privileges from the post-office. The perfumed letter of the millionaire and the post-card of the pauper travel in the same mail-bag. There still survives liberty, equality and fraternity among letters.

Sixty years ago Sir Rowland Hill began his agitation for penny post in England, announcing that the government could

ILLUSTRATIVE PICTURE.
The methods of the Standard Oil Company are the methods of "**business.**"
(For early history, see Author's Autobiography.)

THE "FLOW" FROM AN OIL WELL JUST TORPEDOED.

By permission of Jas. A. Tenlon.
A 35,000 BBL. OIL TANK ON FIRE, PENNSYLVANIA OIL REGIONS.

carry a letter from John O'Groat's to Land's End for one penny. At that time the transmission of letters was in the hands of a few private individuals, and the cost of carrying a letter from London to Liverpool was one shilling. We can hardly comprehend the historical fact that the sweeping proposition of that great and good man was realized within a few years from the time when he began the agitation.

His proposal was at first met with ridicule, with stolid indifference and active opposition. It was called the hare-brained scheme of a dreamer. Tories prophesied that it would plunge the government into debt, and overwhelm it with new responsibilities; but Rowland Hill persevered until the nation discovered that he was right.

An Imminent Change for the Better.

The disposition of the trust here proposed, may seem to many a consummation for the distant future. But it may come in our own generation. That clever English writer, the author of "The Social Horizon," says:

> Imagine if you can that a hundred years ago some preternaturally far-sighted social leader had thought out all the details of our post-office organization, and had predicted that by the close of the nineteenth century every parish of the United Kingdom would have been brought within the scope of it. Suppose he had foretold that the government of the day would have had a permanent staff of about 64,000 people, besides another 55,000 employed by local postmasters; that in every important village, ever so remote, there would have been a post-office official, receiving and distributing letters, postcards, books, circulars, and newspapers, receiving and paying cash, and keeping strict account. Imagine that he had foretold that on every country road from Land's End to John O'Groat's, messengers would have been jogging along with valuable parcels and orders for money and bags full of letters, many of them containing cheques and bank notes — that altogether the packages thus conveyed would have numbered, throughout the kingdom, over two thousand five hundred millions in the year; that in addition to all this, this one government department would have insured the people's lives, and banked

their money, and granted annuities, and issued licenses, and over and above it all would have managed a vast and complicated system of telegraphs, largely of its own creation. Why, how simply ridiculous the thing must have seemed to people who knew that the very seats of justice in the metropolis of the empire had only just been purged of the grossest corruption.

If so crazy a prophecy had been made and anybody had thought it worth while to pay serious attention to it, what a host of objections might have been raised. Just think of the capital you would want. How could it possibly be made to pay? How could you keep the accounts of 20,000 post-offices dotted about all over the kingdom? Think of the pilfering and peculation you would have to contend with; only consider the patronage you would be placing in the hands of the higher officials; look at the opportunities for jobbery and corruption you would be affording, and of the political power such an organization would give to those who had control of it.

And then how would you manage it? Where would you find your trustworthy and competent officials? How could the government, sitting in London, exercise any sort of control in the remote villages of western Ireland or northern Scotland? No, No, the thing is preposterous. If you could make all men honest and disinterested, conscientious and public-spirited, entirely devoted to duty and the public welfare, it might be possible, but so long as human nature is what it is, depend upon it such a fantastic scheme is utterly impracticable.

But here it is, all working so smoothly, and, upon the whole, satisfactorily, and with so little practical difficulty, that when it is proposed that, in addition to all it has in hand already, the post-office shall take over the telephones, or set up a system of express messengers, or of special delivery of letters, the very last thing anybody thinks it necessary to ask is, " Can the department manage it? "

Prof. Seligman, of Columbia University, says:

In all media of transportation and communication there seems to be a definite law of evolution. Everywhere at first they are in private hands and used for purposes of extortion or profit, like the highways of mediaeval Europe, or the early bridges and canals. In the second stage they are effected with public interest and are turned over to trustees, who are permitted to charge fixed tolls, but are required to keep the service up to a certain standard; this was the era of the canal and turnpike trusts or companies. In the third stage the government takes over the service, but manages it for profit, as is still the case to-day, in some cases, with the post and the railway systems. In the fourth stage, the government charges tolls or fees only to cover expenses, as until recently in the case of canals and bridges, and as is the theory of the postal system and of municipal water supply with us at the present time. In the fifth stage, the government reduces charges, until finally there is no charge at all, and the expenses are defrayed by a general tax on the community. This is the stage now reached in the common roads and most of the canals and bridges, which has been proposed by officials of several American cities for other services, like the water supply.

Even the Conservatives See Its Probability.

It is singular that so conservative an organ as the New York "Tribune" should see how inevitably the organization of trusts leads to the conclusion of the necessity of their public ownership. In an editorial on April 27, it says:

> The capitalist and captain of industry in these later days has set himself to demonstrate that the theories of the Socialist are sound. After some centuries of adherence to the principle that individual competition brings the best results and the greatest progress for the individual and for society, suddenly many thousand employers and capitalists rush out of business, give up the positions they occupy and the plants they own in order to avoid competition, and set themselves to prove that society can be best and most cheaply served, and the workers and managers from highest to lowest can get better returns, if all productive work in each branch is performed by a single centralized body controlling prices and wages at pleasure, abolishing agents and middlemen, restrained by no competition and responsible only to society as a whole. If this theory is true, does it not follow as a matter of course that society as a whole might better take possession of the plants and control the business and absorb for itself the profits of production or the gains by cheapening production, at its pleasure?
>
> The philosophy of the competitive period in human development has been sustained by the most rapid and healthful progress ever known thus far, but the Socialist answers that better yet is attainable. Grant that this past stage of development was necessary, its best fruitage is a higher stage in which the costs and the losses of individual competition can be avoided, and in each branch of service all can freely do their best for the benefit of all. Abolish the spur of competition, driving each to seek the latest inventions and the best devices, for they have been secured. Take from traders and manufacturers

the intense pressure of battle against each other, and give all of them a sure profit for a regular service to society. Let the multitude of employees be also emancipated from the tyranny of competition, which closes some works and drives others to reduce wages, and let them all have their regular pay for service to society, increased by the elimination of the losses through competition. When experience proves, as the Socialist holds it will prove, that the greatest progress and the highest conditions yet attained are not comparable to those to be attained by abolishing competition, then no man but an idiot will question the wisdom of society, as a whole, taking control of all the processes of trade and industry, and the harmonious adjustment of all, with power to cheapen products or enlarge profits in each, as may best serve the general welfare.

If the modern combination proves that competition is no longer a benefit, but a curse; that individual struggling for success is no longer needed to evolve the best inventions and devices and bring them into use; that the monster corporation can work more cheaply, and at the same time more wisely and ably in handling many establishments of different kinds, far apart and under different circumstances, than the individual owners who have created them; that it can prevent the frequent stoppage of the weaker works while the stronger continue to thrive; that society no longer needs any defense against monopoly, because the monopoly must always cheapen in order to enlarge business, and that workers, consumers and employers will all gain by elimination of competition, then, indeed, the Socialist has only to demand the logical completion of the journey. There will be no sense in leaving the big corporations to blunder along, sometimes losing and sometimes hurting society by unwisdom, when society itself can appropriate their plants, direct their labor, make and bear its own blunders and pocket its own gains.

THE COMING TRUST — THE AMERICAN PEOPLE (UNLIMITED).

In this, as in every other chapter, I have sought to show the failure of competition, and the necessity and inevitableness of a system of collective production and distribution. I have tried in the foregoing pages to apply a broader view to the trust problem than that of those men who would harass these organizations by legislation that experience shows cannot be enforced, and that, if it could be enforced, would but palliate our evils and miseries. The real thing to be remedied is the immorality that permeates our economic system, that springs from the idea of seeking individual success at the expense of others.

There is just one way by which we shall be able to overcome the trusts, that is, through something better for the people, and that is the Big Trust, the Co-operative Commonwealth, the trust that will take us all in, by all and for all. That is the trust that I am trying to break into.

This ideal is coming; it is coming through the realization of the truth that love is to manifest itself in law. Men are striving to get together; business is to be friendship and government will be love. The growing discontent with our inadequate distribution of the good things that we produce in such lavish abundance, the great increase in organizations of all sorts — fraternal lodges, brotherhoods, trusts, monopolies of all sorts — indicate a world-wide movement towards a better, more just, more honorable and more enduring social relation. The trusts over which we who are not in them have expended much righteous indignation, are really harbingers of better days. It is revolt from competition. Men want to love one another and are determined to love one another even in business, and because it teaches the lesson of co-operation, we shall yet come to see that the trust, which is a combination affording the maximum of production with the minimum of cost, is one of the most striking, wonderful and permanent features of the world's progress. The fight against it is as unwise and foolish and futile as the battle against labor-saving machinery, as is shown in the countless failures that have already been made to enforce legislation against this concrete example of the world's progress. The trust is here, and here to stay. There is but one way in which we can overcome it, that is, we must own it; we must all be in the trust, as we are all in the post-office trust, and as we must all eventually be in the telegraph trust, the railway trust, the flour trust and in every form of trust whereby through the organized love of the municipality, state, and nation, we can minister to one another better than we can in our individual capacity.

In this way shall we learn to appreciate and to demonstrate the Golden Rule applied to government. Then shall we have realized the dream of the founders of this republic and

>	Man to man the world o'er
>	Will brothers be, for a' that.

CHAPTER IX

SHOULD A CITY OWN ITSELF?

At my feet lay a great city. Miles of broad streets, shaded by trees and lined with fine buildings, for the most part not in continuous blocks but set in larger or smaller enclosures, stretched in every direction. Every quarter contained large open squares filled with trees, among which fountains flashed in the afternoon sun. Public buildings of a colossal size and architectural grandeur unparalleled in my day, raised their stately piles on every side. Surely I had never seen this city nor one comparable to it before.—*Bellamy: Looking Backward.*

CHAPTER IX.

SHOULD A CITY OWN ITSELF?

IT has been popularly believed in days gone by, that a serious menace to the perpetuity of our institutions was to be found in municipal ownership. I do not remember ever having heard any one specifically locate the danger, but I am well aware that I, in common with thousands of others, once accepted it as a settled conclusion that the municipality or the government, either state or national, should keep its hands off from business, business being something that only individuals or corporations had a right to engage in. If we define business to be merely making money in order to enrich an individual or set of individuals, I think the point is well taken. Such business should be the prerogative of individuals and private corporations, if of anybody. But when it comes to a question of adding to the Commonwealth, then every consideration, both of selfishness and morals, will agree that it is the business of all the people, whether represented by municipality, state or general government.

No circumstance justifies the granting of franchises. No one wants a franchise but for profit, and if there is a profit in it, the city ought to keep it for the benefit of the people. This sums up the whole franchise question.

Any system of leasing for a percentage of the receipts, or providing checks to keep the corporation regulated, is simply a compromise with the crime. The city should own all values created by society, and use them for public improvements.

A city should have the same privilege with regard to doing work of public improvement that an individual has with respect to erecting a house, building a bridge, digging a sewer, or constructing a highway.

To say that a private corporation can operate a function of this kind and serve the people better than they can serve themselves, is an unwarranted assumption of superiority on the part of those who make the claim. It is a flagrant manifestation of a lack of the spirit of patriotism, for no man who is truly patriotic will be willing to confess to a desire to use the people of his city simply for what he can make out of them. The city and the city government are here for the benefit of all of the people, and the patriots who love the city will be quite as ready to manifest that love and show their patriotism by serving the city in those fields where they possess superiority, whether it be in making gas, operating a public lighting plant, looking after the interests of the library or the public schools, as were the patriots who went to Cuba and gave up their lives in front of Santiago, because they loved their country.

Private Ownership a Public Immorality.

All natural monopolies should be publicly owned, because, in the first place, they cover a class of necessities that are common to all of the people. It may be urged that the poor do not need gas, electric lighting or telephones, etc., but in the most just order of society, into which we are coming, these utilities will be as accessible to the poor as they now are to the rich. It is no stretch of imagination to say that many a poor person has died simply for want of a telephone to reach a doctor quickly, and the only substantial reason why the poor should not have telephones and other things that are now considered luxuries is found in the fact that they cannot have them. Unjust economic conditions have placed them beyond their reach. I fancy that the time will come when the social needs of a city will be so perfectly understood that the telephone will not only be publicly owned, but publicly paid for, and will be as freely used by all classes of citizens as are now the streets, street lighting, the protection of fire and police departments, and public-school education. Man is a social being. We have not yet begun to take in the profound philosophy of the statement that "no man liveth to himself." If we have prosperity that is real, we all share it; in like manner, whether we will or not, we all share in the adversity which to our short-sighted eyes may seem to affect only a few.

A second and perhaps the best reason why these monopolies should be publicly owned is found in the fact that private ownership of a public utility is a public immorality. No legislative body has a moral right to farm out a privilege granting certain individuals the right to rob the people while pretending to serve them. Perhaps the word "rob" may be extravagant in this sense; but I mean to say that no moral right is lodged in any legislative body to grant a privilege to a corporation to make profit from the people by providing a social necessity, when this class of service is the manifest duty of the people. According to any just conception of democracy, it is one of the imperative functions of government. To evade it or avoid it by granting franchises or leases of privileges of that kind is a shirking of responsibility on the part of the leaders amounting to nothing less than a crime against the people.

The Streets the Common Property of the People.

I believe that we are in the beginning of a time when, through the administration of love as law, we are to realize in a larger degree the kind of liberty that Lincoln believed in and died for.

I believe that the wealth created by the people should be used for the people's benefit. The streets are the common property of all of the people. Every wire, every pole, every conduit, every rail — everything permanently in or on the streets should be for the common benefit of all of the people, not for the private benefit of a few.

In his address before the Nineteenth Century Club of New York City, November 11, 1897, Governor Pingree said:

> Good municipal government is an impossibility while valuable franchises are to be had and can be obtained by corrupt use of money in bribing public servants. I believe the time has come for municipal ownership of street railway lines, water, gas, electric lighting, telephone, and other necessary public conveniences, which, by their nature, are monopolies.

The whole idea of granting special privileges to a few people so that they can make profit from the labor of the rest of the people is undemocratic. It prevents the realization of one of our loftiest ideals — the equality of all men before the law. It is contrary to the spirit of republican institutions. It is the same thing as the granting of titles in monarchical countries. It creates gas barons, electric-light earls, and street-car dukes.

A few financiers are given a permit to enrich themselves at the expense of those who do the actual work of the city. Generally their wealth comes from the poorer classes. The hard-earned nickle of the washerwoman and the seamstress go to make up the profits of the street-railway magnate.

Let all those who share this sort of profit understand the source of their wealth. The ladies who wear sealskins and diamonds, and the men who give thousands to colleges and churches and foreign missions, should remember in what way their wealth has been heaped together.

In granting or selling a franchise, the city becomes a party to the crime, and becomes responsible for the misery and wretchedness of the submerged tenth.

Every Man the Servitor of Society.

The fundamental idea of democracy is not that every individual shall be free to seek his own good or to pursue his own ends. You cannot build up a society on those lines. "Every man for himself" is treason to humanity. When men co-operate and build cities, a new set of social duties is created, which men must obey if they wish co-operation to continue. We have been trying as individuals to get all the benefits of co-operation without performing any of the duties.

The moral code of gypsies may do for the woods, but it will not do for a highly organized civilization like ours. We need a new definition of freedom and independence which will harmonize them with co-operation and brotherhood.

The merit of the idea of democracy lies in the assumption that every man will sink his own interest in order to serve his fellow-men. This is by the very law of our being — our only possible chance for permanent peace and happiness. And yet so very dimly is this principle understood that it is the commonest kind of an occurrence to hear a man say that he "cannot afford to take public office"— that he is "too busy with his own affairs."

This assumption is a denial of democracy, and until, through a more advanced system of education, we shall come to understand that the city and nation have the first claims upon our affection and service, in peace as well as in war, we shall not begin to realize the glorious possibilities of collective effort. The evasion of responsibility in public matters is civic treason, and it is by no means a rare crime. It arises from a lack of social consciousness. There are not many as yet who have consciences delicate enough to detect the suicidal nature of selfishness.

Democracy is based on the present-day fact that society is like a human body. Every part, by being the servant of every other part, is initiated into the higher freedom which co-operation alone can bring.

How absurd it would be to grant a special franchise to the left hand, freeing it from the necessity of being useful, and giving it four times its usual supply of blood for remaining idle! It would not only be injurious to the rest of the body, but to the left hand as well. Active service is the price of health. No man or class of men can long escape a share of the common burden. All the laws of nature are against them. "Whatsoever a man soweth that shall he also reap."

Our Constitution rightly prohibits any American citizen from bearing a foreign title. We have abolished at least that kind of aristocracy. Our next task is to make it impossible for any citizen to hold a public franchise. Our system of industry should be as free from aristocratic elements as our politics. The kings of commerce must be dethroned, else they will establish a profit-mongering feudalism which will bring the Dark Ages upon us again.

Prof. Parsons' View.

As to the legal aspects of this question, Prof. Frank Parsons says:

> The truth is that decisions sustaining grants of franchises or other monopolistic privileges are *contrary to the fundamental principles of free institutions*, democratic government, and Anglo-Saxon jurisprudence. No legislature or Congress ever had a right to grant a monopoly or a franchise that practically amounts to a monopoly.
>
> What the sovereign power of Queen Elizabeth could not accomplish against the people's interests is surely beyond the rightful power of legislators elected to serve the people's interest. A private monopoly is just as much against public policy when formed by grant as when formed by combination — more so, if anything, because of the corruption of the government so often incident to such grants. The result is that justice, public policy, and the established principles of our jurisprudence, permit no private monopoly, either by combination or by grant; wherefore, monopoly, wherever necessary in the nature of the case, or for the sake of economy, must be public and not private. That every water, gas, electric light, transit, telegraph and telephone franchise should

be owned and operated by the public is a clear deduction from principles of justice and public policy firmly established in our law for the last 500 years.

A franchise establishing a virtual monopoly, and relating to a practical necessity of civilized life, like transportation, light, water, means of communication, etc., involves a power to exact tribute from the community, a power substantially equivalent to the privilege of levying taxes for private purposes, which is beyond the authority of any legislative body in a free country.

The legislature cannot delegate a power it does not possess, cannot do indirectly through a corporate franchise what it has no right to do directly; wherefore, on the clearest principles of law, every monopolistic franchise our legislators have granted should have been held absolutely void.

Such franchises not only involve taxation for private purposes, but taxation without representation — the people who pay tribute to the street railway, gas, and electric companies are not represented in the deliberation of those bodies.

It is a curious spectacle this, of a government choking monopolies with one hand and granting them in lavish abundance with the other, declaring all the while that monopolies are contrary to public policy, and passing laws to destroy them, while in the very same hall, and, perhaps, in the very same hour, still other laws are passed to create them.

The Root of Municipal Corruption

In reply to the popular criticism of public ownership, on the ground that our civil service is so bad that to do further service would tempt to corruption, the answer is simply that experience proves this charge to be wrong.

Bad as the civil service may be, we seldom hear of any corruption in the post-office department. Our public-school system is surely more free from corruption than our street-railway corporations.

Traveling men who sell supplies to private corporations and to municipal departments tell me that their experience proves almost uniformly that the purchasing agent of a corporation is more easily corrupted than a public official.

As Henry D. Lloyd says, "Our problem is a paradox: we must municipalize in order to have good government; and we must have good government in order to municipalize."

Prof. Bemis says:

The greatest advantage of municipal ownership is its tendency to relieve communities from corrupting relations with men of wealth.

Some believe that merely the form of corruption would be changed thereby; that, instead of the corruption of the city council by franchise-seeking corporations, there would come the corruption of the spoils system. Even if this should at first prove true, the spoilsmen can be cuffed and kicked about in the gutter ad libitum, without the slightest danger to one's social or business position. In fact, it is becoming almost the fashionable thing to express disgust at the political office-seeker. With the growing need of civil service reform, which the increase of public activities is sure to force upon public attention, the spoils system is likely to die unhonored and despised.

Our rich and influential citizens, whose financial interests, as investors in franchises, now prompt them to desire weak or corrupt government, would, under public operation, have no financial interests at stake, except as taxpayers, and in that capacity would desire efficient administration.

To attempt reform to-day in public regulation of private ownership is to endanger one's position as editor, professor, preacher, attorney, or man of affairs, since the men who gain by existing corruption and degradation of government are the leading supporters of our churches, our colleges, and our business. Against such people reform has hard sledding.

Prof. John R. Commons says:

The great majority of the 300 cities and villages now furnishing light are actually getting better service at less cost than those which depend upon private companies. It is objected that such cannot be the case, especially in our large cities, because of the flagrant municipal corruption and inefficiency. Business ability and integrity, it is said, are excluded from municipal office, appointments are made as a reward of political service, and the municipal plant soon becomes burdened with barnacles who draw pay without work. I do not deny that such is often the case. But I maintain that nine-tenths of the existing municipal corruption and inefficiency result from the policy of leaving municipal functions to private parties; and that an essential part of the present unparalleled awakening of civic conscience on the part of all classes of the people is the desire for municipal ownership of franchises. As the people become aroused to the degradation of their politics and to the need of reform, their attention is concentrated on the chief source of that degradation, the underhanded and often highhanded domination of city officials and machine politics by the corporations whose life is maintained by city franchises.

MUNICIPAL ELECTRIC LIGHT PLANT, JACKSONVILLE, FLA.
(Conspicuous example of success in municipal ownership.)

MUNICIPAL LIGHT PLANT, LOGANSPORT, IND.
(Affords the lowest meter rate in the world.)

Unreason of Continuing Private Ownership of Any Public Utility.

I am unable to see why it is not just as reasonable to undertake to make a plan for providing individuals or corporations franchises to build and take care of the city streets, letting them collect their pay by the old-fashioned method of the toll-gate, as to grant franchises to people to furnish us with light I believe that plenty of corporations can be found who will agree to furnish this or any other social service cheaper than the city can do it through municipal ownership. They will agree to police our cities, put out our fires, carry on our schools, take care of our poor as they used to do in days gone by, and proclaim that they can save money for the tax-payer; and to my mind it is just as reasonable in these closing years of the nineteenth century for thoughtful men to set about devising a system of checks and balances that will compel corporations to do as they agree in the management of any one of these privileges as it is in the management of a street railway, an electric-lighting plant, a water plant, or any other public interest of the city. There is no difference. The streets, the schools, the bridges, the fire department, the police department, are pretty generally emancipated from the grasp of the money getter. They have passed beyond his reach; they are now in the domain of the municipally owned and conducted things, where eventually we shall find all such things as water-works, lighting plants, heating plants, telephones, telegraphs, messenger service, city directory, and, in fact, every form of public utility which can be operated by the people for the benefit of all the people, better than an individual or private corporation can serve them.

Through the work that has already been done to control street railroads and electric lighting, thousands of dollars monthly of the people's money that were being heaped up as private wealth are now saved to the people. Selfishness has made and will continue to make every conceivable effort to keep the people from taking what belongs to them, but we are rapidly approaching a period where history, not less than theory, is coming to our aid. Public ownership is only another name for co-operation, and in Great Britain and Europe, where they are older than we, they have come to understand that the good of the individual can only be found and conserved by seeking the good of all. When Glasgow, Leeds and Plymouth adopted public ownership of the street railways, they bettered the service, reduced fares, shortened the hours of labor and raised the wages of the men.

Development of Municipal Ownership.

The man who prides himself on being "practical" is constantly asserting that public ownership is an untried and risky experiment, whereas the evidence of its success is on every side of him. As Sidney Webb says in his "Socialism in England" (page 65):

> The individualist city councillor will walk along the municipal pavement, lit by municipal gas and cleaned by municipal brooms, with municipal water, and, seeing by the municipal clock in the municipal market that he is too early to meet his children coming from the municipal school hard by the county lunatic asylum and municipal hospital, will use the national telegraph system to tell them not to walk through the municipal park, but to come by the municipal tramway, to meet him in the municipal reading room, by the municipal art gallery, museum and library, where he intends to consult some of the national publications, in order to prepare his next speech in the municipal town hall, in favor of the nationalization of canals and the increase of the government control over the railway system. "Socialism, Sir," he will say, "don't waste the time of a practical man by your fantastic absurdities. Self-help, Sir, individual self-help, that's what has made our city what it is."

I do not believe that statistics are the best arguments. *Right is right, whether it "pays" or not.* We should have public ownership because it is the fair and natural way for business to be done among friends.

But for the sake of those who demand figures and facts, the

following are submitted, the authority for them being Prof. E. W. Bemis and Dr. Milo Roy Maltbie:

The city of Watervliet, N. Y., has for seven years furnished its 115 arc lamps at a cost of $75 each, including depreciation, but not interest. Its neighbor, Troy, has paid a private company, during the same time, $146 for like service. Watervliet's plant cost $26,000, but was paid for in two assessments, without the issue of bonds. Distributed over the entire period, this investment would have been equivalent to $31 per lamp-year, making the total expense to the taxpayers $106, against $146 paid by Troy.

Lansing, Mich., bought out the private plant, and reduced rates at once from twenty cents per kw. to eighteen cents, and again to twelve cents, in two years. The city pays its municipal plant $10,000 yearly for 117 2,000 candle-power lamps, moonlight schedule, and the plant receives also $15,000 for private lighting, making a profit for the plant of $7,000 yearly above operating expenses and interest. The rates are twelve cents per kw., being a reduction of eight cents below the rates charged by the private company whose plant the city purchased. The saving to the citizens on commercial lighting is, therefore, approximately $10,000 per year.

Logansport, Ind., established a municipal plant in 1894, at a cost of $90,000. The expenditures in 1897 were $18,946.75, of which $13,206.60 were for operation, and $5,740.15 for new construction. The commercial receipts were $17,442.53, or $4,235.93 in excess of operating expenses, and within $1,504.22 of the total expenditures. Adding $13,442.35, for lighting streets and public buildings, to the commercial receipts, and the income of the taxpayers for the year was $30,884.88 against an expenditure of $13,206.60. Depreciation would increase this to $15,900, leaving a profit of $15,000. The success of the plant has been so great that the rate for incandescent lighting has just been reduced to five cents per kw., probably the lowest meter rate in the world.

Elgin, Ill., prior to city ownership in 1890, was paying $8,000 for thirty-three arcs running till midnight, or $242.42 per arc; but in 1891 the city ran seventy-seven arcs all night on the moonlight schedule, or over one-third more hours, for $4,800 for operating expenses, or $62.34 each, plus, say 10 per cent. of the amount then invested, $17,900, for interest and depreciation. This would make the total cost at that time from $84 to $90, or about one-third of what the city had been paying; while the cost in 1896, even with interest and depreciation, was only about $72.

The oldest electric-light plant in this country, probably in the world, is in Fairfield, Ia. It originally cost $6,000. It was built by a private company in 1880, and was purchased by the city in 1882. No commercial lighting is done. There are six arc lights on a tower, and twelve others which are operated in connection with the city water-works, but the cost is kept separate. For light all night on dark nights, with coal at about $2 a ton, these few lights have cost the city on an average only $64 yearly per lamp, including the average expense of all renewals, but not the fixed charges.

Jacksonville, Fla., is one of the most conspicuous examples of success in municipal ownership. Not only is the net cost of its 122 public arc lights reduced by good management and by the receipts from commercial lighting to less than one-fourth of what the city had been paying a private company, but the commercial rates of the public plant have been reduced one-half, forcing a considerable reduction in the prices of two private electric-light plants in the city, and of gas. These reductions alone are officially estimated to equal a yearly profit to the consumers of light of two-thirds the cost of the public plant.

A decided movement has set in toward municipal ownership of electric light plants in some sections of the country. In 1897, there were five cities of over 100,000 population and fifty-three smaller municipalities with municipal works. The largest city is Chicago, which became owner of an electric-lighting system in 1897. Other cities of importance with municipal plants are Detroit, Allegheny, Columbus, St. Joseph, Bay City, Little Rock, Taunton, Dunkirk, Topeka, Tacoma, Jacksonville, Fla., and South Norwalk, Conn. In nearly every case, however, there are also private companies operating electric-light works in the same town; and in St. Joseph, Mo., the municipal plant alone supplies street lighting.

The recent movement toward municipal ownership has been most active in Massachusetts, where there are now fourteen municipalities which own their electric-light plants. Most of these are small places, but three (Taunton, Chicopee and Peabody) have over 10,000 population each. In addition, some 200 cities and towns in that State are considering the question of municipalizing the local lighting service, and many have taken the first steps in the process. The next few years may, therefore, show a large increase in the number of municipal electric plants, not only in Massachusetts, but throughout the United States.

Of the fifty largest cities in the United States, forty-one have public waterworks, nineteen of these have changed from private ownership, while only one large city, New Orleans, has changed from public to private management. In England and Wales, forty-five of the sixty-four great towns and county boroughs own their water-works, as do all the large towns in Scotland, and Dublin, Belfast and Cork in Ireland.

Some years ago, the sprinkling of St. Louis streets was done by private contract. Some frontages would subscribe, others not. Vacant lots and cross streets were left unsprinkled. The air was laden with dust. An ordinance was passed providing for sprinkling by general contract and assessing the cost on abutting property. The result has been that the city got rid of all dust, and the cost to those who formerly subscribed has been less than half. St. Louis has always owned its water-works. The rates have been as low as those charged by private companies in other places. Out of these rates it has built new and enlarged works several times, until now the value is at least $30,000,000. All of this value has been made out of the profits of the business which otherwise would have gone to private owners. It is commonly believed that it costs the government more to construct works and operate them than private proprietors. Experience proves otherwise. The contracts for building new water-works at St. Louis have each time been taken so low that the contractors were bankrupted. The governments are always favored customers and usually get lower prices than the largest private buyers. In St. Louis there has never been any scandal or corruption in connection with the publicly owned works, such as the water supply, parks, hospitals, fire department, streets and sewers; but its privately owned works, such as gas, electric lighting, and the street railways, have been never-ending sources of corruption and scandal. They have been the forces that have controlled local politics. They have debauched the municipal administration. In the management of the public schools, that part which is actually managed by the public servants has been well done and free from scandal. That part which has been let out to private contractors has been badly done, expensive and corrupt.

The municipal markets in the United States are neither few nor insignificant. The largest are those of New York city, which yield a gross revenue of nearly $300,000. Considering the size of the city, those of New Orleans are most important; the principal ones being leased for $186,000 a year, and an additional $40,000 which the city must use for repairs to the buildings. The municipality also operates directly four markets, which yield a revenue of $10,000 a year. In this instance, the city possesses a market monopoly, and the few private enterprises are carried on under the right of reversion to the city. The Quincy market of Boston is valued at $1,250,000, and produces an annual revenue of $72,000, of which $60,000 is net profit. Baltimore has a revenue of $48,000 from markets, and St. Louis of $28,000. The municipal market buildings of Pittsburgh are valued at $350,000; those of St. Paul at $250,000; and those of Philadelphia, Cincinnati, Nashville, Mobile, and Savannah, at over $100,000 each. Three-fourths of the cities with 100,000 population have municipal markets, the exceptions being San Francisco, Minneapolis, Jersey City, Louisville, Rochester and Providence.

Public baths have been established by very few American cities. It is only about thirty years since Boston established the first municipal summer baths in America, and even this line of action has not been very largely followed. There are now free floating baths under municipal management at New York, Chicago, Philadelphia, Boston, Baltimore, Cleveland, Milwaukee, Newark, Hartford, Des Moines, Lawrence, Springfield, Mass., and a few smaller cities. Municipal baths after the British models have been established in the United States only within the present decade. The first was erected by the city of Yonkers, N. Y. In 1894, Chicago opened the Carter Harrison bath. Two years later, Boston made public the baths at the Charles Bank gymnasium and commenced the erection of new bathhouses. In 1897, Buffalo erected public spray baths, and Brookline, Mass., opened a fully equiped bathing establishment, with plunge, shower and slipper baths. During 1898 municipal baths were opened in Providence and Worcester. In nearly every case the American cities have abandoned the fee system, and made the municipal bath free. The most important municipal baths in the United States are those of Boston, where there are twenty-four establishments, including both inclosed and open-air baths, with an aggregate attendance in 1898 of 1,915,000.

There are in the large continental cities, a goodly number of municipal botanical gardens. At Paris, in addition to the "Jardin des Plantes," there are the noted municipal nurseries and greenhouses in the Bois de Boulogne. Municipal botanical gardens are also maintained at Lyons, Marseilles, Lille, Rouen, Rheims and some other large French towns. In Germany, there are municipal establishments at Munich, Cologne, Frankfort-on-the-Main, Hanover, Hamburg, Brunswick, Stettin, Aachen, Essen, Cassell and other cities. Nearly every Belgian and Dutch city has a municipal botanical garden, as at Brussels, Ghent, The Hague, Liège, Amsterdam and Rotterdam. In Italy, most of the large cities — Rome, Milan, Turin, Palermo, Leghorn and Venice — have botanical gardens. The other larger European cities have also in most cases supplied this combined recreative and educational provision, as for example, Trieste, Lisbon and Stockholm.

In England, municipal botanical gardens are reported only from Glasgow, Leeds, Sheffield, Nottingham and Cardiff. Those in Regent's Park, London, belong to the Royal Historical Society; and the more important exhibitions at Kew, Edinburgh and Dublin are maintained by the central government. In the United States, the only instance of scientific botanical gardens maintained by municipal authorities is at Buffalo and Pittsburgh; but there are important floricultural and horticultural displays in the public parks of New York city, Chicago, Philadelphia, Boston, Cleveland and other cities. New York city has also furnished 250 acres of land in Bronx Park for botanical gardens, which have been placed under the management of the private society controlling the endowment funds. The Arnold Arboretum, at Boston, owned by Harvard University, is administered as part of the municipal park system. The other botanical gardens in America are those at Washington, D. C., owned by the Federal government; at St. Louis, privately endowed and managed; and at Montreal, owned by McGill University.

Public eating-houses are established in a number of German cities, to provide meals for workingmen at cheap prices, so as to do away with the evil effects of the dinner pail. Those in Chemnitz, during 1893, sold 435,000 dinners; receipts were $17,500, and expenditures $15,500. The city of Grenoble, France, also maintains a municipal restaurant, at which about 1,200 meals a day are served. At the outset, the enterprise needed municipal aid, but it is now self-supporting. The municipality owns the property used, for which it receives a nominal rent; and the accounts are reported in the books of the municipality. Any surplus is deposited in the city treasury, as a reserve to draw from when prices of provisions are high. There are also other instances throughout France of similar institutions without municipal aid; several establishments being in operation at Paris, Lyons and Bordeaux.

Somewhat akin to such institutions are municipal bakeries, which are to be found at Rome and at Kovno, in Russia. Stockholm owns municipal liquor stores for the working classes, who cannot obtain drink without ordering food.

The first public open-air gymnasium in the world was that maintained by the city of Boston at one of its small parks, known as the Charles River Embankment. A more complete model playground for children has since been established at Philadelphia; and many other playgrounds have recently been provided (largely through the initiative of private philanthropic organizations) in several American cities,— notably Philadelphia, Boston, Chicago, New York, Providence, Worcester and Baltimore. In New York city, a number of the schoolhouses are used for playrooms during the summer months. Boston has recently been presented with a large and well-equipped indoor gymnasium in East Boston, which is maintained by the park commission free to the public. The London county council has six open-air gymnasia for adults and twelve for children.

In the countries of continental Europe many of the municipalities give substantial aid to theaters and opera houses. The German cities have, perhaps, done most in this direction. Besides state-supported opera-houses in Berlin, Dresden, Hanover, Brunswick, Mannheim and most of the ducal capitals, there are nearly forty municipal theaters in Germany. Fifteen of these are in cities over 50,000 population, including Breslau, Cologne, Frankfort-on-the-Main, Magdeburg, Düsseldorf and Nuremburg. In France, Belgium and Austria, most of the large cities own theaters and opera-houses, as do also Rome, Milan, Bologna, Messina and other Italian cities, Geneva, Basle, Lisbon, Athens and even small Greek cities, such as Patras and Corfu. Paris owns several theaters in addition to the Grand Opera House. Municipal theaters also exist in most of the provincial cities of Russia, St. Petersburg, Moscow and Warsaw having imperial theaters. In North and South America, the only instances of municipal theaters are reported from Para and Maracaibo.

As a rule, these municipal theaters are leased to a company or director, often for a nominal rent, while the city either guarantees a minimum profit or pays a fixed annual subvention. In many towns where there is no municipal theater, and occasionally even where there is one, the city subsidizes private establishments. This is the case at Florence, Barmen, Crefeld, Christiana and Bergen. As a result of this municipal aid, prices are usually fixed so low as to place the performances within the reach of all. Thus, at Marseilles, the prices for the opera fixed by the city council are from fourteen cents to $1.50. Hon. Robert P. Skinner, the United States Consul at that point, writes: "The wealthy do not patronize the opera so much as the comparatively poor, and the keenest enthusiasm comes from the cheapest seats." At Nice, the prices for ordinary performances are from ten cents to $1.60, and on Sundays these are reduced by one-half. On certain holidays, free performances are given at the municipal theaters of Paris, Brussels and other large cities, the expenses being borne by the city.

In addition to the various industrial functions described above, which have been assumed by some considerable number of cities, there remain some exceptional instances where other functions, also of an industrial nature, have been undertaken by a few municipalities.

The ownership of the Cincinnati Southern railway by the city of Cincinnati presents an interesting case of municipal activity. The construction of the road was authorized by a vote of the electors of the city in 1869. It was built at a cost of $18,000,000, and in 1898 the bonds are still outstanding. In 1896, a popular vote was taken on the question of selling the road, which resulted in a small majority against the sale in a vote of less than half the usual vote of the city. Somewhat analogous, but on a much smaller scale, are the cases of Kingston-upon-Hull, which has invested $100,000 in the Hull and Barnsley railroad, and Glasgow, which owns $60,000 of Caledonian railway 4 per cent. debentures. The city of Galveston, Tex., owns stock in the local street railway company.

Los Angeles, Cal., has a public irrigation system to supply water to neighboring farmers, which yields a revenue of about $20,000.

Municipal provisions for sports and games, which afford physical exercise to the general public, such as football, baseball, cricket, tennis, golf, bicycling and skating are general. Nearly all the large cities of Great Britain and the United States have fields in the municipal parks for such of these games as are locally most popular. The county council of London has 284 cricket pitches, 334 tennis courts, 45 skating ponds, 4 golf links, 4 lacrosse fields and 3 bowling greens.

Public pawnshops are operated in France, Holland, Belgium, Austria, Germany, Switzerland, Italy and Spain. The first one was established in Perugia, Italy, in 1462, by the monks of that place. It was designed to liberate the poor from the oppressions of the usurers by accommodating them with loans at moderate rates of interest, or without interest at all.

Those who understand how the needy are obliged to submit to extortion in the private pawnshops in American cities will at once see the benefit of municipal loan offices, where no advantage is taken of the necessities of the poor.

Hartford, Conn., Halifax, England, and Odessa, Russia, each own a municipal quarry, from which stone for street paving and other purposes is obtained. The output at Hartford is about 20,000 cubic yards a year; and the cost of the stone delivered on the streets in 1896 was $1.98 per square yard.

Several English towns take some active part in the chief industries of the locality. Bradford, the center of woolen manufacture, has a conditioning house for testing woolen goods, which, during 1897, made 64,435 tests of goods, weighing over 24,000,000 pounds. The municipality of Manchester has erected a cold-storage plant and warehouse for frozen meats and other perishable goods, which arrive by the ship canal. Oyster beds and herring fisheries are owned by several towns, the Colchester corporation receiving a revenue of $16,000 from its interest in the Colne Fishing Board.

Boston, Mass., has had, since 1897, a municipal printing office, at which municipal printing is done, and which made a clear profit the first year of $8,000.

A Movement Scarcely Begun.

As Dr. Milo Roy Maltbie says, in "Municipal Affairs:"

Whither is all this tending? Whatever a few years since may have been the answer suggested by conservatism, there is to-day but one — and that so obvious as scarcely to be questioned. The extension of municipal functions in the directions in which the city is to act as the servant of the individual has barely begun; and its scope, certain to be indefinitely increased in a comparatively near future, is to be measured only by the resources of developing invention and enterprise, so rapidly developing of late that their early realization will be such as to be unthinkable now. The individual will have cheap facilities for transport and communication. The product of his labor will be multiplied in advantage to him by the co-operation for which cities alone give a chance. He will not be left to the hard paths which chance may afford for education of his mind and his senses, but have this facilitated by every device of civilization. It is, therefore, natural — inevitable indeed — that there should be provided for him, first, water, the prime essential of life and health; next, the first of its conveniences — artificial light; later, those universal incidents of its growth — highway facilities (including power supply as well as a clear path); and, finally, education and recreation.

Another question, however, is coming to the front, in form well calculated to startle even the most radical and enterprising: How far and how rapidly are city services to be offered the individual without condition and without price? Throughout the civilized world, it is now admitted that each citizen should have an abundant supply of water — free, so far as affecting his personal use of it. Of urban aggregations of a million of inhabitants each, one is actually furnishing and others are preparing to furnish free light, not merely for all public places but for private dwellings, whenever a certain degree of aggregation in occupancy has been reached. Turnpikes are rapidly becoming a memory; tolls are steadily dropping from our bridges and canals; and avowedly unremunerative rates of street-car fare for workingmen and students are favored on every hand. The education that used to be charily sold is now not merely free, but compulsory; while, by public funds supporting scholarships and fellowships, the highest and most technical education possible is offered to all under conditions which are scarcely more than tests of capacity freely to improve it. Free libraries and museums, art and musical education are becoming common. In every direction, recreation is being provided free as fast as the public can be taught to use it. The New York Court of Appeals has squarely taken the ground that should invention make it possible, the city might provide its people with improved air.

There seems, therefore, but one answer to the question proposed. Free supply or facilitated provision for each of the more important daily wants of its citizens will be within the functions of the future city. In the concrete, what does this mean? Not necessarily that the city will or should attempt to meet the unlimited want of every citizen for every facility which it might supply him, but rather that to the extent that the resultant of his needs and the ability of the city may determine, it shall offer in every direction a constantly increasing minimum.

Similarly as to street car and rapid transit facilities. The principle of favoring an unremunerative rate for long distance in order to facilitate the settlement in more healthful living conditions of those who must otherwise add to the congestion at our city centers has already been accepted. In this regard, every factor is rapidly becoming more marked, so that the day is close at hand when in each of our leading cities conditions, not merely of health but of business convenience and profit, will demand that what are now largely residential quarters be given over to more and more intense occupation by business structures; and room elsewhere found, even though it involve transport cost, for the multiplying myriads that are still to do their daily work where their homes lately were. Ten years hence, it may seem as ridiculous that free transportation should not be furnished to secure the full use of recreation facilities by our city population, as it would be now to stop the free access to municipal parks and buildings.

Glasgow leads the cities of Great Britain and the world in ministering to the social needs of her people through the medium of collective ownership. Glasgow owns, not only the waterworks, lighting plant, street railway, and parks, but, in addition, public baths, wash-houses, lodging-houses, model homes for widows, model homes for widowers. Tumbled-down rookeries and filthy and disease-breeding haunts for vice and crime were purchased by the municipality, torn down, and in their places beautiful buildings were erected to minister to the social needs of the people in the many ways indicated, the great municipality of Glasgow bringing light, air and sunshine to the downcast men and women who before, on account of their poverty, were compelled to live in the foul tenements that disgraced the city. Public wash-houses for the poor are a public benefaction. The poor woman, living with her children in a rented room, perhaps with no conveniences for washing and drying her clothes, goes to a public wash-house, and for a penny, is furnished with a tub, mangle, wringer, steam dryer, and in an hour's time is back home with her washing nicely done, and for less expense than the cost of fuel that would have been necessary in her own crowded quarters. Workmen unable to find respectable quarters for a lodging, can now go to a lodging-house provided by their mother, the municipality, a beautiful stone building four stories high, where they have bath, laundry, lavatories, library and game-rooms, and all of this at the minimum cost, with no thought of making profit to enrich some individual, but with the thought uppermost in the mind of the municipality of making men, to enrich all and thus enrich the municipality.

Patriotism in Time of Peace.

The League of American Municipalities has brought out the fact that hundreds of cities now operating their own public utilities in one form or another, proves that the question of the wisdom of municipal ownership has passed out of the domain of the problems. The question that the people are now considering is how to get selfishness to release its grasp upon these valuable heritages of the people. I confess I know no better way than to appeal to the patriotism of every loyal citizen. Patriotism calls men to leave home and family or school or shop or farm to go at their country's call, heedless of the weary march and rusting idleness of the camp, the carnage and terrors of battle, and he who shuns his country's call is counted as an ingrate and his name is held in everlasting odium and contempt. And upon the patriots who so nobly responded to their country's call to go and fight for the relief of the Cuban reconcentrados a grateful people is now lavishing its wealth of love and affection. *But why does not patriotism call for service in time of peace as well as war?* Why should the soldier go out to face pestilence, danger and death in order that the good of all may be conserved, while the financier is honored and counted great for remaining at home amidst the luxurious appointments of a comfortable office, seeking to conserve his own good? Why, if we truly love our country, should not our hearts be moved to pity as we contemplate our own great army of disinherited, of disheartened, discouraged, hopeless ones, beaten in the race of life? Why should not our enthusiasm be aroused for them? *And why should not the patriotism of the financiers who have shown conspicuous and marked ability in providing for themselves, so inspire them to come forward in the hour of the city's peril and offer their services for the good of all of the people in the ministry of social need in building a public lighting plant, managing a street railway, or financing any work of improvement for the benefit of all of the people?* I confess that I can see no good reason why. I confess that I cannot see how a man can love his country or love his state, *who uses the people of his city, his state, his country, merely for what he can get out of them.* I believe the time is coming, and may God hasten the day, when our eyes shall be opened to the iniquity of this sort of a life, and we shall make clear distinctions between respectability and righteousness.

Statistics are abundant and easy of access to prove that there is hardly a city in America to-day but has given away franchises for nothing, that would, if now owned by that city, *pay its entire debt,* and, in many cases, place the city beyond the need of levying taxation upon its citizens. We have been in the habit of condoning on the ground that the franchise manipulators " furnished the capital," but we have learned that the people are the capital and that what the franchise-taker usually furnishes is not capital, but cunning.

A Method of Expressing Love.

Through public ownership the municipality, the state, and the nation may find a means of expressing its love for the people, and the people — THE GREAT COMMON PEOPLE — are never wanting, never have been wanting or lacking in appreciation for any sacrifice of service that may be rendered to them. This is shown clearly in the love we have for such service as is now administered by our municipalities and our state and our national government. The state points with just pride to the paternal care exercised over the dependent classes — the aged, the infirm, the blind, the deaf, the insane and afflicted in every class. We have a conscious and just pride in the social service administered by the general government in the post-office department, despite our grief because of the fact that the railroads charge the general government eight cents a pound for carrying the mail, when they perform a similar service for the express companies for about one-seventh of the price, and thus saddle the deficit on the people.

THE GREAT QUESTION.

The question that is rapidly forging to the front to-day in this country is, *"Shall the municipality own or be owned? Shall the general government own the telegraph and railroads, or shall these corporations own the general government?"* We have had a striking example of the lawlessness of capital in the experience of the government in attempting to tax corporations to raise revenue for the war. The government said, "We will tax the telegraph companies so much for each message sent." It would have been easy enough for the framers of the law, if they desired to tax the individuals direct, to say that each person sending a message should pay so much, but they had no such purpose. Their purpose was to tax the telegraph companies, as they plainly stated in as plain language as can be chosen, but what do these anarchists and law-breakers do? The government says "we will tax the telegraph companies," but, "no, you don't," says the telegraph company, "we will tax the people," and immediately an order is issued that every patron of that company shall contribute his mite to relieve the corporation of a share of the burden that the government sought to impose upon it. Identically the same thing is true of the express companies.

IMPROVING CITIZENSHIP.

But the greatest good to be realized through municipal ownership will be found in the improved quality of our citizenship, because of the family feeling, the truly patriotic sentiment, the *love of country which is love of our fellow-men, that will be awakened in the man's breast by the contemplation of the fact that he is a member of a family which owns its own streets, which owns its own bridges, which owns its own water-works, which owns its own electric-lighting plants, which owns its own telephone and express and messenger services; a member of a family which owns and does everything for the family that can, by any possibility, be better done by collective than by private effort.* And whenever the feeling is once awakened that this is our city, this is our country, then a man becomes in the best sense of the word a citizen who loves his country. This feeling will be wonderfully enhanced as the city goes forward in the work of municipal ownership. *The people will learn that they can serve themselves better without profit than any private corporation can serve them with profit as the only incentive for their effort.*

In the parks and public playgrounds in Glasgow I saw neat porcelain signs with the inscription: " CITIZENS, PROTECT YOUR PROPERTY," and when my eyes first fell upon that inscription I confess to such a feeling of delight as I had never before experienced through looking at a dumb sign board. It was in such striking contrast to the "boss" idea expressed in the order, "Keep off the grass," a thing that never should be used except by the man who hangs up on his premises that other iniquity, " Beware of the dog." The policeman's " move on " is another atrocity I should like to see linked to the two I have just mentioned and the hideous trio consigned to eternal oblivion.

AN UNWISE JUDGE.

" Municipal ownership is all right with regard to water-works, but not as to street railways," said a learned judge to me recently. If I were a young man who had been trained to a proper respect for the bench, I presume I should have accepted this declaration as final, because of the learning of the judge; but had this judge used his reason instead of accepting the reasoning of some hired man employed by the corporations, he would have known that the same principle applies to both classes of service, and that if it is good for a city to own its own water-works, it is good that every utility that ministers to all of the people shall be owned in the same way.

The only danger that I can see in the growth of sentiment in favor of collective ownership is the threatened doom of those who seek individual gain at the expense of the people. *Free gifts of franchises worth millions are not as common as they once were;* the people are coming to realize that the source of their wealth is through labor — hard, sweating labor — and with this realization comes a revelation of the truth that those who do not labor do not produce wealth, all the fine-spun theories about brain work and capital to the contrary notwithstanding.

SAVE THE LITTLE CHILDREN.

The little children must be rescued from our factories and sweat-shops no less than from the slums and saloons, if they are to grow up to an appreciation of their responsibility as citizens. All the horrors of our present day industrialism must be changed. Patriotic men and women must no longer be willing to live by robbing children of their childhood and young girls of their maidenhood through taking their toil in stores and factories at $2.50 to $5.00 a week; and the fact that the children and young girls may be hidden from our gaze, or the profit we make come to our hands through the thin gauze of a corporation, should never for one moment hide the wrong from the quickened social conscience of the man or woman who truly loves his country. I deny the right of any man or woman living by such means to claim to be patriotic. It is true there are thousands whose attention has never been called to this wrong, but those of us who have had our eyes opened to this iniquity are nothing less than

ELECTRIC LIGHT TOWER, FAIRFIELD, IOWA.
Here is located the oldest electric light plant in this country — owned by city.

MUNICIPAL MARKET, NEW YORK.

MUNICIPAL QUARRY, HARTFORD, CONN.

particeps criminis unless we cry out against this spoliation of our people for the sake of private profit. When we shall have realized the perfected republic, then we shall find the good of the individual only in the good of all.

Play is the normal condition for the healthy child as work is for the healthy adult; it is necessary for its well-being and proper development, and really another part of its education; and to provide satisfactorily equipped play-grounds for the children is, in my opinion, to minister in a most substantial manner towards the building up of the future citizenship of our city. Give the children play-grounds and lots of them. It will be money well spent, and, without a doubt, in many instances will result in saving children from falling into vice and possibly crime, by providing them a place to go where they can be engaged in healthful recreation; whereas otherwise they might be wandering aimlessly about the streets and demonstrating in their lives the truth of the adage that the "idle brain is the devil's workshop." Keep the children at play and the men at work.

"Train up a child in the way he should go, and when he is old he will not depart from it," is the injunction of Solomon the Wise.

All educators now agree that very much is lost to the work of true education unless it is begun with the child. It is said that the seeds of fundamental truth that form the character of the future citizen must be planted in the child before he reaches the age of seven years. There can be no question but that the thing of greatest importance to a city is the character of its citizens; it then becomes the clear duty of a city to contribute in every possible way to character building, and, to act intelligently, it is important that the contribution should be made at the time when the "apprentice citizen" is most ready and likely to receive correct impressions. This the city can do in one way and no other, and that is by establishing *free kindergartens;* in other words, making the kindergarten a part of the public-school system.

History as well as theory can be cited to prove the correctness of this proposition, and in those cities where the kindergartens have been established long enough to begin to show the fruit of proper training in early years, a canvass of the records of the courts shows most conclusive evidence of the wisdom of thus exercising care over the very young children. Children who have had kindergarten training do not grow up into men and women of criminal character of either high or low class. The way to a good citizenship, without criminal tendencies, is to plant the seed of it in all children through the kindergarten system before they arrive at the age when they are admitted to the public school.

Let us have the kindergartens. "Give the babies a chance." Let them have the right to choose whether they will do right or wrong. It is cheaper to establish kindergartens than to maintain courts and build jails, workhouses and prisons. Give all the children proper kindergarten training, and the supply of bad citizens for our prisons, jails and workhouses will be exhausted in a generation.

Assault upon Democracy.

Nothing that I have yet heard has brought me to see that the policy of granting or selling franchises is anything other than an assault upon the very foundations of democratic government itself; and, as a matter of fact, it is only when we are sunk so low in public morals as to be almost unworthy to be called citizens, that we are willing to make profit at the expense of the comfort and even the lives of our fellows. I have already pointed to the fact that the profits of the street-railway magnates, the silks and satins and lace curtains and lambrequins and the multiplicity of sofa pillows of their wives and daughters, are purchased with the hard-earned nickels of the toiling washerwoman, and certainly any intelligent conception of right social relations would lead every one of these to spurn the thought of living in luxury purchased at such a price. But our attention has not been called to these things; our attention has been centered on the "successful man." Press and pulpit, public school and college throughout the land have sounded the praise of the individual whose only claim to distinction lies in the fact that he has placed a city, state or nation under tribute to himself; and this man, who has been changed from a being created in the image of God into a monster of greed and rapacity, is just what we have made him by the processes I have just described.

Bribed by the Rich.

The movement for public ownership is government seeking the good of all as against the individual who seeks only his own good. It is a recognition of the fundamental fact that the humblest citizen is entitled to the greatest degree of comfort that associated effort can provide. It is organized love, manifesting itself in service. It is patriotism of the highest and purest type. It is the casting down of idols and the lifting up of ideals. It is dethroning the millionaires and exalting the millions. Happily, we are passing away from the abject worship of mere dollars to a realization of the truth so tersely stated by the simple Nazarene nearly nineteen hundred years ago: " Ye cannot serve God and Mammon." And we are coming to measure men not by their ability to organize industry and use their fellow-men simply as profit-making machines, but by their ability to organize industry and serve their fellow-men; and where can we look for nobler examples of patriotism, or love of country, than to the men and women whose lives have been devoted to the service of their fellow-men rather than to mere sordid worship of wealth, rather than to debauching the machinery of justice and the people's legislators in order to serve their own purposes? "BRIBED BY THE RICH TO ROB THE POOR," was the scathing verdict pronounced by the Honorable Wayne McVeagh upon the legislators of Philadelphia, who leased the gas-works created by the vote of the people, without any resort to the vote of the people; and in the address at the commencement exercises of the University of Pennsylvania last year, the same honored gentleman said to the students of that institution, that the " black flag of the corruptionist is more to be feared than the red flag of the Anarchist."

The Briber and His Victim.

It is short-sighted and idle to sneer at bribe-takers without visiting the same condemnation upon those who offer bribes, but the facts are that the men who send their agents out to purchase votes of legislators are our wealthy men who live on the avenues in the big houses and ride behind horses with short tails, while the man whose vote they seek to purchase lives in the narrow street and small house, and probably serves the city without a salary, and frequently finds himself without salary from any source or other visible means of support, when the poison of the briber is offered to him.

Such a system is not worthy of an intelligent people. Yet, you are well aware that I am painting no fancy picture, but that in many of our municipalities to-day we are electing men to positions of trust and responsibility to serve without pay, men who have to confess themselves beaten in the game of life and who have not only failed in the warfare of business, but have even failed to secure a salaried position to provide them and their families with the necessaries of life. In this condition, with the poison of the briber in the air, what hope is there for the man who realizes the need he is in, who realizes the distress that stares his wife and little ones in the face? He is like unto one weakened and emaciated with long fasting, who should suddenly be thrust into a fever-laden atmosphere. Of course, such a man will take the fever. And in the other case, unless a man has in him the blood of the martyrs who suffered death for the truth, of course he will take the bribe. Not long ago the city of Chicago furnished a valuable object lesson, showing the evil of granting municipal franchises, and the resolutions passed at the great Music Hall meeting, condemning the officers and directors of the street-railway companies, placing those leading citizens in the same class with the aldermen whom they proposed to bribe, shows that the people are beginning to see where the real fault lies. *It is idle to talk about " electing honest men" while continuing a dishonest system.* We pray "lead us not into temptation," and yet elect men to serve us, often without compensation, in a position where our leading business men tempt them with an offer of a single bribe that is a fortune in itself. What do we expect them to do while the scramble of " every man for himself and the devil take the hindmost " is our ruling passion? Take the bribe, or die for the truth? Municipal ownership settles these questions once for all by removing the opportunity for bribery, and there is no other final solution.

No War on Wealth.

I am not indulging in a phillippic against rich men, against trusts, combines or monopolies. I point to all of these as legitimate products of our economic system. The folly of legislating against them may be easily understood when we reflect that, almost without exception, our antagonisms against trusts, combines or monopolies lie in the thought that we ourselves are not in them; once let us become sharers or partakers in the plunder and our opposition vanishes. The reason for this is found in the fact that our opposition does not rest upon a pure basis of morality. But the people are rapidly coming to see that the chances for the many to become partakers in this sort of wealth are so very limited that the great masses are made moral perforce — moral because of the absolute inability to be immoral, or to become partakers of the fruits of other people's toil.

Let none seek to befog the real question by saying that I am making a warfare upon wealth. I am pleading for more wealth. I am pleading that more of our people now doomed to hopeless poverty may share in the wealth that their hands have produced. I plead with the captains of industry, the men who are honored for their ability as bankers and financiers, as street-railway magnates, as managers and owners of great railroad corporations, express and telegraph companies; I plead with these as fellow-citizens of a republic of equals; I plead with them from the standpoint of one who loves his fellow-men with a passion that will never die. And I say to you, who hold in your hands the wealth of the world, where is your patriotism? Do you love your country? If you do, then you love your fellow-men, and there never was an hour of greater need that you should manifest your love for your fellow-men than the present hour; that you should cease your hoarding of dollars and turn your attention to your idle brothers and devote your ability, not to amassing more wealth for yourselves, but to saving the people, of whom you are one, from the fearful social distress and agony of this hour. *I am not asking for charity. We have too much of that. Charity seeks to continue the present order, seeks to palliate the trouble for to-day. I am pleading for a social order of fair play, a social order of doing as you would be done by. No man or woman has the right to any claim to love of country unless that man or woman is as ready to serve the people in times of peace as the most devoted soldier in time of war.*

Made of the Same Clay.

I must not be misunderstood upon this point. That man or woman, rich or poor, high or low, black or white, does not live for whom I have in my heart any other feeling than that of brotherly love. I am resting upon a rock bottom conclusion that we are all made of one common piece of clay, that we have one father, even God, and we are all brothers; that if our problems are ever to be solved, they must be solved together. We cannot save an individual here and there and let the masses go tumbling headlong into the cesspools of vice, poverty and crime.

If it is wise for the state to provide for a system of free education, which has been done, then all the reasons that have been urged for that form of Socialism may be brought forward in support of a proposition for free lectures, free music, free baths, free play-grounds, free gymnasia, etc. We are beginning to see that we have been making a narrow use of the word education; a whole lot of stuff has been called education that did not educate. We have separated life into fragments, and the fundamental fact is ever before us that life is a whole, and we are coming to accept the doctrine of the absolute unity of the entire race. This is because of our better conception of democracy and brotherhood, and as this idea of unity takes possession of us, we see the necessity of having every social unit as nearly complete, as nearly perfect, as the socialized energy of the municipality, state or nation can make it.

The acceptance of the idea of democracy involves a dismissal from the mind of any thought of class or classes, a degrading notion that has always hindered the progress of the world. The idea that a few of us are endowed with the " divine right of kings," and are especially fitted to govern or rule what we have called the lower classes, is undemocratic, as well as unchristian and of course unbrotherly; and worst of all, it is unscientific. Emerson says that " the entertainment of the proposition of depravity is the last profligacy and profanation; there is no skepticism, no atheism but that."

If we are a democracy, we must believe in the people; there is no escape from that conclusion. If we believe in the poeple, we must believe that we are going to be saved altogether or lost altogether. It is my belief that we are making progress toward nobler ideals of democracy and brotherhood than we have ever yet dreamed of. I see the promise of this in the growing desire to enlarge the functions of government in ministering to the social necessities of the people; and as we have long since recognized the importance of one part of the thing called education — what is taught from books — and have practically made that as free as the air we breathe, so I believe we shall enlarge our conceptions of what really constitutes education, and make such things as baths, gymnasia, play-grounds, music, lectures, etc., as free to all as the common school now is.

THE SYSTEM TO BLAME, NOT INDIVIDUALS.

The trouble is not so much with the individuals that compose our social structure as with the structure itself. In the scramble for individual wealth, we have fallen into a frightful state of public and private immorality. Everything has been made subservient to the money-getting craze. Social standing, friends, family, home — yes, even life itself, are sacrificed in the hope of private gain. This applies to rich and poor alike. We have yet to learn that life does not consist in things, but we can only learn it through an acknowledgment of our social dependence upon one another, through an acknowledgment of brotherhood.

A scientific engineer understands how to raise one of our largest brick blocks twenty feet into the air and never crack the plaster or interfere with the daily use of the building, but he will not attempt the work piece-meal; he will apply the lifting power of men's hands to hundreds of jackscrews equally to every part of the structure. In like manner, we who have received the illumination of an awakened social conscience may, through the sacrifice of service, apply the lifting power of love to the social structure; but like the building, we must all rise together.

PUBLIC MIND CHANGING.

The growth of sentiment in favor of public ownership indicates that the mind of the people is rapidly clarifying on this question.

The people are beginning to see that no good reason exists why all the people in the city shall say to a few of the people,— the lighting company, the water-works company, the street-railway company, " Now, all of us will give you (a few of us) the right to get rich from the rest of us." Large numbers of the people are beginning to see that the only wealth that is in any sense theirs is the Commonwealth, and with instincts that are perfectly natural, they are striving to regain possessions that have passed out of their hands, usually through the practice of deception and fraud. Though men tramp thousands of miles daily through the streets of our cities, either because they have not or cannot afford to spend the precious nickel to ride, they are still able to understand that the public streets are theirs, are common property; they may walk in them in their weary and hopeless search for the right that is inherent in every man, but which we are to-day denying to millions — that is the right to work, the right to share in the creative effort going on about them, the right to participate in building and making a country that they are asked and expected and want to love. These millions are coming to understand the source of their misery, the cause of their distress. They are coming to see that our policy of granting special privileges in the way of public franchises, contracts and unusual opportunities for profit-getting to a few, is invariably making paupers of the many, and our only salvation from the strain of the present hour is to cease our policy of exploiting all of the people for the sake of enriching the few, and to establish in its stead the purely democratic policy in government of considering the interest of all of the people as always ahead of, and superior to, the rights of any individual or set of individuals.

How to Diminish the Jail Population.

There is no room to doubt that 50 per cent. of the sum now expended in so-called restraining and charity methods, would, if expended in any reasonable way along socialistic lines, so as to enlarge the privileges of the people, and to provide opportunities for them — within twenty-five years place our almshouses, jails, penitentiaries and prisons very largely in the domain of the relics of a hideous past. To appreciate this truth, we first have to understand that the source of our wealth is in "hard bone labor," all fine-spun theories about brain-work and capital to the contrary notwithstanding. Let me illustrate: We might wipe off from the face of the earth all created wealth, all property, manufactured goods of every description, and if we have a healthy, educated and socialized people, ready to work for the good of all, we may reasonably expect to restore, in a short time, all of these material things. I think this will help us to see the relative importance of wealth and health, and along with it, the necessity and duty of providing opportunities for people to be healthy. Then when with our socialized energy we shall provide opportunities for them to work, it will follow as a perfectly natural consequence that they will be wealthy.

It is most assuredly the sacred duty of the state to promote habits of industry and to maintain self-respecting manhood, and the imperative necessity of this hour is that the city, state and nation shall organize in its collective capacity so that the citizens of this growing Commonwealth may live self-respecting lives.

We provide for free education through the manual-training schools; we even teach our children how to work, and then we turn them out into a scrambling, fighting, quarrelling mob (the competitive system), where every man is struggling for himself, in a "grab-all," "catch-as-catch-can," "devil-take-the-hindmost-one" game, foolishly expecting that they will win success; they are helpless babes, pitted against trained fighters. After having taught them in the art and beauty of work, and how to work and how to make beautiful things, we fail to give them an opportunity to work.

We deny them the right to share in making and building a country that we ask them to love, a country that they want to love, and this is where the colossal failure of the present system reveals itself in its most hideous proportions — in the ever-increasing army of the workless, in the growing numbers of those who bear the curse of the wandering foot, and go from place to place vainly seeking and begging and pleading for the right to stand upon the earth, and the right to participate and share in the glory of the work that is going on about them. But all this is to be changed; this air is filled with signs of promise. The manifest destiny of these United States is to save the great peoples from the impending doom that the narrowness of a few would bring down upon them.

Our future is to be heroic, spiritual. We are to be a great people — great in quality, not in mere bigness. We are to manifest our greatness by our love for one another, and in a recognition of the rights of our fellow-men in providing opportunities for every man, for even the weakest child, to live the best possible life that is in him.

Ruskin has said that "the wealth of a nation may be estimated by the number of happy people that are kept employed in making useful things." Some day we shall take account of stock in that way. We shall not go to Lombard street or Wall street; but pointing to the happy people, who are constantly employed in making useful and beautiful things, we shall say, like the mother of the Gracchi, "These are my jewels."

Rainbow of Promise in Public Ownership.

It is because I see the rainbow of promise in public ownership that shall secure for us, as a people, a larger realization of liberty, that I plead for it. It is because I know that only in the good of all is the real good of the individual to be found, that I plead for collective work. It is because I stand, like many of you, day after day, with hopeless and hungry men, pleading that they may be allowed to work, that I raise my voice in their behalf. It is not because I would stir up dissension or cause trouble; it is because I would avoid trouble, and point the way to the smooth sea of prosperity, that I speak for these men.

> Is true freedom but to break
> Fetters for our own dear sake?
> And with leathern hearts forget
> That we owe mankind a debt?
> No; true freedom is to share
> All the chains our brothers wear,
> And with heart and hand to be
> Earnest to make others free.

Democracy has not failed. Like Christianity, it has not yet been tried. Thus far we have only dimly understood the meaning of either word. Hear Walt Whitman sing of Democracy:

> I speak the password primeval,
> I give the sign of Democracy.
> By God, I will have nothing that all cannot
>   have their counterpart of
> On equal terms.

When this kind of an ideal inspires us, the perfected republic, the Co-operative Commonwealth, will no longer be a dream, but a realized possibility. The municipality is the nucleus of government. The state and the nation look to the municipality for their ideal. Let those of us who have a conception of a loftier and better patriotism sound the keynote of a new municipal programme, that shall proclaim emancipation to the enslaved people *who are to-day the mere tools of the profit-gatherers. Let us announce the purpose of municipal government to be that of ministering in every possible way to the social need of the people of the municipality, and let us proclaim as an unalterable principle toward that end: Public ownership of all public utilities. No grant or extension of municipal franchises. No special privilege to any man or set of men to exploit the people for the sake of enriching the few.*

CHAPTER X.

CO-OPERATION AND PROFIT-SHARING.

Out of all the turmoil and confusion of centuries of competition steadily emerges this truth, that it is not by strife and warfare, but by unity and co-operation, that humanity advances. The way of welfare is the way of peace. History, as well as Christian morality, warns us that we cannot mount to power and happiness upon the ruin of our fellows. The law of the unity of human interests is not true because Christ taught it; he taught it because it is true. It is the fundamental fact of human society; any adequate induction of human experience will verify it. Men have doubted it, denied it, fought against it through all the ages, but the word standeth sure, and every generation that passes brings it into clearer light.— *Washington Gladden: Tools and the Man.*

CHAPTER X.

CO-OPERATION AND PROFIT-SHARING.

By N. O. Nelson.

A MAN with prophetic vision looking forward from the year 1799, through the now closing century, and seeing the improvements that have taken place in machinery, the scientific discoveries to aid man in conquering the material world, the rich resources of new lands that have been occupied in all parts of the world, must have reached the conclusion that by the year 1899, every man, woman and child would be abundantly educated, housed, fed, and clothed, and would enjoy abundant leisure. That we still have the problem of the poor and ignorant and unemployed, must mean that something is wrong in our use of the new forces.

The century started out with a rapid growth in manufacturing. The domestic industries were merged into factories, which required large capital and yielded high profits. In the early cotton factories, 100, and even 1,000 per cent. per annum was not uncommon. The master, with his two journeymen and two apprentices all living as one family, gave way to the manufacturing capitalist who bought labor as he bought raw material, and had no connection or concern with the life of the hundreds of "hands." People took more and more to working for wages, and in order to move readily from place to place where work could be obtained, they became tenants instead of home-owners. The classes of capitalists on one hand, and hands on the other, have grown further and further apart. The millionaire district of New York is an entirely different world from the workingmen's sections at the lower end of Manhattan Island. It is so in every city, big or little. Even at farming, we find a large proportion of the work done by renters, who pay one-third or one-half of their crop for the use of the bare farm, and laborers working at fifty cents a day for six to eight months in the year and doing odd jobs or tramping the rest of the time.

Theoretically, every man is given the same opportunity to get along in the world. He is free to work for whom he pleases, go into business if he pleases, sell his labor or his merchandise in any way that suits him. Free scope is given to those who are strongest in the elements that count in trade and management.

The industrial system by which this remarkable and disappointing development of the century has been worked out is generally known as "competition," said to be the life of trade, in reality the death of the best in human life. It has given us the millionaire master class, and it has given us the tramp, the unemployed, and the parasite. "Equality and fraternity" have been the watchwords of prophet and poet and statesman from time immemorial; "capital" and "profit" are the watchwords of nineteenth century commercialism. The tradition of brotherhood has been lost in the scramble for profit and luxurious living by the master class, and a chance to work by the wage-earner. Brothers of the same race, children of the same Father, have engaged in deadly strife. Competition is war, and you can't refine it or moralize it. If this is the best to be gotten out of machinery, is it worth the having?

The Co-operative Principle.

Directly opposed to competition is co-operation. It is the principle of co-operation that has undertaken with varying success to change government by the strong for the benefit of the

N. O. NELSON.
(Founder of the beautiful village, Leclaire, Ill.)

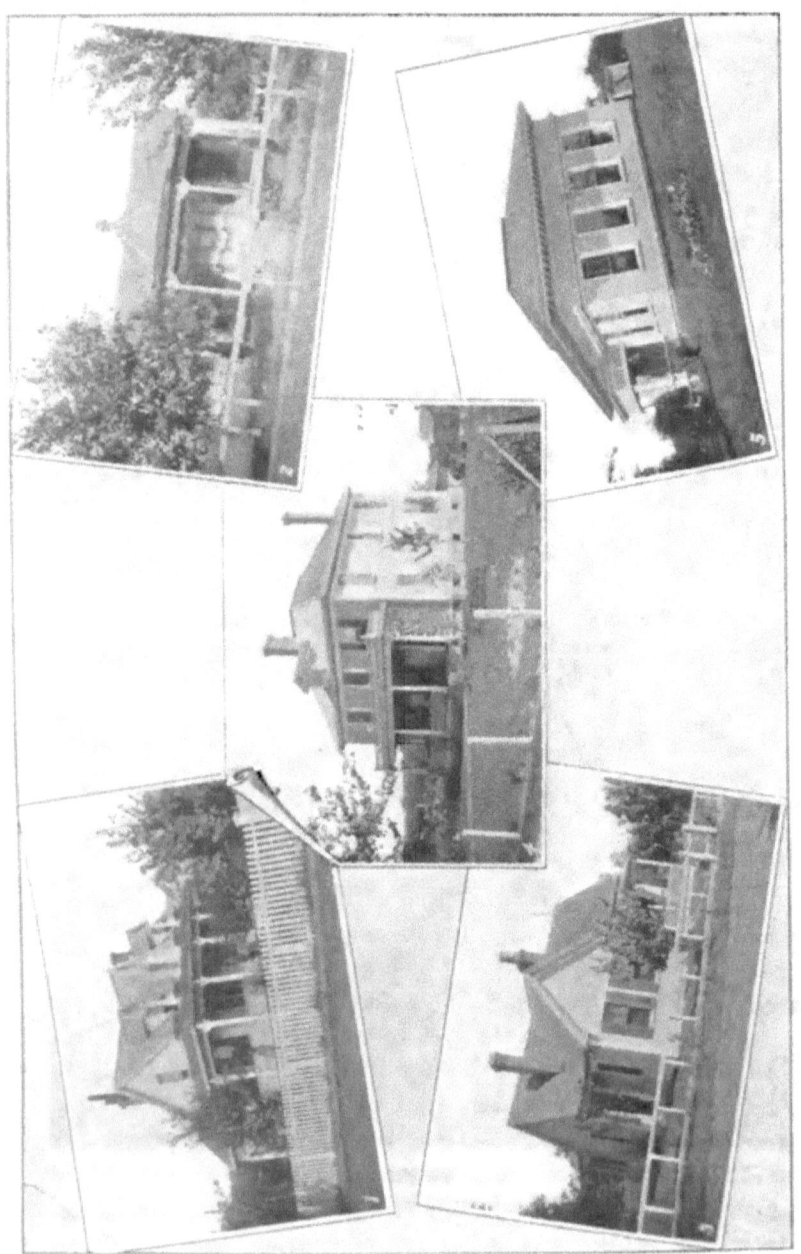

LECLAIRE, ILL.
(Founded by N. O. Nelson.)
Nos. 1, 2, 3, show Homes of Workingmen; No. 4, Home of N. O. Nelson; No. 5, School House and Public Hall.

few, to government by the whole people for the benefit of the whole people. In the public ownership of public utilities, free schools, free roads, free life-saving service on lake and sea, free libraries, the postal service, and in many places the water and light supply — in all of these and many others the whole people co-operate with manifest advantage to all. It must not be supposed that these services were always public. It was about 1750 that Benjamin Franklin first proposed the government postal service. Toll roads and bridges were the rule up to the middle of the century, and are still to be found in some parts of the country. Only gradually has it dawned upon us that no monopoly can be safely intrusted to private ownership and that government can give better and cheaper service.

While it will be said by some that it is monopoly rather than competition that is the root of the commercial evils, the fact remains, as well said by Henry George, that great fortunes are never earned, but are the results of monopoly or spoliation in some form. No man can do much more work than the average man, even as to managing ability; in public or private affairs there are always capable men to take the place of any master who dies or retires. The captains of industry of one decade are at least as capable as those of the preceding decade. Business in the larger view is a monopoly against the consumer and worker.

We have co-operation in government, in education, in carrying on the public utilities, and few there are so belated or reactionary as to wish to go back to the system of private ownership and management in any of them. On the contrary, the trend of opinion in all the foremost nations, notably England and the United States, is in favor of public ownership of all public utilities, including the land.

But the public utilities are only a part of our needs and conveniences; of still greater importance is the industrial and commercial business, which is still almost wholly in private hands and conducted for private profit. After all, a man's chief concern is the vocation by which he earns his living. Whether he is to have steady work, favorable working conditions, the full yield of his work, and to get his wants supplied with pure goods at a fair exchange of labor for labor, are problems that come nearer home to him and mean more to him than the price of his railroad fare or water or light, more even than his rent and his taxes. Usually, he has so little of these that his outlay for them is a small part of his expenses.

Co-operation in the United States.

Business co-operation is not now mere theory; it has had a half century of trial and success. Great Britain and Germany are far in the lead, but even in this country there are many co-operative stores, creameries and shippers' unions owned by hundreds, and in some cases thousands of members, who elect their own officers and managers, and divide the profits among themselves.

The Arlington store, at Lawrence, Mass., has about 3,500 members, does a business of over $300,000 a year, and besides paying its members interest on their investment, and creating a surplus, returns regularly seven and one-half per cent. rebate on purchases.

In Olathe, Kan., there is a co-operative store now in its twenty-third year, a bank in its twelfth year, and an insurance company several years old. They are owned by farmers, are exceptionally prosperous and illustrate beyond question that plain people can conduct their own business better than a private proprietor can do it for them. The Olathe Association has about 800 members, and the largest building, stock and business in that part of the country. The members pay cash for everything they buy, and have saved themselves a great deal of money. The bank is the leading one in that section, and commands the fullest confidence of the entire community. In 1898, I had the pleasure of delivering the address at their annual reunion, at which perhaps 2,000 persons were present.

In San Jose, Cal., the Farmers' Union has been in operation for over twenty years, carries an immense stock, does a very large business, pays cash, and returns a handsome dividend to its members.

The Fruit Growers' Unions and Exchanges in California are now doing about half of the entire fruit shipping of that State. They have resident agents in all the principal Eastern cities to direct the shipments and regulate the supply according to the demands of each market. At home they employ experts to direct the packing and the care of orchards.

There are hundreds of stores scattered throughout the United States that are well established, well managed and profitable. In the states of the Mississippi valley, co-operative creameries, owned and conducted by the dairymen and farmers, are common.

Co-operation in Great Britain.

But we must cross the Atlantic to find co-operation in its most advanced stage. In Great Britain, there are now over 1,500,000 co-operators, representing a population of 7,500,000. There are about 1,800 societies, some of them having from 20,000 to 40,000 members, and twenty to thirty branches. The aggregate annual business is considerably above $300,000,000, and the profits, which are divided between interest on shares, dividends on purchases, and surplus, are nearly $40,000,000. As the members live on their ordinary earnings, most of the profits are converted into share or loan capital, giving the older associations abundant means for productive enterprises of their own, or independent ones.

The co-operators have everything of the best. Their store buildings are noted all over England for beauty of architecture, solidity of construction and perfect adaptation to the business.

The Leeds Society has a stable of sixty draught horses, the finest lot it has ever been my pleasure to see.

About twenty-five years ago, the retail stores in England combined to make a wholesale society. Their business the first year was $3,000,000; in 1898, it exceeded $65,000,000. This wholesale society has resident buyers in all the large markets of the world; has seven ships used in bringing its supplies from France, Denmark, and Ireland; has several highly equipped shoe factories; makes its own soap, crackers, candy, furniture, cloth, clothing, preserves, flour, and many other goods; sends a special buyer once a year to Greece to buy full cargoes of currants and other dried fruit; and carries on banking and fire and life insurance. Of the banking department, the following figures from the Banker's Magazine, for June, 1899, for the year ended December 31, 1898, will be found instructive: "Deposits and current accounts, etc., amounting to $9,078,350; capital paid and reserve fund, $4,540,000; proportion of capital and reverse to deposits, fifty per cent.—which was the highest percentage of all the banks in the table." The headquarters of the society is at Manchester, and there are branch depots in London, Newcastle, Liverpool, and Bristol. Its chief counting room occupies an entire floor of its magnificent central building, with a force of about 250 clerks.

The Scottish Wholesale Society holds the same relation to the Scottish co-operators. As I drove up to its headquarters, on my last visit, I noticed a magnificent new building approaching completion, which I took to be a new city hall. It proved to be the new store of the Scottish Wholesale Society. In the suburbs of Glasgow it has a tract of thirteen acres, on which for the last ten years it has been building factories. In this place, leather, shoes, cloth, clothing, crackers, preserves, soap, flour, are produced, and scarcely a year goes by that some new line of production is not added. The workers receive a dividend on their wages out of the profits of the business, and they are represented on the board of directors.

Both of these wholesale societies are owned entirely by the retail societies, but whether their holdings be large or small, each has only one vote. They receive interest on their respective investments, and the remainder is divided in proportion to purchases. The officers, directors, and managers in the wholesale, as well as the retail societies, are workingmen who have grown up in the business. They are a splendid business school. A man is first elected as a director in his own store, in due time is promoted to the presidency, and finally is elected to the wholesale board, where he is given charge of some department of the business. The increase in his pay is slight, but the honor is much esteemed, and there is an active competition on the part of the societies to get their man elected.

Low Salaries Paid.

In the handling of all this enormous business, no high salaries are paid; in no case, so I am informed, does it go beyond $1,500 a year. Mr. J. T. W. Mitchell, who was chairman of the English Wholesale Society for twenty-one years, being re-elected every quarter, was a man of extraordinary all-around ability, not only in business, but as a writer and speaker. He never accepted beyond $1,000 a year, and when he died, his fortune amounted to $1,800. In discussing a suitable memorial in recognition of his life's devotion, it was proposed to erect an orphanage at a cost of about $150,000, and requiring an annual outlay of about $30,000. This particular project was not carried out, but it showed the views and liberality of the co-operators. Business men have said to me, " Why did he not get a salary in proportion to his ability? " To which I answer that he did not want it. He could easily have had a $25,000 salary from private corporations, but he would have regarded it an act of treason to leave the co-operators or go into the business of making money for himself. He represented, in the best possible way, a large part of the English people. They were his friends and admirers, he loved his work, and no amount of money could have given him so full or useful or agreeable a life.

Mr. Maxwell, who is at the head of the Scottish Wholesale Society, and a leading spirit in co-operative circles, is a machinist by trade, and a business man and speaker of rare ability. I do not know his salary, but I think it does not exceed $1,200. Ability and loyalty are abundant in the co-operative circles, and there is no disposition to claim or to give large salaries. It is a mistake to suppose that a man can or will do work in proportion to his salary. The world's best work has never been done for money.

EXTENT AND PROGRESS OF THE SOCIETIES.

The extent and progress of these societies may be inferred from such news items as these:

A conference of the South Yorkshire Association was held June 24, 1899, at Doncaster. The reports showed the number of members to be 58,944; capital, $3,670,750; value of land, buildings and machinery, $1,437,525; goods, $952,055; investments in co-operative factories, $518,195; dwelling house property, $440,070; other investments, $324,470; net profits, $1,113,645, for the year 1898. In all of the co-operative societies interest, depreciation and surplus are always deducted before estimating the net profit.

The Royal Arsenal Society, at Woolwich, reports sales of $1,260,000 for last year. Its numbers have increased in the last three years from 7,992 to 12,317; its capital from $400,265 to $756,025; sales from $737,310 to $1,260,000. It is one of the most progressive in the kingdom and owns a building department, factories and a farm.

Some samples of recent (July, 1899) balance sheets will be interesting, bearing in mind that all expenses, interest, depreciation of buildings and machinery, surplus fund and educational grants have been deducted before profit is stated:

Rochdale Pioneers, the parent society.— The quarterly meeting of this society was held recently. There was a crowded attendance, and Mr. James Brearley (president) occupied the chair. In opening the meeting the chairman said there had been a gain of twenty-two members during the last month. The quarterly report of the committee stated that the receipts amounted to $363,135. The members' claims amounted to $1,640,175. The total depreciation of buildings and fixed stock to date was $293,030, leaving the present nominal value at $481,010. The buildings of twelve of the society's branch shops had been entirely written off, and were not accounted as any value in the assets of the society. The balance disposable gave a dividend of 15 per cent. on general purchases.

The Leeds Society has over 43,000 members; its annual sales exceed $6,000,000, with profits of $9,000 over and above interest on share capital and depreciation of fixed property.

Sittingbourne (Kent).— The 100th quarterly meeting of this society was held on June 3d; Mr. W. Copping was in the chair, and there was a numerous attendance. The balance sheet was of a very satisfactory character, showing the sales during the quarter to be $78,550, an increase over the corresponding quarter of last year of $6,195. The membership now stands at 1,674, a net gain of fifty-three for the quarter.

Birkenshaw.— The quarterly meeting held July 3, 1899. Sales, $68,400; profits, $11,790. This allowed a dividend of 15 per cent. on purchases and left a balance of $1,825. An additional grant of $50 was made to the Bradford Charities, and the committee was empowered to open a branch store at Cutler Heights.

Birstall.— The sales for the last quarter amounted to $50,840; net profits, $7,130, allowing a dividend of 14 per cent.

Brightside (Sheffield).—Sales, $388,870; net profits, $47,785, allowing a dividend of 13 per cent. on purchases. The purchases from co-operative sources have been $147,110.

Consett.— One hundred and forty-fourth quarterly meeting. Sales for the quarter, $83,735; dividend on purchases, 17 per cent.; number of members, 1,804, who have to their credit, $215,260.

Droylsden.— Sales, $128,565; profit, $19,365; dividend, 15 per cent.

Heckmordwike.— Profit, $37,675; dividend, 17 per cent.; sales, $215,470.

Nelson.— Sales for the quarter, $247,450; profits, $38,600; dividend on purchases, 15 per cent.

A co-operative business, once established, is much easier to carry on than a private business. Its customers are assured, it has no debts, and the dividends do the advertising. The expense rate is amazingly small, being only one and one-half per cent. on the sales in the wholesale stores, and about five per cent. in the retail stores. They pay no rents, do very little advertising, make no useless display and incur no bad debts.

Providing Homes.

A home is as necessary as land or clothing or bread. Only savages and tramps can do without it. It is about as unnatural to rent a house and keep moving about as it is to rent clothing, which some people do. Co-operative building associations have been popular in this country because they enable many members to pool their surplus and build homes for some of their number. But they have suffered from the defects of overcharging the borrower and overpaying the lender, and many have been mismanaged by incompetent or dishonest officers. These wise and affluent co-operators are making homes for their members out of their surplus, charging the lowest interest rate and no extras. Here are some examples:

So far back as 1873 the directors of the Leeds Society decided to assist its members to build houses for themselves; and for this purpose made a grant of $15,000 to a committee, and this amount was subsequently increased to $35,000. Two year later the society built fifty-one cottages, at a cost of $62,500; and in the same year purchased an estate, for the erection of a better class of houses, at a cost of $5,000. But capital continued to grow faster than means came to hand for its safe employment; and so we find in 1896, land was bought in four different places on which to build cottages for the members of the society. Whoever walks or drives about the suburbs of Leeds, and comes upon a bright, well laid-out estate, or streets and terraces of new, well-designed tenements, will probably find that the owners or builders are the co-operators. Three hundred houses erected by the society have been sold to members, but it also advances money to members to enable them to purchase houses not built by the society. About 650 houses have been erected by the society. A number of houses have been bought as investments.

From the last published balance sheet, it appears that the total outlay of this one society in land, stores, cottages, and kindred undertakings has been no less than $2,028,500.

In addition to this property, held by the society itself, the individual members have property, in their own right, to the value of $1,303,500, which has been secured either by purchase from the society or by advances made to them for the purpose of buying houses from other sources. And it appears that these members have already paid back one-half of the sum thus borrowed.

Leeds, however, is a great city, and possesses a society which did a trade of $3,087,000 during the last six months, and the net profit for the half-year, after providing for all expenses, interest on capital, and depreciation of property, amounted to $445,000.

And now a third step in our forward movement is being taken by supplying houses to the members of stores; and this is being done by small stores as well as by the larger ones, even by so small a society as that at Shanklin, in the Isle of Wight, as well as by our great societies at Woolwich, Lincoln and Leeds. The Colchester Wholesale Society likewise has, through various stores, placed some $800,000 in the hands of co-operators for the purpose of building cottage property.

Raising Their Own Produce.

The co-operators take a broad view of their mission. Not satisfied with storekeeping and manufacturing, they buy farms and raise their own produce. I quote from a recent paper by Alfred Hood, a famous Single Taxer and co-operator of Brighton.

The first great step, taken by co-operation about fifty years ago, was the acquisition of freehold land for the purpose of building stores and factories, a step which has been taken by our great wholesale societies, by most of our successful stores, and by the various labor copartnership workshops. But, in addition to this first step, the Colchester Wholesale Society has taken a second step by the purchase of the Roden estate, which was bought in 1896 for the sum of $150,000. This estate consists of 741 acres of land, and comprises five separate farms, together with the buildings, residences, and timber thereon. And now there are eight cottages in course of construction for the workmen employed on the fruit farm, and it is estimated that these additions will cost, with tomato houses, about $25,000.

Then we find that the Colchester store has in its possession a farm of sixty-six acres; that the Banbury store has acquired sixty-seven acres of grass land, which they think of working themselves; that twelve years ago, the Royal Arsenal Society, at Woolwich, then numbering only some 4,000 members, took the bold step of purchasing in public auction fifty-two acres of agricultural land at the average price of $600 per acre. This land is now chiefly used to cultivate market garden produce; and, even already, Bostall Farm, though not one of the most profitable parts of this society's work, is regarded with pride and pleasure by its members.

Advantages of the Cash System.

The absolute cash system is an important economic reform, for one of the worst evils the people have to suffer, from the competitive system, is the panic and consequent depression and loss of work, due chiefly to inflation of credit. In this respect the co-operative movement has in two marked instances shown its ability to withstand extreme disturbances. When the American Civil War resulted in a cotton famine, there was an almost total stoppage of work in the Lancashire district, where the co-operators were the strongest. Because they were out of debt and had money in the store, they were able to emigrate to America or the Australian colonies, or live on scanty work. In the great coal strike of 1897, the fight was won by the Durham miners, because in their great co-operative stores they had money enough laid up to enable them to hold out for several months. No co-operative factory shuts down on account of dull trade. All have plenty of money and simply go on making up goods for the active season of the year. Having abundant capital, collectively and individually, and being engaged in making goods for their own use, they have a steady business, year in and year out.

Protection Against Adulteration.

To protect members against adulterated goods, the wholesale society keeps a complete laboratory, in which all doubtful foods are tested. In view of the recent testimony before the Congressional Food Commission, the value of this judicious care cannot be overestimated. It was found that spurious food products by the hundreds are daily sold as genuine and pure in all the cities of the country. Sausage, for instance, is sold in markets in various places, which contains fifty per cent. meat and fifty per cent. clay; jellies of all sorts are sold which are wholly made out of glucose and sulphuric acid, the fruit flavor being obtained from cores and peelings. Deleterious acids are used in many products sold as pure, and so rapidly is the practice growing that it is difficult to obtain, in a pure state, many things daily in consumption.

METHOD OF PROCEDURE.

The usual plan for starting a store is for a few people who understand and believe in co-operation for its morality as well as its economy, to get together, subscribe enough money to buy a small supply of goods, select their best man as storekeeper, retail the goods to themselves and the public at ruling market prices, and at the end of the quarter, after ascertaining the profit and allowing interest on the shares, divide the net profit on the purchases of each member. They sell to outsiders and give them half the regular rate of dividend. No credit is given, only honest goods are sold, there are no tricks of trade, there is no object in cheating themselves. Members are admitted on the payment of any sum they can spare, and the remainder of their subscription is paid either in weekly installments or by applying their dividends. Thus, any person can become a member and have the same benefits as his richer neighbor. Members who do not want to spend their dividends can leave them on deposit and draw interest, thus making the store their savings bank. The deposit capital is often as large as the share capital. Between the share capital, the surplus and the deposits there is ample means for starting factories and for investment in independent factories started by workmen. Co-operation is equally adapted to any kind of business, stores, factories, banks and farming. It rids business of its fraud and selfishness, and it economizes so largely that it draws customers away from the private stores.

Contrast the self-managed co-operative business of one-seventh of the population of Great Britain with this speech of Congressman Prince to the Illinois Manufacturers' Association:

I was somewhat impressed with the thought uttered by the president of this association to-night; $1,000,000,000 represented by this association; 200,000 men and women, perhaps, including both, working for the men interested in this association. On the ratio of population, 1,000,000 of people are receiving, directly or indirectly, their support from the members of this association.

Illinois, with its population in the neighborhood of 4,000,000; you gentlemen surrounding this board to-night, representing directly or indirectly one-quarter of the people of this great State of Illinois — in your hands you hold this immense sum of money. In your hands you hold the life, the happiness, the hope, the aspirations of 1,000,000 of your fellow beings. What a tremendous power for good or for evil! What a tremendous power to uplift mankind or to toss it down!

In your hands a million of men to-night are resting their hopes and the hopes of their children and the hopes of the state and of the nation.

"The Protest," by Ella Wheeler Wilcox, gives the sequel:

>   Said the great machine of iron and wood,
> "Lo! I am a creature of iron and wood,
>   But the criminal clutch of godless greed
>   Has made me a monster that scatters need
>   And want and hunger wherever I go.
>   I would lift men's burdens and lighten their woe.
>   I would give them leisure to laugh in the sun,
>   If owned by the Many — instead of the One.
>
> " If owned by the People, the whole wide earth
>   Should learn my purpose and know my worth,
>   I would close the chasm that yawns in our soil
>   'Twixt unearned riches and ill-paid toil.
>   No man should hunger, and no man labor
>   To fill the purse of an idle neighbor.
>   And each man should know when his work was done,
>   Were I shared by the Many — not owned by One.
>
> "I am forced by the few with their greed for gain
>   To forge for the many new fetters of pain.

> Yet this is my purpose, and ever will be,
> To set the slaves of the workshop free.
> God hasten the day when, overjoyed,
> That desperate host of the unemployed
> Shall hear my message and understand
> And hail me friend in an opulent land."

Origin and Growth of the Movement.

The movement had its inception in the moral enthusiasm of Christian Socialists, and the desire to secure the workingman's independence. The Pioneer Society was formed by twenty-eight workmen at Rochdale, in 1844. Robert Owen had already widely introduced the ideas of co-operation during the preceding twenty years, but he had too much faith in overcoming in short order the indifference, ignorance and selfishness of the people. He got hundreds of stores and some factories started, but being determined to eliminate the very idea of profit, everything was sold at cost and no capital was accumulated. Most of the associations fell to pieces, but the lessons taught by Owen had been well learned by many people. The Rochdale Pioneers reasoned that by selling at the ordinary prices and dispensing with much of the expense of retailing goods, they could accumulate capital and become personally independent and socially rich. The consumer should get the profits, there should be something set aside for a surplus, something for education, only honest goods should be sold, no credit should be asked or given, all people of whatever class should be admitted on the same footing, a member should have one vote regardless of his money, and the savings thus made should be used for self-employment. They were enthusiasts and believed they could initiate a new social order of fraternity and equality by applying the Golden Rule to every-day business. The Rochdale Store has been prosperous from the day it opened, it has returned millions of dollars to its members, and has now a total capital of nearly $2,000,000. It has large factories of its own, and large investments in other co-operative factories, and in the wholesale society.

The Rochdale experiment proved fascinating as well to the idealists as to the plodding laborer who wished to earn a dividend. The idea spread rapidly and has kept spreading with scarcely any interruption. The increase in membership and in business has averaged almost 10 per cent. annually, and I see nothing to prevent its absorbing the bulk of the English business within the next twenty or thirty years. The economies are so great and the principles so scientific that they must inevitably overcome the wasteful, haphazard and unscientific methods of private business.

It was not long after the start was made that Kingsley, Neale, Ludlow and Hughes, all leaders in the Christian Socialist revival, became closely allied with the movement. They lectured for it, helped shape the laws to fit it, wrote about it and preached the morals of it to the members and the world. Neale became the general secretary of the propaganda and conducted it with great zeal until his death, about ten years ago. Ludlow, who was a barrister, has been a zealous worker in the cause for over fifty years, became the registrar under the Friendly Societies Acts, and helped shape the legal and moral course of the movement. He now lives in a ripe and honored old age at 35 Upper Addison Gardens, Kensington, London. George Jacob Holyoake, the all-around reformer and writer, also joined the movement in its youth and is still one of its most active friends. He is the historian of the movement, having written the "History of the Rochdale Pioneers," the "Jubilee History of the Leeds Society," and the "History of Co-operation." He lives in Brighton, and his pen is as prolific as ever. To get a view of the many reforms that have come over England in this half century, read Holyoake's "Sixty Years of an Agitator's Life." His hardest fight was against the tax on information, twelve cents a copy on newspapers. For publishing his newspaper on unstamped paper he and his brother were arrested and fined, time after time throughout many years, until the government gave up in despair, and without any repeal of the law, it fell into disuse. Holyoake says he is indebted to the Crown in a sum of about half a million dollars for unpaid fines. That he still finds something to reform is shown by the following extract from a recent address he made at the Russian Embassy, in London, as spokesman for the Crusaders of Peace:

> I belong, your Excellency, to a numerous body of the industrial classes to whom reference has been made. I have been concerned with the co-operative movement from its beginning. (Hear, hear.) It now numbers fully a millon and a half of members who are organized, and none of them anywhere have hesitated to express the greatest gratification at the steps which have been taken, and which we have come here to acknowledge, in the promotion of peace. No doubt your Excellency has seen with the astonishment that we have seen it, the declaration made in our own Parliament that the cost to us of maintaining peace is so great that we are no longer able to make provision for the payment of our own debts. (Laughter, in which M. de Staal joined.) We are, therefore, glad of any prospect that these impositions, which are as great as any war could impose, may no longer oppress us. The profession of co-operators is thrift, their pursuit is economy, but when war breaks out then all the earnings are more or less swept away and a good many earners too, which we think might be avoided. Therefore we are very much concerned that war, which hitherto seemed absolutely inevitable, may be rendered subject to conditions which shall establish peace. Those for whom I speak, and whose views I know, are not skilled in compliment to Emperors, but they pay to His Majesty the Czar the highest compliment in their power — that of being grateful for the effort which he has made. (Hear, hear.) I join with them in order to assure you of the reality, the permanence, and the wide extent of appreciation of these efforts. (Hear, hear.)

Acts of Parliament have been from time to time passed so that now the co-operative societies can adopt their own rules, may have an unlimited capital, unlimited number of members, and yet limited individual liability. In several of the states of the Union, co-operative statutes have been passed.

ATTITUDE TOWARD EDUCATION.

Education has always been a leading feature of the co-operative movement. The subject was given prominent place in the articles of association of the first Rochdale co-operative society. What it meant in England fifty years ago, to stand for popular education, may be judged by a perusal of the public utterances of prominent men of the time on the subject. For instance, Dr. Bell, a clergyman and leading educator, somewhat favorably disposed toward an extension of education, wrote, at the time of the introduction of the Whitbroad bill:

> It is not proposed that the children of the poor be educated in an expensive manner, or even taught to write and cipher. * * * There is a risk of elevating, by an indiscriminate education, the minds of those doomed to the drudgery of daily labor above their condition, and thereby rendering them discontented and unhappy in their lot. It may suffice to teach the generality, on an economical plan, to read their Bible and understand the doctrines of our holy religion.

Mr. Davies Giddy, M. P., was not so favorably inclined, and spoke in the House of Commons as follows:

> However specious in theory the project might be, of giving education to the laboring classes of the poor, it would, in effect, be found to be prejudicial to their morals and their happiness; it would teach them to despise their lot in life, instead of making them good servants in agriculture, and other laborious employments to which their rank in society has destined them; instead of teaching them subordination, it would render them factious and refractory, as was evident in the manufacturing counties; it would enable them to read seditious pamphlets, vicious books, and publications against Christianity; it would render them insolent to their superiors; and, in a few years, the result would be that the Legislature would find it necessary to direct the strong arm of power towards them, and to furnish the executive magistrates with much more vigorous laws than were now in force.

The co-operators, however, recognizing that ignorance is the greatest drawback to the workingman, provided, in many of their

NATIONAL CASH REGISTER COMPANY, DAYTON, OHIO.
(Partly profit-sharing.)

HOMES OF THE WORKERS EMPLOYED BY THE NATIONAL CASH REGISTER COMPANY, DAYTON, OHIO.
(Profit-sharing.)

societies, for education. At Huddersfield, Rochdale and many other places they have libraries and night schools. No society is considered well equipped without a reading room. Several societies have valuable astronomical instruments. University extension courses are actively supported, and several Oxford scholarships are endowed in memory of departed leaders, such as Neale, Hughes and Mitchell. In disposing of the societies' profits, there are commonly items like these, which I take from one number of the "Co-operative News:" Carbrook Society (Sheffield), for education, $250; Droylsden; $465; Heckmondwike, $870; Nelson, $955 — each being for three months. In a recent address, before a co-operative body, Mr. J. T. Taylor, of Oldham, strongly urged upon societies the necessity of appropriating a portion of their profits to education, believing that it was the duty of societies to educate the young in the principles of the movement. He also suggested the holding of concerts and entertainments, and pointed out that those societies which did most for education were the most successful.

Propaganda for the co-operative cause is carried on constantly. This movement toward the education of the people costs upwards of $30,000 a year, and is supported by voluntary contributions.

Attitude Regarding the Land.

That they are sound on the land question, is shown by this extract from the Woolwich Society's journal:

> When once a co-operative society has purchased land in such a position as that in which it is bound to increase in value, it ought never to allow that land to pass into private hands; the freehold should remain the common property of all the members, present or future, and be administered for their common good. Once the freehold is parted with there can be no security that it will not fall into the hands of landlords, large or small, who will use it merely as a means of squeezing an unearned income out of their tenants, who will pile up shops and offices and factories upon our cottage sites, or let them degenerate

into crowded slums, or do anything else with the land which will bring an additional percentage upon their outlay.

At a conference of trade unionists, co-operators, and land reformers, recently held at Newcastle, among the resolutions passed was the following:

"That this conference urges all co-operative societies to recognize the duty devolving upon them of extending the principles of their movement to fresh fields, especially to (a) the erection of good houses for the people, such houses on no account to be resold, but retained as co-operative property, and let at rents just covering the cost of erection and charges for maintenance; (b) the application of co-operative capital to agriculture, in such a way as to enable the laborer to obtain access to the land on fair terms, with security of tenure, it being clearly understood that all land acquired for this purpose shall on no account be allowed to again enter the bondage of private ownership, but be held in trust, pending the complete ownership of the land by the whole community."

But in November last this energetic and enterprising society bought another estate of some 122 acres for over £40,000. And the feeling is very strong that this new estate should be laid out by the society, and cottages erected upon it by the society's own works department, so that the most comfortable and convenient type of dwellings may be secured, and the best possible materials used in their erection.

The Lincoln Society has two farms in full working order — the North Hykeham Farm, and the Gregg Hall Farm, both growing garden produce and pigs, and one even going in for wheat. The great society at Leeds, of course, has a farm department; but then they have got almost everything they require.

Is it not possible, by co-operation, to do even those things which seem to be beyond the power both of church and state? Why should not we, as co-operators, solve the modern social problem, and lead the people, by degrees, from the great cities back once again to the more humanizing forms of country life, tempered by the advantages of town without its many drawbacks?

Beyond mere financial success, however, look at the advantages of an intellectual and moral character which such "garden cities" might confer upon the people who would dwell in them. One can even imagine that such co-operative cities would become so attractive and beneficial that the old-fashioned cities would in time entirely cease to exist. One can even imagine, in no very distant future, that not only would every city be thus a co-operative society, but that the whole people would end in being one society, living each for all and all for each, none exploiting his neighbor, but all dwelling together in peace and good will, a brotherhood co-operating in every labor, and sharing in all the pleasures of a common life, the end of which would be the perfecting of human character.

The Movement Makes for Public Ownership.

While economy is an important factor in promoting business co-operation, it is by no means the only or the chief one. In the words of Mr. Lloyd, " The British co-operative movement is an established religion, for co-operation is not a method of business merely, but an ideal of conduct and a theory of human relations. Without cathedrals, creeds, ritual or priests, it has not only openly professed, but has successfully institutionalized the Golden Rule in business."

Manchester is the capital city of the co-operative world. Rochdale, a suburb of Manchester, was its birthplace, and Lancashire is its stronghold. Having discovered its ability to manage co-operative manufacturing and trading on a large scale, we need not wonder at the extent to which that city has increased its municipal activity. It has made a new departure by adding manufactories of soap, tallow, oil, glue and fertilizer to its garbage and sewer department. The city government now owns street car lines, gas, electric-light and water-works, ice factories, fifteen markets, baths, cemeteries, cheap lodging houses and public laundries, slaughter houses, technical schools, art galleries and workshops for the manufacture and repair of its vehicles, tools and implements. It has reclaimed a large swamp by depositing its street cleanings and the solid matter found in its sewerage and is now reclaiming another, by which it is expected to add several millions of dollars to the wealth of the corporation.

Glasgow is a close second to Manchester as a co-operative centre. It is the seat of the Scottish Wholesale Society, with its great system of factories, and it is also the world's foremost example in municipal ownership. Beginning with the deepening of the sluggish little river Clyde at a cost up to date of $100,000,000, a project which has converted Glasgow from an inland town to be the largest ship-building city of the world, and one of the largest ports, it has taken up one public utility after another, including the street car service. It gives more and better free services than any other large city, and the paid services yield it a profit so large that taxes are merely nominal.

The Glasgow "Chronicle" says:

> Since the Glasgow municipality began working the tramways five years ago the revenue has doubled, and is now nearly half a million a year. The lines have been extended during the period, but not in proportion to the increase of revenue. During the last twelve months the overhead electric traction has been put into operation on one route with notable economy in the working, and general satisfaction to the travelling public. Last year the corporation carried 118,775,000 passengers over its forty miles of lines. There was a gross profit of £121,118, and after payment of rents, interest on capital, sinking fund charges and depreciation, the sum of £9,000 was handed over to the common good fund of the city as mileage due, and a surplus remained of £53,772, which was carried over to the general reserve fund.

Evidently co-operation teaches the lesson of public ownership, convinces people that they can do their own business for their own equal benefit. In the forms of storekeeping, farmers' supply associations and people's banks, the movement is making rapid headway in all the European countries. The International Co-operative Congress which met first in 1895, then again in 1897 and 1898, brought representatives from about thirty different countries, with a constituency of several million members. Less has been done in the United States than in most of the great industrial countries, one of the reasons being that we are so large, the stores and factories are so scattered that it has been impracticable thus far to get them together in a union or federation. We do not know one another nor have we the influence on the general public nor the facilities for helping along the new beginners. There is a union and monthly publication with headquarters at 744 Massachusetts avenue, Cambridge, Mass., their activity being confined mainly to New England.

A MATTER OF EXPERIENCE, ADJUSTMENT AND GOOD FAITH.

The co-operative movement illustrates in a perfectly fair and conclusive way, the feasibility of public ownership of any kind of business. What the Leeds Society can do for 43,000 members, what the English and the Scottish Wholesale societies can do for a million and a half of members, what the people's banks of Austria and Germany can do for a million or more of agriculturists, all the people of any community, large or small, can do for themselves. It is only a matter of experience, adjustment and good faith. The trusts and department stores exhibit one side of cooperation, the utility and power of unified management and large operations, but having no permanent hold on their customers they are always in danger of other equally strong competitors. The advantages of operating on a large scale with plenty of capital and an established market are so great that ordinary competition cannot maintain itself against either the co-operators or the trusts.

It is not a communistic plan of business or life, it is not perfect either in its theory or its working, but it is a long stride ahead. It gives a chance for normal human feeling, it cultivates fellowship and it is going forward to equality and brotherhood. It has much of the same fraternal spirit in it that we have in our churches, clubs and associations. Through these we get many things more economically than we could otherwise do; we abandon our selfishness and we find in them the best association with our kind. In their business, in their numerous meetings, in their congresses and social functions, the co-operators are equals and brothers.

THE CO-OPERATIVE PRESS.

There are many publications representing the movement, among them the "Patron," of Olathe, Kan.; the "American Co-operative News," Cambridge, Mass.; the "Co-operative News," Manchester, England, a very able and extensively circulated weekly; the "Wheat-Sheaf," Manchester, representing the English Wholesale Society, and many weeklies of the retail societies. The best books on the subject are Holyoake's "History of Co-operation," Beatrice Potter-Webb's "Co-operative Movement," H. D. Lloyd's "Labor Copartnership" and the "Wholesale's

Annual." E. F. Adams, of the San Francisco "Chronicle," has just published the "Modern Farmer," 600 pages, largely devoted to co-operation.

Profit-Sharing.

Profit-sharing is a form of co-operation between proprietors with an established business and their employees. It consists in dividing a portion of the profit among the employees. Interest is charged on capital, and the remaining profit is divided by some fixed proportion between wages and interest or wages and capital. Splendid examples of this kind are the Godkin Company, Guise, France, a well-established and profitable foundry concern, employing about eleven hundred men, and the painting and decorating house of Leclaire & Co., Paris, France. In each of these the business has fully passed into the hands of the employees. They have been far more prosperous than those working under the ordinary competitive conditions. An educated self-interest leads to better work and less waste.

The company with which I am connected commenced profit-sharing in 1886, and has distributed dividends on wages amounting to about two-thirds of one year's pay, besides sick benefits. No change is made in the management, salaries or wages, but at the end of the year the profits in excess of 6 per cent. interest on capital are divided at the rate of 2 per cent. on wages for each 1 per cent. on capital. There are about 400 employees. In a magazine paper, Mr. N. P. Gilman, the historian of profit-sharing, says:

> On the 18th of December, 1892, exercises took place at Leclaire which deserve the most careful attention of the great body of employers of labor in this country, as well as of all students of practical social reform. An excursion train from St. Louis carried to Leclaire the city employees of the N. O. Nelson Company, and some forty invited guests. At the business meeting, held during the day, one of the employees was elected chairman, and Mr. Nelson gave his annual report, from which these sentences are taken:

"The annual meeting this year has been turned over to the employees of the company. The officers are here as your guests, with no duty on their hands except to enjoy themselves and announce the result of the year's business. The year just closed has been one of depression and low prices, especially the last half of the year. Construction of all classes has been neglected, owing to the scarcity of investment capital. Under the circumstances we deem it a matter of congratulation that the company is able to declare a dividend of 7 per cent. on wages and 14 per cent. on capital. This makes a total of 50 per cent. dividend on wages paid during the six years of profit-sharing. Those of you who have invested your dividends from the beginning in the stock of the company have up to date received just 72 per cent. on your wages, or $449.28 on $12 a week wages, $561.25 on $15 a week wages, and $1,080 on a $1,500 salary."

Later in the day, the employees, with their guests, assembled and passed the following most significant resolutions. They may have a precedent in the history of American labor movements, but I am not aware of the fact. Certainly they are the best expression yet given of the sober judgment of employees under profit-sharing; and the thoroughness with which they commend the system is striking. There has been no utterance from any body of working people in this country in recent years which more deserves to be pondered alike by employers of labor and by their employees than these resolutions so different in their tone from the fiery and indiscriminate denunciation of the employing class with which too many organizations have made us familiar. This is the full text:

"Inasmuch as society in general, and the wage-earning class in particular, have an interest in knowing the practical results achieved through any marked departure from ordinary business methods; and, inasmuch as the profit-sharing plan of manufacturing and merchandizing is a comparatively unknown thing in the United States, we, the employees of the N. O. Nelson Manufacturing Company, deem it proper to put upon record some expression of our views in relation thereto, based upon years of experience with it. Therefore, be it

"Resolved, That the system of profit-sharing constitutes, in our judgment, a long step toward that emancipation of labor for which wage-workers have for generations prayed, fought, and hoped, with but pitiful results.

"Resolved, That while, on its face, profit-sharing seems to take from the employer a part of his rightful share, and to give to the employee that which is in excess of his due, yet we are convinced that it does neither, but conduces to the betterment of both when both act with an honest conception of the responsibility which it imposes.

"Resolved, That in our judgment, profit-sharing means the application to the every-day business of the world of those governmental principles — independence, justice, and equality — for which men have fought through all ages; and that when these principles have been as firmly established between employer and employee as they have been between the government and the governed, there will be little occasion for apprehension concerning the future of our country or the character of its citizenship.

" Resolved, That in our opinion, profit-sharing, when generally adopted, will give to the broad-gauge, liberal capitalist the advantage over a selfish, narrow business rival which should be his by right, but which is denied him under the commercial system prevailing to-day; and that when this new departure becomes the rule, prosperity will come only to those who live fully up to its spirit.

" Resolved, That we recognize that profit-sharing puts new obligations upon labor as well as upon capital; that it emphasizes the fact that there is a moral as well as a mathematical element in the contract between the two; that to make success possible the wage-earner must enlist the earnestness, the vigilance, and the industry which too often are absent where there is no proprietary interest. But we confidently believe that these qualities will develop rapidly in the wage-earners of America under opportunity and education."

The Village of Leclaire.

In a more co-operative way, this company established the village of Leclaire, about eighteen miles from St. Louis, in 1890. It acquired a tract of 125 acres of beautifully situated land, upon which it has built a number of factories and established a village adjoining. This village is intended to be one of home-owners, not renters; it has no boss and no political organization. The intention is to provide out of the common fund earned by the joint effort of the management and employees, all the public and private facilities desirable in a community. It is laid out with winding roads, has well-made cinder streets, board sidewalks, plenty of trees, a greenhouse to supply flowers for the public grounds and for private yards; it has a school house and large lecture room, a baseball campus which is very much used, a bowling alley and billiard room. It has a course of lectures every winter, interspersed with spelling matches, musicales and dances. The residents all have flower and vegetable gardens on their own one-third of an acre and as much additional ground in the adjoining farm as they wish to cultivate.

There is a children's club of twenty-five, ranging from six to sixteen, who cultivate about three acres of garden, the proceeds of which are not to be divided, but used for joint purposes. A good library supplies the village, the adjoining city of Edwardsville, the neighboring farms, and also sends traveling libraries or book boxes into different states.

All of these public utilities are free to the world. There is no price for anything. The plan has worked most excellently, and the influence is evident on not only the residents but the neighbors of the larger town of Edwardsville. These neighbors do much of their driving and wheeling on our good roads, they come to our lectures and dances, they play ball on our grounds, they bring their visitors to see us, and in every respect show their appreciation of our high quality of public utilities. We sometimes facetiously say that we carry on this village on the Single-Tax theory, first, by turning the price of lots into public improvements; second, by providing for all the public services out of a single tax on the earnings of all. We are Socialists in the sense that we care more for social good than personal gain or personal advantage. We are pure Individualists in the sense that we do everything voluntarily. There is no compulsion either by law or by the influence of a boss. With my wife and daughter I live in a house that is a little larger and little finer than my neighbors', all of whom are mechanics, but we are neighbors in all respects. My daughter teaches in the school and has a reading club of the larger children, which meets weekly in our home. My married daughter, son-in-law, and grand-children also live in the village. All like it better than the city. It is clean, breezy, and all the surroundings are well kept. Several of the residents, plain, everyday workingmen, have as handsome yards as can usually be found in the suburbs occupied by the rich.

The Next Great Word is Association.

Co-operation is rapidly coming to take the place of competition in the form of public ownership and voluntary associations, but in the meantime the employers of other men, those who have charge of the active capital of the country, can relieve their consciences to some extent, lessen the strain of business and do some measure of justice, by adopting a profit-sharing plan and by using a goodly part of the income from the joint labor of the employees and themselves in making the conditions of living better for the workers and their families. It is simple enough to do, and there is a great deal of satisfaction in doing it.

Mazzini said the next great word was Association. We must associate for mutual good if we wish to avoid the destruction that self-seeking has brought upon all nations of the past, and if we wish to bring on the reign of the Golden Rule and Brotherhood.

Let us co-operate, let us stop fighting. There is enough for all if we but work moderately and share brotherly. Why must we quarrel and feed soldiers and policemen and jailers and lawyers? Why must we drudge to build unnecessary stores and factories and feed unnecessary managers and clerks? What we all ought to want is a chance to work moderately, live comfortably and have the full returns of our labor, with the privilege of sharing with our fellows in a generous way.

CHAPTER XI.

PROGRESS AND POLITICS.

We hear a great talk about the failure of our institutions as applied to cities, as if it were our incapacity to deal with masses of people and with the problems of city expansion that wrecked us. It is nothing of the sort. There is intellect and business capacity enough in the country to run the Chinese Empire like clockwork. Philosophers state broadly that our people "prefer to live in towns," and cite the rush to the cities during the last thirty years. The truth is that the exploitation of the continent could be done most conveniently by the assembling of business men in towns; and hence it is that the worst rings are found in the larger cities. But there are rings everywhere; and wherever you see one you will find a factory behind it. If the population had remained scattered, commerce would have pursued substantially the same course. We should have had the rings just the same. It is perfectly true that the wonderful and scientific concentration of business that we have seen in the last thirty years gave the chance for the wonderful and scientific concentration of its control over politics.—*John Jay Chapman: Causes and Consequences.*

CHAPTER XI.

PROGRESS AND POLITICS.

THE late political campaign in Toledo affords one of the most instructive lessons tending to show the real difficulty that confronts us in solving the problem of governing ourselves. In short, it is our bondage to commercialism.

So completely are we in servitude to the thing called business and its customs, that the stoutest heart well-nigh quails as one comes to see clearly the causes that chain the people in economic bondage.

The trouble is not, as is popularly believed, with the thing called "corrupt politics." The root of the whole matter lies in the business corruption that persistently injects itself into our politics, our religion and our life, often corrupting the very fountain of justice itself, so that to a very great extent the thing we call government has been controlled by capital — been bought and run for revenue. On this point Mr. John Jay Chapman says:

> At the very moment when the enthusiasm of the nation had been exhausted in a heroic war, which left the Republican party managers in charge of the ark of the covenant, the best intellect of the country was drawn from public affairs and devoted to trade. The name of king was never freighted with more power than the name of party in the United States. The change of motive power behind party organization from principle to money was silently effected during the thirty years which followed the war. There was a steady degradation in public life, a steady failure of character, a steady decline of decency. Only quite recently has the rule of money become complete, and there are reasons for believing that the climax is past.

The country finds in the recent independent movement in Toledo sound reason for believing that the people are at last tired of being governed by cash, and the toilers, at least, have taken a stand in favor of governing themselves. The enthusiastic thousands assembled at our meetings proved that the crack of the whip that places party above principle no longer strikes terror to the hearts of men who are born free and have come through that citadel of liberty, the free school. They understand that a degree of freedom that means nothing to a man but liberty to exist on a crust and live the life of a dog is not liberty in any just sense, and that to be contented with such conditions of life is treason to the republic wherein we are all equals before the law, and a blasphemy of Almighty God, who is the father of us all and who through His divine Son has said, " A new commandment I give you, that ye love one another even as I have loved you."

Business Methods and the Press.

This is the doctrine of equal opportunities for all and special privileges to none; and for interpreting these words to mean just what they say I was stigmatized throughout the campaign by all of the partisan press as a dangerous man.

The average party organ is perhaps the most instructive example of the corrupting influence of business methods to be found in our social system to-day. A professed distributor of intelligence, its news columns are distorted with falsehoods and cunningly devised statements intended to mislead; a professed teacher, the influence that directs its policy is worked from behind the scenes by a business house, a corporation or a self-seeking clique, and its editorials are freighted with sophistries justifying, under specious names, nearly every species of robbery and extortion. It must stand for the god of " Business Interests " at all hazards. The political machine is only the ignoble go-between.

The local party organs sought to make it appear that their antagonism was directed to me personally, but the people were not so easily gulled. It was the principles of human liberty that I stood for that the party organs feared. They tried to make an example of one who had the effrontery to stand for the rights of the common people against the rights of a political machine. A well-trained politician always puts the collar on when it is presented to him. My offense consisted in violating this sacred tradition, and so they found it convenient to ignore the fact that practically all labor, organized and unorganized, in Toledo had indorsed the principles for which I had stood in the mayor's office during the previous two years. There was little or no quarrel between the newspapers over political questions, but all three turned their guns on the Independent candidate.

Alarmed with the thought that through the Independent movement the people might find a larger degree of liberty, the partisan press forgot that there is " honor even among thieves," and, with shameless effrontery, slandered the fair name of the city, stating that it was run by gamblers and prostitutes; that during my term in office the number of saloons had increased from 600 to 840; that crime was increasing; that the police were inefficient, and intimating pretty strongly that I was in league with most of the disreputables.

These charges were all answered in the common-sense of every person acquainted with the facts; but specific answers were directed to each of the allegations. We showed from the books of the county auditor that the number of saloons in the city had been 589 in the December preceding my inauguration, and was 581 in December, 1898; we showed that open gambling had been suppressed, and further that crime had greatly decreased; that the police were vigilant and that we had as orderly a city of its size as could be found in America. An extract from an article prepared at this time from the records of the police department will doubtless be found interesting:

During the past ten years there were 42,450 persons arrested by the Toledo police, an average of 4,245 per year; during the year 1889 there were 3,950 arrests; during 1896 there were 4,938 arrests; during last year there were 3,432 arrests, 518 less than ten years ago, when the city was half its present size.

Look at a few of the figures of arrests for the class of misdemeanors involving violence, licentiousness and intrusion upon the rights of others for the years 1890 and 1898. Remember that Toledo has increased 92 per cent. in population in these eight years, and that the figures for 1890 should be approximately doubled to give the real ratio between the disorder of the first-named year and that of the last:

Charge.	1890.	1898.
Drunkenness	992	326
Disturbance	734	335
Drunk and disorderly	382	154
Abusing family	79	33
Resisting officer	43	12
Indecent exposure	35	3
Reckless driving	18	1
Insulting females	15	4
Shooting in city limits	6	2
Total	2,304	870

To keep up with this old-time record, Toledo should have had about 4,000 such violations of law and decency, instead of 870.

But, say the advocates of jail morality, this low record is due to police leniency; the police wink at violations.

Is this true? It is either an ignorant or a deliberate lie. One rarely sees a drunken man on the streets of Toledo. Still rarer is the sight of a disorderly drunken man. One never sees a case of police outrage on a citizen, and the spectacle of resistance to an officer is so uncommon that, perhaps, not twenty citizens of Toledo have witnessed it during the last two years.

This is the testimony of every common-sense individual, either residing in or visiting Toledo.

But there is another class of charges under which the number of arrests may serve as indications of the relative leniency or vigilance of the police. These are the three charges, suspicion, safe-keeping and suspicious person. The suspicious person is one who has committed a crime at some previous time, and is found in a locality or under particular circumstances where and when he ought not to be. The person "suspicioned" may possibly be connected with some crime or misdemeanor. The person taken in for "safe-keeping" may be any one of a number of things, and is worth holding a few days to await developments. There may be few among these who are liable to punishment, but lest no guilty man escape it is for the best interests of society that, when circumstances are unfavorable, these persons be gathered into the fold. With an honestly organized and sanely administered police force, an increase in the number of arrests on these charges is an indisputable evidence of police vigilance. The number of these arrests has grown from 537 in 1890, to 936 in 1898. Allowing for the increase in the population, the ratio is about the same. Allowing for the marvelous diminution in the volume of misdemeanors and crimes, the figures constitute an unanswerable argument in favor of the efficiency and watchfulness of the present police force.

I further answered specifically, lest some credulous persons might take silence for admission, that I did not know a half-dozen saloonkeepers in the city and that I had never, even by implication, entered into any agreement with any one for the purpose of "easing up" on the enforcement of any law or ordinance.

Did the attacks cease? Not at all. With never a mention of the *respectable thieves* who were seeking to get control of the city, the papers kept crying "Stop thief!" at the Independent movement. Their attacks increased in number, and in venom. The two most striking examples of partisan journalism kept whipping themselves into a fury as the days dwindled toward election, and the last issues were the most flagrant of all.

I do not believe that permanent injury can be done the cause of truth by such campaigns of wholesale lying and slander, though unquestionably much transient harm is done; there are many people who read only the partisan papers, and these are as hopelessly shut out from a knowledge of the truth as if they were in the heart of Africa.

Either Party, So It Stands for "Business."

From the time of my first introduction into public life, I have sought to fix the attention of the people upon the principles that determine government, on measures, not men. The subject of public ownership of a lighting plant came up last spring. Our contract expires at the end of the present year, and I asked the council to let the people vote on the question of owning our own plant, provided it could be had without a bond issue. I offered then, and do now, to provide a construction company that will complete a plant for us and take its pay in the saving that we make between what it is now costing us and what it will cost under municipal ownership. The board of aldermen, by a vote of eight to seven, refused to let the people vote on this reasonable proposition. There was no politics in this vote, for the majority was made up of four democrats and four republicans.

You see it is not corrupt politics that is troubling us; it is corrupt business, and business never disturbs the relation between the political parties. Said a business man, who testified before a Senate investigating committee: "It costs us a good deal for campaign expenses." "What political party do you usually contribute to?" was the next question. "In republican districts to the republicans, and in democratic to the democrats," was the reply.

The fact is that a legislative body to-day is like a raft in the middle of the ocean. It is attacked on all sides by men who desire special favors and are willing to pay for them. The shrewd agents of franchise-grabbing corporations take advantage of every weak point, and obstruct, by every technicality devised by law, any reform that would subtract from their employer's profits.

In the strong words of Prof. George D. Herron:

> Organized money menaces the integrity and perpetuity of every existing government. It is causing the peoples international to question, as never

before, the utility of government; they are beginning to distinguish between government and the nation, between legalism and law, between power and liberty.

From St. Petersburg to the plains of the Dakotas, toilers and producers are asking why they should toil to produce billions to support governments which are the instruments of the privileged classes to further exploit them. They are asking why they must support navies, armies and parasitic legislatures to protect them from each other, when they are in reality brothers and need no such protection. The idea of government as fraternal co-operation, as brotherhood, as friendship, is the living dynamite that is getting underneath the thrones of the Old World, and underneath the legislatures of our American money lords. * * * Any genuine religion must be a science of righteous politics,— a science of individual liberty. It is a Hegelian principle, as well as the substance of Hebrew social philosophy, that the political life of the nation is the final revelation of the moral worth and living power of religion. The real religious creed of the people, the unmistakable evidence of what they actually believe, is their politics.

The Senseless Clamor for a Business Administration.

Politics is not a matter of business alone; it concerns the home, and the intellectual and moral life of a city.

I do not think that people ordinarily mean what they say when they declare that they are in favor of a " business administration " of the affairs of a city, state or nation. They do not take in the meaning of the word in all of its modern significance. So far as I am able to interpret it without any particular reference to dictionary definitions, a " business administration " of affairs is such an administration as will get the " best bargain," is such an administration as will make profit — in short, is such an administration as will get something for nothing. I think it will be generally conceded that this is a fair statement of the case. To attain what is known as business success to-day, one must make profit, and I do not understand this to be any part of the purpose of organization known as government. We can imagine a government living wholly to itself. We talk freely of a government of the people, for and by the people, as Lincoln put it, though on account of the injection of the business idea into every conception of life we really have little understanding of what is meant by the words; but I think all will readily see that a government living within itself would have no place to which it could look for profit; and, therefore, in such a condition of affairs what we now understand as a business administration would be an impossibility, as there would be no one to make profit from. Indeed, I am of the opinion that the injection of the business idea into government is the cause of much of our social distress to-day. I do not see how what is known as a business training can help in preparing a man to serve as a public official. The whole idea of business is based upon the thought of individual success. Everything else must be subservient to that one idea. It is true we have, or think we have, a certain code of ethics governing our business transactions, our relations with one another, and this code we attempt to enforce by various forms of law, but our laws, our ethics and our morals are pretty generally suited to the prevailing idea of the necessity and importance of individual success. When I say success, all know what I mean. I need not define the word. We hear two men chatting in a hotel or on the street; they are talking of some one who has made a success; we know at once what the man has done; we have no need to ask; he has made money.

The most superficial student of municipal life will admit, I think, that it is no part of the legitimate work of a city to devote itself to money-making, and as money-making is the only purpose of a business life, is the sole reason for carrying on all of our manufactories, mills, workshops, stores, mines and commerce from top to bottom, is to make profit, make money, we see that a "business administration" is just the thing that we do not want in the affairs of a city.

THE PUBLIC AND THE PRIVATE MANAGER.

It is sometimes thoughtlessly said that the successful management of a city requires the same kind of ability that is required for the successful management of the affairs of a large private corporation. Nothing could be further from the truth. The very purpose of the existence of a large corporation is antagonistic to everything that is best in a lofty municipal ideal. The affairs of a municipality should be conducted in the interest of all of the people of that municipality, and the aim and ambition of every public official from top to bottom should be so to administer the responsibilities of his office as to contribute to the social welfare, to the well-being, to the comfort and happiness of all.

The mayor should have a broad — shall I say big? — conception of the responsibilities and privileges of his office. Truly *the interest of all* should be his constant study; how to direct, to lead, to guide the various departments of municipal life so as to bring them to co-operate, to pull together, for the benefit of the whole people; how to get such conceptions of liberty and freedom, of civic pride, of loyalty and patriotism before the people as to bring them to unite their efforts for the common good. This should be his constant study and care. Carrying out the thought suggested here, I have said to the Police Department in Toledo: "Your duty or the duty of a good police officer is to use your best endeavor to make it easy for the people to do right and hard for them to do wrong." A patrolman can often serve his city better by saving the city the necessity of arresting one of its citizens than by dragging him a culprit to prison, thus disgracing the man and degrading his family.

To arouse, to awaken, to stimulate the social conscience in the people, the sense of social dependence upon one another, to present anew, as often as possible, the old truth that "no man liveth to himself," that a successful administration of each of the various departments of the city depends upon the intelligent co-operation of every other department, and to inspire the public officials with the spirit of emulation and ambition to serve rather than the ignoble jealousy and strife that arise from the *boss* conception of government — these are the purposes that should inspire the chief executive of a city.

Let us contrast these ideals with the qualifications required for an ideal manager of a large money-making corporation. I do not think that our captains of industry, or, indeed, that any so-called successful business man, would agree that the qualifications I have enumerated as desirable in a mayor are at all essential to the successful management of a business corporation. Most will agree that a city should be managed in the interest of all of the people, all of the inhabitants. The corporation, on the other hand, operates the railroad or the factory not at all in the interest of all concerned, of the workers and patrons, but solely in the interest of the owners; the operatives or employees being mere instruments or cogs in the wheels of the machine that is run to make profit for the stockholders. Up to date it has not been considered, nor is it now, any part of the duties of a business manager of a large corporation to look after the welfare of the families and dependents of the employees and patrons. It is his business, as I have been told repeatedly by managers, to make dividends, and dividends are made out of people; and as the labor market is and always will be, under existing conditions, overstocked, the *interest of all*, which should be the whole concern of the mayor and of a city government, is no part whatever of the concern of the managers of a business corporation. In saying this I have no thought or intention of saying hard things of managers of business corporations. I am such a manager myself. I am simply stating a fact with reference to the purpose of business. It is carried on with the one idea of getting profit; and while a manager here and there may be inspired with humane and kindly motives, and incidentally, as far as he can, may look after the welfare of those under his charge, it is not, as I have said, any legitimate part of his work. The work of a profit-getting corporation is, therefore, distinctly different and distinctively sordid — it is using human beings for what can be made out of them — while the work of a public official is or should be spiritual and ennobling in the highest and best sense.

The real purpose of the work of the public official is so to administer as to contribute to the good of the whole community, and he should find his greatest recompense in the fact that service brings its own reward. The inspiration of the private manager is found alone in the cash compensation, and this is increased in proportion to his usefulness as a dividend-producing machine. This is the reason that, while to a certain extent, the same kind of skill may come in play either in administering public or private functions, we find that there is the thing called honor attached to positions of trust in public life that is hardly known with respect to private positions of apparently greater importance. The life of the private manager is without noble purpose; it is almost without inspiration. I think private officials in charge of large properties are very few who do not at times feel a sense of shame and ignominy; feel, indeed, that they themselves are slaves to a tyrannical and unholy system largely of their own creation, the one purpose of which is to use their cleverness to convert the talents of their fellow-men into profit for private owners; indeed, many private managers have told me as much as I have here stated, and more, and all over this country those may be found who are looking and longing for some way of escape from the industrial bondage of the system in which they are caught.

No Common Ground for Comparison.

There is no common ground for comparison between serving the public for the good of all and serving a private corporation for the good of the capitalist. This idea of making comparison between the management of the affairs of a city and the management of the affairs of a private corporation has led to much confusion, and to the failure to understand the difference between the two classes of service may be attributed many of the shortcomings of municipal administration. The individual seeking his own good or the private manager seeking the good of the few whom he serves according to the narrow conception of the day, pursues a line of study that is antagonistic to any growth or development calculated to fit him for the public service. With him it is individual salvation first, last and all of the time, and, if on special occasions he makes a demonstration of so-called patriotism or loyalty or love of country, as a good business man, his first thought should be to see how his demonstration or exhibition can be arranged so as to bring most certainly a substantial return in increased profits. If he consents to serve his fellow-men even temporarily, it is because he believes he will get a larger reward in return, and if he for one moment loses sight of this idea he is at once pronounced a failure as a business man and business manager.

A Summing-Up of the Advantages of a Business Administration.

The vigorous words of Dr. C. W. Wooldridge sum up the situation in an admirable way:

Business men's government! Who are the business men? Not the men who sow and plow and reap the harvests. Not the men who carve the wood, or forge the iron, or mine the ore, or tan the leather, nor the men who handle the lever that pulls the throttle of the engines that move the mighty machinery of our times; not even those who oversee and direct the workings of this machinery; all of these are hirelings, or slavish supplicants for a job. No refuge can save the hireling and slave from the danger of want and the fear of the grave.

But who are the business men? Not they who do any useful thing in all the world, that is labor, which they despise and turn over to hirelings. These are the business men: They who buy that for which they have no need in order to sell it again at a profit to those who must use it. They who, looking to their neighbor, and not to nature, for their sustenance have for the law of their being that they must take more than they give or perish, and forget that, in taking more than they give they require others to give more than they take, and perish by that same law.

They who hold cities in bondage and lay taxes upon their people for the privilege of using their own strength and their own skill, their own tools and their own materials before they build a schoolhouse, or pave a street, or dig a sewer, or do any manner of public work for their convenience or need — these are business men; and without business men's government they could not thus hold the energies of great cities subject to their nod and make them do, for their enrichment, one day's work per year for twenty years for every twenty days' work they do for themselves in any one year, collecting it from themselves in taxes, all for no service rendered, except to unlock for the occasion the fetters with which business men's government has fettered them.

They who bribe councils and legislatures to give them franchises to enrich themselves at the expense of the people for services which the people might better do for themselves at cost, but are, by business men's government forbidden — these too are business men, and it is through business men's government that they do these things.

They who have so shaped the financial system of the world that nothing may be bought or sold or exchanged, without paying tribute to those whose only service it is to paralyze the energies of mankind — these are business men, and by business men's government they have done this.

Jefferson declared that to secure to the people their rights to life, liberty and the pursuit of happiness, was the purpose for which governments were instituted among men, and that when government shall fail to accomplish that purpose it is the right and duty of the people to alter or abolish it; but business men's government is the antithesis of this; its purpose, in the language of its advocates, is to protect property and to enforce its prerogatives, and before this purpose the rights of man are as dust before the gale.

Jefferson thought and said that for the preservation of liberty a revolution about once in ten years was necessary. A very crude, unsafe and unsatisfactory way of accomplishing that end. But certainly it is true that through all history, all the efforts of business men's government have tended to the overthrow of liberty and the establishment of despotism.

From time to time men have risen in revolt against business men's government; these have been the epochs when patriotism has kindled the fires of revolution, when heroes have fought and died that freedom might live — heroes whose names, when success has crowned their efforts, have been handed down for the admiration and example of future generations; but where business men's government has been strong enough to crush them they have sunk as rebels and criminals into dishonored graves. At the time of the American Revolution nearly all the business men were tories, who would have hanged Jefferson and Washington if they could.

Business men's government is worse than war, pestilence and famine; for war, pestilence and famine are but a few of the evils which business men's government creates. Lest it might be thought that this statement is an exaggeration of rhetoric, let me refer to what Julian Hawthorne, only two years ago, wrote of the famine in India. You all remember the horrible pictures in the magazines at that time of men, women and children, with their skeleton arms, legs and hips, heads and necks, their staring ribs and their swollen abdomens, the seal of death upon them — 20,000,000 was Julian Hawthorne's estimate of the number of deaths which that famine would cause — but Julian Hawthorne, himself an adherent and supporter of business men's government, wrote to warn the hand of pity to send no food to the hungry and dying. "Send no grain to India," he said, "send money, for if you send grain it will disturb the course of trade. Every grain merchant in India will immediately lock up his stores, and unless you are prepared from the very outset to feed the whole 80,000,000 of people in the famine district, which is impossible, you will only make a bad matter worse. Send money; there is grain enough in India to feed all the hungry, but the starving cannot buy it." Thus he advised the world to try with money to satisfy the insatiable greed of the fat buniahs who had all the grain in India locked up in their stores, and could set what price they pleased on it, whom he described loading this precious grain on camels before the eyes of the dying, reduced by hunger to that extremity that they could neither stand nor speak, but only with hollow eyes watch the food as it was carried out of their sight, into regions where the famine was not quite so bitter, where there was something left that the buniahs could sell it for, before they had stripped the country clean and left its people like these, dying of hunger in their nakedness. "Send no grain, send money, lest you disturb the course of trade." If government had existed there for the purpose of protecting the lives of the people, even though the intelligence of the administration had been no higher than that of a new-born babe, they would have known that the thing to do was to seize every bushel of grain in India and distribute it in rations, and the pitying world would very gladly have made up any deficiency; but that would not have been business men's government. Business men's government prevailed there as it prevails here, and the idea and practice of business men's government is, never disturb the course of trade. Thus in India, where, to horrify the world, missionaries have held up the picture of the car of Juggernaut crushing the life out of a few fanatical devotees who have thrown themselves beneath the wheels. The course of trade crushes the life out of 20,000,000 in a single season, and the business world approves, and business men's government warns a pitying world not to interfere. And yet, among a people devoted to business, as the American people are, business men must govern, business men's government must prevail; and establish pure democracy and freedom as often as you may, with the certainty of the recurring seasons business men's governments will put despotism, degradation and death again on the throne. Nearly 2,000 years ago one to whom the world has ever since accorded divine honors, told business men that they made the place where they did business a den of robbers.

Property in excess of personal needs must lose its value — not be taken away from those who hold it, but lose its value because none shall be so poor that they need to buy the use of it. Government by and for the people must secure them in their right to life, liberty and happiness by helping those who need, to create for themselves the things they need.

Exploiting the People by Criminal Labor.

In many places in this country we can find that the business idea has gotten into the administration of public affairs to such an extent that city, county and prison managers are pointing to the fact that they "make money" out of their criminal classes; they point to this fact with pride, with no thought of a sense of shame that such a condition ought to induce. Just a few days ago I stood on the rear end of an observation car on a railway in the State of Texas; the train moved very slowly along through a group of seventy-five convicts of the state, who were employed in ballasting the track of this privately owned railroad. On either side of this track there were a number of guards, each armed with a Winchester and several revolvers hanging in his belt. As the train moved along I was within a few feet of the faces of many of these men; nearly all were young men, and as I looked upon them and thought, "These are American citizens," and then turned my eyes to the walking arsenal represented by the guard who stood over them, I could not but involuntarily exclaim, " In God's name, if this be civilization, what sort of a condition would we find where anarchy prevailed?" Upon inquiry I learned that these men are furnished by the State of Texas to work for private owners at forty cents a day. All will admit that with the present cost of living in these United States, it is impossible for a free man to live a decently human life and sustain a family on forty cents a day; but by this very act the State of Texas sets the pace, makes the wages of its free men. We have only to carry out this principle far enough until we shall have filled the place of every free laborer with a convict, for in doing the work with convict labor we leave no work to be done with free labor, and therefore make it impossible for a man to get employment until he first becomes a criminal. Yet so abjectly do we worship our system, so much are we given to mere idolatry of everything that we call American, that we blind ourselves to the defects of a plan of government that is surely destined to overthrow itself unless there shall be radical reform. The State of Texas is not unique in this infamy. The State of Ohio is doing the same thing, differing only in degree; our convicts are employed within prison walls to make private profit for private contractors, and the contractor pays a trifle more to the state for their service than is paid for the Texas convict. This evil is the outgrowth and direct result of our monstrous conception of the purposes of life in the thing we call business.

The notions about business success, with which we are saturated from our early youth, blind us to most of the possibilities of this life. Two modern business men were on shipboard when a big storm came up; there was great excitement and fear that the vessel would be wrecked. One of them came pacing down the deck in a great state of alarm, and his fellow-traveler, who was quietly smoking a cigar, inquired what was the matter. "Why, don't you hear? The captain says there is no hope, the ship must be lost!" Placing his thumb in the armholes of his vest, his friend calmy inquired, "What do we care? We don't own the ship."

Fellowship Instead of Business.

I am not trying to picture my fellow-man of the business world as a monster or as an unnatural human being; I am simply doing my best to portray him as he is, doing my best to present the facts as they are, fully believing that when people come to see clearly both the hideousness and hopelessness of our modern conceptions of business, they will only be too eager to turn from a system that is constantly degrading human life, and devote their talents to providing a plan that will exalt it. I think it will be a long step in advance when we can drop the word business out of its ordinary association with the administration of the affairs of a city, and instead of clamoring for a "business administration," ask for a scientific administration; an administration that will consider the rights of the weakest child in the city as being equally important with those of the greatest and wisest man. A scientific administration will be an administration of justice, and a just administration will take away from life in the city of to-day all of the hideous phases that make existence a curse and life an intolerable burden to thousands upon thousands of the American people. Indeed, it is due to our failure to govern justly that we are now brought face to face with questions of the greatest moment in our cities, not only affecting the life of the city and nation, but even leading thoughtful people to question whether the thing we call civilization itself is much longer to endure.

"Fellowship," says William Morris, "is life, and the lack of fellowship is death." Let me ask you to consider calmly for a moment what the average fortunate workingman (and by that I mean the man who has a job) knows about fellowship in any just sense? Take the case of thousands upon thousands who are working for $1 and $1.50 a day, and who, with the casual work they obtain, are only able with the most careful economy to meet the daily expenses of life. The man who comes home at night without ambition enough left within him to scrape the mortar off his shoes or from under his finger nails — what, I say, does such a man know of fellowship? And if he seeks fellowship in the only social centre that we provide for him, in the saloon, instead of seeking to make opportunities for men to live better lives, we exhaust our energy in fulminations against the saloon evil, in attempts to enact laws to coerce people into living righteous lives that we make impossible by a business system that makes the many continually mere objects to be plundered for the benefit of the cunning and clever few. Sometimes it almost seems to me as if the thing we call government had, in many respects, been deliberately planned in cold blood to plunder those who are unable to fight for themselves.

Something Better Wanted.

I have dwelt at length on this subject for the purpose of emphasizing that the thing above all which we do *not* want in connection with the affairs of a city is a business administration. It is no part of the legitimate work of a city, state or nation to make money, to convert men, women and little children into profit; but the business idea has seized upon us and so thoroughly blinded us to any spiritual conception of the purposes of life that we are doing this very thing daily and hourly in all of our cities. The business idea has brought us the infamy of the system of fines, through which in our police courts we extract from the poorest and most wretched of our citizens tribute to carry on the work of further despoiling them of their liberties. Hundreds and thousands of cases occur annually in this country where men and women are driven into pauperism and crime because they are denied the God-given right to work and they have no other resources. Denied the right to work, they are denied the right to beg, and for the mere asking for bread many an American citizen has been dragged a culprit to prison; the business idea carried further, he is fined $5 or $10 and costs and sent to the workhouse or prison to work at from forty to sixty cents a day, while his dependent family is driven into pauperism; and then the managers of our prisons, wholly unconscious of the part they are playing in the infamy, point with pride to the fact that the prison or workhouse has been self-sustaining or even has made money. The further we can keep the business idea away from the city government, the better it will be for the people. The purposes of business are directly opposed to the purposes of governmental administration, and it is because this new conception is taking hold upon our life that I feel optimistic in regard to our American cities. The true conception, that there can be no prosperity for some that does not mean opportunity for at least some prosperity for all, is taking hold upon our people, and in the cities particularly they are making a concerted movement looking toward a scientific administration for the good of all.

An Instance of Scientific Administration.

I had the pleasure of visiting the city of Boston last winter. In Mayor Quincy we find an official who regards his place as a means of enhancing the social welfare of the community, with no thought of building up individual prestige. Mayor Quincy is comparatively a young man, just forty, but he has shown a degree of wisdom and lofty purpose in connection with the administration of the municipality of Boston unparalleled, I think, in the experience of American cities. Evidently he has not surrendered to the business idea, for idealism and imagination form a large part of his programme. Though elected as a partisan, he has stood closely by the spirit of the civil service law, and is clearly of too large calibre as a man to be anxious about the loyalty of subordinates. The city of Boston has, perhaps, made greater advances in municipal Socialism than any American city. The iniquitous system of doing the public work of the city by contract to the lowest bidder has been abolished, and instead the work is done by the day-labor plan, with a minimum rate of $2 for a nine-hour day. The great city recognizes the fact that it is impossible for a man to be a good citizen unless he receives enough from his toil to enable him to live decently.

Mayor Quincy has led the people of Boston into a recognition of this truth of social obligation and responsibility, and during the last few years they have established free baths where nearly two million people last year obeyed the injunction to "wash and be clean." Boston also owns its own municipal printing plant and a municipal electric repair department. The city provides music for the parks in summer; provided, last summer, a week's outing for 14,000 children; gave a series of orchestral concerts at Music Hall during the winter, and made an appropriation of $2,500 for public lectures on topics of popular interest, the lectures to be delivered in various schoolhouses of the city.

Every act of this kind, as I have said before, is in direct opposition to the business idea, but it is in strict harmony with the awakening spirit of liberty — a spirit that is manifesting itself in the increasing discontent of the great masses with a conception of life so narrow that it provides a plan for only a small portion to live in comfort, and even these must live at the expense of the lives of their fellows. This sort of a programme will not do for Americans. Let us have a scientific administration rather than a business administration. The New Time is already here, and we are soon to see the day when business will be transformed — when the good of all, the welfare of the whole body politic shall be the inspiration that sings us to our work; when the sordid idea of administering and grinding, of turning every act of life into a profit-getting device shall have disappeared; when the motto of St. Simon, "From each according to his ability, to each according to his need," shall have supplanted the business maxim of, From each according to his necessity, to each according to his greed. This is the new conception, the new patriotism that is inspiring the heart of the waiting people with a new hope.

Non-Partisan Political Action.

One important essential to the establishment of free government under our system is the absolute destruction of party machines, and there is one way to accomplish this that is easily within the reach of workingmen of this country, and that is through entire independent political action.

The great political parties in this country have been without a moral issue for the last quarter of a century. A great hullabaloo has been raised every now and then over some question that has been dragged into prominence and which party leaders have made a great effort to prove was important, but the chief importance of most of the questions that have formed the issue between the parties has been their value as an agency to fool the people, to rally them to the call of party machines in order that they might be in a convenient position to be plundered.

We hear much about "loyalty to the administration;" the question of "imperialism and expansion" will be pushed to the front; it is even quite likely, as in the campaign of '96, there may be much florid excitement over the "money question," and there will probably be much pronounced "condemnation of trusts" in general terms, without any proposed remedy. But it is not a question of endorsing the administration, or what to do with the Philippines, or the question of our foreign relations that is disturbing the average workingman and farmer in the country to-day; it is, on the contrary, the question of what the future may have in store for *him*. The peculiar kind of money or what our monetary system may be, is of little interest to these. They know by bitter experience that from day to day it is a life and death struggle to get enough of any kind to keep soul and body together. The debt-ridden thousands of our people, and the other thousands who are too poor to be able to get into debt, are eagerly looking for a new social order that shall lift them out of the perpetual bondage in which their lives have sunk through the iniquities and crimes of our competitive social order.

The Two Old Parties Alike.

But no realization of this new state appears in the promises of the two great parties. They do not differ in their moral purposes. One is as bad as the other, and both are against the best interests of the greatest number. They are greedy for spoils and plunder. They do not care for social conditions. They do not seek to improve society. They foster nothing so much as place-getting. There is a constant evasion of real issues in the platforms and in the resolutions of public assemblages. No mention is made of the appalling condition of distress which exists among the masses in our cities. Not a word is said about the throngs of unemployed men and women, who are tramping the well-beaten road to beggary and crime. Everywhere in the public utterances of party leaders we hear a soothing and pleasant optimism that is wholly unsupported by the facts of our everyday life.

In partisan politics we have the worst expression of the evils of our competitive life. First, it is a " fight between partisans," who pretend to hate one another in order that they may make tools of the people. After the contest between the parties is decided, then the " fight " is carried on between the victors over the question of who are to have the post-office and revenue office, who are to have the other offices, and so the never-ending struggle goes on.

The basis of partisan politics is the machine. It is formed by, or in the interest of, those who want to " get something out of politics." Its engineers run it for one purpose only — and that is to win. No public need, no urgent problem of humanity, is permitted to interfere with this purpose: the spoilsmen must have the offices. Says James Bryce, in " The American Commonwealth " :

> The class of professional politicians was the first crop which the spoils system -- the system of using public offices as private plunder — bore. It is these spoilsmen who have depraved and distorted the mechanism of politics. It is they who pack the primaries and run the conventions, so as to destroy

the freedom of popular choice; it is they who contrive and execute the election frauds which disgrace some states and cities, repeating and ballot-stuffing, obstruction of the polls and fraudulent countings in * * *. The civil service is not in America, and cannot under the system of rotation become, a career. Place-hunting is the career; and an office is not a public trust, but a means of requiting party services, and also a source whence party funds may be raised for election purposes. * * * Politics has become a gainful profession, like stock-broking, the dry-goods trade, or the getting up of companies. Republicans and Democrats have certainly war cries, organizations, interests enlisted in their support. But those interests are in the main the interests of getting or keeping the patronage of the government.

A political machine is a joint-stock corporation run for the benefit of the directors or managers. Where is the business man that would take stock and pay good money for it and have any faith in a business corporation operated on such a basis? And yet all know that this is the truth. The dividends are the spoils; no spoils and no party. There is no difference between Hannaism, Crokerism and Plattism — they all mean bossism. Political bosses are uncrowned kings who have held dominion over our people, and the almighty dollar has been the political sceptre that has threatened the very citadel of our liberties.

The Boss System Doomed.

But these monarchs are to be dethroned; already their pedestals are tottering to a fall, and the destruction of this iniquitous system of enslaving the people through party bosses is to be brought about through independent political action. Through the Initiative and Referendum the people are to do their legislating; through the amendment of the bribery laws, punishing only the bribe-giver, we are to put an end to the rule of commercialism in politics; and through voting for "principle before party," through voting in our respective localities for men rather than for money and for measures even before men, the American people are to realize their emancipation.

The only way to prevent bossism is to cultivate the spirit of independence in every voter. As long as men say "My party, right or wrong," politics will be controlled by bosses. Even the small Socialist party which exists in a few cities is as much troubled by bossism as any other, because it lays more emphasis on adherence to party than on devotion to principle.

The independent vote is the factor that is always feared by the selfish business man and the politician; it is through independent action in our politics that we are to make progress.

The municipal election in Toledo is invaluable to the American people as an object lesson that the power is with them, that they are not dependent upon party bosses or party machines; that whenever and wherever the rule of money and corrupt men becomes odious, they have the power within themselves to throw it off.

Very little can be done by changing parties, or organizing new ones, until the common conception of life is elevated. So long as the "party" idea dominates us, and our chief endeavor is to get our men in and the other men out, every election will be a source of disappointment. As for an independent party, the history of the nation is crowded thick with such attempts. About forty such organizations have sprung into being, with a result of almost invariable failure. We must conceive of politics as the science of doing good through government, and then machine politics will become as extinct as chattel slavery. When men have so divorced themselves from party fealty that they are ready to ally themselves at any time in free associations, for the purpose of supporting a principle, just as the soldiers of a volunteer army enlist for a campaign, and on its conclusion are mustered out and go back into the general citizenship, unfettered by any chain — when we reach a voting citizenship such as this, any needed reform will be within our reach.

I have been criticized somewhat freely by members of the several reform parties for the attitude just outlined. They have not shaken my judgment, nor can they. To one of these I recently replied as follows:

TOLEDO, O., July 22, 1899.

MY DEAR FRIEND.— If you are a Christian, I think you will repudiate the idea of party in toto. I believe in *all* of the people, and in a programme or plan of government broad enough to involve the welfare of all. The very idea of party is in the interest of the few. The purpose of party machines is to capture the functions of government (the offices) and operate them for the benefit of the party, that is, so as to keep the machine intact; and no man can hold office and stay in a party who will not conduct his office in the interest of the party first. The only charge laid at my door by the Republicans was that I did not conduct my office in a way calculated to keep up the organization. Had I been in the Democratic party, they would have made the same criticism.

The fundamental principle that keeps party spirit alive is selfish; its intent is to succeed by shutting out from any possibility of success a large percentage of the people. The common people understand this, and have given up all hope of any relief to come through or from political parties. Relief must come through political action, but it must come in spite of, rather than because of, parties. No party ever did or ever can reform itself. The only hope of the people is in absolute independent political action, not always an independent movement, but independent voting. Voting for principle before party will destroy parties and save the people. We must organize, but it must be for educational rather than for party purposes. When the people become educated, when they understand that ours is a wrong social system, that the competitive system is a denial of brotherhood, is unchristian and unscientific, they will lay off the chains that bind them. The power is with the people, but they must be brought to see and understand that men are brothers and that they can never hope for peace through war (competition). I am happy to say that I believe competition has failed; that we are now in an era of combination (trusts), and that we are rapidly passing to co-operation, which will lead to brotherhood, the kingdom of heaven on earth.

Very sincerely yours,
S. M. JONES.

WHAT THE AGGRESSIVE NON-PARTISAN CAN DO.

It is, of course, unjust and unwise, to denounce and anathematize indiscriminately those who belong to either of the two parties. It is the general ignorance and indifference of the people which should be blamed, not the individuals alone who manage the party machinery. The rank and file of the two great parties must be reached and educated, and whatever method will soonest accomplish this, is the wisest method to adopt. Until the majority of voters have a clearer understanding of their duties as citizens and of the sanctity of the ballot, political parties, no matter what their names and principles may be, are bound to be ruled by place-hunters and schemers.

The party candidate should be made to place himself. Whenever a politician stands upon a public platform asking for your votes and influence, ask him to define his position on the real issues of our times. Ask him how he proposes to give work to the unemployed, and how he intends to prevent little children from working in factories. Ask him what he has done in favor of the eight-hour day and the abolition of the contract system. Ask him to declare his views on municipal ownership of electric light, telephones, gas and street railways. Compel him to state whether or not he upholds an industrial system which breeds the twin curses of competition and monopoly.

Don't let him escape the point by assuring you of his loyalty to the Stars and Stripes. Loyalty too often covers a multitude of sins. There is a sort of boisterous lip loyalty which is very conspicuous at election time; and there are plenty of politicians who are willing to get rich for their country's sake. Inquire into his record. If he has voted always for party, and never for principle, he is not worthy to receive an intelligent citizen's vote. If he can give no answer to your questions except to assure you he has always been faithful to his party, then he is a common heeler, and has no business to aspire to public office.

The disruption of the machine is a task that rests largely with the workers, for the business world is either passive in the face of its aggression, or, as is often the case, a sharer in its acts and its plunder. In the words of W. E. H. Lecky, in his "Democracy and Liberty,"—

> There is one thing which is worse than corruption. It is *acquiescence in corruption*. No feature of American life strikes a stranger so powerfully as the extraordinary indifference, partly cynicism and partly good nature, with which notorious frauds and notorious corruption in the sphere of politics are viewed by American public opinion.
>
> There is nothing, I think, altogether like this to be found in any other great country. It is something wholly different from the political torpor which is common in half-developed nations and corrupt despotisms, and it is curiously unlike the state of feeling which exists in the French republic. Flagrant instances of corruption have been disclosed in France since 1870, but French public opinion never fails promptly to resent and to punish them. In America, notorious profligacy in public life and in the administration of public funds seems to excite little more than a disdainful smile.

A striking confirmation of this judgment is to be found in the following words, credited by Prof. Andrew D. White, to a city business man:

> We have thought this thing over, and we find that it pays better to neglect our city affairs than to attend to them; that we can make more money in the time required for the full discharge of our political duties than the politicians can steal from us on account of our not discharging them.

Remedial Makeshifts Proffered.

Whatever our statesmen may think to the contrary, it is clear that the question of right social relations is the next great problem that must be solved by the American people. Public officials and would-be political leaders very much prefer to talk about the Philippines, about revenue and protection and increasing the standing army, but the poverty question cannot be kept down much longer.

We have all the race problems that we can attend to at home. The average American "white man's burden" is heavy enough, without putting any islands on top of the load. Before we start to export civilization, we should manufacture a better brand.

If a laborer's family were faint from lack of food, he would be a fool to go to the store and buy a package of fire-crackers and a dozen sky-rockets. And so, when millions of our useful workers are only a day's march from starvation, it seems like a foolish expenditure of money to vote hundreds of millions for a petty foreign war.

Hunger cannot be appeased with glory and military grandeur. Our first duty as a nation is to the people within our own borders, who find themselves to-day up against the stone wall of hard times. They are the taxpayers, the producers, the people without whom the republic could not exist. They are men and women altogether human, not chattels nor machines.

There is a conception among business men that tinkering with the tariff, or finance, will give us good government; but I am fully convinced that our trouble is only incidentally a trouble of either tariff or finance.

Neither high tariff nor free trade, neither free silver nor single gold standard, can bring us prosperity so long as this competitive struggle is allowed to continue, and so long as a few giants of wealth are permitted to monopolize the means of employment. Free trade means simply that our industrial battle is open to the world, and contestants in other countries may take a hand in it. Protection means only that the fight is limited to our own citizens, and no foreigner may take part without handicapping himself by the payment of a tax. But the unnatural fight goes on in either case. So far as the working people are concerned, protection does not protect them, and free trade does not make them free. The whole question of tariff or no tariff is a problem for employers only, and does not deserve the attention of the great bulk of our people who work for wages.

What does our "protection to American labor" amount to when our American laborers are denied even the right to work? How much "protection" did the miners of Hazleton receive?

The working people are not protected from hunger, or cold, or from cut-downs, or lock-outs, or exorbitant rents, or from any evil that poverty creates. The barring out of foreign competition simply leaves the market in the control of a few trusts, which are operated to enrich the handful of people inside of them and to impoverish the millions of people outside of them.

It is now a well-known fact that we can produce goods cheaper than Germany or England, and that America is steadily wresting from England the doubtful honor of being the "workshop of the world;" so that the politicians who promise to protect us from the "pauper labor of Europe" by a high tariff are either insincere or else have no conception of the present industrial situation. No raising or lowering or abolition of the tariff would have the slightest effect upon the condition of our wage-earners, and it is time for the whole tariff question to be ruled out of order.

As to our monetary system, the real question is not what sort of money to use, but how to get it properly distributed. The free coinage of silver would likely improve conditions for a short time, but only until our money-lords adjusted their methods of appropriation. No matter whether gold, silver, paper or clam shells is the currency, so long as business is a battle between the weak and the strong, the money will go to the strong. There is poverty in gold countries, and there is poverty in silver countries. There is poverty where there is high tariff, and there is poverty where there is free trade.

The Growing Unrest.

None of these makeshifts will do. The great commoner, Abraham Lincoln, said, "You can fool all the people some of the time, and some of the people all of the time, but you cannot fool all of the people all of the time," and the great masses of the people of this country are coming through that bulwark of our democracy, the public schools, and through their own bitter experience in gaining a livelihood, to such a degree of intelligence that they will not much longer submit to a system that is using them as mere instruments of profit for the benefit of the cunning few.

Every year the people are growing more impatient at the enormous burden of class legislation and unfair legal decisions which they have had to carry. Patience with politicians of the capitalistic stripe has ceased to be a virtue. The time is not far distant when the cause of humanity will become practical politics, when the principles of love and industrial freedom will become the inspiration of a great movement. Such a movement will sweep the country like a whirlwind and carry everything before it, creating a political revolution unequalled in American history. Whether it will take form as an old party reborn, cleansed, educated and inspired, or a new one created for a new purpose, is impossible to foresee. The name and genealogy of it are of little consequence,— the main thing is the work it will accomplish.

When Nansen, the explorer, found himself running short of food for his dogs in the Arctic regions, he killed the weakest dog and fed his flesh to the others. At first they refused to eat their fellow-comrade, but starvation soon brought them to it, and once they had tasted the meat they seemed to enjoy it better than other food; so with the strength they had gained by feeding in this way, they pulled the sledges until the supply was exhausted, and the knife was applied to another dog. Every thoughtful man knows that it is no great stretch of imagination to say that Nansen's policy with his dogs is being carried out in modern industry to-day. Men and women and even little children are being ground up into increased gain for the profit-gatherers in a hundred ways by legalized and respectablized means. But the American people are not going to stand and wait to be killed and eaten one by one like Nansen's dogs. As George D. Herron, the prophet of a better day, has well said:

"The sin that is destroying American souls is that of ignorance, apathy and indifference concerning the political and economic evils that are eating out the heart of the nation and making every man guilty of his brother's blood. The evangelist who really wants to save American souls from spiritual death and not get success for himself and approval for his doctrines, will set about arousing these souls against the national evils that darken and destroy."

Political Betterment and Public Ownership Linked Together.

The purification of politics and the public ownership of industries must and will go hand in hand. The complex and contradictory jumble of decisions which we call legislation and law will be reduced to order and simplicity by public ownership. Law will no longer be a tangled network which none but the rich can escape. When the conflict between capitalistic interests is ended, law will become simple enough to be taught in the public schools.

To quote from Rev. Charles H. Vail:

Industrial democracy would greatly simplify legislation. What is the nature of legislation to-day? If you examine our statute books you will find that nine-tenths of the legislation concerns private property, as represented by instruments of production. Look at the laws enacted at any session of our legislatures and you will note that they deal chiefly with private interests. Study the records of our courts and note how continually the railways figure in law suits. Now, compare the privately owned railways with the publicly owned post-office. The postal law is simple and concise, and we seldom hear of a law-suit connected with this service. We see by this comparison how public ownership would simplify government. The abolition of the private ownership in the instruments of production would remove all these laws from our records.

Private ownership of capital is not only the chief cause of legislation, but also of litigation. Abolish private capital and most of the litigation of the courts would disappear. Under socialism law-making would be reduced to a minimum. The chief cause of the endless laws under which we groan to-day is individualism,—the rule of private employers and private proprietors.

Great Forces Moving Upward.

There is a great evolutionary force in the world which overmasters the selfish schemes of cliques and individuals. The earth is rolling up into the sunlight of a better day, and no tiny threads of prejudice and greed can hold it down.

All we have to do is to co-operate with the divine spirit of progress. We merely have to tend the machinery, see that the fires are kept burning, the engine well oiled, keep a firm hand on the lever and a sharp look ahead. In spite of the swarm of politicians that cling to office, like barnacles to a ship, in spite of the noisy prominence in Congress and legislatures of incompetent bribe-takers, and in spite of the silence, and, too often, the apathy of honest men, this period of corruption and class rule is bound to terminate before the twentieth century is out of its cradle.

> We know that by and by a better day will come,
> When hate and strife shall die and each man own his home;
> When "mine" and "thine" are ours, and every law is good,
> And all are pure as flowers in one grand brotherhood.

No one can number and realize all the elevating and purifying influences that are aiding the growth of civilization to-day. Sympathy is everywhere sending out the green shoots of a new life; and we have a tenderer, more considerate feeling for the unfortunate and the poor. Even the songs of our theaters show a degree of sympathy and tenderness which a few centuries ago was not to be found in the hymns sung in the churches. We have societies for the prevention of cruelty to animals, and to children. We have fresh-air funds, and orphans' homes, and houses of refuge, and newsboys' clubs, and scores of societies for the amelioration of human evils and misfortunes. There never was a time when there was so much family affection, and so many homes that would be perfectly happy if the fear of poverty were but removed. Our whole system of teaching children, in the public and high schools, tends more and more to make them humane and bright-minded. Corporal punishment, both in the home and in the school, is, comparatively speaking, almost abolished. The harsh, rough school teachers of forty and fifty years ago, whose method of teaching was a word and a blow, have been superseded by gentle-mannered young ladies, who endeavor to rule their pupils by kindness.

Now, all life is one, whether in the home, school, shop or polling booth; and our piratical politics cannot escape the uplifting forces that are at work, any more than snowdrift can outlive the warmth of the summer sun. Private ownership of government is as certain to be abolished as private ownership of railroads.

THE REAL WEALTH OF A NATION.

"The wealth of a nation," said John Ruskin, "may be estimated by the number of happy souls that are employed in making useful things." This is the way we shall measure our wealth in the future; not by the number of millionaires and billionaires, plutocrats and aristocrats, but by the degree of equality of opportunity that we have made possible under our government, by the extent to which we have manifested our love for our fellow men by providing means for them to live in a manner becoming self-respecting citizens of a free republic. Said Whitman, the prophet of democracy:

> Come, I will make the continent indissoluble.
> I will make the most splendid race the sun ever shone upon;
> I will make divine magnetic lands,
>   With the love of comrades,
>   With the life-long love of comrades.
> I will plant companionship thick as trees along all the rivers of America,
>   and along the shores of the great lakes, and all over the prairies.
> I will make inseparable cities, with their arms about each other's necks,
>   By the love of comrades,
>   By the manly love of comrades.

I have an abiding faith in what Lincoln called "the common people." I think they are always right when they have an opportunity to express their honest convictions. They are often made the tools of designing and unscrupulous men, and for a time they may seemingly go off with "false gods," but in the long run, and the short run, too, for the matter of that, I believe that the great mass of the people are right; that the great majority of them are honest and their purposes are pure; and above all, they desire that justice shall be done in what they call government.

Who Are Really Dangerous Men.

It is not pleasant to be counted among the disreputable, to be classed as "a demagogue" and "a dangerous man," to feel that one is ostracised from those who call themselves the "best people;" and to me it is a great grief to feel that I am misunderstood by those whom I believe to be as earnest in the search for truth as I. But there is comfort in the reflection that men at whose feet I would count it an honor to sit have been called demagogues, and that in our own history the very brightest and best were so characterized; such, according to some, were Jefferson and Jackson and Lincoln and Wendell Phillips. The mild-mannered and gentle-spirited Sumner was clubbed in his seat in the United States Senate by the fiery Brooks, and William Lloyd Garrison, an absolute non-resistant (who, by the way, Lincoln said was the man who actually brought about the freedom of the slaves), was dragged at a rope's end through Boston's streets by a mob dressed in broadcloth. His statue now adorns Commonwealth avenue, where, the other day, I read on it this inscription:

"I will not excuse, I will not evade, I will not equivocate, I will not yield a single inch, and I will be heard."

Garrison was pleading for the black slaves, I am pleading for my fellow-men, doomed to a servitude no less galling, and I plead for such a degree of liberty as will grant to every man in this country the right to work and the right to live the life of a freeman. I ask nothing more than equal opportunities for all men, and I will be satisfied with nothing less.

To realize this better government, I believe we must rely wholly and solely upon the divine power of love, upon the spirit of pure patriotism so aroused in the human breast that it will not see the slightest wrong done to the weakest child in all of our glorious country.

To aid in bringing about conditions that will make these things possible and secure for the toilers who produce all and have so little, a more just share in the fruit of their labors, is the ambition, the inspiration, and shall be the purpose of the remaining years of my life.

Longfellow beautifully expresses my thought and position in these lines:

> I am strong
> In faith and hope and charity;
> For I have written the things I see,
> The things that have been and shall be,
> Conscious of right nor fearing wrong;
> Because I am in love with Love,
> And the sole thing I hate is Hate;
> For Hate is death, and Love is life,
> A peace and splendor from above;
> And Hate a never ending strife,
> A smoke, a blackness from the abyss,
> Where unclean serpents coil and hiss!
> Love is the Holy Ghost within,
> Hate the unpardonable sin!
> Who preaches otherwise than this
> Betrays his Master with a kiss!

CHAPTER XII.

THE GOLDEN RULE.

A man has a right to be employed. to be trusted, to be loved, to be revered. The power of love, as the basis of a state, has never been tried. We must not imagine that all things are lapsing into confusion, if every tender protestant be not compelled to bear his part in certain social conventions; nor doubt that roads can be built, letters carried, and the fruit of labor secured, when the government of force is at an end. * * * There are now men — if, indeed, I can speak in the plural number — more exactly, I will say, I have just been conversing with one man, to whom no weight of adverse experience will make it for a moment appear impossible that thousands of human beings might exercise towards each other the grandest and simplest sentiments, as well as a knot of friends or a pair of lovers.— *Emerson: Politics.*

CHAPTER XII.

THE GOLDEN RULE.

EDWIN MARKHAM, author of "The Man with the Hoe," heard his poem exquisitely read in a San Francisco church. The clergyman had persuaded Mr. Markham to be present and speak, the following being his remarks:

It is always difficult for me to speak to my fellows. It is difficult to say the right word. I am not any man's teacher; I am only a pupil; but there are times when a man is drawn by a power greater than himself. I have been asked to say a few words about "The Man with the Hoe," and my solution of that problem. The men who built the pyramids struggled with that problem. The men who are building San Francisco are struggling with it to-day. I have but one solution — that is the application of the Golden Rule. We have committed the Golden Rule to heart; now let us *commit it to life.* I believe the industrial question is a religious question. I believe everything that has to do with the welfare of men, in politics, in industry, is religious at the bottom; everything shows our relation to one another and our relation to the Father of Life. I believe Jesus of Nazareth is the Father, the Saviour of the human race. In His principles of justice, in His principles of brotherhood, we find the solution of these questions. Fraternity to me is the dearest of all words, and in that word is the hope of the human race.

In the above words we find the remedy for our social diseases. We have had the prescription for centuries, but we have only recently begun to think that we ought to get it filled and take the medicine. For thousands of years men have said: "Self-preservation is the first law of nature," forgetting that it is a still more important law of nature that you make yourself worth preserving.

We have been thoroughly committed to the idea that self-interest is the only real interest, very much of the teaching of the church itself having been to the effect that a man can do nothing more important than save himself, or his soul, as it is commonly put. We have nursed the idea with our mother's milk that to save ourselves — to succeed, as we call it — is an object worthy our best ambition and effort.

From a Christian and scientific standpoint, this assumption is false, mischievous and misleading.

In thousands of our homes, schools, colleges and churches, throughout all Christendom, to succeed means simply to get rich. Our children, our youth, are having their attention constantly directed toward men whose only claim to attention is the fact of their great acquisitiveness, and, in most cases, a wholesome disregard of the rights of weaker fellow-men and an utter ignorance of the application of the Golden Rule. The result of such teaching is a class of men entirely given over, from infancy to old age, to the pursuit of getting money. What for? In order that they may get more money and so on, ad infinitum, ad nauseam — a mania as unreasonable and irrational as that for opium, cocaine or alcohol.

The Rage for Making Money.

One hundred and thirty-five years ago Oliver Goldsmith wrote:

> Ill fares the land, to hastening ills a prey,
> Where wealth accumulates, and men decay.

During the last two years I have asked more than fifty rich men — men worth from one hundred thousand dollars to fifteen millions of dollars — this question, "What do you want to make money for?" Not in one single instance did it elicit an answer that would do credit to the intelligence of a ten-year-old boy.

One man replied: "Because I love my family." There were three in his family, and he was already worth half a million.

I suggested that one hundred thousand apiece was doing fairly well by them. Raising his hand and striking the table, he said, with a great oath: "If I could leave them one hundred million apiece I would do it."

Another man, said to be worth fifteen millions, replied: "What does anybody want to make money for? I never heard of such a question before!"

It is a spectacle to make men and angels weep. Able-bodied men, intellectual men, men capable of serving and loving their fellow-men, engaged in a fierce warfare — wherefor they know not. This is not the Golden Rule, but the rule of gold. To dethrone this monarch is the duty of every one who loves his country and his fellow-men.

Henry D. Lloyd says:

> The precept "Love thy neighbor as thyself," is not the phrase of a ritual of sentiment for the unapplied emotions of pious hours; it is the exact formula of the force to-day operating the greatest institutions man has established. It is as secular as sacred. Only by each neighbor giving the others every right of free thought, free movement, free representation which he demands for himself, * * * only thus is man establishing the community, the republic, which, with all its failings, is the highest because the realest application of the spirit of human brotherhood.
>
> Wonderful are the dividends of this investment! You are but one, and can give only yourself to America. You give free speech, and sixty-five millions of your countrymen will guard the freedom of your lips. Your single offer of your right arm puts the sheltering arms of sixty-five millions about you.
>
> Does business pay such profits? Wealth will remain a secret unguessed by business until it has reincorporated itself under the law which reckons as the property of each one, the total of all the possessions of all his neighbors.

The belief that this precept — to love your neighbor as yourself — is beyond the reach of common people, and is the prerogative of religious devotees, is, to my mind, a wicked and devilish heresy.

I do not believe the Founder of Christianity ever gave a single rule of life that He did not expect His followers to obey. I believe He meant that the mistress of a household should love the servant in the kitchen, not as a servant, but as a human being capable of loving, of feeling, of sympathizing. I believe that He expected his followers to be servants. I cannot understand why it should be thought strange in this nineteenth century of Christian history that a man should work for the good of others as well as for his own.

What plea, other than that of downright insanity, can excuse a man for devoting the energies of a lifetime merely to piling up wealth? Why should not a spirit of love and helpfulness inspire us to far nobler effort than the brutally selfish idea of toiling and scheming — even to the sacrifice of life itself — for the sake of having a larger pile of money than our neighbor across the street?

Putting the Golden Rule Into Practice.

About five years ago, a short article from the pen of Prof. Herron, on "The Philosophy of the Lord's Prayer," made a lasting impression on my mind. It begins something like this:

> Our Father, means that all men are brothers — the tramp is the brother of the railway president; the wild-hearted woman is the sister of the clergyman, and her shame is his, because she is his sister.

Such a comprehensive setting forth of man's relation to man, and of my relation to my fellow-man had never been presented to my mind, though I had been taught this prayer at my mother's knee and had been, for years, a regular attendant at church.

Reflecting upon these serious words and dwelling upon the utter hopelessness of our social situation, troubled beyond expression by the wrong of my fellow-men who toil with their hands, and the greater wrong of those denied the right to work, I resolved to make an effort to apply the Golden Rule as a rule of conduct. I determined to do something, yet I knew not what. But the important point had been reached — I was ready to begin, and the opportunity came, as it is sure to come to every one filled with a purpose to do instead of to wait. We had just started a manufacturing enterprise in Toledo — not on a large scale. For the first six months we employed fifteen or twenty men — not women nor children — able-bodied and full-grown men. We fixed wages, not on the basis of what others paid, or what hungry men would consent to work for, but on the basis of what was needed to enable men to live decently and to fit them and their families for citizenship in a free republic. We had social gatherings of various sorts for employers and employees and tried to disseminate a spirit of brotherliness. There was a disposition to shyness, for employers as a rule do not deal so with employees.

One day, in a spirit of desperation, I had the Golden Rule painted and nailed up on the wall of the factory as the only rule that should govern that factory. It is there to-day. We have not perfectly fulfilled the divine command, but it is our aim. We said to the men: " This rule is a double-acting rule; it works both ways; it means that you are to do your work as you would want us to do it, if you were in the office and we were in the shop."

You will ask how we can compete with those who pay smaller wages. We cannot fairly compete. What is left of the competitive system is wrong from top to bottom; a system that pits men against one another, as wild animals, is outrageous; it goes without saying that it is unchristian and unscientific.

We are able to carry on our business only because we have an advantage in a little patent that keeps the competitive wolf from our door. But even if we did not have this patent we should not be justified in employing child labor, or in paying starvation wages to men and women, degrading them below the level of citizenship in a republic. "But you must do it," you reply, "you must meet prices."

No, you must not. There is always one avenue left open to a self-respecting man — he can fail; and it seems to me we have reached the period in our history when men are wanted who are willing to fail for principle.

Competition is a failure — demonstrated by the fact that in the important industries of to-day we have no competition; it has been superseded by the trust, and the trust foreshadows the coming of our deliverance, which is finally to be found in the corporated brotherhood.

It is time that the church and the world learned that the utterances of Jesus are not platitudes, not sentimentalism, but statements of profound scientific principles, and that all we have to do to prove their efficiency, is to put them into practice.

The application of the Golden Rule to real life will shorten the hours of labor, divide up the work of the world, employ all of the workless and give those who are now employed for long, wearisome, heart-breaking hours, leisure for recreation, rest, study and improvement.

Sad Need of the Golden Rule in the Administration of Justice.

A look at the machinery of justice in our land to-day will lead one to think that the Golden Rule has never been heard of.

A jury, failing to agree in a certain city in this state, not long ago, tossed up a copper to determine whether the verdict should be acquittal or manslaughter. The prisoner was sentenced to twenty years in the penitentiary upon the turn of the coin; and, so intricate is the law, that, the fact becoming known, it took two years to set him at liberty.

In our police courts are daily enacted the tragedies of human life. In Toledo and in most cities of the land, we actually imprison men for being poor. We first deny them the right to work, and then if they fall into our police courts, we send them to prison for being poor.

Recently two young men were brought up in a certain police court for the crime of disturbance. One, the son of a rich father, paid his fine and walked away; the other, whose father had been unable to find employment for six months, went to the workhouse to work out his fine. Out upon such a system! If a man ought to be imprisoned at all, it is because his liberty is a menace to society. No amount of money or influence should give him that liberty. The prison population of Ohio has doubled within the last eleven years. Viewed in the light of the Golden Rule, the operation of our system is calculated to destroy, rather than to save, men.

It is time we should agree to try the programme of Jesus in real life.

How can we be contented with present conditions? Why should we be? We should not. If we are patriots, if we love our country, then we love our neighbors, and cannot silently consent to the unrighteousness of the social situation.

> Man is not Man as yet,
> Nor shall I deem his object served, his end
> Attained, his genuine strength put fairly forth,
> While only here and there a star dispels
> The darkness; here and there a towering mind
> O'erlooks its prostrate fellows; when the host
> Is out at once, to the despair of night,
> When all mankind alike is perfected,
> Equal in full-blown powers, then — not till then —
> I say, begins man's general infancy.

Worship of the God Success.

The favorite Americanism that "Nothing succeeds like success" should be paraphrased into the paradoxical statement that the most complete success is failure, and the most complete failure is perfect success.

We have been worshipping a false god; we have compassed the earth in searching for "groves and high places" where we may prostrate ourselves before the altar of this Moloch. It is the one word to-day that, more than any other, has commanded the universal worship of the nations. To achieve the mythical thing called success has been deemed a goal worthy of the highest and noblest ambition, and yet we must confess that it is a thing so mythical that hardly any two can be found who will agree upon a definition of it. All will agree that one who accumulates large sums of money is a "success," but all alike fail to agree upon how much money, how many dollars, how big a pile one must acquire before he can have placed upon his forehead this much-coveted crown. I am inclined to the opinion that there is no greater delusion in the world to-day than that of success; that there is no one cause responsible for so many disappointments, heartaches and heart-burnings as this dreadful delusion. From our very childhood we have been taught that success is a thing easily within our grasp if we have the necessary ambition, pluck, energy, nerve, push, etc. On the right hand and on the left there are pointed out to us striking examples of success in the persons of men and women who were poor boys and poor girls, who, by reason of their indomitable energy, pluck and luck — generally the latter — have achieved fortune and fame.

My mother used to teach me that it was a part of God's plan that a few should be rich and the many poor, that a few should be masters and the rest servants, and at a very early age I began to see it was more advantageous to be a master. So before the age of twenty I became an employer, and began to make slaves of a few of my fellow-men. I was enabled to eat my bread, not in the sweat of my face, but in the sweat of other men's faces, as every "successful" man must do in the present system.

With this heresy early implanted within our breasts, we start out into what is properly called life's battle. We are determined that, come what may, we are going to succeed, and so we enter into the game, the life-and-death struggle, that most of us very soon find out is after all a game of chance; for, were we not "blind leaders of the blind," a moment's reflection would bring us to see that so far as achieving what is called success is concerned we may with equal reason direct a young man or woman to the roulette wheel, to the faro bank, or to such a gambling scheme as was the Louisiana lottery in its palmiest days, as to hold out before either the hope of winning success in the fratricidal struggle for supremacy that is now going on throughout our Christian civilization.

Much has been said and written about the advantage that an education gives one in winning success. Not long ago I heard a prominent lawyer address a graduating class. In the course of his talk he said that "the advantage of a college education may be seen when we reflect that 53 per cent. of the political offices in the country, from the President on down through the cabinet officers, heads of departments, Senators, Congressmen, down to Governors of states, are held by college graduates," and, taking this as his text, he urged upon the young men the importance of securing a college education at any cost. Now, let us see what there is of real encouragement in this lawyer's statement for the average young man of to-day. More than half of the "good jobs" in political life are held by college graduates; quite a pleasing prospect to the young man with his diploma in his hand, indeed, but when we take into account that a college education to-day is almost exclusively the prerogative of the well-to-do and especially the rich, and that but 2 per cent. of all the men in the country ever saw the inside of a college, the prospect is indeed a discouraging one for the masses of the people. All right for the select classes, I admit, but when the welfare of all the people is considered, the prospect of success, so-called, in this field is truly most discouraging.

But I am talking about the failure of success, and I call pointed attention to these statistics in order to show that even the so-called success or supremacy of a few men in political life must be purchased at the cost of the failure of the many of their brethren. We seem to have an unfortunate and deplorable misunderstanding of the purpose of life. God never placed a human being in this world without having a purpose in doing it. That purpose never was that he should find the thing called success through compassing the failure of his fellow-men. We are all His children, entitled to share alike in His bounty and care, and only as conditions are such that they will allow us all to share alike in His bounty and the prosperity arising from it,—only with such conditions, I say, can God by any possibility look with pleasure upon the children of this earth. But the popular measure of success to-day, as I have already said, is money, and I think all of us alike, in church and out, Christian, pagan, heathen, Jew, pretty generally accept the possession of money as evidence of success, with no questions asked as to how it has been acquired.

What Jesus Thought of Success.

Is it not a little strange that Christians should so easily fall into this delusion, in the face of the plain statement of Jesus in regard to this poison? "A man's life consisteth not in the abundance of the things which he possesseth." "A man's life is more than food and raiment." "No man can serve God and Mammon," which means money of course. "What shall a man give in exchange for his life?" The world is filled with men to-day who are willing to give their life in exchange for money. "How hardly shall they that have riches (success) enter into the kingdom of heaven." "It is easier for a camel to go through the eye of a needle than for a rich (successful) man to enter into the kingdom of heaven." Finally, "What shall it profit a man if he gain the whole world and lose his life or himself be a castaway?"

Here we have the most unqualified declaration of the failure of success from the lips of our Lord himself, from the lips of the loving, tender-hearted Jesus, who was moved with compassion when He saw the multitude that were like "sheep without a shepherd;" whose tender, loving heart was touched with sympathy for the leprous, for the blind, the infirm, the lowly, the poor, the depressed, who were His daily companions. How thoroughly do the standards of Jesus cast down the idols of to-day! The successful man, the rich man, whom we ignorantly worship, the leading citizen, the best people and the higher classes — all of this phraseology is pure blasphemy when considered in the light of the teachings of Jesus, whose broad sympathies reached out for all of the people. What condemnation do His words visit upon our measure of success to-day as we contemplate the horrors of modern industry, as we contemplate our men and women riding in costly equipages, bedecked with diamonds and jewels and royal apparel, purchased at the price of the destruction of the lives of little children and underpaid men and women in sweat-shops, factories and stores, and this wealth we are exhorted to " use for God's glory." We make much ado about the generosity of the rich man who gives a dole to feed the poor, when by the operation of the clever machine called business, he wrings from the same classes dollars in return for his doles.

Service for Service the Just Recompense.

The Golden Rule in its last analysis requires one to do as he would be done by, i. e., render service for service. This is impossible in the present social order, and consequently a strictly Christian life, according to the life and teachings of Jesus, is incompatible with what is known as "success" in business. No man can succeed in business to-day and be Christian. He may be a very good man, a very pious and religious man, but Christian, according to the life and teachings of Jesus, no. Can you imagine that Jesus would be content to have, while others have not; to abound while others want; to sit in an office and make money; draw dividends, clip coupons, etc., while all around people were standing in want and every imaginable condition of distress, who were denied the right to work in order to extricate themselves from their dilemma? I think not.

According to my understanding, there is no room for profit-making in the ethics of Christianity. I cannot imagine Jesus as a "successful business man" or financier any more than I can imagine him a successful general, leading an army into battle, and letting the warm life-blood of his brethren crimson the ground.

No man would willingly cheat himself, and the teaching of Christ is that every man should love his neighbor as himself. We are to act as if every man and woman was a partner of ours,— as if a wrong done to any one was a wrong done to the national firm.

Oh, that the standards of the simple Nazarene might be our standards! Oh, that we were ready and willing to apply the scientific gospel of overcoming evil with good to real life, rather than merely to exhaust ourselves in worship of the rich man, in merely attending the "means of grace," and simply saying nice things about God. The most pathetic utterance recorded as coming from our Lord, save His last expiring cry upon the Cross, it seems to me is this one: "Why call ye me Lord, Lord, and do not the things that I say?" The gospel plan, the plan of Jesus, contemplated nothing less than the success of society, the success of all, for in any proper sense there is no other success. That city, that state, or that country, can only be said to be really rich in which all have something, in which all have some measure of real success. In the ideal society, the little gathering of early Christians, of which we have a record in the fourth chapter of Acts, we are told that they "had all things in common, neither was there any among them that lacked, for as many as were possessors of lands and houses sold them and brought the price of the things that were sold and laid them down at the apostle's feet, and distribution was made to every man according as he had need."

Evidently the money-making craze was not a part of the training of the early Christians. According to the measure of to-day, this little company would hardly be able to produce a successful man, but if we were governed by the simple rules of justice that inspired the lives of these saints, we should have no problem of the starving miners in Ohio to-day. Our successful coal operators may point to the failure of the starving miners as the legitimate corollary of their success.

Pitted Against One Another Like Wild Animals.

I am not arraigning individuals; I am arraigning a system that is as unchristian as it is unscientific, in which men are pitted against one another as wild animals in the fierce warfare for supremacy, and in which we point to the strongest man and most unscrupulous man as our model of success. It is vain that a man with a streak of tenderness in his bosom shall try to apologize for this iniquitous system by gifts to churches and universities or by dealing liberally with his employees. All such efforts, while inspired by worthy motives, no doubt, are at best but mere apologies for a system that is inherently wrong, and that is as certainly doomed to failure as is a system for playing faro or roulette. The fact that we have thousands of people in the great State of

Ohio annually brought to the verge of starvation ought to bring the blush of shame to the cheek of every honest man, and yet this is a periodical curse that has happened before, and it will happen again; it will be so next year and the next and perhaps oftener than annually, while this fratricidal strife continues.

Men must come to realize that this program of Jesus is the only program, that salvation can be found only in the recognition of the imperishable fact of Universal Brotherhood; and no matter what thin gauze of corporation or trust or monopoly may hide it from our eyes, the sacrifice of life that is going on to make our profits, all of the ill-gotten gains that are wrung from the toil and tears of underpaid men and women, and the avalanche of failures in the business world that continually confronts us (according to some statistics 95 per cent. of all who ever engage in business) are a most comprehensive and sweeping indictment of our whole cut-throat system.

Referring again to the periodical trouble of the coal miners. One of the most distinguished, as well as most thoughtful and most loving of the Christian teachers of this state, wrote me recently in regard to this subject: "The condition of the coal miners is truly deplorable, and I can see no possible solution of the question except that the state shall take possession of all of the mines and operate them for the benefit of all of the people." Here the successful man has made failure most complete and dismal. The coal miners of the country are now, and have been for some years, living in a state of degradation that can only properly be called serfdom; their freedom is a mockery and their liberty is liberty only in name.

It is not the fault of the captains of industry that their success is purchased at the price of the failure of so many, but it is rather due to a system in which there is no possibility of any other result than failure colossal for every instance of success infinitesimal.

What the Success of a Few Means.

"It is because of monopolies which we permit and create and the advantage which we give to one man over another that some are tramps and some are millionaires," said Henry George. These words serve as perfectly as any I have ever heard to reveal the the iniquity of our whole selfish system. As I have said before, I do not arraign particular individuals or classes. We are "all in the swim," all relatively guilty, for the system is made up and lives by the consent of society, and we are the units that make up this aggregate whole that we call society.

It is only when we look at a subject in the aggregate that we are able to see what a colossal failure the success of a few of us has really wrought. Dr. Spahr's tables tell us that one-half of the families of the nation own practically nothing, and I think if you look about you, think of your situation and that of your neighbors with whom you are intimate, you can easily understand this is not an over-statement. One-eighth of the families own seven-eighths of the wealth, and 1 per cent. of them own 59 per cent. of the wealth.

With this outlook before you, young men; with discrimination everywhere in favor of the privileged classes; with the necessity upon you who are poor of doing what the farmer and wage-earner to-day must do, that is, sell your product in a competitive market and buy to a very large extent in a monopolized market; with such tremendous competition for a "job" that more than a thousand applications are on file in a wholesale house in this city employing only about fifty men, and where only about a half-dozen changes occur during the year; with the battle for place and the right to live becoming fiercer and fiercer, sharper and sharper, year by year, by reason of the development of machinery, and of the means of transportation and the perfection of the instruments of production; with all of the benefit of the marvelous improvements of the century captured and enjoyed by the employing classes — with these conditions before you, the prospect of finding the kind of success that may be more properly called failure is certainly not alluring, is certainly not such as to draw to the game any who have clear ideas of the purpose of life, any who understand that we are not put here for the purpose of exploiting one another, or exhausting ourselves in ceaseless energy to try to make profit at the expense of the comforts of our fellow-men.

Two Futile Agencies for Reform.

"It is selfishness up and selfishness down," said Miss Addams to me recently, and to my mind, selfishness is the sin and despair of our age to-day. "Man must be born again," it was said. We have lulled ourselves in fancied security to believe that this had reference to an indefinable, spiritual, mysterious transformation that, so far as my own personal experience went until the awakening of the social conscience within me, was wholly a nondescript, meaningless thing. I now believe that to be born again means to be teetotally made over, with other purposes, other hopes, other aspirations and ambition; ambition to serve others only instead of self; for the teaching of Jesus shows, if it shows anything, that only in the service of others can our own intelligently selfish good be found. "If any man would be chiefest among you, let him be the servant of all," or as one who serves. There are the conditions, there the prescription. Do you want to succeed? Do you want to know success that shall not be failure? Then take this prescription, apply it to your life, bid farewell forever to the money-making craze as a thing that has any part, lot, or place in true success; bid farewell forever to the delusion and snare that with money you could do great good.

Reflections like these have led me to see that we have been relying upon two agencies to do good that are both futile, and neither of which Jesus ever employed at all. These agencies are first money, and second physical force in one way or another. Did you ever think that Jesus never used either of these? As for money, He never used it " to do good," for He tells us that He "had not where to lay his head." Equally did he shun the use of force. Now, please do not quote that one instance, the " whip of small cords." I think that poor, lone instance has been badly overworked, when we reflect on the great weight of testimony against it. Jesus recognized no power of force as a constructive agency other than that of love, and His whole life was a protest against the exercise of physical force upon our weaker brethren. If there ever was an occasion in the world's history when the use of physical force was justified, it was when Peter drew his sword and cut off the ear of the servant of the high priest; for surely sword never was drawn in a more worthy cause than in the defense of a loved friend, and yet the loving Jesus said " Put back thy sword in its sheath, for they that take the sword shall perish by the sword." If we are to credit His written word He might have resorted to superior force to overcome His enemies, for He told His disciples that He could summon " more than twelve legions of angels " to His relief. But He quietly submitted to arrest, conviction and execution, all the time knowing that He was guilty of no crime.

Yet here we are, 1,900 years after, still denying the power of love, and killing people " for the sake of humanity." I am with Franklin, Garrison, Tolstoi and Christ on the question of war. I don't believe there ever was a good war or a bad peace.

America the Workman's " Paradise Lost."

"America is the workman's ' Paradise Lost,' " said Herbert N. Casson, and think of the pathos of his description: " Our carpenters build magnificent mansions with pillared hall and mosaic floor, and as soon as their work is done, they pick up their tools and leave and never come there any more. They build carriages and electric railway cars, and walk thousands of miles daily in our streets with their dinner buckets in their hands. Our miners dig gold and die poor; they delve in treacherous coal mines and lack fuel in December." And to my personal knowledge, some of our oil-well drillers, who, with their hands, have uncovered millions of barrels of oil, were in such destitution last winter, through the depression in that industry, that they were unable to buy a lampful of the oil their hands had produced, and so they sat in darkness. This misery, this despair, this wretchedness and disappointment of the many is the source from which the success of failure is so often obtained. It is idle and useless for us to rail against millionaires, monopolists and capitalists while we ourselves have within us the ambition or desire to take their places.

The Tangle Wherein We Are All Caught.

It is equally idle for us to rail against special evils, as the saloon, the gambling den, the brothel, and charge these institutions with our misery and wretchedness. Thousands of men and women can be found in every city who look like squeezed oranges, who are leading miserable, wretched, pinched, half-starved lives, who never had any direct connection with any of these institutions.

But the state and the successful and highly respectable merchant have connection with them, and thrive by that connection. In my city we draw upon the saloon for every dollar that we have in the public fund for the relief of the poor. Other city governments fatten their revenues from them. Our leading bankers do not hesitate to take the deposit of the saloon-keepers, our manufacturers supply them with bars and ice-boxes and all the paraphernalia that go to equip their places, for the sake of the poison of profit, which is something for nothing; our jewellers will gladly supply them with costly jewels, the money merely passing from the hand of the drinker through the hand of the saloon-keeper to the merchant. And so in a thousand ways we are in a hopeless tangle with wrong, revealing clearly the utter hopelessness of a reform that proposes to reform only a part. As Isaiah says, " the whole man is sick from the crown of the head to the sole of the feet," and our attempt to cure the evil by the application of physical force to one part, is like applying salve to one of the scabs of a man's body who is dying with the disease of smallpox. These popular evils are merely the scab; the disease is found in our Christless social system, our denial of brotherhood with these men and women; for once we have admitted that relation, we shall apply the same remedy to them to heal their disease that we should apply to our own flesh and blood; not physical force, not vituperation and abuse, but the healing power of the helpful hand and loving heart, of the open door to some other avenue for a livelihood.

The foregoing would be a discouraging picture, indeed, were I not able to present to you the other side, the side in which there is room for all, in which there is hope for all, and reward for all. I point you to the one possible phase in life in which you may hope to win a real success, that is, the life of self-renunciation, a life in which you shall give yourselves up with a surrender as complete as was that of Jesus for the good of all other lives.

All Life Is One.

Let us remember that all life is one, and let us dismiss from our minds forever the horrible blasphemy of the class idea. There is no man or woman, there is no human being on this earth to-day that has not in him something that is good. Emerson says:

Nothing shall warp me from the belief that every man is a lover of truth. There is no pure lie, no pure malignity in nature. The entertainment of the proposition of depravity is the last profligacy and profanation. There is no skepticism, no atheism but that. Could it be received into common belief, suicide would unpeople the planet. It has had a name to live in some dogmatic theology, but each man's innocence and his real liking for his neighbor has kept it a dead letter.

Let us go forth with larger hopes because we have nobler purposes; let us set ourselves to the task of making practical these things that we have looked upon as ideal; let us give up the notion that the world is irredeemably bad, that we are to regard the Bible merely as a lamp to our feet and a light to our path out of the world into a heaven in some future world; let us, on the contrary, find in it a clear and definite exposition of principles by the application of which this world may be transformed into heaven. It is impossible to look out upon life from the standpoint of one who believes in its sacredness and glory, and teach the dishonorable doctrine that this world is under the dominion of the Evil One. However difficult to break away from old associates and proclaim the falsity of what once seemed true, there is no choice left to those who realize what a barrier in the way of true progress this perverted sentiment has been and must ever be. It has been made the bulwark of social injustice of every kind, and from social injustice proceed conditions which produce and perpetuate vice and crime. "Let us stand fast in the liberty wherewith Christ has made us free." Let us ourselves become Christs, willing servants and ready to take up the cross of self-sacrifice and bear our part in the salvation of a world that he died to redeem.

Let us remember that, measured according to the measure of to-day, the life of Christ was the conspicuous failure of all history. Let us look about and behold " the fields white for the harvest." Let us consecrate our lives, not to the idea of getting profit out of our fellow-men, but to the idea of service for the good of all of our fellows, knowing that in no other direction may we ever hope to realize the success that knows no failure, and that in every avenue to which we may turn our attention we are certain that we shall find but one result, and that will be the realization that the success we had hoped for is indeed after all but the success that is better named failure.

Said Theodore Parker:

> Give me the power to labor for mankind;
> Make me the mouth of such as cannot speak;
> Eyes let me be to groping men and blind;
> A conscience to the base; and to the weak
> Let me be hands and feet; and to the foolish, mind,
> And lead still further on such as Thy Kingdom seek.

CHRISTIANS AND ATHEISTS ALIKE IN BUSINESS METHODS.

It is a terrible but constantly noticed fact that no difference can be seen between the business methods of those who are in the church and those who are out of it. Religion has been separated from real life in the minds of the people, and does not really have much effect upon their lives.

With the early Christians religion was a new method of business as well as a purer type of worship. Every convert placed all his property upon the altar of the common good, so that it was said of them that "no man said that aught he possessed was his own, but distribution was made unto every one according as he had need." Certainly nothing short of communism is Christian if the fourth chapter of Acts is to be believed.

Every great revival in the Christian church has been in some way connected with the material welfare of the working people. Savonarola denounced those who enslaved the Italian peasantry, and banqueted while the people starved. Luther declared against those who made religion a thing to be purchased,— an additional luxury for the rich. He thundered against the sale of indulgences, by which ecclesiastical sanction was given to the crimes of the wealthy. John Wesley was a social reformer as well as an evangelist. He bade his converts help one another in business, and what was better still, he endeavored to provide employment for his adherents. He started several industries for those who were out of work. He did not believe that starvation is a regenerating force in the world, nor did he teach, as some of his modern followers seem to think, that religion was wholly a matter of spiritual ecstacies and inward assurance of one's own personal salvation.

He believed in the right to work, and as far as he understood industrial questions he was on the side of the poorly paid wage-earners of England, among whom his whole life was spent. He advocated the doubtful maxim — "Get all you can; save all you can; give all you can;" but at the same time be entirely disregarded the first two-thirds of his rule, and after a long life of almost unequalled activity, he died almost penniless.

Even the Salvation Army, which began its career by completely ignoring the material necessities of the poor, is now building lodging-houses for the homeless, and establishing farm colonies for its unemployed members. General Booth has been for several years devoting more time to the social side of his work, and less to the spiritual and individual side of it.

Wherever men have an earnest desire to do good to their fellows, and leave the world better than they found it, they are sure to realize very quickly the spiritual and intellectual evils which poverty brings into the world. The mind-life and the body-life cannot be separated. There is no holiness except wholeness. To be a Dr. Jekyll on Sunday and a Mr. Hyde on Monday is not to be a Christian. A religion that will do for a prayer-meeting and not for a factory or a store is like the scissors that are made to sell and not to cut.

To quote from "Between Caesar and Jesus," Prof. Herron's inspired book,—

> If the teachings of Jesus are dangerous and destructive, if He spake impracticable things which He did not understand, if His words are the cries of an overwrought enthusiast, then let us quit worshipping Him, and put an end to this colossal thing we call Christianity. If Jesus is the Son of God and the Redeemer of man, if He is the true teacher of practicable teachings, then while it is yet day, before dreadful judgment comes on, let us begin to preach what He taught, and to divinely enforce the justice of His love.

We have been treating Christianity as if it were a mere metaphysical theory, as if it were something to be believed, instead of something to be lived. The one great difference between Christ's teachings and the various religions of the world is that he emphasizes the relations between man and man, and the others emphasize the relations between man and God.

If His precepts are not practical, they are nothing. If they are not for our guidance in this everyday life on earth, then they are a delusion and a snare, and we had better exchange our New Testaments for "Getting on in the World."

The Church Too Often in the Rear.

It is a sad and strange truth that the church generally brings up the rear in the march toward freedom and brotherhood. Prior to 1776 the ministers preached from such texts as "Honor the King" and "The powers that be are ordained of God." Before the Proclamation of Emancipation they thundered from their pulpits against abolitionists, and said, "Servants, obey your masters, for this is right in the Lord." And to-day, with a few rare exceptions, they misunderstand the movement for industrial democracy, rebuke reformers with the words which Christ addressed to Judas, "the poor ye have always with you," and pronounce a benediction over the inhuman and immoral strife which we dignify with the name of business. The only union which did not indorse the independent political movement in Toledo, which upheld the political machine and the corporations, was the minister's union. This is not a remarkable thing. When Lincoln ran for President, there were seventeen ministers in Springfield, Ill., and only three of them were for Honest Abe. And yet the ministers wonder why workingmen don't go to church.

"The greatest enemy of Christ and humanity," said Rev. Gustavus Tuckerman, "is not the saloon, but pharisaism," and the same sentiment was voiced by Bishop Potter in a recent letter to the New York "Outlook," in which he said: "It is the same old story — as old as Christianity — the scribes, pharisees and hypocrites on one side, and over against them the truth."

THE PRAYER OF SELF.

They have piled theological books around them so that they have shut out all view of the world and its miseries. They go up on the mountain apart to pray, but they rarely go among the multitude below to teach and heal. Their unthinking and selfish worship is well rebuked in the following poem on " The Prayer of Self," by Priscilla Leonard:

> One knelt within a world of care
> And sin, and lifted up his prayer:
> " I ask Thee, Lord, for health and power
> To meet the duties of each hour;
> For peace from care, for daily food,
> For life prolonged and filled with good;
> I praise Thee for Thy gifts received,
> For sins forgiven, for pains relieved,
> For near and dear ones spared and blessed,
> For prospered toil and promised rest.
> This prayer I make in His great name
> Who for my soul's salvation came."
>
> But as he prayed, lo! at his side
> Stood the thorn-crowned Christ, and sighed.
> " O blind disciple,— came I then
> To bless the selfishness of men?
> Thou askest health, amidst the cry
> Of human strain and agony;
> Thou askest peace while all around
> Trouble bows thousands to the ground;
> Thou askest life for thine and thee,
> While others die; thou thankest me
> For gifts, for pardon, for success,
> For thine own narrow happiness.
>
> " Nay; rather bow they head and pray
> That while thy brother starveth to-day
> Thou mayst not eat thy bread at ease;
> Pray that no health, or wealth, or peace

May lull thy soul while the world lies
Suffering, and claims thy sacrifice;
Praise not while others weep, that thou
Hast never groaned with anguished brow;
Praise not thy sins have pardon found,
While others sink, in darkness drowned;
Canst thou give thanks, while others nigh,
Outcast and lost, curse God and die?

"Not in my name thy prayer was made,
Not for my sake the praises paid.
My gift is sacrifice; my blood
Was shed for human brotherhood.
And till thy brother's woe is thine
Thy heart-beat knows no throb of mine.
Come, leave thy selfish hopes, and see
Thy birthright of humanity!
Shun sorrow not; be brave to bear
The world's dark weight of sin and care;
Spend and be spent, yearn, suffer, give,
And in thy brethren learn to live."

Evade, avoid, apologize and explain as we may, the fact remains that we have made over our religion to suit our business, instead of our business to suit our religion. Our ideals have all been low. We have assumed that "peace on earth and good will among men" was a dream, and not a moral command. We have exhausted ourselves in the impossible service of God and Mammon, ignoring the plain statement that it could not be done. We have taken Adam Smith's "Wealth of Nations" as our Bible, and relegated the teachings of Christ to the realm of sentiment. Instead of classing our New Testament with works of political economy and practical ethics, we have placed it among the poets. Religion in many a church has dwindled down to a Doxology and a collection-plate. The poor, among whom Christ spent his life, sit hungry and homeless on the church steps, while the church door is locked and the cushioned seats are vacant.

Why People Do Not Go to Church.

The question, "Why do not people go to church?" is one that has been much discussed in the last few years. Many thoughtful men and women have given it their best attention without a satisfactory solution. I do not claim an original discovery in the answer that I offer, but I have an opinion, and here it is:

We read of Jesus that "the common people heard Him gladly." I believe they are just as glad to hear the message of love and sympathy that He preaches to-day as they were when He was on earth, and the evidence of it is the fact that those who "come to preach the gospel to the poor and to heal the broken hearted" do not lack for hearers.

The message of Jesus was almost wholly social, having to do with the conditions of life that He found people in. With the thing technically called "religion" in His day or ours Jesus had little to do, and He evidently did not interest himself in it.

He said very little about anything that would be construed as a reference to some place beyond the skies; He had much to say about living here on this earth, and "the common people heard him gladly" because He pointed them to true ideals of life that would make this earth a heaven, and He taught the beautiful law of love so simply and yet so forcibly that they could easily see the possibility of a realization of the delightful life of brotherhood was easily within their reach.

Moreover He insisted upon the practice of the precepts that He taught. "Why call ye me Lord, Lord, and do not the things that I say?" was one of the searching questions that He put to those who found it easy to "worship" but failed to carry out the fundamental principles of His gospel, such as "Love your enemies, do good to them that hate you," and "as ye would that men should do unto you do you even so unto them."

The man who preaches that the carrying out of these principles is an absolute essential to a Christian life to-day will not be without hearers — but he is pretty sure to be without a place in a first-class pulpit.

Because much of the preaching of to-day has little or nothing to do with real life, because it does not help a man working for a dollar a day to understand the mysterious philosophy that makes it right for his brother employer to make a profit of from two to ten times that amount from his labor — because religion has been separated from real life as something having to do with the next world, while men are chiefly concerned about this world — these are the reasons mainly why people don't go to church. I believe there are more men among the clergy that are seriously studying this question to-day than ever before, and I think it is a hopeful sign that we are to have a purer gospel;— a season of Christianity applied to everyday life is ahead of us and in the near future to be realized in these United States.

It more and more appears that the church is not "Christian," that by separating life into fragments of sacred and secular, she has misled the people, and there is very little of the Christianity of the carpenter of Nazareth, as I understand it, in our churches to-day. But it is useless to spend time railing against the church. It is best simply to go ahead and apply, as well as possible, the Christianity of Jesus in the everyday affairs of life, allowing the church to hang back and exhaust itself in so-called worship and adoration. Thousands of men and women, both inside and outside of the church, are wondering why there are —

> So many gods, so many creeds,
> So many paths that wind and wind,
> While just the art of being kind
> Is all this sad world needs.

The conviction has come to my mind that to be Christian means to be, and "to be" means to do. I assure you that I have no other purpose than to be Christian on the basis of loving my neighbor as myself, whether my neighbor is a church member or a non-church member, a saloon-keeper or a store-keeper; a gambler or an oppressor of labor; always remembering that he is my neighbor, God's child and my brother — an erring brother, perhaps, but my brother, just the same.

The Immorality of Business.

It seems to me the chief difficulty in the way of social reform lies in the fact — FACT, I repeat — of the immorality of business, in which we are all, more or less, involved. I have come to regard any way of getting something for nothing, whether called profit, interest, rent or any other name, as an immoral way of getting a livelihood. I do not believe that I have a right to live at the expense of some other man's toil, nor that any one else has; this, however, is so radically at variance with popular ideas that there are very few people in the churches to-day ready to accept it. I believe thoroughly with St. Paul that "If any will not work, neither shall he eat." Understand, that implies willingness to work, of course; one who is not able is not expected to, but the willingness is the equivalent of work. I do not understand that St. Paul exempted any from this classification; not even the "best people," or those who have inheritances or who are the beneficiaries of any of the multitude of schemes in the way of business, for getting a living without work, or at the expense of other people's toil; I do not believe one can entertain a just conception of brotherhood and deny the truth of these propositions.

The brutal assertion that every man must look out for himself has place no longer in my declaration of creed. No more unchristian statement ever was uttered, and yet it is uttered daily by church members, or if they do not give utterance in words they do it by their acts and lives. Practical demonstration shows that the very contrary is the truth, that the man who looks out for others,— who forgets self, if possible, is sure to have others look out for him. The great majority of people are keen to appreciate and quick to respond with a deep degree of affection to the touch of love. Instead of the world being cold and heartless, as we hear it continually charged, by the application of the Golden Rule, which is only the law of love after all, one may have the wealth of the world's affection lavished upon one.

By strange distortion of the simple teachings of the gospel of Jesus Christ we have construed His religion, which He said consisted entirely in ministering to others,— in "loving our neighbor as ourselves," into a system of ceremonies under the name of "worship," whereby we have led ourselves into the belief that in some way we can square accounts with God, even while we are denying our brother the right to work, or causing him to toil ten, twelve or eighteen hours a day.

We have come to think we can square accounts with God while tolerating all this wrong, by simply going to church, singing "All Hail the Power of Jesus' Name,"— when it has no power to make us sacrifice or surrender anything,— and say complimentary things of Jesus in the name of worship.

This sort of heresy is destroying the church. The church is deceiving itself, the people are not being deceived by it. As Rev. Josiah Strong says: "Instead of seeking to save men the church is seeking men to save itself."

Our Real Needs Much the Same.

There is no satisfactory reason why some men should have so much more money than others. Our real needs are all very much the same. We all have free access to the air and the sunlight. There is a limit to what we can eat and wear and use.

If millionaires had stomachs and bodies in proportion to their wealth, then there might be some excuse for their millions. If they were like the giants in the fairy tales, who could eat a bullock or two at a meal and drink their wine by the barrel, then extraordinary wealth would be very necessary to preserve them from privation.

Of course there are differences of ability and character and energy, but these differences are not so great as to justify the possession by one man of two hundred and fifty millions, while another has not a nickel to pay for a loaf of bread. If millionaires were three miles high, if they were a class of higher beings upon whom we depended for our cleverest inventions, our most arduous undertakings, our noblest literature, if they were our guides, philosophers and friends, then the tremendous disparities in matters of wealth might be overlooked. But the fact is that they differ from other men only in the line of ability to capture and keep. Their physical and intellectual wants are the same as those of the peanut vendor on the street. The application of the Golden Rule to business would not injure any of their real interests.

"Men," says Prof. Herron, "you are brothers; in your heart of hearts you know it. The chasm which the social crisis has opened between classes, right here in our American life, had no right to be. In your better moments, you know that the feeling of manly comrade love you have for your fellows brings you more of joy, more of all that makes life worth while, than all the possessions of the earth. This affection and brotherhood of sympathy are your inheritance from the ages of sacrifice, bloodshed and heartache; they are your birthright. You cannot, men, you will not, let strife over mere things, over pieces of iron and paper and gold, array you against each other, and steal your birthright away. You are not enemies; you are not classes; you are not the guardians of interests; you are friends, comrades and lovers one of another. Your fears about your rights are unmanly and unworthy; your interests are superstitions; your gains are delusions; your classes make you ashamed, for you know that they are not noble. Do not suffer *things and prejudices* to rob you of your fellowship, for that is your life. Rise to the noblest that is in you and dare to trust it. Act as men too strong to be made the tools of interests and things,— men too brave to become the slaves of fear and prejudice, and in the conquest of your fears, you will conquer yourself; and the God in you will conquer the world for love and liberty."

Dr. Washington Gladden.   Ernest H. Crosby.
Nathan Straus.   Dr. George D Herron

A GROUP OF PROMINENT REFORMERS.

MR. JONES ADDRESSING A VAST AUDIENCE AT GRAND CENTRAL PALACE, NEW YORK, UPON THE SUBJECT OF "THE NEW RIGHT."

Love the Only Power.

The best way to obtain your own rights is to be diligent in securing the rights of others. Whatever you gain by the overthrow of a fellow-man is a moral loss. Wrangling law-suits, enlarging of jails, increase of the police force,— all these methods of force and coercion cannot establish justice or abolish crime.

I have never yet had a law-suit, never yet have sued a man or been sued. Law-mongering breeds only hate and malice. It is no cure for evil. No punishment is adequate which does not prevent the crime from being repeated. Love, after all, is the only power there is in the world for the accomplishment of good. We may make a show of doing good with physical force and legal restraint, but it is only a show. Paint a tiger pink, but he remains a tiger still. The only way to influence men permanently is to change their dispositions. Clubs and chains and prison cells have been tried for thousands of years, and they have only increased the evils they professed to prevent. It is time we tried a wiser and humaner plan. Government should seek to educate rather than compel.

Love is the true inner evolutionary force of the world. It alone can melt prejudice and expand the heart. All social reforms boil down to this. All parties, creeds and civilizations exist only for this,— to hasten the reign of love in every department of life. Little good can come from these ready-made reforms that are being suggested on every hand, and which rely upon organization or legislative coercion for their success, unless the citizenship back of them is inspired with the spirit of love. Have we not discovered that tyranny can be as real in a republic as in a monarchy?

Love is the only regenerative force. To teach love to individuals by personal kindness and helpfulness is to do well; and to mould love into law and thus uplift and enlighten a whole city or state is to do better. Organizations, political parties and churches are of value only so far as they teach and embody the spirit of brotherhood; and even government itself has no other justification for its existence than the upbuilding of a fraternal civilization.

More laws and more policemen will not convert people to lives of brotherly kindness. More than anything else we need men and women "of the truth," who are willing to do as they would be done by, actually willing to go out and be poor as Jesus and St. Francis did, and show by their lives their faith in human nature and their love for their fellow-men.

The People Sick of Canting Words.

We must have brothers before the people can understand what brotherhood means. The people are sick of words. Liberty, justice, truth, love,— these words are used so often by unworthy men for unworthy purposes that men's eyes do not brighten at the sound of them. These words must become flesh, and dwell among the people before they can be understood. A true life is the best definition of truth, and a loving act does more to define love than all the explanations of all the dictionaries.

The work of the geographical explorer is almost finished. There are no new oceans or continents to be discovered. But the work of the moral explorer is as yet scarcely begun. Columbus, Magellan and Balboa will have their counterparts in the future in the men and women who will dare to venture their lives for a principle, and thus by their courage and self-sacrifice pioneer the way to a regenerated world. But let it always be remembered that the Golden Rule is a precept which no solitary hermit can obey. It is thoroughly social. There must be not only yourself, but "others." The old monkish notion that solitary confinement was essential to holiness was a serious mistake. Morality is a social as well as an individual virtue, so that while as individuals we can do much to teach and practice a higher truth, we cannot do so perfectly without the co-operation of others.

As Henry D. Lloyd says:

"Regenerate the individual" is a half-truth; the reorganization of the society which he makes, and which makes him, is the other half. Man alone cannot be a Christian. Institutions are applied beliefs. The love of liberty became liberty in America by clothing itself in the complicated group of structures known as the government of the United States. Love is a half-truth, and kissing is a good deal less than half of that. We need not kiss all our fellow-men, but we must do for them all we ask them to do for us — nothing less than the fullest performance of every power. To love our neighbor is to submit to the discipline and arrangement which make his life reach its best, and so do we best love ourselves.

History has taught us nothing if not that men can continue to associate only by the laws of association. The Golden Rule is the first and last of these, but the first and last of the Golden Rule is that it can be operated only through laws, habits, forms and institutions. The Constitution and laws of the United States are, however imperfectly, the translation into the language of politics of doing as you would be done by — the essence of equal rights and government by consent. To ask individuals to-day to lead by their single sacrifices the life of the brother in the world of business is as if the American colonist had been asked to lead by his individual enterprise the life of the citizen of a republic. That was made possible to him only by union with others. The business world is full of men who yearn to abandon its methods and live the love they feel, but to attempt to do so by themselves would be martyrdom.

As to how far an individual can go ahead of the generation in which he lives, is a question which every one must answer for himself.

It is my opinion that the life of Jesus furnishes the answer as to how rich it is right to be, and I do not believe there is any peaceful solution for the thoughtful person this side of such an admission. Every one is entitled to what he justly earns, and he is not entitled to the earnings of any other one. No man ever earned a million of dollars. I very much doubt if any one ever earned and saved a hundred thousand dollars. Though many honest men have gotten that sum, it has come to them through a dishonest system that has made respectable various forms of robbery under the guise of profit, and in this system I think every man is a law unto himself unless he is willing to accept the law of Christ. If he is willing to accept that as his guide, I am sure he cannot have while others have not, he cannot abound while others want.

Show Your Love for God by Serving Your Fellow-Man.

According to the teachings of Jesus the way to prove we love God is to serve our fellow-men. How can a man be a thorough Christian while he is content and proud to have this world's goods and see his brothers in the most dire and abject need? Who can explain the consistency of those rich church members who are daily making money at the expense of the beaten lives of other men and women?

"Inasmuch as ye have done it unto one of the least of these ye have done it unto Me," said Christ. The poor represent not only humanity, but God. Civilization as well as religion is measured by the amount of sympathy we have for the helpless and unfortunate.

Surely this state of things which we have pictured cannot be permanent. This society which permits such deadly parallels as we see, "the gorged few, and the hungry many," cannot last. A nation which has produced such marvels of material progress in less than a century must certainly have the ability to find a better plan for dealing with these problems than we now know.

I believe that the new century upon which we shall soon enter will see a wonderful spiritual development and uplifting, far outdoing the material of the one about completed, not only in this country, but the world over. Already there is much righteous discontent, which makes itself felt by speeches, newspapers and books. There is nothing so persuasive as a story, and many modern novels are full of the social questions of the day, and are sold in large numbers.

There is to-day a wonderful awakening of the social conscience far and wide. Miss Addams describes the "social conscience" as that feeling which will not permit a man to sit down to a meal at a bountiful table and enjoy it, with hungry, starved eyes looking in upon him through the windows, broadened and enlarged till it takes in the sufferers about us everywhere, who are out of sight, but should not be out of mind. I believe that never before have people cared so much about other people.

What is possible for a few to-day may, after generations of development, become possible for all. When we begin to study and to cultivate human nature as wisely as we have studied and cultivated flower nature and horse nature, we shall have men and women worthy of the beautiful world in which we live.

Once banish the maddening fear of poverty, and the perpetual suspicion which mars almost all human intercourse in matters of business, and Emerson's hope will be realized. The conditions which surround the lives of most of us would make an angel from heaven selfish. When generosity means bankruptcy, and bankruptcy means hunger and cold, what wonder that generosity is a rare virtue!

See how a mother sinks her own comfort in the comfort of her child. Think of the daily martyrdoms of motherhood, of the love that pours itself out in service and asks for nothing in return but love. Every human being is a living proof that love is in the world, that the strong care for the weak, and the wise for the ignorant, else no one of us would have survived the helpless, moneyless days of infancy and childhood. These ideas may be "peculiar" and even "dangerous" to some people; but they have the merit of great age, and having been in the possession of the race for nearly two thousand years, it does not seem that society is running any very great risk if it tries the Golden Rule, as the other schemes that have been tried up to date are colossal failures.

We have given selfishness a thorough trial, and it won't work. The general break-down of our industrial system proves it. The more we rush and grab, the poorer we get. It is a natural law and not a fancy that "it is more blessed to give than to receive." Every self-centered millionaire, dwelling in loveless and isolated luxury, has discovered that happiness does not come by the acquisition of much property.

The Era of Peace on Earth and Good Will to Men.

Nearly 1,900 years ago the angelic voices rang out on the midnight air of Judea's plain, proclaiming the dawn of a new era, for which the world still waits, the era of "peace on earth and good will to men." Are we idly waiting for this good time, or are we helping to make it a reality? Nothing is plainer to me than that the mission of Jesus was to establish a new social order on earth, which He called "The kingdom of heaven," and "The kingdom of God." Jesus never once used the term, "Kingdom of heaven" or "Kingdom of God" as meaning a place, but always a condition of mind, a social order in which men (Christians) would love all men as brothers, and live and act toward them like brothers. He taught that men should be governed by the law of love, instead of hate — for hate, then, to a much greater extent than now, sought to rule and govern the world. In order to help the world to understand this new social order, He gave us a number of very plain and simple rules which you will find written in the gospels of Matthew, Mark, Luke and John. I particularly invite you to read the fifth, sixth and seventh chapters of Matthew, for here you will find practically all of the rules that Jesus gave for the ordering of our lives in our relations with our fellow-men. This portion of the teaching of Jesus is known as the "Sermon on the Mount," and I think that when you read it, as you read the sayings of any other teacher, you will admit that it is the most revolutionary document that has ever come to your notice. Before the birth of Christ, the law that ruled the world was truly a law of " blood and iron."

> Eye for eye, and
> Tooth for tooth;
> Hate for hate,
> And ruth for ruth.

The history of the time that has come down to us is black with the record of hatred, bitterness, revenge and murder of the foulest description — hatred and vengeance that in its desire to "get even" spared not the lives of innocent little children. If, through their veins coursed the blood of an enemy, their doom was sealed as surely as that of the offender himself.

But all this was to be changed — that's why the dawn of the new era was heralded by the angelic song of peace on earth!

The Christ, the loving, forgiving, gentle, compassionate Christ, if He were to visit this earth would find many, many things in our so-called civilization that I think would cause Him to weep even as He wept over Jerusalem. As He looks on our millions of disinherited poor I fancy I hear Him repeating the reproach that He pronounced on the civilization of His time when he said, " The poor ye have always with you." Evidently they did not know enough to be ashamed of their paupers, and we are very much in the same state of mind, for we point with pride to the fact that we " take care of our poor." We have not yet learned to be ashamed of a civilization that makes some of our brothers paupers. But we have sound proof that the world is awakening, and before many years we shall awake to see a time when poverty shall be banished from the earth.

Shame on us that we have tolerated it so long. The Rev. Heber Newton, of the Madison Avenue Episcopal Church, New York, in a recent sermon said that " the kingdom of God was a new order of society, which men themselves should bring about, from which should be abolished poverty and misery." The time would come, he said, when men would consider it a crime and an outrage that any person should starve to death in the midst of plenty. He for one looked to see poverty abolished in our own generation. So do I. I am looking for a time when every man shall have the fruit of the labor of his own hands, and no man shall, either by the methods of the gambler or the methods of respectable business, have the fruit of the toil of some other man's hands. Then poverty will be a thing of the past because the real cause of poverty — the man that lives at the expense of other people's toil — will have disappeared. Brotherhood is, and the manifest destiny of mankind is to live it, and in order that men can do so the present social order — that is, the present way of carrying on business known as competition, which is only another name for war, will have to disappear. And it will, and in its stead we shall have a system of co-operation that will govern all industry and business — a system in which it will be possible for all men to love one another and act and live like brothers. That's the kind of Christianity we all want.

Let us have a system in which every man shall have just what he earns, and nothing more, a fair-play, Golden-Rule system, and twenty-five years of that sort of a system will relegate all of our prisons, jails and almshouses to the domain of the past. Social systems, like individuals, may be known by their fruits. Men do not gather grapes from thorns, nor figs from thistles. Our thousands of paupers, tramps and criminals are not the result of chance or accident; they are the legitimate fruit of our wretched social system. As long as the system continues, we may expect the fruit.

Mrs. Stetson has given us a beautiful picture of the new kind of Christianity that we are working for, in these lines:

> Do you think that the love which has died for the world
> Has not lived for the world also?

The Golden Rule.

    Filling man with the fire
    Of a boundless desire
  To love all with a love that shall grow?
It was not for nothing the White Christ was born
  Two thousand years ago.

The love that fed poverty, making it thrive,
  Is learning a lovelier way.
    We have seen that the poor
    Need be with us no more,
  And that sin may be driven away;
The love that has carried the martyrs to death
  Is entering life to-day.

The spirit of Christ is awake and alive,
  In the work of the world it is shown,
    Crying loud, crying clear,
    That the Kingdom is here,
  And that all men are heirs to the throne —
There was never a time since the making of man
  When love was so near its own!

CHAPTER XIII.

THE BROTHERHOOD OF MAN

As we believe in humanity as the sole interpreter of the law of God, so do we believe in the people of every state as the sole master, sole sovereign, and sole interpreter of the law of humanity, which governs every national mission. We believe in the people, one and indivisible; recognizing neither castes nor privileges, save those of genius and virtue; neither proletariat nor aristocracy, whether landed or financial; but simply an aggregate of faculties and forces consecrated to the well-being of all, to the administration of the common substance and possession, the terrestrial globe. We believe in the people, one and independent; so organized as to harmonize the individual faculties with the social idea; living by the fruits of its own labor, united in seeking after the greatest possible amount of general well-being, and in respect for the rights of individuals. We believe in the people bound together in brotherhood by a common faith, tradition, and idea of love. * * * Equality, liberty and association: These three elements constitute the true nation.—*Mazzini: Faith and the Future.*

CHAPTER XIII.

THE BROTHERHOOD OF MAN.

THE great increase in the number of organizations and associations of all sorts that have gotten together during the last twenty years is very significant. Men in vast numbers are becoming convinced of the failure and folly of competition, and are beginning to realize that their normal condition is one of association.

The race may be said to be groaning in travail in the effort to realize relationships to one another, in the effort to comprehend the purposes of our being, and to understand what is a self-evident fact to every thoughtful person,— the imperishable fact of our universal brotherhood.

In the earlier history of this country, social ties were weaker than they are to-day. Society was less complex, less interdependent. Every little community in the woods planted its own wheat, and sawed its own lumber, and had little to do with the rest of the world. The functions of government were minimized, and the spirit of independence overpowered the spirit of co-operation. So long as the doors of the Great West were wide open there was not so much need of an organized social system; but to-day, without organization, our civilization would become an anarchistic brawl. We are none of us separate creatures any longer. We are fractions, and the unit is the nation. The co-operative forces have for a long time been operating without our notice, but they are now being recognized as the only hope and salvation of the world.

In the words of Washington Gladden:

> There has always been a great deal of competition in the world, but there has always been some good measure of co-operation also. Men have been striving with one another for certain ends, and they have also been combining with one another for certain ends; their contests divided them, but their mutual interest united them; the repulsions of self-interest have been balanced, and often over-balanced, by the attractions of sympathy and good-will. Men compete in their business relations; on the streets their rivalries, even if honest and fair, are sharp and incessant; each is trying to get the lion's share. But they come together in the neighborhood, in the school, in the church, in the secret fraternity, in the literary fraternity, in the literary or musical society, in the political party, and in other associations where their interests are no longer divergent, but common, where the good of each is seen to be the good of all, where they find their profit in combining; and thus they learn to think of one another and to care for one another, and the social sentiments and activities are healthily developed. The co-operative principle and habit are really the cement of society; competition develops individual powers; co-operation develops social relations. As society advances from barbarism to civilization, men compete less and co-operate more. The principle of competition is the law of the survival of the fittest; it is the law of plants and brutes and brutish men; but it is not the highest law of civilized society; another and higher principle, the principle of good-will, the principle of mutual help, begins at length to operate.

How the New Inventions Make for Brotherhood.

All the new inventions in the industrial world, especially in the line of transportation and communication, tend to bring people to a better understanding of one another. The cable, telegraph, telephone, railroads and steamers have transformed the whole world into a village. San Francisco and New York are in reality nearer to each other than were farmers who lived in the same county in pioneer days.

In an article advocating the municipalizing of the telephone, Prof. Frank Parsons says:

> There is no better social cement or business developer than the telephone; and besides the utility, think of the happiness of conversing at will with friends

in every part of the country. A nation that is not well telephoned is losing one of the best and cheapest of the comforts and utilities within its easy reach.

Suppose the country were netted with telephone wires, and the rates were such as to bring the service within the reach of the great body of the people, what a mighty power the telephone would be for unifying and solidifying the nation, uniting and harmonizing the interests and sentiments of north, south, east and west. If the trunk lines ran freely across the Rhine, and every town in France could communicate, at a reasonable cost, with any part of Germany, it is probable that, in spite of the limitations of race and language, the telephone would be found a potent means of healing the breach between those two great peoples, which, more than any other thing, except, perhaps, the Turkish and Egyptian questions, threatens the peace of Europe.

If the new telectroscope can be practically applied at low cost, so that we may see the face of a distant person while we speak with him over the telephone wire, distance will, indeed, be vanquished. Friends may talk with each other face to face in spite of intervening mountains and seas. Niagara may be seen and its thunder heard without leaving our homes. The world will be at our feet.

Labor Organizations Contribute to Brotherhood.

Brotherhood is really what men have always been seeking. They do not really rejoice in warfare. They have sought by various ways to escape the battle of life. They have organized themselves into guilds, lodges, unions, and other protective and fraternal organizations. Few men to-day actually stand alone. We are blindly seeking to get closer together, to know one another better and help one another more.

Trade-unions point in this direction. They are in reality colleges where the first principles of industrial brotherhood are being taught. Workingmen of various nationalities, who had been taught in Europe to hate and make war upon one another, come together as brothers in the trade-union, and realize their common interests. What is called the sympathetic strike is also, in its way, a proof that workers are beginning to regard "an injury to one as the concern of all."

As we have shown in the chapter on "The Organization of Labor," it is the trade-unions, more than any other organizations, which have endeavored to put in practice the truth that America is to be the brotherhood country of the world. They have not despised any man because he was poor or of foreign birth, but welcomed him into their union and given him the right hand of comradeship.

ALL — FROM HIGHEST TO LOWEST — PEOPLE.

They who speak of the "scum of Europe," and the "scrub emigrants" fail to catch the true American spirit. No man is a foreigner in this country, save perhaps he who wishes to perpetuate the prejudices and tyrannies of older lands. This is an international republic,— the first of the kind the world has ever seen. All the way from a poor, ditch-digging Polack clear down to the richest plutocrat in the land, a man is a man and nothing more.

There are whole volumes of evidence to prove that babes taken from the very worst surroundings make good men and women when they have the chance. Dr. Barnardo's tables, which have been carefully kept for twenty-eight years, prove this beyond question. At least, the so-called dregs of our society are as worthy as is the froth. A just and orderly economic system would wipe out both,— it would remove the parasitic poor and the parasitic rich, and oblige every citizen to be a useful partner in the national industry. Uncle Sam is still rich enough to give every newcomer a farm, but the old gentleman is not so wise and impartial as he used to be. He has become the protector of the "Haves," and entirely ignores his duty to the "Have-Nots." When we pay the same attention to making men which we now pay to making profit, we shall have no "scum" in our cities.

THE RACE PROBLEM.

The so-called "race problem," that for so many years has troubled the Southern states, is in reality only another phase of the social problem. The people of the South do not object

JANE ADDAMS.
(The founder of Hull House, Chicago.)

A SUNDAY AFTERNOON MEETING IN GOLDEN RULE PARK.

to the negro simply because he is a negro; let him "content himself in the social grade to which Providence has decreed him," and he remains a very acceptable being. He is not looked down upon because he is an intellectual inferior; Booker T. Washington is certainly the intellectual equal of thousands of men and women, either in the North or South, who have white skins, but he would not be accorded terms of equality by the prevailing sentiment of the South any sooner than would be accorded the most ignorant negro. His color is a badge of previous servitude and of perpetual inferiority, and he must remain a member of a lower caste. The negro is freely accepted in the South, as well as in the North, as a servant or laborer. Indeed, it is not an uncommon thing to see a negro woman employed as a wet nurse for white babies, even to-day. Negroes are familiarly accepted in all such capacities as porters on Pullman cars, about hotels and railway stations and as cooks, dish-washers, house servants, barbers, farm-hands, etc. In all of these capacities indeed there is no objection at all to the negro. The white men do not object to converting negro flesh and blood into profit to be expended in wanton luxury, while the lives out of which it was ground are doomed to hopeless poverty.

It is when he steps out on the plane of equality, and indeed the kind of equality set forth in the Declaration of Independence, that is, "That all men are created equal and entitled to certain inalienable rights, among which are life, liberty and the pursuit of happiness"—when the negro assumes to stand upright as a man under the rights set forth by this declaration, the rebellion is aroused in the breast of his white brother, who insists and declares that the "whites have been born to rule and the blacks to serve," wholly unmindful of that other declaration more ancient and perhaps more authoritative than the Declaration of Independence, the statement set forth in God's word, that "He hath made of one blood all nations that do dwell on the earth."

EQUAL RIGHTS OF BLACK, WHITE, BROWN, AND YELLOW.

It seems to me that this statement from the Bible and the one quoted from the Declaration of Independence are both strictly scientific; they recognize the idea of unity, and I do not believe that any system based upon a narrower philosophy can ever solve our problems and bring social peace. I believe in the absolute unity of the entire race. When I say that "I believe in all of the people," I make no exceptions. I believe that I have as much right on the earth as any other man, black or white, brown or yellow, and I do not claim any greater rights for myself than I am ready to accord to every other being. The very fact that we are on the earth is proof, primal, conclusive and final, that we have equal rights to the earth. God did not except black men; neither does the Declaration of Independence except them. How, then, can I except them? "Each of us is here as divinely as any is here." I think this is the platform on which we must work out the problem.

I have repeatedly stated that I do not think our problems are to be fought out; they are to be thought out. How shall we get justice among men? How shall we get into right relation with our fellows? These are the questions that confront us. As no question is settled until it is settled right, so this so-called race problem can never be settled by ignoring it, as seems to be the policy of the present administration. Neither can it be settled on an unjust basis, either to black or to white as some seem to suppose. "Might does not make right," and our policy of conquering the little brown men in the Philippine Islands, simply because we are stronger, will not prove that we are right, nor will it bring social peace any more than the exercise of superior force on the negroes in the Southern states will bring us social peace. The question of the relation between the negroes and the whites is, as I have said, a social problem, more than a "race problem."

Peace and Fellow-Love the Solution.

It is no part of my purpose to enter into a discussion of the physiological causes that have produced the sensual brute in either the negro or the white man. I have repeated often in this book that all of our misery, every form of distress that afflicts humanity to-day, can be traced to social injustice, and I believe it as I believe in my own life. Furthermore, I believe that it can never be eradicated, except through the application of a just system of social relations that will give to every man and every woman their rightful place in society. This is the basis upon which I look for social peace to be realized in these United States, a basis of justice to every man, black or white; and I believe that the realization of this hope is much nearer than the most sanguine expect. People are losing their faith in the power of coercion, in the power of hate to regenerate and save society. All that is needed to-day to put an end to war for all time, so far as this country is concerned, is that the men who do not believe in hate, and do not believe in war, but do believe in love and peace shall say so plainly and loudly, and once having said so that the same men and women shall set themselves about the task of inaugurating a just social order and Golden Rule, do-as-you-would-be-done-by plan of life for every man and every woman of every race and color. With a program of this kind applied to our lives, applied to the lives of the little babies born into this world of ours so that each shall have equal opportunity with every other, we shall find that in twenty-five years the horrid spectacle of murders, lynchings, burnings and the various forms of crucifixion that now horrify us — all the legitimate products of a wicked social system — will have disappeared and the Kingdom of Heaven will have been realized on earth.

A Plea to the Men of the South.

I want to say in all earnestness to my brothers of the South, the most warm-hearted, loving, hospitable and generous of all the people of these states, I see no other opportunity for a settlement of this dreadful problem save along the lines that I have indicated. I do not set myself up as an empiric, presenting a plan and program and insisting upon its adoption; I simply say as a man and brother who loves you and loves every soul into whom "He has breathed the breath of life," that I see no opportunity of making peace through war, but I do see the realization of the dreams of the prophets, sages and poets yet to be fulfilled in our glorious country. It can never come until we recognize the fundamental fact of brotherhood and adjust every relation in life to that scientific truth. Brotherhood is, and is as inevitable in the spiritual realm as in the physical or material. It matters not whether you believe 2 and 2 make 4 or not. The fact is ineradicable. Two and two cannot become any other sum, and if you have a system of arithmetic by which you get another result, it is simply a false system that must lead to endless confusion in your mathematics.

A denial of brotherhood is exactly the same thing, and is the cause of the dreadful strain and social agony of the race in the present day. So thoroughly am I under the conviction of the importance of this truth that, quoting the great emancipator of the black race, William Lloyd Garrison: "I will not excuse, I will not evade, I will not equivocate, I will not yield a single inch, and I will be heard." It is because I see in every man a brother and in every woman a sister, and because I see no possible solution of the problem of life on any other basis, that I plead for the recognition of this fact and for the incorporation of the idea of love into every law of our land, providing equality of opportunity for every one, black, white, brown or yellow. "Equality," "Unity," "Brotherhood"—these are the foundation principles upon which our social fabric must be builded, if we build to endure. There is no other foundation that any man can lay. This is not a statement of sentiment; it is a statement of a fact as scientific and as easily demonstratable as any fact of arithmetic, and because there is no escaping it, I urge its consideration upon every lover of liberty, and, indeed, upon every lover of humanity.

True Greatness Among Humble Men.

One of the great men of my acquaintance was a blacksmith who was in our employ. He was of foreign birth, had not had very much of the finish that comes from books, or association with so-called cultured people. He was not a member of any lodge or any church, but he was a *man* in all that the word means. His society was more enjoyable and profitable than that of the average learned personage, whose education has been a matter of memorizing rather than of observation and reflection.

The "masses" whom we speak of as if they were human nature in bulk are better than our thought of them. As Doltaire, in Gilbert Parker's "Seats of the Mighty," said of the French peasantry: "These shall save the earth some day, for they are of it, and live close to it, and are kin to it."

I like the "common people" because they are most democratic. They believe in one another. They are neighborly and helpful. The rich man has no neighbors — only rivals and parasites.

The uncommon people who are too clever and cultured to render any useful personal service to society could easily be spared without seriously injuring our civilization. They have not sufficient self-respect to be ashamed that they eat food others have prepared, and wear clothes others have sewed, and live in houses others have built, without doing anything for those others in return. They are but wealthy mendicants after all. Their lives are built upon an unnatural and dishonest foundation. Ruskin says that "only the ignorant can enjoy luxury; the cruelest man living could not sit at his feast did he not sit blind-folded."

In spite of all the miseries and hardships that poverty brings, there is more genuine happiness among the working people than there is among the very wealthy. They are free from the ennui which is the curse of luxurious idleness. They live closer to one another and to Nature. There is little that is artificial about their lives. Whatever faults they have are on the surface. Their defects are not so apt to be concealed behind a mask of piety or a veneer of so-called " refinement."

" Better be a fool in revolt against oppression," said Kossuth, " than a learned philosopher forging an excuse for his chains." The workers at least are not parasites in a world where labor is needed. They are standing on their own feet, and not riding on any one's back. The money they put in their pocket on Saturday night is all honestly earned, and no widow or orphan has been made poorer because of what they receive. Their characters have not been blighted by that curse of the ages, irresponsible authority.

Life to the working classes is not a well-devised system of polite hypocrisies. It is not a game of make-believe. It is not a substitution of etiquette for affection, and good manners for brains. It is not a matter of millinery and upholstery.

Political economy to them is not an abstract theory, as it is to the professors; it is a terrible every-day fact. The social problem is to them not a " matter of interest," but a matter of life and death. The evils and abuses which the rest of us discuss in the magazines, they are compelled to endure.

The Workers Not Intrinsically More Moral than the Idlers.

Do not understand me to mean that the working people are essentially more moral and intelligent individually than the wealthier profit-taking classes. The poor are not poor from choice. They deserve little or no credit for their safety from the dangers that property-owning brings. With scarcely an exception every one of them would be a millionaire if he had a chance. The disease of ownership infects us all. There is an equality of folly with regard to wealth. Almost every man is governed by the delusion that riches and authority bring happiness; and no industrial change will regenerate us as long as that delusion has influence over our conduct.

The sturdier virtues of the poorer classes and the selfish frivolities of the wealthy are both caused by their environment. The lives of the poor are more natural, honest and transparent, not because they do not wish to be parasites, but because they are unable to become such. It is as if there were a beautiful castle in the midst of a malarial swamp. Only a few dozen people could occupy it at the same time, and millions gathered on the highlands round about the swamp, and fought daily for the privilege of entering the castle.

Those who succeeded and became dwellers in the castle were constantly suffering from chills and fevers, so that their lives were made miserable. The defeated millions, on the other hand, were quite free from sickness and ill-health, because, though the land on which they lived was hard and rocky, it was high, and the air was purer.

Neither those inside the castle, nor those without, realized the unhealthiness of the swamp. Their one constant endeavor was to get into the castle and leave the highlands behind; so the better state of health among the outsiders was not due to their wisdom or sanitary precautions, but to conditions which they never thought of and even endeavored to escape.

Our present unbrotherly social system afflicts us with two opposite evils — those of idle luxury on the one hand and poverty on the other,— the hardships of the mountains and the malaria of the castle in the swamp. Both these evils can be removed when our irrational warfare is ended, and we have common sense enough to drain the swamp and make the castle large enough for us all.

Real Education Needed.

When we partition our neighbors off into educated and uneducated, we generally have a wrong standard of learning. College degrees are too often like the brands on adulterated goods. What is labelled "Choice Dairy Butter" may be the rankest oleomargarine. There are more valuable subjects of study than Latin and Greek and ancient history. To know and appreciate human nature, to detect vice and falsehood under all its disguises, to honor truth and courage, to preserve a healthy mind in a healthy body, to understand how to cultivate the soil, how to build a house or train a horse or do any of the numberless practical things of everyday life, to reverence the mysteries of life and death, and to be open-minded for the reception of every new truth,— these things are not taught in the colleges, but they must be included in any definition of education which the future will indorse.

What we lack is ideals, not idols. Our idol has been the practical man; we must find the ideal man. We have pointed to the individual who, by his superior cunning or prowess and strength has amassed the wealth of his fellow-men, as our model of success. But we are coming to see that all such success is purchased at the price of the failure of the many. Our greatness is to be proved in the days to come, not by pointing to the individuals here and there who are like the anaconda, gorged with wealth for which they have no use, at the expense of an army of paupers and tramps who have no wealth to use, but rather by pointing to a citizenship that is made up of people truly free and truly happy — a republic in which there are neither drones nor idlers, and wherein the interest of all sings us to our work. When we shall have passed up the broad avenues of collective ownership to a realization of that condition, who shall be able to fathom our productivity and cheer?

The movement for public ownership is government seeking the good of all as against the individual who seeks only his own good. It is a recognition of the fundamental fact that the humblest citizen is entitled to the greatest degree of comfort that associated effort can provide. It is *organized love*, manifesting itself in service. It is patriotism of the highest and purest type. It is the casting down of idols and the lifting up of ideals. It is dethroning the millionaires and exalting the millions. Happily, we are passing away from the abject worship of mere dollars to a realization of the truth so tersely stated by the simple Nazarene nearly 1900 years ago: "Ye cannot serve God and Mammon." And we are coming to measure the great captains of industry, not by their use of their fellow-men simply as profit-making machines, but by their ability to organize industry and serve their fellow-men. Where can we look for nobler examples of patriotism, or love of country, than to the men and women whose lives have been devoted to the service of their fellow-men rather than to mere sordid worship of wealth, rather than to debauching the machinery of justice and the people's legislators in order to serve their own purposes?

Always Believed in People.

I am inclined to the opinion that I was always a Socialist, and the awakening to the fact was evolutionary. I do not remember the time when I did not believe in people. As far as I was able to think contrary to the prevailing ideas around me, I was inclined to think that we are all very much alike. I remember when I was quite young, saying to my mother, "I do not see how God can be fair if He planned, as you believe, that some were to be rich, others to be poor; some to be overfed and others to hunger," yet I lived for a large part of my life under the dark shadow of that superstition, trying to make myself believe that all of the wretchedness and misery, the woe and want, the wrong and outrage, were in some way in harmony with the divine plan. I remember having been told again and again that if it were not so, God would not permit it; the very fact that evil existed was evidence that he permitted it.

It has been through Socialism that I have stepped out into the larger liberty that Paul saw when he exhorted men: "Stand fast in the liberty wherewith Christ hath made you free;" but as Paul says of his Roman citizenship, "it was at a great price that I purchased this liberty." It was only after years of struggling with superstitution that I finally came to realize liberty in my own person; and after having once tasted of life, having once caught a glimpse of the joys and the glories that await all of us, that are for all and to be enjoyed by all, I find my chief joy in contributing to build up the new, heroic and spiritual world that I seem to feel and know, though I cannot argue out just how, is the manifest destiny of this great American nation. We are coming to a day, and it is not far distant, when one purpose shall inspire us all, and that purpose will be to make conditions of life such that every one will be free to live the largest and best possible life, to bring out the best that is in him. At present very few of us have that liberty; existing conditions tend very largely to develop and promote the very worst that is in us instead of the best.

An Economic System that Denies Liberty.

Have you ever thought how very little real liberty there is about us after all? It is true we have political liberty and religious liberty, but we are, to a very great extent, yet in industrial and economic slavery. Very few people have the liberty that will allow them freely to speak their minds on topics of the day, on questions of politics, religion, etc.

In every large city letters come to the mayor and public officials suggesting wise reform, but they are often anonymous; the writer might lose his or her place, if he were known to entertain opinions that might seem to be against the interest of his employer. During the senatorial contest in Ohio last winter, one of the leading editorial writers of the State told me that the articles he was writing daily most thoroughly misrepresented his honest convictions; but, said he, "the policy of the paper is dictated by my employers, and I get $65 a week." This practice prevails all through our social fabric, and it can have no possible effect but to stifle and hinder the struggle that is ever going on within the human breast to realize liberty. Look at it frankly and carefully, and I think you will admit that this is the effect of competition.

So far as we are collectively concerned, the present industrial and economic system is purposeless, planless and hopeless. We are trying to make individual success, but the main purpose of our life, our daily work, our industry, our business, has no collective relations, and if what we do in striving for individual success contributes to the building up of the social fabric, it is an incident merely and not a part of the purpose we set out for. We are all engaged in a wild, harum-scarum, rough-and-tumble scramble for things. There is no point in the scramble where we may cease struggling, but the appetite, feeding upon itself, is ever crying for more, more; and, as a natural consequence of a race in which there was no classification of the participants, in which the strong and the weak, the cunning and simple, the fleet of foot and the laggard, the lame and halt and blind are all entered indiscriminately and told to run for the prize,— we have a few prize-holders, some who catch a glimpse of it, and many who never even catch sight of the coveted goal. Such is the distribution of what is called our national wealth under competition. A few of us are rich, some are in circumstances of reasonable comfort, millions are poor, and many are in pauperism.

The Real Incentive for Work.

Men want to help one another. We like to work together. Individualists see no incentive to action save the prospect of getting, but these view the question from the very lowest possible plane, the business plane —" What is there in it for me?" A moment's reflection will convince any of us that this position is not the true one. The best goods are not bought goods. Solomon said of wisdom: "It cannot be purchased with silver, neither shall gold be weighed as the price thereof," and yet it must be said that the prevailing idea to-day is that the best things can be had for money.

The fact is, that the best work of the world has never been done for money.

I cannot recall an instance where a poet has been inspired to write or a singer to sing through the love of money. All of the great poems and pictures have found their inspiration in something nobler than dollars and cents.

Burns found the theme for his greatest songs in the common life about him. Neither he nor any other poet was ever inspired to write by contemplating our idol of to-day — the successful business man. Money did not inspire Leonardo da Vinci to paint his immortal picture, "The Last Supper." Wordsworth could say, in 1830, after thirty-two years of literary activity, that he had not earned enough in that time to pay for his shoe-strings.

Money may inspire such stuff as passes for poetry in the magazines. It may call into being the "pot-boilers" that degrade the name of art. It may guide the thought of many a sermon and control the vote of many a legislator.

But money loses its magic power when a St. Francis, a Thoreau, a John Brown, a Frances Willard, or a Whitman appears in the world.

Noble souls will do their work, will speak their message, whether the world pays them for it or not. Many a great thinker has spent money for pens and ink when he was in need of food and clothes.

The Ideal of the Common Good.

It is only a lower-natured man who can be dazzled by the bauble, gold. Men who have discovered the true wealth of mind and character care little for the wampum of commerce.

I fancy there is to be a change in all our ideas of the thing we call education. The day is coming when all school children will be exhorted to strive to do well instead of to strive to excel. When the better day comes, children and grown folks will strive to outdo one another just as much as now, but it will be striving to outdo one another in doing for others, and people will come to understand what a few of us can already see, that service brings its own reward, and that in serving others we are really serving ourselves. "Love thy neighbor as thyself," or, as being part of thyself, is not the expression of a bit of sentimentalism; it is a command to be wisely selfish.

The civilized world is getting tired of competition. We are getting ashamed of the horrors that are produced by our fratricidal strife. Business men of large experience often tell me that they heartily wish for some way out, but they know not what to do. I believe the way out is easier than we think; it is the evolutionary way, and we are coming to it by leaps and bounds. Here are two facts: the first, men want to love one another; the second, they want to work together. Competition seeks to ignore both of these facts. Men cannot love one another while working against one another, and they cannot work together while continuing in the competitive system; and it is this spiritual fact that is fundamental in human affairs.

In the words of Henry D. Lloyd:

> If all will sacrifice themselves none need be sacrificed. But if one may sacrifice another all are sacrificed. That is the difference between self-interest and

other-self-interest. In industry we have been substituting all the mean passions that can set man against man in place of the irresistible power of brotherhood. To tell us of the progressive sway of brotherhood in all human affairs is the sole message of history.

Mrs. Stetson's poem on "Nationalism" strikingly illustrates this truth. She says:

>The nation is a unit. That which makes
>You an American of our to-day
>Requires the nation and its history,
>Requires the sum of all our citizens,
>Requires the product of our common toil,
>Requires the freedom of our common laws,
>The common heart of our humanity.
>Decrease our population, check our growth,
>Deprive us of our wealth, our liberty,
>Lower the nation's conscience by a hair,
>And you are less than that you were before!
>You stand here in the world the man you are
>Because your country is America.
>Our liberty belongs to each of us;
>The nation guarantees it; in return
>We serve the nation, serving so ourselves.
>Our education is a common right;
>The state provides it equally to all,
>Each taking what he can, and in return
>We serve the state, so serving best ourselves.
>Food, clothing, all necessities of life,—
>These are a right as much as liberty!
>The nation feeds its children. In return
>We serve the nation, serving still ourselves.
>   Nay, not ourselves — ourself! We are but parts,
>The unit is the state — America.

Since this close social unity has become a fact, every one who has not become deaf to the voice of his better nature is becoming aware of his responsibility for the well-being of his fellows. Our business affairs have suddenly become enlarged, so that they include the affairs of the whole city and nation. We feel the force of those words spoken by Marley's ghost in one of Charles Dickens's Christmas stories: "Mankind was my business. Justice, mercy, truth, were my business. The dealings of my trade were but a drop in the comprehensive ocean of my business."

Our Common Responsibility.

If we do not know that there are any worthy, industrious, intelligent men and women who are on the verge of starvation in our own city because they cannot find work, it is because we have been too blind to see them and too deaf to hear their cry.

As an able English writer says:

A few weeks of frost, some little dislocation of industry, some exceptional depression of trade, and the amount of suffering down in the lower industrial classes of London is something unspeakably sad.

I have visited their rooms and listened to their tales of sorrow and suffering, and seen it all written in their haggard faces and in the squalor and destitution of their surroundings, and I have come away sick at heart and positively ashamed of the very modest comfort of my own home. May it not be just possible that we may gradually develop some better social and industrial system than that under which any falling off from the highest point of commercial prosperity plunges whole strata of our population into such depths of destitution and despair, and entails upon the rising generation all the physical, moral and mental mischiefs of chronic starvation?

Is it not, I earnestly ask you, the bounden duty of us all to be extremely careful that we do not allow mere bogus objections to stand in the way of any possible remedy for evils of so serious a character?

"I didn't make the world, and I am not responsible for it," said a country clergyman to me, when discussing with him some of our social difficulties. No, sir. You didn't make the world, and you are not responsible for it. But if the power that did make the world is manifestly working out under your very eyes a grand scheme of social redemption for those suffering masses, and you, in your willful blindness and culpable ignorance, set up your puny back to hinder and obstruct it, if you do your best to thwart and discredit movements which you have not taken the trouble to understand, if you nurse your class prejudices and defend your class privileges, and are ever ready to stand forward as the upholder of things as they are, and to oppose all efforts to put them as they ought to be — then, sir, I say you are responsible, even though you didn't make the world.

We have been on the wrong track in our Christian work. We have been building costly churches, with cushioned seats, stained-glass windows and expensive pipe-organs; we have been supporting an immense standing army of ministers, singers and organists; we have been spending millions for display and comfort, while hungry men walked past the church doors in an agony of despair and bitterness of heart, unable to provide bread for their wives and children.

We have been "worshipping" in comfortable pews with the complacency of Pharisees, and singing hymns of consecration to the Divine will, while around the corner and up four flights of stairs, a friendless factory girl lay on her narrow bed, gasping in the last stages of consumption, and destitute of every sick-room comfort. We have driven in our carriages on Sunday evening to hear an exquisite song-service by the high-salaried quartette choir, and on the way we have passed throngs of unemployed laborers, with desperate thoughts in their minds, and bitter feelings in their hearts against God and man; and we have gone past them with an indifferent glance and a half-conscious feeling that it was very disagreeable to have such rough, uncultured creatures in the world. It has never dawned upon us in the blindness of our selfishness that Christ referred to just such people when he said: "Inasmuch as ye did it unto one of the least of these, ye did it unto Me."

Pink teas and necktie socials and boys' brigades and jolly Christian Endeavor conventions are not Christianity. They do not constitute religion any more than a few dead autumn leaves make a forest. It is well enough to have a pleasant clubhouse, such as many churches are becoming, where we can meet congenial friends and hear essays on ethical abstractions once a week, but our duty to our unfortunate fellow-creatures is not fulfilled by such church membership.

"If a man love not his brother whom he hath seen, *how* can

he love God whom he hath not seen?" This is the unanswerable riddle which condemns all such exclusive, pleasure-worshipping churches.

There is still a multitude to feed, to heal, to teach, to love, to lead into the straight path of honesty and truth. If the church ever intends to follow Christ again, it must take up the question of the loaves and fishes. We have not yet discovered a plan by which they can be fairly distributed among the people. Christ never insulted an audience of poor people by talking to them of the joys of heaven while they were suffering the pangs of hunger. His plan was first the loaves and fishes and then the Sermon on the Mount. The social problems of our day are all spiritual problems. They concern the welfare of man's whole nature, and our attitude toward them is the real test of our religion.

Preaching Christianity and Practicing Paganism.

We all profess to believe that the life of Jesus was a perfect life; we all know that measured according to the standards of to-day his life was a perfect failure. He had not the den of a fox nor the nest of a bird that he could call his own; moreover, he repeatedly warned his followers against the danger of subordinating their lives to things. "A man's life consisteth not in the abundance of things which he possesseth," yet the whole thought of the business world to-day is how to get more things. "Lay not up for yourselves treasures on earth," yet we ignore the plain teaching of the life which we profess to believe to be divine, which we profess to believe to be perfect, and we are exhausting ourselves in either striving to lay up treasure, or in formulating rules to guide our children in so doing.

I know that the republic cannot endure and that our mock Christianity must perish from the face of the earth unless those of us who claim to be both patriotic and Christian are able to demonstrate by the sacrifice of service that our claims are well founded, by redeeming our beloved country from the cruel grasp of selfish greed that would destroy, and make it what God designed it should be — a haven for the oppressed of all the earth. This we can only do by or through the realization of brotherhood, and even organized greed in the form of the trust and the monopoly is aiding on the glorious work. They are teaching society a valuable lesson. They have ceased to destroy one another, and have combined in a brotherhood (limited) and turned their attention to plucking the people. Let the people be wise. Let us enlarge the present idea of the trust and the monopoly until they shall take us all in on the basis that every man who is willing to work has a right to live.

To quote from that interesting book, " The Social Horizon:"

> For nineteen centuries men have been preaching peace, and praying for peace, and proclaiming the Gospel of the Prince of Peace, and now that an era of social and industrial concord really begins to slant its first rosy beams over the hilltops, many of them are crying off in dismay: " Peace, if you please, but not to this extreme. Put down competition, indeed! Abolish industrial rivalry, bring all men into harmonious and helpful relations with each other, and how in the world are you going to get along? Where is your motive power?
>
> " What will become of your race of heroes," we used to be asked, " if you put down the clash of arms? Men must fight or they will degenerate into spiritless poltroons." And just in the same way we are assured now that they must exert their strength, one against the other, if they are to develop characters with any muscle and sinew in them. It is absolutely necessary that they shall wrestle in competitive strife, and if you don't appeal to their individual self-interest, how are you going to get them to strive?
>
> " Blessed are the peacemakers," we would remind them, and we point to the fact that the Bible is full of prophetic visions of a time of universal peace, even for this poor, old world of ours — visions all untroubled by any fear of stagnation and decay. And what the grand, old seers of the Bible saw far away in the distance, so clear and so sweet, our own prophets, the modern poets, see actually on the horizon, and they sigh for its speedy advent:
>
>> Ah! when shall all men's good
>> Be each man's rule, and universal peace
>> Lie like a shaft of light across the land?

This doctrine of Jesus that man must be ruled by love instead of hate, although taught so plainly by the Nazarene 2,000 years ago, comes to most of us to-day, and especially to the members of Christian churches, with the shock of a new revelation. In the beautiful words of Sir Edwin Arnold:

> The echo, not the meaning, of Christ's speech
> Lives; and men tell it sadly each to each,
> With lips, not hearts; sadly, from tongue to tongue,
> The Ages, unpersuaded, pass along
> The dulcet message, like a dream bygone
> Which was for happy sleepers, but is flown.
>
> *　　*　　*　　*　　*　　*
>
> What man could do, man hath well done
> To blot with blood and tears his track divine,
> To sweep his holy footsteps from the earth.
> In steel and gold, splendid and strong and fierce,
> Host after host under that Mount has marched
> Where he sate saying: "Blessed are the peacemakers!"
> In rage and hatred host with host has clashed
> There where he taught: "Love ye your enemies!"
> Banners which bore his cross, have mocked his cross,
> Scattering his land with slain.

The seed of Christ's teaching was planted deep in the soil of human life. It was covered with the rubbish of superstition and the stones of militarism, so that for a score of centuries it seemed to be lost or trampled under foot by warring men. But in these more fortunate days, we can see the green shoots appearing above the ground, not so often in the ecclesiastical gardens as here and there beside the roads and highways, and in the "waste places of the earth."

That which has been barren faith is becoming fruitful fact. The tree of morality is beginning to have fruit as well as leaves. Human brotherhood is being proclaimed in the streets and in the daily press. Progressive and altruistic ideas which would have led the thinker to the rack and the stake a few hundred years ago are now freely spoken everywhere. There is, in spite of the bitterness of competition, more " peace and good will among men " than there ever was before.

The very influences which to-day are causing poverty and suffering will yet bring prosperity and pleasure, when we have learned how to direct them. For instance, the machinery which is now throwing workers on the street will, when it is socialized, cut down the hours of labor to five or six a day, and bring leisure to all the overworked toilers. The trusts which are bankrupting and impoverishing so many, and causing business to be so uncertain, will under public ownership establish business upon a rock and bring peace and plenty to every home.

No change for the better can come save by education and the awakening of the public conscience. Reformers cannot work in any more effective way than by holding up to view the hideousness of our economic conditions. I really believe people can be reformed through being made ashamed to live by eating the flesh and drinking the blood of their fellow-men, that is, by denying them the chance to work and thus taking away their lives, and by working them and taking the product of their toil in profits.

More Thoughtless than Heartless.

We are more thoughtless than heartless. Thousands of kind-hearted men and women actually do not know that there is any undeserved poverty in the country. Their horizon is no wider than the small circle of their friends and relations. They imagine that wealth is obtained by labor and thrift, and are under the hallucination that fortunes are still possible to all who are worthy of them.

They are completely unaware of the omnipotence and despotism of trusts, or of the influence of labor-displacing machinery. The tramp at their back door is to them an abnormal and vicious creature, whose proper habitation is the jail or workhouse.

When they understand the real conditions of the struggle for bread, they will interest themselves in social reform, and cease to be indifferent to the cry of the poor. It is ignorance, not wilful sin, that perpetuates the miseries of the world.

A vast amount of educational work must be done to prepare the people for their industrial inheritance. It is a sad fact that most of those who are now the "under dogs" in the fight, who are denouncing monopolists and bankers, would be quite willing to be capitalists themselves if they had the chance. The capitalist is just what we have made him — he is the natural product of a vicious system. We have admired and taught our children to admire the "successful man;" and by success we meant nothing more than money-getting.

The average young man growing up in America has no conception of success that is not associated with wealth. While this ideal of success remains, all of our raillery against capitalists will be insincere and futile.

We must persuade people to give up the money-getting craze as a hopeless delusion, and to see that the good of the individual is only to be found and conserved in the good of all. So long as men believe in, and uphold by their votes, a dog-fight industrialism, it is impossible to abolish poverty for any save the victorious few.

Service for Service the Only Just Recompense.

Service for service is the only final and just payment, but we might as well attempt to get a race of idolators who had been trained for ages to worship a graven image, to rise at a single step to the realization of the spiritual truth of the unity of all things and to the fact that God is love, as to expect the wrongly taught masses to imagine the possibility of a moneyless civilization.

"The next great word is 'Association,'" says Joseph Mazzini.

Opportunities for the thing called "success" are so nearly exhausted under present commercial and industrial conditions that the outlook for that thing is practically hopeless for the masses. The great field that is "white for the harvest" and that is positively alluring to every man, young or old, who has the Christ spirit, may be found in the enlarged opportunities for work for the good of all. I would not lift my finger to help any individual young man to get rich, because I would not know how to tell him to do any good with the riches obtained in a dishonest social system; but I gladly give my life to the work of helping all men to realize the kingdom of God, which consists of brotherhood relations, of men looking upon and acting toward all men as brothers. This is what Frances Willard called Christian Socialism and of which she said, "Oh, that I were young again, it should have my life! It is God's way out of the wilderness into the promised land. It is the very marrow and fatness of Christ's gospel. It is Christianity applied."

No Immediate Panacea.

Social reformers are frequently unjustly blamed because they have no definite, "presto, change" plan by which the masses can at once be extricated from all their difficulties and made prosperous in the twinkling of an eye.

Social regeneration is not a small half-day's task. Millions of men and women labored for it before we were born, and we simply continue the work from where they left off. It is a terrible fact that countless thousands will yet be ground to powder by the merciless wheels of our present industrial system, before the people are educated up to the level of co-operation and brotherhood.

By another class, social reformers are sometimes called "young men in a hurry." Compared with the apathy of most people, it is natural that the earnestness of those who wish to make the world better should seem to be rash and iconoclastic. Those who have studied the causes of poverty and social evils have discovered that nine-tenths of the world's misery is *preventible*, and they are of course eager to prove it to those who stand still, with folded hands, and say " These things always were and always will be."

But every student of social evolution knows that it takes more than a well-devised plan or code of by-laws to regenerate society. Ready-made millenniums are always a poor fit.

These pert young interrogators of social-reform lecturers who inquire for a " definite remedy," and seem to expect some " Patent Prosperity Restorer," put up in bottles and marked down to thirty-eight cents for this day only, have not the slightest conception of the nature of a *social* reform.

The main thing is not to plan a " model city " somewhere in the woods, or to devise some marvellous system of currency that is warranted not to get into the control of usurers, but to move along step by step as opportunities present themselves, always teaching the doctrine that men are brothers, and that business and politics and religion and everything else must rest on a basis of fraternity.

We must always take into consideration the various kinds of people who compose society.

For this reason the colonization idea is not the highest or most useful method of social reform. Little can be gained by segregating. We are in the world, and there is no advantage in playing the part of a monk by retiring from it. Better stay in it and save it by making it intelligent.

Moreover, people can live more comfortably in cities when they become socialized than they can in small isolated communities. It is collective effort which is to make life easier for us.

Our work is not to select a few who are fit for the brotherhood life and pull them away from the thoughtless selfish masses, but rather to encourage them to remain where they are and educate their less fortunate fellow-workers.

The few colonies, or socialist monasteries, which have been formed, prove by their financial failure and internal dissensions that it is unwise to leave the great social current and try to dig little short-cut canals of our own. The people whom we may call stupid and selfish need light and love so much the more. As Christ said, " I come not to call the righteous, but sinners."

The more knowledge we have of these perplexing industrial problems, the greater is our responsibility to those who cannot understand them. " We are all bound up in one bundle of life;" we cannot separate ourselves from our fellows without suffering an irreparable moral loss.

Democracy means, not the survival of the fittest, but the fitting of all to survive, as has been well said. We are not to be like John Bunyan — so anxious to save our own souls that we rush off and leave our wives, and children, and fellow-citizens behind.

The Curse of Private Property.

Richard Wagner was not far from the truth when he said: " From possessions which have become private property and which strangely enough are considered as the foundation of good order, proceed all the crimes of myth and history."

Private property has done us great injury in character and morals. A wealthy employer of labor in St. Louis recently said to me: " I feel a personal resentment against private property; it has been a grave injury to me and mine. It enslaves me now; I don't know what to do with it. I can't sell it, and if I did I shouldn't know what to do with the money. It is a poison wherever you put it, in the present industrial scheme."

We are all suffering from what Whitman calls " the mania of owning things." We have written upon our door-posts,— " It is more blessed to receive than to give." We have turned the law of Christ upside-down.

The craze for private property mars every relation of life. It turns the marriage altar into an auction block. It commercializes even the intercourse of the home. It sunders friend from friend. It breeds suspicion, envy, hatred and crime. It takes men who might have been useful and public-spirited citizens and transforms them into forgers, burglars, gamblers and murderers. It hardens the heart against the cry of the unfortunate. It clenches the hand that might have been opened in generosity. It dries up the fountain of tears. It narrows the mind, so that the true and the beautiful and the good become as unreal as the rainbows that hover in the mists of Niagara Falls.

It is private property that creates the partitions of pride between men who would otherwise have been congenial and affectionate comrades. The work of our own hands has enslaved us. We have become the chattels of our chattels,— the unhappy slaves of our own possessions.

We, as a people, are wearing ourselves out in the busy rush and push of business. The most abject slave among us to-day is the successful business man. One of our wealthiest merchants said to me the other day:

> I am the worst slave in my whole establishment, chained to my post like a galley-slave. I am here at 7 in the morning and not home till after 6 o'clock in the evening, five days in the week, and on Saturday from 7 a. m. till 11 or 12 at night. On Sunday I am so worn out with the labors of the week that I just throw myself on my bed and lie the whole day in the vain effort to regain strength for the conflict of the coming week. Such is my life. I have no time with my family. I have no time for social intercourse with my friends; and it is perfectly clear to me that I am engaged in a purposeless grind where, after all, I am little better than a galley-slave.

I hail with great delight the signs of the times that point to a growing desire for leisure, rest and recreation. We are a nation of over-worked people. Those who have employment are over-taxed, while on the other hand thousands have no work at all, and are goaded to desperation by the fear of starvation.

We are yet in an immature stage. Our civilization is crude and unfinished. We have no wise plan for the division of labor, or the fruits of labor. Consequently some of us who do not work at all are gorged like anacondas, through other people's toil; while others who labor long and weary hours are starved to the leanness of the "seven lean kine" of Pharaoh's dream.

A man's life is more than "food and raiment," more than working, and getting, and hoarding, and investing; and in our few oases of recreation we learn to know one another better, and find that the men whom we had regarded with suspicion are not bad fellows after all. Only as we learn to respect and help, and love one another better do we really become better citizens, or really learn to work for the perfected republic which was the dream of our forefathers. Deny it if you please, proclaim against it if you will, but we are working toward industrial equality, when business will be so thoroughly organized for the benefit of all that our daily work will be as easy and natural as breathing.

Notwithstanding the craze for property that has cursed this country for so many years, I believe human brotherhood will be realized first in America. There is a heroic and spiritual core to our national life. Less national prejudice exists here than among any other people. We are developing a free-spirited, tolerant robustness of character which will set us free from small and petty conceptions of life. We shall yet have *men to match our mountains, rivers and prairies* — large-natured men, too generous to be tyrannical and too strong to be selfish.

As yet, the American nation is composed chiefly of raw materials. We have gathered together people from every country in the world, full of superstition and national prejudices,— people who have never known the meaning of liberty or democracy, or who have never even dreamed of a world-wide brotherhood, and we are rubbing away their sharp angles, and mixing them together in factories and trade-unions and political parties, until they discover that a man's a man and that the whole human race is one large family.

America's Task.

This is the task which America has the privilege to be the first to attempt. No work could be more moral or spiritual. It is the practical fulfillment of every poet's dream.

This is to be the "land of comrades,"— the land of large thoughts, large hearts, and large conceptions of the value of every human soul.

What we call ignorance is in reality nothing more than smallness of mind. The ignorant have no comprehensiveness of view. They can see nothing but their own relations and village and personal interests. They do not realize the connection between the past and present, and neither can they conceive of the possibilities of the future. They are like ants who live under a tea cup, and know nothing of the great dome of the skies.

They conceive patriotism to be a hearty hatred of every country except their own, and a bulldog's stupid willingness to fight in defense of their foolish prejudice. Loyalty is to them an unreasoning adherence to "the powers that be," however tyrannical and unwise. Religion to the ignorant is the conceited belief that the Creator of countless worlds is their especial protector, and can be coaxed and bribed to confer personal benefits by songs of flattery and gifts of gold.

The small-minded have no sense of proportion. The tiny spot where they happen to be born seems to them to be the center of the earth. Everything is viewed from their own standpoint. A mole-hill beside their feet appears to them as large as a mountain twenty miles distant. The faults of their own nation seem to be virtues, and the virtues of other nations seem to be faults.

If they happen to be in comfortable circumstances, then —

> God's in His Heaven;
> All's well with the world.

But when trouble and adversity come to them, then they become pessimists at once and declare that the whole world is going to the dogs.

America's task is to teach larger views of life and duty. We are to interpret that great word, *Humanity*, to the world; so that when travelers from other nations visit us they can understand it. The petty distinctions of birth and wealth have no place in this republic. If we are to have any upper classes, they will be composed of those who know most, and love most, and help most. We shall allow nothing to elevate a man but love for his fellows.

Instead of armories we shall have kindergartens, in which the little children will be taught how sacred a thing human life is. Instead of cannons we shall have electric fountains, tossing the colored spray high in the air. Instead of battle-ships we shall have excursion steamers, giving health and pleasure in place of pain and death. Instead of blaming and punishing those who are foolish enough to sin against the public welfare, we shall teach them, with pity and love, that the path of happiness is the path of useful service.

To quote from "Wealth Against Commonwealth:"

We are to become fathers, mothers, for the spirit of the father and mother is not in us while we can say of any child, "it is not ours," and leave it in the grime. We are to become men, women, for to all about reinforcing us we shall insure full growth, and thus insure it to ourselves. We are to become gentlemen, ladies, for we will not accept from another any service we are not willing to return in kind. We are to become honest, giving when we get, and getting with the knowledge and consent of all. We are to become rich, for we shall share in the wealth now latent in idle men and idle land, and in the fertility of work done by those who have ceased to withstand, but stand with each other. As we walk our parks, we already see that, by saying "thine" to every neighbor, we say "mine" of palaces, gardens, art, science, far beyond any possible temptation to selfishness, even the selfishness of kings. We shall become patriots, for the heart will know why it thrills to the flag. Those folds wave the salute of a greater love than that of the man who will lay down his life for his friend. There floats the banner of the love of millions, who, though they do not know you, and have never seen you, will die for you, and are living for you, doing in a thousand services unto you as you would be done by. And the little patriotism, which is the love of the humanity fenced within our frontier, will widen into the reciprocal service of all men. Generals were, merchants are, brothers will be, humanity's representative men.

We are rapidly approaching a time " when business will be friendship, and government will be love;" when a new system of political economy will be evolved that will perform as well as promise, and "rain the luxuries of nature into the laps of the starving poor."

The old form of business, by which the man who got the most property from his fellow-men for the least personal service was rated the most successful, must be laid away in the museum of antiquities in the same room with feudalism and chattel slavery.

The old form of government, which meant the ensnaring of the workers by legal technicalities so that a political clique might become enriched, must pass into the oblivion that hides the dead despotism of ancient times.

The old form of political economy by which a very few ideas were buried under a mountain of words, and the prevailing greed for gold was dignified by being elaborated into a philosophy, must be ranked among the curiosities of literature and laid away upon the top shelves.

Whatever separates man from man, and labor from wealth, and the worker from employment, must go. No matter how firmly entrenched an institution may be, no matter what prejudices may rally to its defense, if it stands in the way of human brotherhood it is bound to be removed. This dark, sad little world of ours is rolling up into the light, and all the hosts of darkness cannot stop it.

" No question is ever settled until it is settled right," and democracy is right. The people make mistakes, but they seldom commit crimes. They are learning rapidly what their rights and their duties are, and when the time for industrial equality arrives, they will be as well prepared for it as any select and cultured class of society.

Every labor organization has been teaching the practical meaning of brotherhood to wage-earners. The co-operation of the workers in factories and mills and large department stores has prepared their minds for the application of co-operative principles to every department of business. Our large cities have taught us that every individual is only a small part of the whole; and our swift means of transit have broken down the local prejudices which are so common in older countries.

In fact, the civilization of the nineteenth century has been but the scaffolding by means of which we are to build the great *Home* of the human race. It has been but the means to a glorious end, and will pass away only to bring to view the perfected structure of democracy.

The Movement Onward and Upward.

The moment we begin to look upon our present civilization as a finality, it will begin to deteriorate and decay. Progress is the law of life. The nation that ceases to develop begins to degenerate. Egypt stood still, and was turned into stone. China stood still, and became a nation of human vegetables.

> New occasions teach new duties; time makes ancient good uncouth;
> They must upward still and onward, who would keep abreast of truth.

Society is like a river, not like a lake. It must, if it is healthy, be continually flowing.

No sensible man to-day uses the old argument: "It always was, and it always will be." We do not value institutions because of their age, and prize them because of their mould and rust. Usefulness is the only excuse which any institution can give for its existence.

The search-light of the press is flashed in every direction, and wherever we discover a defect it is our privilege to point to it and demand a remedy.

If our constitution, written when social conditions were entirely different from what they are to-day, stands between the people and a just income tax, or any other reform, then common sense teaches us that "man is more than constitutions," and amendments to the latter are in order.

If our form of government becomes at any time unwieldy, expensive and oppressive, then we have the same right which Jefferson had, to criticise, oppose or remodel it.

If our system of doing business fails properly to distribute the wealth that is created, if it rewards the unworthy and neglects the useful members of society, then it is not a final system, and is bound to change.

Whatever is injurious to the public welfare should not be regarded as permanent. It may be allowed to remain until some better way is found and agreed upon, but no longer. The well-being of the people is the first thing to be considered. All laws, customs and institutions are secondary to this.

As to the limits of improvement no one can be dogmatic. So far as we can see to-day, the horizon is boundless. Every day some hitherto impossible task is accomplished. Science has countless treasures yet to be revealed. No man is so foolish and blind as he who imagines he can perpetuate things as they are. As well might he attempt to stop the revolution of the earth, and tie it to a hitching-post in the moon. Even Huxley, the cautious, exact scientist, once said: "I see no limit to the extent to which intelligence and will, guided by sound principles of investigation, and organized in common effort, may modify the conditions of existence."

So far as our present duties are concerned, it does not matter to us whether this ideal state is a hundred or a thousand years distant. I know that brotherhood *is*. It is our realization of the fact that comes so slowly. As Mrs. Stetson says:

> We shut our eyes and call it night;
> We grope and fall in seas of light,
> Would we but understand.

Electricity has always been in the world, but its power was never utilized until the last few years. Water and fire have existed side by side since the earliest civilization, but steam is a recent discovery. Men lived in the sunshine for thousands of years before they even dreamed of photography. They paddled their tiny canoes for ages before they thought of iron steamships.

And so it is in the social and moral realm. We have not discovered and applied all the altruistic forces that exist. The electricity of sympathy has been too much overlooked. But we can even now see the beginning of new influences which promise much for the future. This is the springtime of evolution, and if we never live long enough to reap, we should rejoice that we have at least the privilege of planting.

This capitalistic system is individualism gone mad, and it is doomed as certainly as to-morrow's sun will rise. This is the march of a better civilization. The forces at work just now are preparatory. Many an ancient snowdrift must be thawed out of the path. On the surface, business seems to be a hopeless, reckless jumble, but all things are really " working together for good." There is a " power that makes for righteousness " in human evolution. We cannot always detect it at the time, but those who shall come after us will be able to see it clearly.

> Yet I doubt not through the ages one increasing purpose runs,
> And the thoughts of men are widened with the process of the suns.

As I grow older my faith in humanity increases. All that is moral and intellectual in the world is human. The remembrance of the struggles for freedom and truth, which fill the pages of history, should make every fellow-being sacred. "It doth not yet appear what we shall be," but we can see that the centuries bring improvement, not retrogression. Love is the goal of our stumbling feet. We were never so near to it as we are to-day, in spite of the frantic efforts of a few to corner the wealth of the world.

BROTHERHOOD.

By Edwin Markham.

The crest and crowning of all good,
Life's final star, is Brotherhood;
For it will bring again to Earth
Her long-lost Poesy and Mirth —
Will send new light on every face,
A kingly power upon the race;
And till it comes we men are slaves,
And travel downward to the dust of graves.

Come, clear the way, then, clear the way;
Blind creeds and kings have had their day.
Break the dead branches from the path;
Our hope is in the aftermath —
Our hope is in heroic men,
Star-led to build the world again.
To this Event the ages ran:
Make way for Brotherhood—Make way for man.

www.ingramcontent.com/pod-product-compliance
Lightning Source LLC
Chambersburg PA
CBHW051855300426
44117CB00006B/410